Baltimore Revisited

Baltimore Revisited

Stories of Inequality and Resistance in a U.S. City

EDITED BY P. NICOLE KING, KATE DRABINSKI,
AND JOSHUA CLARK DAVIS

Rutgers University Press

New Brunswick, Camden, and Newark, New Jersey, and London

Library of Congress Cataloging-in-Publication Data

Names: King, P. Nicole, 1976– editor. | Drabinski, Kate, editor. | Davis, Joshua Clark, editor.
Title: Baltimore revisited : stories of inequality and resistance in a U.S. city / edited by
P. Nicole King, Kate Drabinski, and Joshua Clark Davis.
Description: New Brunswick, New Jersey : Rutgers University Press, 2019.
Identifiers: LCCN 2018037166 | ISBN 9780813594026 (cloth) | ISBN 9780813594019
   (paperback)
Subjects: LCSH: Urban policy—Maryland—Baltimore. | Sociology, Urban—Maryland—
   Baltimore. | Income distribution—Maryland—Baltimore. | Equality—Maryland—
   Baltimore. | Baltimore (Md.)—Social conditions. | BISAC: HISTORY / United States /
   State & Local / Middle Atlantic (DC, DE, MD, NJ, NY, PA). | POLITICAL SCIENCE /
   Public Policy / City Planning & Urban Development. | SOCIAL SCIENCE /
   Discrimination & Race Relations. | ARCHITECTURE / Urban & Land Use Planning. |
   SOCIAL SCIENCE / Sociology / Urban. | SOCIAL SCIENCE / Ethnic Studies /
   African American Studies. | SOCIAL SCIENCE / Social Classes.
Classification: LCC HT395.U63 .B35 2019 | DDC 307.7609752/6—dc23
LC record available at https://lccn.loc.gov/2018037166

A British Cataloging-in-Publication record for this book is available from the British Library.

www.rutgersuniversitypress.org

Manufactured in the United States of America

We dedicate this book to all the students, teachers, researchers, librarians, archivists, activists, artists, journalists, and people of Baltimore.

All royalties generated by this book will be donated to the Enoch Pratt Free Library. Public libraries make cities better places.

Placed Love

He rode me thru' dysphoria
Where the buildings called out their pain
And the bodies laid waste in vain
And the minds were crowded with crud
Where it was hardest for flowers to bud
Pac, I want the rose to grow from concrete
The jungle where haunted souls meet
I tried running from this space
But my heart ran in place
Because my solace is tied to this locality
Have I adopted a privileged mentality?
Where I offer sutures not solutions
To defend my social position
No, this is not the case
For I love the face of my race
How do I grow me and add more growth to our tree
Without giving into capitalist desires that say to sew into me and my legacy
And leave those who ain't surviving the fight like me—be.

—Shawntay Stocks

Contents

Foreword

LINDA SHOPES

Baltimore Revisited: Stories of Inequality and Resistance in a U.S. City (2019) calls to mind the publication, a generation earlier, of *The Baltimore Book: New Views on Local History* (1991). Both are driven by a passion for our beloved and deeply flawed city; both present a critical local history directed at the general reader and seek to connect that history to broader national and global themes. Both also hold out the hope that knowledge of past failures, struggles, and achievements—and the deep roots of structural inequality—can point the way to a more just, equitable future. Yet the two books also differ significantly: *Baltimore Revisited* is no mere update. It is perhaps useful to consider what these differences tell us about changes during the past twenty-five-plus years in our knowledge of the city's past, how we present that knowledge, and what we make of it.

First of all, *Baltimore Revisited* is a bigger book, with more content. Happily, this points to a growing body of research on the history of Baltimore and a welcome shift away from its status as a secondary city within U.S. urban history. Perhaps this explains why *Baltimore Revisited* is also more scholarly in its approach. Although both books are well grounded in careful research, *The Baltimore Book* adopted a narrative style akin to journalism, whereas articles in the current work are well footnoted, their arguments denser and more deeply situated in relevant literature, their reach extending to larger contexts and trends in fields from history to anthropology.

The subject matter of the two books is also different. If there is an overriding theme in *The Baltimore Book*, it is class relations and working-class struggles for justice, reflecting the twinned interests of social historians of the 1970s and 1980s and the authors' involvement in the dissident politics of the 1960s and 1970s. In accord with current scholarly trends, *Baltimore Revisited* offers a forceful critique of neoliberalism as it has played out in Baltimore. It also includes several articles related to environmental and cultural history, as well as a piece on LGBTQ history and articles on two groups of relative newcomers to Baltimore, Lumbees and Koreans. In addition, where *The Baltimore Book* devotes proportionally more attention to events of the nineteenth and early twentieth centuries, *Baltimore Revisited* focuses on the recent past and, with greater temporal distance than the earlier work, on the city's post–World War II history.

The books' contrasting emphases suggest the very different contexts within which each was written. *The Baltimore Book* sought to counter the booster narrative of local history then dominating contemporary civic discourse as the city, in the throes of deindustrialization, sought to reinvent itself as a tourist destination and attractive home for the professional class. And so it included chapters that emphasized social conflict and the active agency of local people to improve the circumstances of their lives. In contrast, *Baltimore Revisited*— under development in 2015 when protests arose following the death of a young black man, Freddie Gray, while in police custody—is more intent on addressing the enormous consequences of redevelopment schemes and resulting gentrification beginning in the postwar period and accelerating in more recent years, actions that reinforced existing, often-racialized structural inequalities or what is sometimes termed the "two Baltimores."

There is also the related matter of interpretation. Both books adopt an unabashedly critical perspective, yet in different ways in accord with the intellectual landscape at the time of their writing. Consider how each approaches the topic of race. *The Baltimore Book* presents race as primarily about the social experience of African Americans within the context of white prejudice and discrimination. Chapters in *Baltimore Revisited*, however, in line with current scholarship understand race as a constructed cultural category that defines whiteness as well as blackness. This difference is strikingly evident in the way each book handles a single source inflected with racial meaning, a 1907 report on housing conditions in Baltimore focusing on four areas of the city: two dominated by immigrants and two by African Americans. My chapter on Fells Point in *The Baltimore Book* quoted from this report as evidence of the way (implicitly white) Polish immigrants in that neighborhood, despite living in overcrowded, rundown dwellings lacking indoor plumbing, nonetheless managed orderly households and, it was implied, lives:

> A remembered Saturday evening inspection of five apartments in a house in Thames Street, with their whitened floors and shining cook stoves, with dishes gleaming on the neatly ordered shelves, the piles of clean clothing laid out for Sunday, and the general atmosphere of preparation for the Sabbath, suggested

standards that would not have disgraced a Puritan housekeeper. The home-staying Polish woman usually takes pride in keeping her domain clean.[1]

In his chapter in *Baltimore Revisited*, Mike Casiano draws on the same report to consider how the description of residents in the black districts as "possessing 'low standards,' an 'absence of ideals,' and 'irregular life and habits'" was part of a Progressive era "comparative racialization" that "pathologized black culture" even as it valorized white immigrant culture—a reading of the document absent in the earlier work.

Consider too the notion of place, a governing theme in both books. *The Baltimore Book*, reflecting the empirical tendencies of social history, conceives of place as a structure, whether extant or not, that housed something noteworthy or an actual site where something significant occurred. Neighborhood, which defines several of the chapters, is assumed to be the locus of both social solidarity and competing interests, both of which can be connected to specific sites. This sense of the term "place" is consistent with the book's origin as a bus tour of the city, which by definition requires something "there" to stand on, look at, or imagine; the chapters themselves are organized as armchair tours.[2] In *Baltimore Revisited*, although it is replete with references to specific sites, place itself is less a container for the stories being told and more the dynamic center of the story. We read of how geographic spaces—East Baltimore, downtown, South Baltimore, Port Covington—have become human places and how they have been created, degraded or destroyed, and re-created, often within the context of the class and racial inequalities that have shaped so much of Baltimore's history. Still, place in both books reflects the editors' intent to encourage readers literally to see the city in new ways, to visualize, if only in the mind, the layers of history that surround them, so that they see themselves as similarly situated in history.

Finally, we might note a difference in the tone of the two volumes. *The Baltimore Book*, for all its critical intent, maintained a cautious optimism about contemporary changes that is not present in *Baltimore Revisited*, even as it called for a more democratic and humane city. One significant instance of topical overlap illustrates this point. Linda Zeidman's chapter in *The Baltimore Book*, "Sparrows Point, Dundalk, Highlandtown, Old West Baltimore," focuses on the rise of the Sparrows Point plant of Bethlehem Steel, including the successful drive to organize two United Steelworkers of America locals to represent workers at the plant in the 1940s. Noting massive job losses in the 1980s, the chapter concludes with these words: "Steelworkers and their daughters and sons . . . will now have to forge new alliances with one another, devise new strategies for unions, and explore new ways to create a working future."[3] That did not happen, and Michelle Stefano's piece in *Baltimore Revisited*, "Finding Closure: The Poets of Sparrows Point Steel Mill," quotes from poems written by one-time steelworkers mourning the loss not only of jobs but also of an entire way of life as the mill finally shut down for good in 2012. It is a poignant reminder of the shift from manufacturing to service sector jobs in the city's economy in the past quarter-century.

Several chapters in *Baltimore Revisited* suggest that both gentrification and racial divisions addressed in *The Baltimore Book* have continued unabated—indeed have intensified—in recent years. Other comparisons indicate a similar sense of opportunities lost, of struggles that remain. Despite continued activism, the Baltimore presented in the current volume is hardly the more democratic and humane place the earlier work called for. Historians are not inclined to predict the future, but the evidence presented in these two books, written a generation apart, does not suggest optimism, even as it opens pathways to it.

Notes

1   Linda Shopes, "Fells Point: Community and Conflict in a Working-Class Neighborhood," in *The Baltimore Book: New Views of Local History*, ed. Elizabeth Fee, Linda Shopes, and Linda Zeidman (Philadelphia: Temple University Press, 1991), 137, 139.

2   For a discussion of the tours from which *The Baltimore Book* developed, see Elizabeth Fee, Sylvia Gillett, Linda Shopes, and Linda Zeidman, "Baltimore by Bus: Steering a New Course through the City's History," *Radical History Review* 28–30 (1984): 206–216.

3   Linda Zeidman, "Sparrows Point, Dundalk, Highlandtown, Old West Baltimore: Home of Gold Dust and the Union Card," in *The Baltimore Book*, 174–191; quoted material, 191.

Baltimore Revisited

Introduction

• •

Why Revisit Baltimore Now?

P. NICOLE KING, JOSHUA CLARK

DAVIS, AND KATE DRABINSKI

Every city is complicated, but Baltimore is a city whose complexities and contradictions defiantly thwart easy explanation. Even the city's seemingly contradictory nicknames—Mobtown and Charm City—conceal more than they reveal. Baltimore has often been understood as the North's most southern city and the South's most northern city, a liminal space where the question of who belongs is always on the table. Baltimore is the biggest city in a border state where slavery flourished, where affluent whites enslaved people of African descent and forced them to perform a wide variety of labor, and where many white residents intended to join the Confederacy until the insistent artillery of Union troops convinced them otherwise. And yet, Baltimore also had the largest free African American population of any city in the country by 1850. After the Civil War, however, Baltimore's white residents eagerly rejected the spirit of Reconstruction.[1] In 1911, Baltimore eagerly assumed the role of Jim Crow pioneer, becoming the first municipality in the country to mandate racial segregation in housing. And having reluctantly sided with the Union, those nostalgic for the "Old South" built memorials to the Confederacy that stood in the city's public spaces until August 2017, when the mayor ordered them hauled away in the dead of night.[2]

Meanwhile, Baltimore was home to one of the most active local civil rights movements in the United States. The city claimed one of the country's largest local chapters of the National Association for the Advancement of Colored People (NAACP), an organization of more than 17,000 members headed by the indefatigable Lillie Carroll Jackson.[3] At the same time, one of the city's native sons, Thurgood Marshall, was a prominent intellectual and legal architect of desegregation as lead counsel for the NAACP, claiming victory in the landmark *Brown v. Board of Education* case decided by the U.S. Supreme Court in 1954 and ultimately becoming the first African American to serve on the Court. Baltimore was a manufacturing and shipping hotbed that boomed amid the Industrial Revolution of the nineteenth century and continued to prosper in the first half of the twentieth century, especially because of growing American consumer expenditures and the expansion of the military-industrial complex during World War II. But during the postwar period, the city experienced a swift economic and population decline as factories began to close and white residents moved to the suburbs in the 1960s. By the 1980s, when Baltimore had lost many of its white middle-class residents, the city turned its working harbor into a tourist destination to lure back a new generation raised in the suburbs. Since the 1980s, the city has continued to lose residents and has become increasingly known as a major hub of the North American narcotics trade. Baltimore has experienced boom-and-bust cycles throughout its history. It is a city of fits and starts, a place where deep inequalities of income and race persist block by block and where some neighborhoods boom but others go bust, often at the same time.

Baltimore encapsulates the bundle of contradictions—the inequalities and traumas but also the joys—that characterize life in U.S. cities in the twenty-first century. It is a model of the neoliberal city: a place where corporate interests eagerly privatize public goods and services to maximize profits. We define neoliberalism as an ideology that privileges profits and prizes private and corporate entities as the ideal providers of public services. As geographer David Harvey has convincingly argued, it is an economic and political belief system that government officials in the United States, the United Kingdom, Europe, and South America have embraced as a rationale for privatizing a wide array of social services and state functions since the late 1970s.[4] This ideology is connected to state violence and surveillance, which are methods to "protect" (manage and control) private property in its many forms. As a fitting symbol of the struggle for survival in the neoliberal city, people in Baltimore like to compare the competition for extremely limited resources to crabs climbing over each other in a barrel, always knocking each other down on their way up.

These trends toward privatization are not altogether new, but the pervasiveness with which they have become normalized in Baltimore is troubling, as is increasing anti-urban political sentiment in the United States, which can be seen in multiplying claims that cities are home to liberal elites, criminals, and undocumented immigrants. As a result, Baltimore is a strategic place where citizens wage the battle for the "right to the city," to borrow a phrase the French philosopher Henri Lefebvre coined just before student protests broke out in Paris in 1968.[5] As David Harvey argues, the right to the city "primarily rises up from the streets, out from the neighborhoods, as a cry for help and sustenance by oppressed people in desperate times."[6] This concept has gained prominence among scholars and activists because of the large numbers resisting the neoliberal turn and fighting for truly democratic public spaces and for justice: from the Arab Spring and Occupy Wall Street to Black Lives Matter and the Women's March, people have taken to the streets of cities in record numbers during this past decade.[7]

Political scientist Lester Spence updates thinking on the right to a city in his 2015 book *Knocking the Hustle: Against the Neoliberal Turn in Black Politics*, which he presciently wrote in the period leading up to the Baltimore Uprising that occurred in the wake of Freddie Gray's death in police custody. While Spence supports Lefebvre's argument that those who live and struggle in a city have more of a right to it than corporations, he argues that race is a central yet underanalyzed linchpin in the neoliberal turn in American politics. Spence details how the public's right to the city "has been effectively transferred" through public–private partnerships, prosperity gospels, the militarization of the police, and the respectability politics of the black elite, a process for which he has found ample evidence in Baltimore.[8]

These trends have hit aging industrial cities with large black populations like Baltimore particularly hard. Exploring the intersectional vision needed to challenge neoliberalism, Spence writes, "Even solutions touted as progressive rely on the hustle for their energy. The city will likely remain ground zero for the battle against the neoliberal turn."[9] We argue that Baltimore is also ground zero for rethinking how "legacy cities"—historic cities experiencing a decline in jobs and population due to a host of local and global trends—might become progressive places where everyday people enjoy a right to the city.[10] We therefore look to Baltimore's past because it can offer important lessons for the future.

This collection has eighteen essays and nine shorter "snapshots." An introduction opens each of the five parts of the book, and a map the first four. Each part takes the reader on a journey through the city and addresses the neoliberal turn using various theories and methods. Part I examines the roots of injustices in Baltimore ranging from segregated schools to the dawn of the criminalization of drug possession. Part II looks at how local residents contest these inequalities by organizing work against the entrenched interests that perpetuate them. As powerful institutions take over neighborhoods and social services are cut, people still fight for their neighborhoods and their rights. In Part III, we listen to the voices of everyday people in various parts of the city, from the "reservation" of Lumbee Indians in East Baltimore to a "toxic tour" of South Baltimore. Part IV delves directly into how people struggle and survive in a neoliberal city. We conclude with a reflection on the raw material of history—the archives—and the potential of future scholarship on Baltimore to illuminate and reveal our right to the city. We have also developed a website, http://baltimorerevisited.org/, to accompany the book and provide more information on researching and understanding a complex city that is essential for analyzing inequality and resistance in the United States and beyond.

Baltimore Revisited is an interdisciplinary collaboration based in the humanities rather than a systematic history of the city. As Spence writes in *Knocking the Hustle*, "neoliberal ideas radically change what it means to be human, as the perfect human now becomes an entrepreneur of his own human capital . . . freedom is redefined as the ability to participate in the market unfettered."[11] The goal of the humanities is to essentially *remain human and block the dehumanization of others* (to paraphrase Toni Morrison).[12] One way to remain human within the context of Baltimore is to understand where our city has collectively come from and then to determine which of our stories and narratives can sustain and connect us over differences and distances, be they physical, temporal, or existential. We believe that research into the people and places of Baltimore and cities like it can make a modest contribution to our society by identifying a better way forward. This collection, like a city, is a collective of people working on the ground and learning to speak different languages to move practices and theories forward. The authors of *Baltimore Revisited* include artists, doctors, social workers, poets, preservationists, community activists, and archivists. Others are scholars of gender and sexuality, public health, anthropology, public humanities, place, and architecture. While some are historians, all of us express a respect for studying the past as a way to better rethink the future.

Historian Linda Shopes writes in the foreword that this book is "not a cause for optimism," which is true. These are troubled times, especially in Baltimore. However, neither is this book a cause for pessimism. We prefer to see it as a reflection on a moment, a teaching tool, and a call for action, including engaging in more rigorous and collaborative research and public programming on the past and present stories of Baltimore. If Maryland is "America in Miniature," as the state's tourist office claims, then Baltimore is the U.S. city that struggles and perseveres, which is the closest thing to hope we might find in the early twenty-first century.[13]

Baltimore, like many other cities struggling with shifting and challenging social and economic conditions, inhabits a tense space between renaissance and revolution.[14] Politicians and city boosters have long touted a vague "Baltimore renaissance" to lure tourists and new residents, while the people of the city have again and again taken to the streets to call for revolution—from the railroad strike of 1877 to the uprising of 1968 and then again in 2015. The chapters in this book address the conditions that created the current need for revolution in this city. We hope this collection starts many difficult but necessary conversations within and beyond Baltimore.

Baltimore Revisited: Stories of Inequality and Resistance in a U.S. City joins previous essay collections on the city's social history that focus on issues ripe for public debate. Perhaps the most influential essay collection on the city has been *The Baltimore Book: New Views of Local History.* Published in 1991 and coedited by Elizabeth Fee, Linda Zeidman, and Shopes, the book focuses on the city's working people from an "admittedly partisan" perspective that was "nurtured in the dissident politics of the 1960s."[15] *The Baltimore Book* remains a go-to introductory text for thinking and teaching about the city; for its histories of working people, union organizing, and residential segregation; and for its other stories of those who built Baltimore from the ground up. Yet every collection of essays has gaps, as ours certainly does. We saw a need to amplify the voices of another generation working on Baltimore research and create a twenty-first-century-style update that addresses how the increasing decline in manufacturing jobs, the rise of public–private partnerships, and continued racial inequality are central to the city's current status. In Baltimore, like other deindustrializing cities in the twenty-first century, work in "eds and meds," growing tourism, and the service industry have taken the place of unionized manufacturing jobs; yet most of these jobs do not come close to offering workers the living wage and benefits that paved the way for class mobility in the middle of the twentieth century. Indeed, the inequality allowed to fester in Baltimore and many of our U.S. cities pervades our criminal justice system, our schools, our government, and even our homes. Freddie Gray was fatally injured in the back of a police van, but he was poisoned by lead paint in the house he grew up in before he was even two years old.[16] We need more research and writing on how such things can happen in our cities in the twenty-first century.

While *The Baltimore Book* grew out of a bus tour called the People's History Tour of Baltimore, *From Mobtown to Charm City: New Perspectives on Baltimore's Past* (2002) emerged from the Baltimore History Conferences of the late 1990s.[17] Both collections thus came out of public programming and reflected a strong interest in the complexities of Baltimore's history in the final decade of the twentieth century. Like *The Baltimore Book, From Mobtown to Charm City* addressed everyday working-class citizens, as well as the importance of race and gender in understanding the city. However, the evocative title, *From Mobtown to Charm City,* reflects a central tension in historic cities: from clean booster image of "Charm City" to the rebellions of "Mobtown," American cities vacillate between wanting a renaissance and needing a revolution.

In 2011, twenty years after the publication of *The Baltimore Book,* another important collection, *Baltimore '68: Riots and Rebirth,* evoked a similar tension in its title.[18] Does a riot lead to a rebirth? Do we need a revolution to start a renaissance? The "new views and perspectives" on Baltimore's past seemed to focus on this tension, a central and productive tension of a city that is constantly in flux. Historic U.S. cities can offer case studies for rethinking space and justice in the twenty-first century. Like the two previous collections, *Baltimore '68* came out of public programming based in the humanities, specifically a 2008 conference at the University of Baltimore that helped to jumpstart a long deferred process of scholarly reflection on the 1968 uprising, including the first set of oral histories conducted with witnesses to the original events. The *Baltimore '68* project and book bring attention to the history of unrest in Baltimore following the assassination of Martin Luther King Jr. that is still relevant to scholars and the public today. This research and the conversations it started were invaluable resources when a city long on edge rose up and took to the streets in spring 2015. We hope that this volume will contribute to the historiography of Baltimore that includes not only these three previous edited collections but also the rich body of monographs on the city's history.[19] We also hope that this book inspires more scholarship that takes Baltimore and other historic neoliberal cities seriously.

We study Baltimore's history to, among other reasons, take stock of where we are and what we are thinking about our city today. This approach provides an opportunity to remind ourselves why social history is important and why we have to fight for our right to the city. Scholarship on U.S. cities may not provide the solution to such problems; however, such work can provide context and uncover some of the patterns that undergird why so much has happened but not nearly enough has changed in Baltimore since the upheavals of 1835, 1861, 1877, 1911, 1968, and 2015.

Notes

1 Christopher Phillips, *Freedom's Port: The African American Community of Baltimore, 1790–1860* (Urbana: University of Illinois Press, 1997), 235.

2 Colin Campbell and Luke Broadwater, "Citing 'Safety and Security,' Pugh Has Baltimore Confederate Monuments Taken Down," *Baltimore Sun*, August 16, 2017.

3 Lee Sartain, *Borders of Equality: The NAACP and the Baltimore Civil Rights Struggle, 1914–1970* (Jackson: University Press of Mississippi, 2013), 8.

4 See David Harvey, *A Brief History of Neoliberalism* (Oxford: Oxford University Press, 2005), and on neoliberalism in Baltimore, see "A View from Federal Hill," in *The Baltimore Book: New Views on Local History*, ed. Elizabeth Fee, Linda Shopes, and Linda Zeidman (Philadelphia: Temple University Press, 1991), 227–242.

5 Henri Lefebvre, "The Right to the City," in *Writings on Cities*, ed. Eleonore Kofman and Elizabeth Lebas (Cambridge, MA: Wiley-Blackwell, 1996), 147–149.

6 David Harvey, *Rebel Cities: From the Right to the City to the Urban Revolution* (London: Verso, 2012), xiii. Also see Harvey, "The Right to the City," *New Left Review* 53, no. 2 (2008): 23–40.

7 For more on this scholarship see: Jeff Maskovsky, "Beyond Neoliberalism: Academia and Activism in a Nonhegemonic Moment," *American Quarterly* 64, no. 4 (December 2012): 819–822; Michan Connor, "Uniting Citizens after *Citizens United:* Cities, Neoliberalism, and Democracy," *American Studies* 54, no. 1 (2015): 5–27; Mark Purcell, "Possible Worlds: Henri Lefebvre and the Right to the City," *Journal of Urban Affairs* 36, no. 1 (2016): 141–154.

8 Lester Spence, *Knocking the Hustle: Against the Neoliberal Turn in Black Politics* (Brooklyn, NY: Punctum Books, 2015), 32.

9 Spence, *Knocking the Hustle*, 51.

10 Klaus Philipsen, *Baltimore: Reinventing an Industrial Legacy City* (London: Routledge, 2017).

11 Spence, *Knocking the Hustle*, 113.

12 Toni Morrison, "The Fisherwoman." foreword to *A Kind of Rapture* by Robert Bergman (New York: Pantheon, 1998).

13 "Maryland Facts," Visit Maryland, accessed April 27, 2018, http://www .visitmaryland.org/info/maryland-facts.

14 The term "renaissance" equates with a form of gentrification, redevelopment, and boosterism that is in line with the neoliberal turn in U.S. cities. Historically, developers and scholars have used the term "Baltimore renaissance" to represent the redevelopment of the city's Inner Harbor and central business district from the 1960s through the 1980s (see chapter 21 by Mary Rizzo for more context). In addition the city has the Renaissance Hotel downtown and Renaissance Academy, a public high school is West Baltimore. In 2010, *What Weekly*, a website that states that it "harnesses and organizes the power of many local creatives," claims that it "was created to 'Document the Baltimore Renaissance,' and to share amazing stories about Baltimore that were often overlooked by mainstream media (https://whatweekly.com/). In 2017 a developer used the term for a redevelopment scheme he presented to the Baltimore City Council; Luke Broadwater, "City Council Greets $10B 'Baltimore Renaissance' Idea with Skepticism," *Baltimore Sun*, July 27, 2017. For more see Davide Ponzini and Ugo Rossi, "Becoming a Creative City: The Entrepreneurial Mayor, Network Politics and the Promise of an Urban Renaissance," *Urban Studies* 47, no. 5 (May 2010): 1037–1057.

15 Elizabeth Fee, Linda Shopes, and Linda Zeidman, "Introduction," in *The Baltimore Book*, vii.

16 Jean Marbella, "Beginning of Freddie Gray's Life as Sad as Its End, Court Case Shows," *Baltimore Sun*, April 23, 2015.

17 Jessica Elfenbein, John R. Breihan, and Thomas L. Hollowak, *From Mobtown to Charm City: New Perspectives on Baltimore's Past* (Baltimore: Maryland Historical Society, 2002).

18 Jessica I. Elfenbein, Thomas L. Hollowak, and Elizabeth M. Nix, *Baltimore '68: Riots and Rebirth in an American City* (Philadelphia: Temple University Press, 2011).

19 In addition to the edited collections mentioned, key historical works on Baltimore include Phillips, *Freedom's Port*; Sartain, *Borders of Equality*; Sherry H. Olson, *Baltimore: The Building of an American City* (Baltimore: Johns Hopkins University Press, 1997); Seth Rockman, *Scraping By: Wage Labor, Slavery and Survival in Early Baltimore* (Baltimore: Johns Hopkins University Press, 2009); Harold McDougall, *Black Baltimore: A New Theory of Community* (Philadelphia: Temple University Press, 1993); Ed Orser, *Blockbusting in Baltimore: The Edmondson*

Village Story (Lexington: University Press of Kentucky, 1997); Kenneth D. Durr, *Behind the Backlash: White Working Class Politics in Baltimore, 1940–1980* (Chapel Hill: University of North Carolina Press, 2003); Andor Skotnes, *A New Deal for All? Race and Class Struggles in Depression-Era Baltimore* (Durham, NC: Duke University Press, 2013); Howell S. Baum, *Brown in Baltimore: School Desegregation and the Limits of Liberalism* (Ithaca, NY: Cornell University Press, 2010); Antero Pietila, *Not in My Neighborhood: How Bigotry Shaped a Great American City* (Chicago: Ivan R. Dee, 2010) and *The Ghosts of Johns Hopkins: The Life and Legacy That Shaped an American City* (Lanham, MD: Rowman & Littlefield, 2018); Matthew A. Crenson, *Baltimore: A Political History* (Baltimore: Johns Hopkins University Press, 2017); Deborah Rudacille, *Roots of Steel: Boom and Bust in an American Mill Town* (New York: Anchor Books, 2010); Paige Glotzer, *Building Suburban Power: The Business of Exclusionary Housing Markets, 1890–1960* (New York: Columbia University Press, forthcoming); Mary Ellen Hayward, *Baltimore's Alley Houses: Homes for Working People since the 1780s* (Baltimore: Johns Hopkins University Press, 2008); Adam Malka, *The Men of Mobtown: Policing Baltimore in the Age of Slavery and Emancipation* (Chapel Hill: University of North Carolina Press Books, 2018); and Mary Ellen Hayward and Charles Belfoure, *Baltimore Rowhouse* (Princeton, NJ: Princeton Architectural Press, 1999). For a more extensive bibliography on Baltimore scholarship and suggestions on research tools see the *Baltimore Revisited* website.

Part I

Place and Power

• •

Roots of (In)Justice in the City

Part I of *Baltimore Revisited*, "Place and Power: Roots of (In)Justice in the City," examines how structural inequality is grounded in place and how it manifests in unequal access to the city's public resources. The authors in this part explore how residents have dealt with entrenched power structures in both successful and unsuccessful ways, as their chapters interrogate what *the public* really means in a city like Baltimore and how public life unfolds across the city's streets and neighborhoods (see Figure 1).

The opening chapter by Robert Gamble begins in the mid-eighteenth century when Baltimore's city government established public markets as part of a larger strategy to ensure residents had access to safe and clean food. Gamble presents Baltimore's earliest public markets as microcosms of the city, urban spaces where citizens asserted but also disputed hierarchies of race, class, and gender. As he argues, the public market "illuminates the intrinsic relationship of food, power, and urban space," a history that anticipates Baltimore's recent push to privatize the city's public markets as the city becomes a national leader in crafting public–private partnerships for urban redevelopment. Moving from public markets to public schools, Emily Lieb argues that Baltimore's segregated schools during the late nineteenth century *created*, and not only reflected, residential segregation by race. She contests the myth that, when African American homeowners moved into white neighborhoods, housing values automatically declined. Her research instead shows how school segregation helped further other forms of racism, such as racial covenants and white supremacist violence.

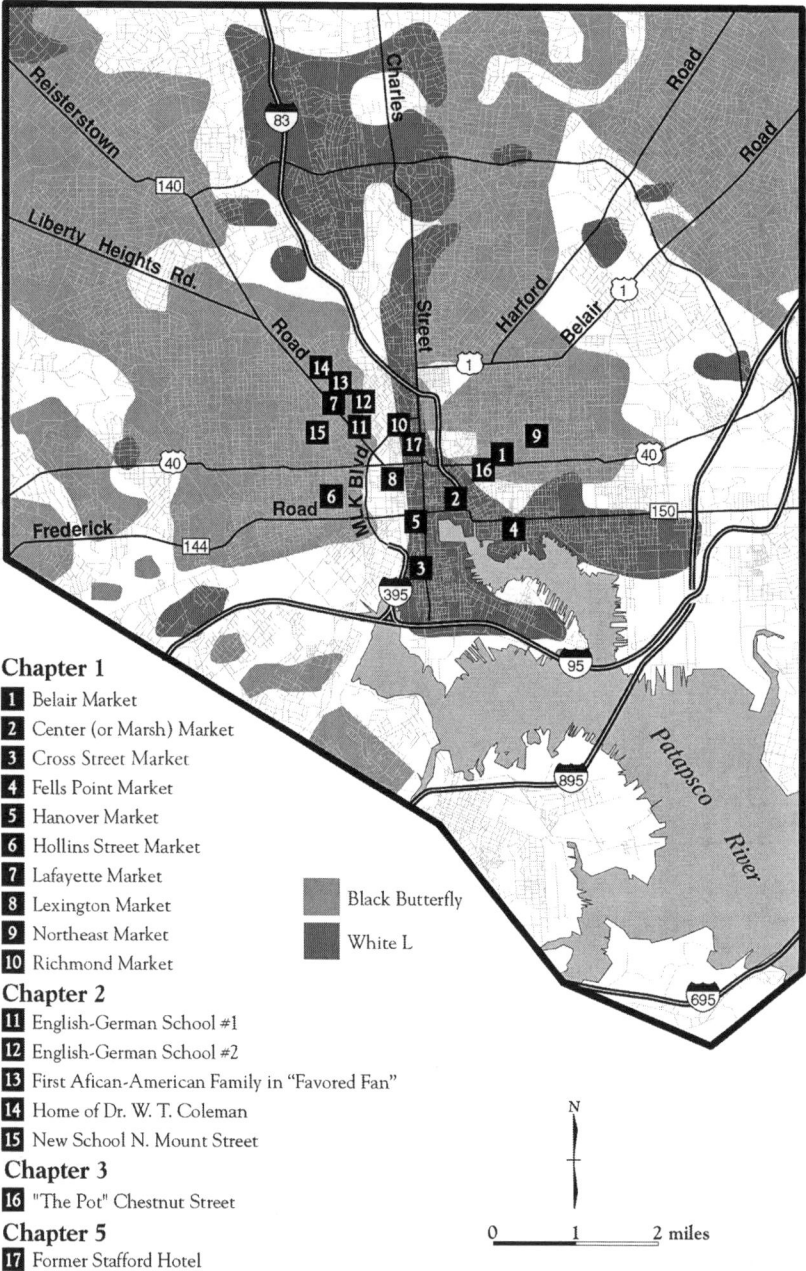

Chapter 1

1 Belair Market
2 Center (or Marsh) Market
3 Cross Street Market
4 Fells Point Market
5 Hanover Market
6 Hollins Street Market
7 Lafayette Market
8 Lexington Market
9 Northeast Market
10 Richmond Market

Black Butterfly

White L

Chapter 2

11 English-German School #1
12 English-German School #2
13 First Afican-American Family in "Favored Fan"
14 Home of Dr. W. T. Coleman
15 New School N. Mount Street

Chapter 3

16 "The Pot" Chestnut Street

Chapter 5

17 Former Stafford Hotel

N

0   1   2 miles

FIG. 1 Map of locations described in Part I. Created by Joe School, 2018.

Homeowners still use the red herring of threats to property value as code for racist and classist views in today's neighborhood Listservs and safety groups. Lieb's chapter pushes us to consider how the blind glorification of private property undergirds an ongoing system of racism and inequity in American cities.

Michael Casiano's chapter focuses on the early twentieth century, when corrupt cops in a neighborhood known as "The Pot" invoked public health concerns and pseudoscience about black criminality to carry out the city's first "war on drugs." This historical moment foreshadowed a current-day war on drugs in Baltimore and throughout the nation's cities, resulting in the frequent incarceration of young black and brown people for nonviolent drug offenses. This legacy continues as the federal corruption trials aimed at members of the Gun Trace Task Force in 2018 found city police officers guilty of stealing and robbing citizens of money and drugs.

The final three chapters investigate inequality as it emerges in an array of forms: vacant housing, psychological trauma, and public health disparities. Eli Pousson addresses the fraught social and racial politics of neighborhood change through an analysis of the city's vacant homes, whose prevalence in Baltimore he traces to the early nineteenth century. Dan Buccino and Teresa Méndez show how many Baltimoreans endure unequal levels of psychological trauma. Buccino and Mendez employ a psychoanalytic framework in assessing this suffering that the city's residents experience because of overpolicing, as well as the murder and violence they all too frequently encounter on the streets of Baltimore. Lawrence Brown addresses white supremacy's critical role in creating major public health disparities in Baltimore. Brown lays bare the disparate realities of what he refers to as the city's "White L," an L-shaped area that is disproportionately white and middle class and enjoys ample services and resources, and the Black Butterfly, the east and west sides of the city that are disproportionately poor and black and are plagued by disinvestment and deteriorating housing. Brown not only shows how racial and class inequality determine life expectancy and other key determinants of survival but he also offers a plan for addressing this inequality with a public policy of increased investment and action he terms the Racial Equity Social Impact Bond.

1

The City That Eats

● ● ● ● ● ● ● ● ● ● ● ● ● ● ● ● ● ● ● ●

Food and Power in Baltimore's
Early Public Markets

ROBERT J. GAMBLE

In his 1855 autobiography, abolitionist Frederick Douglass related one of the
first times he heard Baltimore described. It was sometime in the late 1820s,
shortly after he learned he was to move there from the Eastern Shore, where he
had spent his first decade enslaved. His cousin, just back from Baltimore, "said
a great deal about the market-house." Learning of the market's cacophony of
sights, sounds, tastes, and smells eased young Douglass's nerves, stirring up
"hopes of happiness in [his] new home."[1] For Douglass, as for most Baltimoreans,
the public market represented something more than just a place to purchase
peaches and eggs. It was a gathering spot, a badge of civic identity, a symbol of
municipal authority, and a hub of commercial exchange. With so many functions, meanings, and users, many of them at odds with each other, the market
was both a contested space and a microcosm of the city and its people: diverse
and vibrant, growing and changing, and buffeted by the convulsive forces of
slavery, capitalism, and democracy.[2]

The first attempt to establish a public marketplace in Baltimore came in 1751.
Sensing the village was on the verge of takeoff, fourteen prominent men pledged
funds "to Build a Market House, Town House, and other Necessary Buildings
for the Benefit of said Town, and conveniency of such Persons as bring their

Butcher's meat, and other commodities to sell at Market in the said Town."[3] A decade later, officials contracted with local builders to erect a long and narrow shed on a patch of empty marshland just north of the harbor and west of Jones Falls. The open-air structure was designed with access, cost, maintenance, and adaptability in mind, and architectural embellishments were few. Centre (or Marsh) Market served the town until the early 1780s, when town commissioners authorized three more market houses: Hanover, Fells Point, and Lexington. Despite persistent flooding and mosquitoes, Centre Market anchored an increasingly fashionable and bustling business district. As the city fanned out, Belair (circa 1813), Richmond (1831), Hollins (1835), and Cross Street (1845) Markets followed.[4]

Public markets gave shape to the rapidly growing city's physical and social landscape. Retailers of all stripes congregated in nearby streets and storefronts. Boardinghouses, taverns, and brothels serviced farmers and other travelers. Shopkeepers and auctioneers took advantage of increased pedestrian traffic on market day, festooning sidewalks with their wares, while wholesalers clustered around Centre Market and adjacent wharves. Itinerant hucksters, a notorious group of men and women who bought food from market vendors and resold it at a markup, sized up goods and haggled with farmers and customers. With so much activity, travelers saw markets as windows onto the city's true character. For a visiting Washingtonian in 1824, Baltimore was "the most illiterate, proud and ignorant city, excepting Richmond, in the Union," but the markets' abundance of fruits and vegetables underscored its potential.[5] On the other hand, when New Englander Frederick Law Olmsted toured Washington, D.C., in the 1850s, he saw people in tattered clothes buying food from "small, rickety carts, drawn by the smallest ugliest, leanest lot of oxen and horses" he had ever seen, confirming his view that slavery tainted all it touched.[6]

Versatility defined the market house, as the space morphed over the course of each day and week. Trade was the market's primary function from daybreak to the early afternoon, punctuated occasionally by festivals, artisans' parades, magic demonstrations, outdoor sermons, rabid dogs, runaway horses, and altercations. Some market houses shared spaces with other civic institutions like volunteer fire companies. The Maryland Institute for the Promotion of the Mechanic Arts (later the Maryland Institute College of Art) built its lyceum on top of Centre Market, where it remained until 1904.[7] Some markets also functioned as military depots, feeding soldiers and housing armories. The Maryland National Guard's Fifth Regiment drilled on the second floor of Richmond Market, gathering there before marching on Camden Station one violent night in July 1877 during the Great Railroad Strike. No matter what time of day, the markets were above all social spaces woven into the fabric of the neighborhood. On Saturday evenings, Lexington and Centre Markets became gas-lit spectacles of cross-class sociability, "not only a sight for an epicure but for an artist." One such artist, Fielding Lucas Jr., portrayed Centre Market as a bountiful space, unable to contain all its people and food. In his cross-sectional illustration, hundreds of men, women, and children, black and white, huddled in the shadows of the market house, buying, selling, and conversing with seemingly no regard for social or economic distinctions.[8]

As Lucas's vivid illustration of an 1832 scene shows, public markets reflected the diversity of early Baltimore, where class, racial, and ethnic segregation was not yet widespread or ossified in law. As was the case elsewhere in the black Atlantic, Baltimore's markets permitted a temporary, carnivalesque suspension of racial and class hierarchies. In 1855, an English visitor saw black servants appropriating, and perhaps mocking, the rituals of their white masters and mistresses. "They are exceedingly formal and ceremonious one towards another," he wrote. "They curtsey and bow to each other half a dozen times, and then come a series of giggles and shakings of the hand, interspersed with questions about uncle Johnson, cousin Jackson, and twenty other darkeys of their acquaintance."[9] Markets gave free and enslaved people of color a degree of economic and social autonomy, but they did not insulate them from the omnipresent dangers of the domestic slave trade, Baltimore's other notable "market." The two markets were spatially and legally inextricable: auctioneers conducted slave sales in market courtyards, traders like Hope Slatter jailed their human property in pens at Lexington and Hanover Markets, and slave patrols searched for runaways trying to blend into market-day crowds.[10]

Baltimore's public markets were contradictory spaces for women as well. On the one hand, they provided a respite from the patriarchal ideal of separate spheres that governed other antebellum public spaces. Women across the social spectrum engaged in the same rough-and-tumble practices of negotiation as men. As working- and middle-class women increasingly did the work of shopping for their households—a task long shared by men and women—they seized a larger role in everyday municipal politics. When the city proposed shifting Belair Market from an afternoon to a morning market in the 1840s, thousands of women signed petitions for and against the change. Lucretia Bond expressed the feelings of many when she wrote, "We are as much interested as any other in this change, and as the duty of purchasing principally devolves on the ladies, we as purchasers at this market, ask that some attention be paid to our convenience."[11] As Bond's petition implied, however, women's growing influence as consumer-citizens was made possible by the unpaid labor they were made to do. Moreover, women's prominence as marketers did not grant them more political influence, nor did it promote equal access to other public spaces in the antebellum city.

At the other end of the power spectrum were butchers. These men, and in rare cases women, were deeply invested in the city's markets, having paid as much as $1,000 at auction for the ability to rent their stalls. Stalls, like butchering skills, passed from generation to generation. Prominent victuallers like Henry Pentz and George Rusk held stalls in several markets, rotating among them daily. As they had been for centuries in Europe, butchers in Baltimore and other American cities were politically potent and well organized. Whether leading workers' parades or pressuring city commissioners to maintain and improve market houses, butchers styled themselves defenders not merely of the public market but also of the public good. Customers developed strong loyalties to particular butchers, and the mutual trust undergirding those relationships was—and still is, anthropologists note—what made the public market thrive as an economic and civic institution.[12] This is not to suggest that harmony reigned; haggling often ended in verbal or physical altercations. Writing in the 1860s, New York butcher Thomas DeVoe lamented that cutthroat competition had dissolved the market's self-governing customs of negotiation, as customers became obsessed with price alone and vendors turned to more deceptive practices.[13]

Given the omnipresent potential for conflict and disorder, city authorities took great care to establish market regulations. Among the first provisions in Baltimore's city charter was the "full power and authority to enact and pass all ordinances necessary" for the erection and policing of markets.[14] The very act of establishing a public market was an audacious attempt at governance, delineating where, when, and what people could buy and sell. Residents viewed the regulation of the food trade as an appropriate, indeed vital, governmental responsibility because of its importance to the city's physical and economic health. Clerks were assigned to each market to inspect products exposed for sale, confiscate rotten or adulterated food, check weights and measures, keep the peace, fine or ban wrongdoers, collect rent, clean the common areas, and ring a bell to signal the start and end of market day. The City Council spared little ink to curb fraud, disorder, and disease, passing some two hundred market ordinances between 1797 and 1861.[15]

These efforts met with mixed results: as ambitious as the laws were, enforcement was difficult, particularly for perennially overworked and underpaid market clerks. At their annual sessions, councilmen pored through dozens of petitions from city residents complaining about the conditions of the markets. Horses galloped through crowds, wagons blocked sidewalks and stalls, hucksters harassed farmers, children picked shoppers' pockets, poor men and women vended and begged on street corners, and rotting food and trash assaulted the senses. In an 1845 petition, neighbors of the market in Fells Point informed the City Council they were "greatly anoyed by those who deal in fish" dumping wastewater "indiscriminately where they stand."[16] When the Council proposed building fish stalls at Lexington Market in 1826, one resident predicted they would become a profound nuisance to "the many thousands of citizens, who either reside Westerly, or are in the habit of walking through that very public part of the city." For their part, clerks like Robert Lawson grumbled about the lack of support from the city and marketers in their efforts "to arrest & destroy evil practice[s]." More than any other urban institution, markets tested the small, cash-strapped city corporation's capacity to govern before the Civil War.[17]

To their critics, the markets poisoned not just the physical environment but also the body politic. In 1830, Thomas Griffith groused to the mayor that Centre Market had become a "positive nuisance" that marred the neighborhood. "The Crowds assembled at that Market," he continued, "induce many to keep Tippling-Shops, and no Police [can] prevent Steal, Fighting and many other crimes and vices, contaminating and demoralising those who frequent it."[18] Griffith, like Olmsted (designer of New York's Central Park) and many other nineteenth-century urban observers, believed in a direct link between environment and behavior. The markets' inherent disorder—their congested walkways, chaotic assemblies of people and animals, and dirt and decay—bred coarseness and petty criminality in anyone who spent time there. Commentators worried about the farmers who spent hours on end at their market stalls, whose rural innocence was said to be corroded by constant exposure to urban vice. The *Baltimore Sun* ruefully noted that thieves and swindlers ("sharpers") made quick work of country marketers ("flats").[19]

Hucksters were especially troublesome. To bar them entirely from Baltimore's streets and markets would only add to the public burden. Or, as a group of widows in 1816 put it, "An Alms house then, if they must be fettered from possible industry, must be their final resource."[20] In addition, by vending damaged, overripe, or otherwise unsalable food, hucksters provided a key service both for poorer Baltimoreans who could not afford the freshest goods and for farmers with unsold products on their hands. At the same time, shopkeepers, middling and elite property owners, and moral authorities decried hucksters as a menace to the commonweal: they disturbed the peace, manipulated the price and availability of essential items, sold unhealthy or tainted food, and fenced stolen goods. In 1823, grocers called the City Council's attention to "the practice prevalent in this city, of hawking about the streets candles on poles or otherwise and imported fruits, such as oranges, lemons, limes &c." These hucksters not only defrauded poorer customers, they alleged, but also committed "most of the petty thefts" in the city.[21]

Race figured prominently in critiques of huckstering. Segregation may not have been formalized in law, but white elites nevertheless saw interracial sociability as a threat to public order. An 1806 petition condemned "Disreaputable Inhabatants" in Hanover Market: "from 6 to 8 Lewd women and Black & White and some yellow & as many men of Different Caulers—also fighting & Drunkiness Disturbing the Neighbourhood in the Dead Hour of the Night &c." These "inhabatants" most likely were hucksters intending to negotiate with early arriving farmers.[22] For another group of petitioners in 1824, black vendors attracted unsavory figures to the streets surrounding the market: "by the general introduction of a class of hucksters who occupy the west side of Harrison Street in the sale of old cloathing &c, it has become a mere harbour for drunken disorderly persons & crowds of people of color." After Nat Turner's slave rebellion in 1831, authorities called for stricter surveillance of black customers and vendors in the city's markets. The *Sun*'s report of a peach theft by a "colored hanger-on" in Centre Market ended with a racially coded warning: "Never turn your back on anything that you should keep your eyes upon."[23]

Public markets magnified Baltimore's sharpening racial animosities; they also mirrored the city's deepening economic rifts because of their evolving role in working-class life. Sabbath laws long had targeted laborers' access to markets on Sundays, their lone day off, to prevent places like Centre Market from becoming "the resort of idle and dissolute persons," as petitioners in 1811 put it.[24] Over time, however, these formal restrictions crumbled under the weight of working-class politics. Laborers converted the open-air spaces into meeting sites for citywide strikes in 1833 and 1853. When the Bank of Maryland failed in 1834, wiping out the savings of its mostly poor customers, outraged Baltimoreans gathered in market houses before proceeding to attack symbols of entrenched wealth in the city, including the homes of bank directors. Unsurprisingly, rioting was commonplace in the city known widely as Mobtown, and ethnopolitical turf wars often spilled into the markets. On multiple election days in the 1850s, members of the nativist American Party, or Know-Nothings, exchanged gunfire and brickbats with rival Democrats in Lexington Market, while marketers scattered and took shelter behind stalls.

There were other, less eventful ways that public markets reflected the disruptive forces of capitalist development. Architecture was one ready indicator of shifting urban priorities. Before 1850, Baltimore's market houses were unostentatious: they were low, long, and narrow and open on all sides—a humble combination of brick, timber, and tin sheet. That changed in 1851 with Centre Market's reincarnation as the majestic Maryland Institute Hall.[25] It was Baltimore's first enclosed, multistory market hall, a trend gaining steam in other European and American metropolises as commercial and political leaders reformed the urban retail experience. By sealing out weather and the streets, introducing new amenities and wider walkways, and beautifying its façade, the Institute Market appealed to coalescing middle-class tastes and sensibilities. The City Council removed the fountain from the courtyard—the converging point of all classes and races in Fielding Lucas's sketch—so the market hall could extend to the street and appear "as imposing and ornamental as possible," fit for well-dressed promenaders and shoppers. Market halls like the Maryland Institute Hall contributed to a larger middle-class reform movement to segregate, police, and marginalize the poor in the second half of the nineteenth century.[26]

Most notably, shifting residential patterns necessitated new approaches to urban provisioning. As residential neighborhoods sprouted farther from the harbor and industrialization made possible new, more privatized retail and distribution methods, the system of municipal marketing faltered in the 1840s and 1850s. Aggressive land speculation and cheap housing drew working-class residents to the south and west—closer to emerging industrial areas like Mount Clare, but beyond the reach of traditionally popular markets. Newer markets failed to attract customers and suppliers, even as Belair and Lexington Markets swelled past capacity. In 1852, one hundred residents west of Poppleton Street bemoaned the expansion of Cross Street and Richmond Markets while they faced the "great inconvenience of travelling more than a mile to the Lexington Market." Meanwhile the nearby Hollins Market sat mostly vacant. In 1855, Mayor Samuel Hinks asked the City Council to sell Richmond and Cross Street Markets: "They are used mostly as lounging places for idlers, and playgrounds for boys."[27] As a sign of the skewed demand for market stalls and the trade's high barriers to entry, many upstart butchers took their chances selling without licenses outside Centre Market, rather than rent in one of the newer structures.

The costs of inconvenient market access were dearest for poorer households. Limited market hours restrained working-class Baltimoreans' ability to buy provisions, as petitioners routinely reminded authorities. In 1849, a group of East Baltimore's Old Town "mechanicks and Labouring men" asked that Belair Market be made a morning market so they could shop and "get to our work at the usual hour." Other residents called for different market days altogether. City officials resisted change out of fear that it would upset the delicate competitive balance among the different markets—and diminish their profitability to the municipal corporation.[28] Poorer Baltimoreans were left to shop at more distant markets or find alternative food sources closer to home. Nascent forms of mass transit like omnibuses and horse-drawn streetcars arrived in fits and starts after 1840, but they catered mostly to affluent day trippers, not working-class families on the city's outskirts. Those dislocated from the municipal market system turned to hucksters or small shops known as green groceries for their daily bread. These shops resembled and in fact paved the way for the ubiquitous corner stores that overspread Baltimore during the twentieth century.[29]

Green groceries proliferated across Baltimore in the early 1850s, sparking heated debates about public health and working-class consumer practices. Market butchers led the attack against the new food outlets, many of which were opened by journeymen and apprentice butchers unable to rent stalls in the city's older markets. City delegate (and master butcher) Stirling Thomas introduced a bill in the State Assembly in Annapolis to allow the city to restrict meat sales to the markets, which was eventually passed.[30] Consumers and the City Council were split in their reaction to the new law, however. A March 1856 petition signed by 1,433 men and women deplored the market butchers' "selfishness" and asked that the "honest and enterprising" green grocers' "great public conveniences may be continued, because of the accommodations they afford to the neighborhood in which they are established." Critics of green groceries alleged they sold "cattle which would not be admitted to the slaughter-yards of respectable butchers" and would turn Baltimore into "a vast slaughter house"—endangering both public health and property.[31] Fearing working-class unrest during the economic downturn of the late 1850s, the City Council decided to allow green groceries to continue their march across the city, though it passed regulations governing these new retail outlets. For the next century and a half, these privately owned, small-scale convenience stores would sustain neighborhoods during periods of disinvestment in the municipal market system and the arrival and departure of chain grocery stores. These shops would also serve as frequent talking points in late twentieth- and early twenty-first-century debates about food deserts, public health, and criminality. When Mayor Catherine Pugh called for a reduction in the number of corner stores in April 2018, attributing a rash of criminal activity as well as ongoing public health problems to them, she was entering into a debate that went back more than 150 years.

Privatization of the city's food trade carried many unforeseen costs. As farmers did more business with wholesale merchants, rather than selling directly to consumers in the markets—facilitated by new railroad linkages stretching across the country—Baltimore's geographic sources of food, or foodshed, grew, isolating eaters from their food sources both geographically and psychologically. Green groceries brought food to working-class neighborhoods in the nineteenth century, but they helped create the conditions for food deserts to emerge in the twentieth century. When access to fresh food came to be seen not as a public good but as something best left to abstract market forces, poorer consumers—for whom freedom of choice did not mean the same thing as it did for wealthier shoppers—ultimately suffered. As residential segregation took root in the second half of the nineteenth century, African Americans bore the burdens of unequal food access most of all. Specialized hucksters known colloquially as arabbers first began to sell fruit and vegetables from the back of their horse-drawn carts in the 1860s, and for a century these African American street merchants were crucial links between black neighborhoods and the broader food system. Beginning in the 1960s, however, the number of arabbers dropped from several hundred to perhaps a dozen today, as a battery of health regulations, among other factors, have marginalized the trade.[32]

Despite the green grocery insurgency of the 1850s, public markets remained key economic and civic institutions, adapting to meet the needs of the changing urban population. Officials even erected two new structures: Lafayette Market in 1871 (now Avenue Market) and Northeast Market in 1885. Early twentieth-century photographs of Centre and Lexington Markets reveal how

European immigrants made these spaces their own. As in the early nineteenth century, market stalls passed from generation to generation, and customers remained loyal to particular vendors whom they trusted. The arrival of automobiles in the 1920s prompted a host of spatial transformations to the city's market houses, which saw available space converted to parking lots and docking facilities for another novel technology, refrigerated trucks. Such innovations in refrigeration unlocked new economies of scale, and Baltimore's public markets gradually shifted toward the wholesale trade in the middle third of the century, supplying much of the East Coast with fresh fruit, vegetables, meat, and fish, as customers increasingly relied on grocery stores for their weekly provisions. Myriad interconnected forces eroded the municipal market system in the second half of the twentieth century, particularly white flight and the rise of grocery store chains, which drove consumer spending away from the redlined areas of the city where the public markets were located. Burned down in the Great Fire of 1904 and rebuilt, Centre Market languished in the heart of the declining city core and closed for good in the 1980s when the city embarked on its Harborplace experiment: what developer James Rouse envisioned as "a festival marketplace."[33]

Drawing from celebrated examples of market revitalization in Seattle, San Francisco, and other North American cities, recent years have witnessed repeated efforts to restore Baltimore's extant markets, most notably Lexington, Cross Street, and Hollins, to their former glory. Yet the new markets do not resemble the boisterous, almost chaotic, institutions of the nineteenth century. Baltimore's markets are now viewed as potential agents of gentrification, with developers devoting more space to restaurants—often at the expense of vendors of food staples. To proponents, renovated markets will spur new business and invigorate neighborhood life. Critics worry that the emphasis on a clean, safe, and ultimately mall-like shopping experience will drive current users from the markets and reinforce food inequalities. Like many urban institutions in the early twenty-first century, public markets are at risk of becoming a mere symbol of civic vitality, rather than an actual force for it. Most recently, the city has initiated the process of turning over ownership and management of the six remaining markets to private groups, drawing one of the nation's longest municipal marketing traditions to a potential end.[34]

Debates over the future of Baltimore's public markets fall into another 250-year-long tradition. Since the 1760s, Baltimoreans have battled—in petitions, newspaper editorials, City Council meetings, and the markets and streets—over a fraught question: What and who is a market for? Were market houses designed for farmers and butchers, for poor men and women to make a living, for neighborhoods to gather, for the sale of fresh food or all things, for the promotion of public health or the promotion of property values? Markets were, as this chapter has argued, made and maintained with all these disparate aims in mind, though shifting dynamics of class, race, and gender led certain objectives to be privileged over others. Still, markets' versatility and openness allowed them to weather the economic, social, and environmental transformations wrought by industrialization, slavery, and immigration. As more Baltimoreans crowd farmers' markets, work to overcome food deserts, and tout the city's rich epicurean traditions, the history of the city's public markets illuminates the intrinsic relationship of food, power, and urban space.

Notes

1 Frederick Douglass, *My Bondage and My Freedom* (New York: Dover, 1969 [1855]), 136.
2 Helen Tangires, *Public Markets and Civic Culture in Nineteenth-Century America* (Baltimore: Johns Hopkins University Press, 2003); Cindy R. Lobel, *Urban Appetites: Food and Culture in Nineteenth-Century New York* (Chicago: University of Chicago Press, 2014).
3 J. Thomas Scharf, *History of Baltimore City and County* (Philadelphia: Louis H. Everts, 1881), 205–208.
4 "A New Yorker in Maryland: 1793 and 1821," *Maryland Historical Magazine* 47, no. 2 (1952): 140–141; Sherry H. Olson, *Baltimore: The Building of an American City* (Baltimore: Johns Hopkins University Press, 1997), 19–20. Determining a market's opening date is subjective, because the market houses themselves were erected piecemeal, as funds, materials, and labor permitted. Dates are generally based on when state or municipal laws authorizing new markets were passed, though it often took several years for a building to go up and occasionally even longer for venders to show up.
5 Raphael Semmes, *Baltimore as Seen by Visitors, 1783–1860* (Baltimore: Maryland Historical Society, 1953), 98.
6 Frederick Law Olmsted, *The Cotton Kingdom: A Traveller's Observations on Cotton and Slavery in the American Slave States* (New York: Alfred A. Knopf, 1953 [1861]), 28–29.
7 *Baltimore Sun*, March 5, 1851, and May 14, 1851.
8 Jacob Frey, *Reminiscences of Baltimore* (Baltimore: Maryland Book Concern), 395–396.
9 Alfred J. Pairpoint, *Uncle Sam and His Country; or, Sketches of America, in 1854–55–56* (London, 1857), 223.
10 City Council Records, 1846:372, Baltimore City Archives (hereafter BCA); Christopher Phillips, *Freedom's Port: The African American Community of Baltimore, 1790–1860* (Urbana: University of Illinois Press, 1997).
11 City Council Records, 1849:629, 621, 626, BCA.
12 Stuart Plattner, "Economic Decision Making in a Public Marketplace," *American Ethnologist* 9, no. 2 (May 1982): 399–420; Elijah Anderson, *The Cosmopolitan Canopy: Race and Civility in Everyday Life* (New York: W. W. Norton, 2011), 31–71.
13 Thomas Farrington DeVoe, *The Market Assistant, Containing a Brief Description of Every Article of Human Food Sold in the Public Markets of the Cities of New York, Boston, Philadelphia, and Brooklyn* (New York: Hurd and Houghton, 1867), 21–26.

14 Ch. 68, sec. 9 (1796), Ch. 54, sec. 2 (1797), and Ch. 108, sec. 3 (1805). Clement Dorsey, ed. *General Public Statutory Law and Public Local Law of the State of Maryland, 1692–1839* (Baltimore, 1840).

15 William J. Novak, *The People's Welfare: Law & Regulation in Nineteenth-Century America* (Chapel Hill: University of North Carolina Press, 1996).

16 City Council Records, 1845:282, 284, 703, BCA.

17 *Baltimore Gazette and Daily Advertiser*, February 22, 1826; City Council Records, 1812:547, 1816:467, BCA.

18 Mayor's Correspondence, 1830:1006, BCA.

19 *Baltimore Sun*, September 22, 1842.

20 City Council Records, 1816:327, BCA.

21 City Council Records, 1823:241, BCA.

22 City Council Records, 1806:206A, BCA. See also Seth Rockman, *Scraping By: Wage Labor, Slavery, and Survival in Early Baltimore* (Baltimore: Johns Hopkins University Press, 2009).

23 Mayor's Correspondence, 1824:831, BCA; *Baltimore Sun*, August 18, 1848.

24 City Council Records, 1811:294, BCA.

25 *Baltimore Sun*, March 3 and May 14, 1851; *Charter, Constitution, and By-Laws of the Maryland Institute for the Promotion of the Mechanic Arts* (Baltimore, 1852).

26 City Council Records, 1852:450, 453, 844, BCA; James Schmiechen and Kenneth Carls, *The British Market Hall: A Social and Architectural History* (New Haven: Yale University Press, 1999).

27 Mayor's Correspondence, 1830:1006; City Council Records, 1848:537, 1852:456, 1855:427, BCA; *The Ordinances of the Mayor and City Council of Baltimore, 1855* (Baltimore, 1856), Appendix, 8.

28 City Council Records, 1849:413, 628, 632, BCA.

29 Mary Ellen Hayward, *Baltimore's Alley Houses: Homes for Working People since the 1780s* (Baltimore: Johns Hopkins University Press, 2008), 63–144; David Schley, "Tracks in the Streets: Railroads, Infrastructure, and Urban Space in Baltimore, 1828–1840," *Journal of Urban History* 39, no. 6 (November 2013): 1062–1084.

30 Ch. 333 (1856), *Session Laws of Maryland*, Archives of Maryland Online.

31 City Council Records, 1856:377–382, 388, 383–387, 389–396, BCA; *Baltimore Sun*, March 22 and 26, 1856.

32 "For Want of a Horse: Will This Generation of Arabbers Be Baltimore's Last?," *City Paper*, April 28, 2010; Alison Hope Alkon and Julian Agyeman, eds., *Cultivating Food Justice: Race, Class, and Sustainability* (Cambridge, MA: MIT Press, 2011).

33 Tracey Deutsch, *Building a Housewife's Paradise: Gender, Politics, and American Grocery Stores in the Twentieth Century* (Chapel Hill: University of North Carolina Press, 2010); Shane Hamilton, *Trucking Country: The Road to America's Wal-Mart Economy* (Princeton, NJ: Princeton University Press, 2014).

34 Natalie Sherman, "Plan Calls for Razing, Rebuilding Lexington Market," *Baltimore Sun*, December 2, 2016.

2

"Shove Those Black Clouds Away!"

• • • • • • • • • • • • • • • • • • • •

Jim Crow Schools and Jim
Crow Neighborhoods in
Baltimore before *Brown*

EMILY LIEB

Starting in 1872, when Baltimore opened its first public school for "colored" pupils, the city's black and white children attended legally segregated schools. Municipal policy held that white schools could be converted to black ones "when the neighborhoods in which such schools were situated became colored neighborhoods"—a guideline that left far more to speculation than it proposed to settle.[1] What was a "neighborhood"? How should one determine its boundaries? Likewise, what did "become" mean? Who counted as a black neighbor— and how many black residents did it take to turn a "neighborhood" into a "colored" one?

These taxonomies of race, geography, and community mattered a great deal to many of Baltimore's white homeowners, even those who did not have children in the city's public schools. For them, the most important matter was not the schools themselves; instead, it was the idea that an officially "white" school would create an officially "white" neighborhood, and that a house in an officially "white" neighborhood was worth more than a house someplace else. In

West Baltimore especially, this idea had catastrophic consequences—and it persevered for generations. In fact, the real estate mythology that connects high property values to segregated schools continues to shape American places today.

For the policy's first thirty years, officials rarely applied the secondhand-schools rule: both old schools and newly constructed ones tended to be reserved for the children of white voters, which meant that there actually were not many "colored" schools in Baltimore at all. But in 1898, the state General Assembly approved a new charter for Baltimore City that established several new boards, including a citywide School Board, "designed," one historian writes, "to place critical decisions beyond the reach of ward heelers and machine councilmen."[2] In 1900, the reform-minded mayor Thomas G. Hayes chose a new Superintendent of Public Instruction, James Van Sickle of the Denver School District. Van Sickle was no integrationist, but he did believe that the city's children ought to be able to go to school in the neighborhoods where they lived, and shortly after he arrived in Baltimore he set about reclassifying the city's public schools so that black children would have more options closer to home. He started with the English-German School No. 1 at the corner of Pennsylvania Avenue and Dolphin Street, one of five bilingual public schools established after the Civil War to serve immigrants and their children. By the turn of the century, however, few German speakers still lived in that part of West Baltimore, and half the chairs in the school built only fifteen years earlier sat empty. Furthermore, School Board president Joseph Packard told the *Baltimore Sun* that "the school is located in a section in which the colored population largely predominates." "It is evident," Packard continued, "that if the white school is continued there the attendance will still further decrease, so that the city will have on its hands a large school building with few pupils in it."[3] Thus Van Sickle and his School Board decided on what seemed to them a simple solution to a mathematical problem: to close English-German School No. 1 and open in its place the city's first Colored High School and Polytechnic Institute.[4]

But to many of the English-German School's white neighbors, the problem was neither simple nor mathematical. Most of the men—and they were almost always men—who inveighed against the board's decision spoke English at home, not German, and many did not even have school-age children, but still their dedication to the preservation of the English-German School was absolute. "We are not actuated by race prejudice," explained Lewis Hirshberg of the Northwest Improvement Association at an emergency School Board meeting convened in June, "but we desire to preserve the value of our property, which has taken some of us a lifetime of hard work to accumulate."[5]

Contemporary scholars have developed a sophisticated understanding of the many complicated ways in which cities have evolved: we now know, for example, just how segregation ordinances, restrictive covenants, and exclusionary

zoning and mortgage-lending laws created and perpetuated neighborhood segregation. The story of Progressive-era Baltimore reminds us of the important
and too often overlooked role that schools played then. Indeed, segregated
schools do not just reflect neighborhood segregation; they also create it.[6] In
Baltimore, they were the very first tools that white homeowners used to police
the mapped and unmapped boundaries of their neighborhoods, and they would
turn out to be among the most durable.

Superintendent Van Sickle's instincts were correct: English-German School
No. 1's neighborhood *was* getting blacker. For much of the nineteenth century,
Baltimore had no identifiably African American neighborhoods: as historian
Karen Olson has noted, "although African Americans constituted ten percent
or more of the total population in three-fourths of the city's twenty wards, no
single ward was more than one-third black."[7] But as lawyer W. Ashbie Hawkins
explained in the NAACP journal *The Crisis,* beginning in 1888, when the residents of nearly twenty square miles of Baltimore County to the north and west
voted to join the city proper, "the opening and development of large suburban
tracts for residential purposes by the middle class of whites . . . threw great
blocks of handsome houses [in West Baltimore] on the market, and they had
to be disposed of to anybody, and often on any terms."[8] As one result, those
African Americans who could afford to move to West Baltimore did so.[9] Most
settled in the wedge-shaped area bordered by Druid Hill Avenue, Dolphin
Street, Gilmor Street, and North Avenue.[10]

That West Baltimore wedge had more black residents in absolute numbers
than any other part of Baltimore, but by the School Board's fuzzy standard,
was it a "colored" neighborhood?[11] Other newcomers to the neighborhood comprised what historian Gretchen Boger calls "a tier of whites with a tenuous
hold on middle-class reputation": people like Lewis Hirshberg, who sold insurance; McCulloh Street plumber William Dunnett; and Frank Bartholomee, a
wallpaper hanger whose house, on Pennsylvania Avenue at the corner of Mosher,
was the first he had ever owned.[12] In 1901, Hirshberg's block of Druid Hill Avenue was still all white. Over on Pennsylvania Avenue, according to the 1900
census, Bartholomee's neighbors included a house painter, a carpenter, two
locksmiths, a shoemaker, two dressmakers, and one milliner, all white; the sole
black family on the block was that of John Russell, a merchant sailor.[13] Just
around the corner on Mosher, however, the racial landscape was much less
homogeneous. At 551 Mosher, grocer John Treffinger and his family were white;
just next door, at 549, waiter William Gassaway and his family were African
American. An Irish marble polisher lived between a white butter dealer and a
black musician.[14]

Up and down West Baltimore's rows of houses, this pattern repeated itself.
Some blocks were all white, some were almost all white, and some more closely
resembled what historian Thomas Hanchett calls "salt and pepper."[15] Very few

were all black. Consequently, when School Board president Packard told the newspaper that "the neighborhood . . . [is] at least on two sides surrounded by colored people," he was not tallying up census data or presenting the results of a house-to-house headcount.[16] He was making a more general statement: that a neighborhood with "colored" children needed colored schools, and the question was where, not whether, to create them. A few years later, Superintendent Van Sickle would sum up this way of thinking: "My duties are confined entirely to the educational features of the affair. I have nothing to do with the effect [of school conversions] on property values and social conditions."[17]

In contrast, for the white improvement associations, "property values and social conditions" mattered far more than "the educational features of the affair"—and because people would not live where their children could not go to school, Van Sickle and the School Board had *everything* to do with it. According to the school officials' system of classification, there was no such thing as an integrated neighborhood—a place was "white" or it was "colored," with no in between—and West Baltimore's white property owners believed that keeping the schools "white" would keep the neighborhood from becoming "colored." They wanted schools to serve as chess pieces—rooks and bishops blocking black migration onto white blocks; moreover they wanted *formally* white schools to brand the homes and streets over which they stood sentry. Thus, to the improvement associations and the white homeowners they represented, the fact of black neighbors mattered less than their presence, taxonomically, in the official record.

Why? As many writers have noted, the mythology of market preference for segregation was one of the most powerful forces shaping the twentieth-century American city—not least because, especially after the New Deal, federal housing policy made that mythology true. For example, the Federal Housing Administration's mortgage-redlining rules made sure that a house in an integrated neighborhood *was* worth less than a house in an all-white neighborhood, thereby levying on integration a real financial cost—one that many families, no matter how open-minded, could not afford.[18] But even during the Progressive era, the idea that black neighbors meant lost property values generated its own momentum. That there was no reason why it should be true did not stop people from acting like it was—and their actions made fact out of fiction by enabling a kind of blackmail, later known as "blockbusting," in which realtors used the threat of integration to frighten whites into selling their houses, often for much less than they had paid, to be resold at enormous markup to black families desperate for decent housing.[19] Thus, Jim Crow schools were more than just schools. As far as the white "improvers" were concerned, they were an insurance policy, a promise from the city to keep white assets safe from black encroachment.

And so at the beginning of the 1901 school year, the Northwest Improvement Association and the McCulloh Street Improvement Association sued the

Baltimore City School Board over the planned conversion of English-German School No. 1. The plaintiffs argued that when the City Council had created the school in 1891 it had meant it to always be an English-German school; in other words, the School Board had no flexibility to decide what kind of schools its buildings should house.[20] They also argued that to build a "colored school" at the corner of Pennsylvania and Dolphin would devalue all of the white-owned property in Baltimore. The courts disagreed on both counts.[21] Ruled the Court of Appeals in 1903:

> The ordinance in question could never have intended that the premises could be used only for the uses of one particular school . . . [and] apart from this it seems clear that the complainants suing as taxpayers have no standing in court. It, perhaps, may not be difficult to perceive how the establishment and maintenance of a colored school in the building might result injuriously to the property in the immediate vicinity, but the plaintiffs do not charge that their property will be specially injured by the proposed change, but aver that all the property in the city will be injured—a conclusion very difficult to reach.[22]

In other words, the judges ruled that the School Board could do what it wanted with its property.

Still, West Baltimore's white residents kept fighting. In 1903, Frank Bartholomee and the Northwest Improvement Association rallied the neighborhood's white parents against School Board plans to put another black school a block away from English-German School No. 1, on the site of a white grammar school at Division and Lanvale Streets. The Division Street school had once served so many white students that the district had to annex two nearby buildings to house them all, but lately it was only about half-full. "The school building will inevitably soon be empty," Superintendent Van Sickle told a reporter, and "we have a large number of colored children that we are unable to house, and who live contiguous to the building. The question for the board, and the taxpayers to settle is whether they will allow this building to become empty and build a new one for the colored children, or utilize this one for the purpose."[23] President Packard likewise pleaded with the neighborhood's white parents to "make room for colored children."[24] However, his appeals foundered in the face of what the *Sun* called the "self-evident fact that the presence of a negro school, or of any negro institution whatever in a neighborhood where white people reside, will lower the value of their property and that the presence of such a school will be an incentive for negroes to move into the neighborhood and by so doing further lower the value of property and reduce the taxable basis of the city."[25] The obstreperousness of the community's protest led Van Sickle to change his mind about the Division Street school, but he cautioned parents that "it is plain . . . that No. 46 must become a colored school unless the board has the earnest and hearty co-operation of the white people of the neighborhood in keeping it a white school. They must not send their children to schools further away, and then protest the school, which they have thus helped to deplete, being changed to a colored school."[26]

Meanwhile, the *Afro-American* newspaper kept on pointing out that the *Sun*'s "self-evident fact" was not a fact at all. "Not satisfied with doing the colored children out of the school on Division street," the paper reported a few months later, "the white people are now making a fight to prevent the new school building on N. Mount street, which is being erected for the use of colored children, being used for that purpose."[27] The Southwest Baltimore Improvement Association did not dispute that African Americans comprised the majority of the school-aged children in the neighborhood just then; as the *Afro-American* pointed out, "the Macedonia Baptist Church, which is next door to the school, had been there for twenty years and had not depreciated the property, and . . . the neighborhood was now largely colored."[28] However, the improvement association argued that this would not be true for long. A pair of developers had a few months earlier purchased an old playground not far from the Mount Street school site and announced plans to build more than 100 new houses there—houses that would be reserved for white buyers.[29] This would seem to be perfect evidence that property values did *not* automatically plummet in the presence of black institutions, but the improvement association did not see things that way. Instead, it floated two somewhat contradictory arguments: first, that the occupants of the new houses would tip the balance in favor of the neighborhood's white pupils; and second, as one white neighbor put it, that "if given over to the use of colored children, [the school] will prove an attraction for colored persons who will have children attending, and many of these . . . will have a tendency to move into that neighborhood."[30] Either way, to the community's white improvers, the Mount Street school was unwelcome.

Clearly, West Baltimore's white homeowners felt entitled to the protection they believed Jim Crow ought to provide, as if keeping their neighborhoods segregated was the city's side of the social contract. They embraced the paradox of segregation's self-regulating invisible hand: the *Sun*'s "self-evident fact" that the presence of black people "always causes a marked and immediate depreciation in the value of property" and the equally self-evident fact that integration was a real bonanza for the real estate men who trafficked in it.[31] Only the School Board had the power to defend their property by declaring it officially "white"— and yet the School Board would not act. So West Baltimore's whites embraced an unprecedented expansion of local government's regulatory powers via what one called a "legislative enactment to prevent the encroachment of negroes in the white residential sections."[32]

By 1910, West Baltimore below Druid Hill Avenue was pretty well integrated. According to historian Gretchen Boger, "if the development of streetcar suburbs had been the initial pull for departing white residents, the arrival of increasing numbers of African Americans was a push," until by the end of the decade the neighborhood was "home to almost half of the city's black population."[33] But Druid Hill Avenue itself was the limit, because above it lay what Baltimoreans called the "favored fan": McCulloh Street, Madison Avenue, and especially Eutaw Place, known as the "Champs Élysées of Baltimore."[34] To whites below the line, integration was, by now, a fact of life.[35] To whites above it—and especially to the neighborhood's relative newcomers, people who had scrimped and saved to say they had a Eutaw Place address—the idea that they might live in a "colored" neighborhood was still thoroughly repugnant. The neighborhood had no schools for African American pupils and none were proposed, but the School Board had proven itself to be an unreliable ally. No other city official had the power or the grounds to protect white property from integration. There was nothing to do but worry and wait.

And then, at the end of June 1910, it happened: a black family moved into 1834 McCulloh Street, one block north of the Druid Hill line. (These first migrants were George McMechen, Ashbie Hawkins's law partner, and his family.) On July 5, the day after boxer Jack Johnson beat the "Great White Hope" Jim Jeffries to become the first black heavyweight champion of the world, the white property owners of the "favored fan" formed the Madison Avenue, McCulloh Street, and Eutaw Place Improvement Association. They were determined to win the passage of an "ordinance . . . for the prevention of further invasion" that would "permanently fix the value of real estate [and] remove a large percentage of the risk now involved in investing in Baltimore property."[36] Such a law would not require white homeowners to rely on schools as proxy for neighborhoods. It would buoy the housing market and keep white blocks white while eliminating the problem of the perfidious Superintendent Van Sickle—who in October 1910 alone had proposed the conversion of three more neighborhood schools from white to black.[37] Perhaps elected officials would make better allies than appointed reformers had.

Everything south of North Avenue lay in Baltimore's 14th Ward, represented on the City Council by the "thoroughly Republican" Augustus C. Binswanger.[38] Almost half of the voters in the 14th Ward were black, and Binswanger knew it: among other things, the *Afro-American* reminded voters before the 1911 election, he had "protected the colored man's right to register and vote . . . for many years" and pushed for the construction of more and better public schools for the black pupils in his district.[39] For Councilman Binswanger, a vote in favor of any kind of Jim Crow law would have been politically suicidal. For Councilman Samuel West, who represented the all-white 13th Ward just to the north, the opposite was true.[40] Councilman West spent August in his office with Milton Dashiell, an attorney and exuberant racist who lived down the block from the McMechens, and together they drafted what they called "an ordinance for preserving order, securing property values and promoting the great interests and insuring the good government of Baltimore city." The new law was forthright. "In the territory bounded by North avenue, Charles street, Baltimore street and Fulton avenue," it said, "no negroes shall move into houses on streets on which a majority of whites live."[41] In other words, in theory, the ordinance would freeze West Baltimore just as it was: white blocks would stay white, and black blocks would stay black.

Immediate objections to the West law fell into three categories. The first was legal. "The negro has been endowed with civil rights," one segregation-sympathetic white lawyer reminded the newspaper, "and any attempt to challenge this might be declared illegal by the United States Supreme Court."[42] The second was ethical. "When a man own[s] a piece of property," said Councilman Binswanger, "he own[s] it from the centre of the earth to the heavens and no ordinance, building inspector or anybody else ha[s] any business saying what he should do with it."[43] The third was practical. "Residents of sections contiguous to the segregation area," reported the *Sun*, "feared that other parts of Baltimore would have to take care of a possible exodus of colored residents."[44] In other words, should some whites have to suffer more black neighbors because other whites wanted none? This last line of reasoning persuaded Dashiell and West that residential segregation would have to be an all-or-nothing enterprise, and in October they submitted a revised law to the City Council. The adjusted law said that no black person could move onto a majority-white block anywhere in Baltimore; it also said that no white person could move onto a majority-black block.[45] From city line to city line, Baltimore would be a Jim Crow town.

Except that it was not. In the end, Baltimore ran through several segregation ordinances: the City Council kept on tweaking them from 1910 until 1917, adjusting their language over time to make it easier and more profitable for real estate men to flip blocks from "white" to "mixed" to "black."[46] Consequently, none of the ordinances did what West Baltimore's white homeowners wanted. Almost every day the newspapers printed another jarring headline about the advancing "negro invasion" of West Baltimore—the 800 block of McCulloh; the 200 block of West Lanvale; the 1300 block of Eutaw Place, Stricker Street, and Mosher Street, and Myrtle Avenue. Just as they had given up on Superintendent Van Sickle's School Board, the neighborhood's improvement associations gave up on the West ordinance.

"Feeling that there is no law under which they can prevent further inroads," the *Sun* reported in 1913, "the white people [of West Baltimore] have openly declared that they will use their own method in the disposing of the unwelcome neighbors" and restoring legally "white" blocks.[47] Mobs of white men, some of whom were paid by local neighborhood protective associations, smashed rocks through every window of black-owned houses. They fashioned medieval-style catapults and trebuchets for bricks, marbles, and rotten vegetables.[48]

They dumped old garbage on stoops and splashed paint on doors and windows. They sawed off someone's front porch and tipped it into the street.[49] And it got worse: on Mosher Street that September, one African American woman was shot in her house while her neighbor was stabbed in the street.[50] Everywhere in West Baltimore, houses burned—even houses on legally "colored" blocks, even houses that had been black owned for years.[51] This violence was personal, aimed straight at African American families—no city councilor ever came home to find a bottle bomb alight in his front hall—but it seemed to be making a political argument: for the white homeowners of West Baltimore, public policy had failed.

In contrast, for realtors, and especially for developers in the "restricted" western suburbs, it had been a wild success. Just past the old city line in Edmondson Terraces, for instance, the Piel Company's neat, affordable rowhouses sold almost as quickly as they could be built.[52] Ads boasted that a person could "Buy a Piel Home for $300 Down and $9.32 Per Week—And Live Happy Ever After."[53] He would have "good, substantial neighbors," "no alley houses," and "no saloon corners." In-town realtors pressed some advantages, like moving doorways and mailboxes (and therefore addresses) from one side of a house to another so that a house on an all-white block could be sold to a black family on a "mixed" one, while their suburban counterparts promised permanently white schools and a "community spirit" that could be centered around three-legged races and pie-baking contests instead of racist invective and terrorist plots.[54]

Elsewhere, in places like Kansas City, New Orleans, and Montgomery, Baltimore-inspired laws took different forms. In 1914, the Louisville City Council passed a law making it illegal for African Americans to live on majority-white blocks and for whites to live on majority-black blocks.[55] Unlike Baltimore's ordinance, this law effectively made blockbusting illegal—undermining the interests of realtors as well as African Americans—and so the local branch of the NAACP found an eager ally in Louisville's all-white Real Estate Exchange and took the law to court.[56] In 1917, in the case *Buchanan v. Warley*, a unanimous Supreme Court ruled against the Louisville housing-segregation law—and if realtor Buchanan had the right to do with his property what he pleased in Kentucky, did he not have that same right in Maryland or anywhere else? At the end of that year, the last violation of the West ordinance reached the city's courts; and though his white neighbors vowed to keep on exercising all of the "ways and means whereby the negro can be compelled to move," the judge ruled that Dr. W. T. Coleman had the right to stay in the house he had bought at 2039 McCulloh.[57] "We all have to bow to the Supreme Court," Coleman told the *Sun*.[58] The city government had lost some of its power to tell Baltimoreans where they could and could not live.

But it had not lost *all* of its power. Instead, West Baltimore's whites were back where they started, depending on the School Board to keep their neighborhoods segregated. In 1911, Superintendent Van Sickle had lost his job, and throughout the 1910s, while the battles over the segregation ordinances raged, school conversions virtually stopped. In 1918, the city annexed dozens more square miles of its suburbs, whose new developments were often restricted by deed covenants that made the color line seem permanently impregnable. There white Baltimoreans who had the money could live securely in the knowledge that their white schools and neighborhoods would stay that way for (they thought) generations. Meanwhile, inside the old city line, white homeowners spent the 1920s fighting one school conversion after another. They used the same language their forefathers had: their arguments were seeded with phrases like "property values," "neighborhood stability," and "homeowners' rights," and they were steeped in the idea that public policy's primary obligation was to protect white investments. And as it happened, after the 1918 annexation, the pace of school conversions accelerated again, pushing whites to pack their belongings, sell their houses to blockbusters, and head to the west: to the covenant-segregated urban suburbs just inside the city line that filled as fast as developers could build them.[59]

What happened before Baltimore passed its segregation ordinances tells us a great deal about urban growth and neighborhood change at the beginning of the twentieth century and about the ways in which schools—the anchor institutions of every community—shape and are shaped by the city around them. In Baltimore, segregated schools created segregated neighborhoods, not the other way around. Even more, once segregated, neighborhoods tend to stay that way—and as present-day Baltimoreans can attest, neighborhood segregation has real, bitter consequences.

Notes

The chapter title is taken from J. Nelson Grim, letter to the editor, *Baltimore Sun*, July 31, 1903.

1   "To Remain White School," *Baltimore Sun*, August 8, 1903.
2   Robert J. Brugger, *Maryland, A Middle Temperament: 1634–1980* (Baltimore: Johns Hopkins University Press/Maryland Historical Society, 1988), 404.
3   "Board Explains Why," *Baltimore Sun*, June 29, 1901.
4   "To Combine Schools," *Baltimore Sun*, May 9, 1901.
5   "Protest to Board," *Baltimore Sun*, June 20, 1901.
6   For more examples of this way of thinking about schools and neighborhoods, see Andrew R. Highsmith and Ansley T. Erickson, "Segregation as Splitting, Segregation as Joining: Schools, Housing, and the Many Modes of Jim Crow," *American Journal of Education* 121 (August 2015): 563–595; and David G. Garcia and Tara J. Yosso, "'Strictly in the Capacity of Servant': The Interconnection between Residential and School Segregation in Oxnard, California, 1934-1954," *History of Education Quarterly* 53, no. 1 (February 2013): 64–89. See also Ansley T.

Erickson, *Making the Unequal Metropolis: School Desegregation and Its Limits* (Chicago: University of Chicago Press, 2016).

7　Karen Olson, "Old West Baltimore: Segregation, African-American Culture, and the Struggle for Equality," in *The Baltimore Book: New Views of Local History*, ed. Elizabeth Fee, Linda Shopes, and Linda Zeidman (Philadelphia: Temple University Press, 1991), 59.

8　Historical Growth Map of City of Baltimore, Department of Public Works, 1977, http://mdhistory.net/msaref14/bc_maps/bc_historical_growth_sc5458_4_134 -0006.pdf; W. Ashbie Hawkins, "A Year of Segregation in Baltimore," *The Crisis* (November 1911): 27.

9　Olson, "Old West Baltimore," 59.

10　Hawkins, "A Year of Segregation in Baltimore," 27.

11　Hawkins, "A Year of Segregation in Baltimore," 27; Olson, "Old West Baltimore," 57–81.

12　Gretchen Boger, "The Meaning of Neighborhood in the Modern City: Baltimore's Residential Segregation Ordinances, 1910–1913," *Journal of Urban History* 35, no. 2 (January 2009): 238.

13　Bureau of the Census, *Twelfth Census of the United States*, Year: 1900, Census Place: Baltimore Ward 15, Baltimore City (Independent City), Maryland, Roll 614, p. 10, Enumeration District 0198, FHL microfilm 1240614.

14　Bureau of the Census, *Twelfth Census of the United States*, p. 11A.

15　Thomas W. Hanchett, *Sorting out the New South City: Race, Class, and Urban Development in Charlotte, 1875–1975* (Chapel Hill: University of North Carolina Press, 1998).

16　"The Germans Object," *Baltimore Sun*, June 13, 1901.

17　"Why He Advised Move," *Baltimore Sun*, July 27, 1903.

18　As writer Ta-Nehisi Coates puts it in the June 2014 issue of the *Atlantic*, "When the mid-20th-century white homeowner claimed that the presence of [an African-American family] decreased his property value, he was not merely engaging in racist dogma—he was accurately observing the impact of federal policy on market prices. Redlining destroyed the possibility of investment wherever black people lived." Ta-Nehisi Coates, "The Case for Reparations." *The Atlantic* (June 2014): 66. See also David M. P. Freund, *Colored Property: State Policy & White Racial Politics in Suburban America* (Chicago: University of Chicago Press, 2007).

19　See, for instance, W. Edward Orser, *Blockbusting in Baltimore: The Edmondson Village Story* (Lexington: University Press of Kentucky, 1994).

20　"Want No Colored School," *Baltimore Sun*, September 17, 1901.

21　"Object to Negro School," *Baltimore Sun*, May 8, 1902.

22　"Decisions in Four Cases by the Court of Appeals," *Baltimore Sun*, January 24, 1903, 10.

23　"Why He Advised Move."

24　"Just think of such an answer as that to a body of white men," one snarled to a reporter. "We [won't] stand by and see our children turned out of a school that has always been a school for the white children of this neighborhood and . . . see it turned over to a lot of negroes." "Indignant at School Board," *Baltimore Sun*, July 15, 1903.

25　"Section Is up in Arms," *Baltimore Sun*, July 16, 1903.

26　"To Remain White School," *Baltimore Sun*, August 8, 1903.

27 "Mount Street School," *Baltimore Afro-American*, September 26, 1903, 4; "Too Old for School," *Baltimore Sun*, October 15, 1903, 7; "Maryland Telephone Ordinance Now Goes to Mayor," *Baltimore Sun*, May 10, 1904.

28 "Protest Meeting," *Baltimore Afro-American*, October 3, 1903.

29 "Garrett Park Bought," *Baltimore Sun*, December 11, 1902.

30 "Object to Colored School," *Baltimore Sun*, September 10, 1903.

31 "Oppose Negro School," *Baltimore Sun*, July 23, 1903.

32 The *Baltimore Sun's* account of the meeting continued: "To this was added the reverse proposition, which created much laughter, that no white person should occupy a house in a block occupied by negroes without the consent of the majority of the dusky residents." "To Keep out Negroes," *Baltimore Sun*, November 8, 1907.

33 Boger, "The Meaning of Neighborhood," 240.

34 Carl H. Nightingale, "The Transnational Contexts of Early Twentieth-Century American Urban Segregation," *Journal of Social History* 39, no. 3 (Spring 2006): 673.

35 In *The Crisis*, Hawkins explained, "More or less friction had been caused whenever a block was invaded—in several instances harsh measures were taken, such as breaking window lights, putting tar on the white marble steps, and in other ways mutilating the property. In one or two cases the families moving in were frightened away, but the great majority stuck, and after a short time the excitement wore off, the whites either moving themselves or resigning gracefully to their fate." Hawkins, "A Year of Segregation in Baltimore," 27.

36 "Residents Are Aroused," *Baltimore Sun*, September 26, 1910.

37 These were School 39 (Carrollton and Riggs), School 30 (Hollins and Monroe), and School 21 (Pennsylvania and Robert). In response, a representative from the Northwest Improvement Association made a familiar argument: "It has been the custom of the School Board in the past to establish colored schools at the outposts of colored districts. This had a tendency to attract negroes into the white districts. The board should establish these schools in the central section of the negro population." "If the board finds no need for a white school at Pennsylvania avenue and Robert street," he continued, "then it should sell the present building and establish a colored school somewhere among the negro residents." "Against Negro School," *Baltimore Sun*, October 13, 1910.

38 Eugene Fauntleroy Cordell, *University of Maryland, 1807–1907: Its History, Influence, Equipment, and Characteristics*, vol. 2 (Baltimore: Lewis Publishing Company, 1907), 158.

39 *Baltimore Afro-American*; *The Baltimore Sun Almanac for 1910* (Baltimore: Sun Printing Office, 1911), 151.

40 Of 5,000 eligible voters in the 13th Ward, just 58 were black. *The Baltimore Sun Almanac for 1910*, 151.

41 Ordinance No. 610, *Ordinances and Resolutions of the Mayor and City Council of Baltimore, Passed at the Annual Session, 1910–1911* (Baltimore: Meyer & Thalheimer, 1911), 204.

42 "Negro Homes Stoned," *Baltimore Sun*, September 9, 1910.

43 "Fight over West Bill," *Baltimore Sun*, March 21, 1911.

44 "West Plan Is Amended," *Baltimore Sun*, October 10, 1910.

45 Ordinance No. 610, 205.

46 See Emily Lieb, "Row House City: Unbuilding Residential Baltimore, 1940–1980" (PhD diss., Columbia University, 2009) and "Shove Those Black Clouds Away!

Inventing Segregation in Baltimore," in *The Suffocated Suburb: How Planners and Policymakers Sabotaged a Baltimore Neighborhood* (unpublished book manuscript). See also Boger, "The Meaning of Neighborhood," and Garrett Power, "Apartheid Baltimore Style," *Maryland Law Review* 42 (1983).

47 "Negro House Attacked," *Baltimore Sun*, September 18, 1913.

48 "Negro Homes Stoned," *Baltimore Sun*, September 24, 1913, 16.

49 "Negro House Attacked."

50 "One Shot, One Stabbed," *Baltimore Sun*, September 27, 1913, 16.

51 "One Shot, One Stabbed."

52 "Come out to Fairmount Today," *Baltimore Sun*, May 30, 1913.

53 Piel Co. ad in the *Baltimore Sun*, November 1, 1913.

54 For instance, 1336 Laurens Street, a white block, became 1301 Calhoun—a "mixed" block. 2001 McCulloh became 406 Presstman, and the architect of the new Colored Y.M.C.A. placed its entrance on Dolphin Street instead of McCulloh. "Segregation Case Argued," *Baltimore Sun*, April 2, 1915; "Angry at Negro Lawyer," *Baltimore Sun*, August 4, 1915; "School Board Protests," *Baltimore Sun*, February 1, 1917; "Single Block Holds Fete," *Baltimore Sun*, July 5, 1912.

55 Power, "Apartheid Baltimore Style," 311.

56 In "Apartheid Baltimore Style," 312, historian Garrett Power tells the story of the ensuing court challenge:

> The scenario had William Warley, president of the Louisville branch of the NAACP, contract to buy a corner lot from Charles Buchanan, a white real estate agent. The lot in question was in a "white block" but was surrounded by black residences. The contract provided that Warley was not required to perform "unless I have the right under the laws of the State of Kentucky and the City of Louisville to occupy said property as a residence.
>   . . . Hence the case of *Buchanan v. Warley* had been staged to work a role reversal. Buchanan, the plaintiff challenging the constitutionality of the ordinance, was a white real estate agent. Warley, the defendant defending the ordinance, was the black president of the Louisville branch of the NAACP. . . . In *Buchanan*, the NAACP hoped to convince the Court to protect Buchanan's constitutional right to engage in the real estate business without meddlesome interference from the City of Louisville (and thereby incidentally to protect blacks from residential housing segregation).

57 "Resent Negro Invasion," *Baltimore Sun*, November 18, 1917.

58 "Resent Negro Invasion."

59 See Emily Lieb, "*The City's Dying and They Don't Know Why*" (unpublished manuscript).

3

"The Pot"

• •

Criminalizing Black
Neighborhoods in Jim Crow
Baltimore

MICHAEL CASIANO

On June 21, 1902, on the last page of the *Baltimore Sun*'s morning edition, there appeared a small news bit titled "Cocaine and Beer Cause Trouble." In it, Henrietta Woods, a black woman, was reported to have created a commotion on downtown Baltimore's Chestnut Street, in a neighborhood the *Sun* coined "The Pot."[1] According to the story, Woods shattered a beer glass over the head of one woman and a lampshade over the head of another because she supposedly "couldn't get enough beer to wash down a quantity of cocaine." Woods then reportedly threw another beer bottle in the direction of a patrolman who detained her.[2]

In the early twentieth-century white press, this type of story was not uncommon.[3] Nationally, cocaine, though seen as useful for its anesthetic qualities in dentistry and for its flavor profile in tonics and soft drinks following its explosion in popularity during the late nineteenth century, was seen by some whites as an intensifier of black aggression. The white press frequently published stories in which black behaviors were interpreted through the prism of cocaine's supposed effects on physical and mental prowess, attributing social disorder—including race riots, breaches of the peace, and moral degradation—to the drug.

Such moral panic culminated in the drug's nationwide regulation with the passage of the Harrison Act of 1914.[4]

In Baltimore, during the drug's heyday, the combination of cocaine use and criminal activity was distinctly associated with black women in the city's slums. For instance, three years after the article on Henrietta Woods's activities on Chestnut Street, the *Sun* published a much longer story on cocaine use with this subheader: "Nearly Every Negress Arrested Is a Victim of the Drug."[5] The story was written with descriptive prose and documented what was considered a common cocaine narrative. In it, a black woman managed to procure the drug after borrowing ten cents from a friend, typically on Chestnut Street, also called the "great cocaine way." She probably bought it from a druggist or a drug dealer, many of whom worked for a druggist. Once the woman's body absorbed the drug, she became enraged and created an uproar, ending in a violent act or some other crime that would get her imprisoned. Tucked in her cell, the woman's "shrieks and yells, curses and blasphemies" shook the station house. Unable to control herself, she became at times despondent, at times energized, and could dance the entire night without a break: a victim of her uncontrolled freedom.

In recounting this generalized scenario and the commotion in The Pot, the *Sun* joined many early twentieth-century U.S. institutions in characterizing crime as a cultural particularity of black life. This chapter demonstrates how white institutions used these characterizations to justify the criminalization of black communities. It does so through an intersectional framework that accounts for the ways that black men and women were subject to political and civil subordination based on the construction of racial and gendered perceptions that manifested in institutional repression and the reproduction of social hierarchies of power that continue to exist in the present.[6]

The setting of this chapter is The Pot, a neighborhood in downtown Baltimore bounded by Fayette, Gay, Exeter, and Aisquith Streets. The Pot's moniker was popularized by the *Sun* and was intended to conjure images of a metaphorical "boiling over": an excess of illicit social customs that had reached critical levels. Using archival documentation—including newsprint, city records, and Progressive publications—this chapter details how perceptions of and interventions in The Pot led to the criminalization of drug possession. In doing so, it demonstrates how the period's Jim Crow preoccupations with black adaptation to city life, the development and reinforcement of racialized and gendered narratives in the press, and the institutionalization of invasive policing and reformatory practices in city policy were intricately connected to and justified by critiques of black life and culture.

The chapter first introduces Swann's Cocaine Ordinance and contextualizes the national and local debates that animated perceptions of black urbanites during the early twentieth century. It then details the geographic and cultural particularities of the neighborhood known as The Pot using *Sun* exposés and other archival information to show how The Pot itself was a geographic construction articulated in the press as an example par excellence of black unfitness for city life.[7] The chapter then highlights the cocaine trade in the city and provides biographical sketches of two black Potters—Daniel "Big Dan" Waters and Alverta "Sweetie" Bailey—demonstrating how raced and gendered meanings were attached to Potters in ways that illuminate the Progressive era belief that black antisocial mores served as grounds for reform and penalization. Finally, the chapter describes the trial of five white police officers charged with abetting cocaine traffic in The Pot. The press accounts of the trial's proceedings and black witness testimonies illustrate how characterizations of black criminal activity shaped perceptions of black unworthiness. They also serve as evidence that this political theater was in some way connected to the passage of Swann's Cocaine Ordinance because the bill's author, Colonel Sherlock Swann, also presided over the trial of the officers while the ordinance was debated and rushed through City Hall.

Framing Black Criminality in the Early Twentieth Century

In 1908, the City Council passed Swann's Cocaine Ordinance, named after Colonel Sherlock Swann, the grandson of Maryland governor Thomas Swann. Colonel Swann was a notable public servant in Baltimore who came to prominence in 1904 as chairman of the Burnt District Commission, which oversaw infrastructure rehabilitation after the Great Fire. In 1908, after withdrawing from the race for mayor, Swann was appointed chairman of the Board of Police Commissioners.[8] During his tenure with the Police Board, Swann drafted and advocated for the passage of an ordinance that would expand the scope of state legislation regulating narcotic traffic to criminalize the *possession*—rather than just the distribution—of illicit drugs.

The ordinance's passage is worth noting because of the enduring legacy that charges of drug possession have had on Baltimore's black residents, particularly in an age of mass incarceration. Though the War on Drugs is popularly understood as a product of the 1970s, there is substantial and compelling evidence to suggest that a "war on baneful drugs" that had uncannily similar features to the modern incarnation—though at an apparently smaller scale—occurred in the first two decades of the twentieth century.[9] Swann's Cocaine Ordinance, the first of its kind in Baltimore, represented one of these features. More than the ordinance itself, the circumstances behind its passage are illustrative of the persistent strategies that characterize antiblack racism in American cities wherein behaviors, such as cocaine use, are racialized through the construction and repeated reproduction of the figure of the black criminal in multiple institutional realms, such as the press, the police, and the Progressive movement.

Swann's Cocaine Ordinance passed during a period of broad national debate surrounding the question of black fitness for civil life in the cities of the North. As black populations in cities rose because of increased migration from the South, so too did the scrutiny under which black city dwellers were forced to live. Many Progressive reformers around the country, as well as in Baltimore, came to agree that the increased presence of black people in urban centers would invariably cause the spiking of social problems, such as crime, juvenile delinquency, and potential "race wars."[10] The justifications surrounding these beliefs resulted in what Khalil Gibran Muhammad refers to as the systemic "incrimination of culture," by which black social customs and ways of life came to be seen as peculiar and unique aspects of blackness that predisposed black people to antisocial activities, including crime.[11] At the turn of the century, this incrimination of culture was, as Chad Heap argues, instituted through the activities of public and private reform organizations that "battled to control the moral construction of the urban landscape." These battles criminalized areas within urban geographies through the racialization of sexual and social deviance that articulated blackness as a problem that had to be solved.[12]

In Baltimore, reformers like Helen Pendleton, Janet Kemp, and J.H.N. Waring articulated the "problem" of black poverty and criminality as intrinsically tied to and informed in some way by black culture. Pendleton and Kemp were members of the charity organization society movement, which emerged during the Gilded Age and was founded on principles of moral uplift that located the roots of poverty within the morally reprehensible behaviors and cultural predilections of the impoverished. Charity organization society members frequently went on "friendly visits" to poor neighborhoods to document urban mores and facilitate moral betterment.[13] Drawing from her friendly visits in Baltimore's black neighborhoods, Pendleton, in an article on "negro dependency," concluded that black antisocial behavior was an outgrowth of the abrupt removal of the regulatory mechanisms present in African slavery, which, hypothetically, had suppressed the emergence of these inherent antisocial behaviors. Particularly, Pendleton found black women's sexual promiscuity and violent tendencies to threaten family values and therefore to require increased social control. Kemp, in a report on housing conditions in Baltimore, attributed deteriorating residential landscapes in black neighborhoods to idleness, drug use, and alcoholism. Juxtaposed against European immigrants and their offspring, whom Kemp viewed as virtuous despite their difficult surroundings, the reformer concluded that black cultural customs uniquely precipitated the decline of black neighborhoods in Baltimore.[14]

J.H.N. Waring, a black educator from Washington, D.C., and the principal of the Colored High and Polytechnic School starting in 1902, echoed these cultural critiques. Writing in a special issue of *Charities,* Waring warned of a "Black Plague" of violent crime that would overtake the city unless drastic measures were undertaken to control the city's slums and indoctrinate the city's black children with bourgeois moral values. For Waring, rearing black children to become well-adjusted members of the American polity was immensely important, but the effort was encumbered by the lack of strong role models and deteriorating family units.[15] Waring's visible position as a black educator, combined with his condemnation of black parenting, represented a black bourgeois investment in "respectability" that decentered environmental and structural critiques of racism and placed the onus of social progress on the oppressed.[16]

Because of these ideas, many of which were formalized in publications and accepted as empirically grounded "truths," black communities around the nation and in Baltimore became the subjects of reformatory experimentation and, as we see, increased police inquiry and control. Lacking the structure of the plantation, some reformers reasoned, black city residents needed something to control what was perceived as their cultural predisposition to crime and self-destruction. As these broad debates echoed on the national level, the popular press reinforced notions of black cultural deficiency locally through exhaustive coverage of black communities.

Creating "The Pot": A Black Neighborhood under Scrutiny

On May 31, 1908, the *Sun* published an exposé, "Quiet Region of Homes, and Later a Resort of Bad Men, 'The Pot' Is Now the Center of the Cocaine Trade." The newspaper described the neighborhood residents as "beautifully indolent," noting, "They all remind you of a bunch of overgrown children." The houses on Chestnut Street, the "great cocaine way," were characterized as shoddily built, susceptible to destruction by a strong gust of wind or small fire. These houses were overcrowded with teeming tenants, a condition the paper noted as a contributing factor to the ongoing "race suicide" it perceived among black Baltimoreans. The streets and sidewalks ran amok with "little half-dressed pickaninnies," "lounging men," and "dirty hucksters." The blocks were dotted with saloons that served as institutions for the immoral Potters in the place of church and school. It had not always been this way, however. According to the paper, in the "good old days," The Pot served as home to respectable white working families who were soon replaced by the incorrigible black hucksters of the present and "a poor grade of whites."[17]

The precise origins of the neighborhood's nickname are unknown. Evidence suggests that the name was derived from the symbolism of a community "boiling over." The "evil influences" of racial mixture, drug use, and prostitution stewed within The Pot's back alleys. These conditions made the neighborhood, as far as the press was concerned, a melting pot of vice. Like many slums of the period, residences were located alongside industrial factories, including a fruit and oyster packing plant and numerous coal and stone yards. The mixing of living quarters with potentially toxic and germ-ridden influences was not unheard of before (and even after) the city formalized zoning controls. It was not uncommon to encounter livestock, unregulated butchery, and other environmentally hazardous conditions in poor neighborhoods, and The Pot was no exception.[18]

In addition to industry, The Pot boasted several commercial establishments, including Hines & Sons, the "cheapest furniture and carpet house on Earth," and William H. Dull's pharmacy, located on the corner of Gay and Exeter Streets. Dull, the son of German immigrants, was raised in Federal Hill in the 1870s. During the 1890s, Dull bounced around pharmacies in West Baltimore before relocating to The Pot around 1900. In short order, the modest young man from Fed Hill became the city's "Cocaine King" and ran his operations out of his drugstore and through a "cigar store" front located on 325 Chestnut Street.

Much like its land use, the demography of The Pot was mixed. While most of the inhabitants were Russian Jews and black people, there were notable Italian, Austrian, and German clusters. Russian Jews dominated Exeter and Aisquith Streets, while black residents occupied most of the homes on Chestnut Street, as well as the small dwellings on Hull's Lane, Half Moon Alley, and Necessity Alley. Although uncommon, some black people even occupied homes on white blocks and vice versa: it was possible to see a white boarder living in a black household. While most of the black Potters were Marylanders, some had migrated—or were the children of migrants—from Virginia, North Carolina, and Georgia. Additionally, The Pot presented living opportunities for outlier minorities, including the Chinese and Cubans. Since these groups had not yet established ethnic enclaves as did other immigrant groups in the city, they could settle in areas like The Pot where race mixing was, at the very least, resentfully tolerated. This aspect of The Pot made the neighborhood a menacing threat to well-to-do whites, who had by this time developed a reputation for intimidating potential black residents or forming protective societies to prevent settlement in their neighborhoods: common tactics in the Jim Crow era ensuring that parts of the city remained heavily segregated and sheltered from the perceived corruption of racial mixture stewing in places like The Pot.[19]

For the *Sun*, the supposed disintegration of The Pot was directly related to the settlement of black and ethnic white families. Its reporting implied that, if the neighborhood had remained racially pure and white as it had once been, the conditions would undoubtedly be much better. Instead of interpreting the issues besetting the neighborhood as structural or environmental in nature, the paper viewed the community's health as a reflection of the cultural inadequacy of its residents. Given the residents' innate inability to adapt to civil life, it was unsurprising, the paper concluded, that The Pot became "the cocaine center of the city."

Cocaine Dealing in "The Pot": Constructing Black Criminality

Derived from the cocoa leaf, cocaine was a versatile agent from its emergence in the late nineteenth century. The substance could be employed for medical and therapeutic use through incorporation into topical anesthetics, lozenges, and medicines to treat asthma, catarrh, and other sinus-related ailments. Recreationally, the drug was present—in trace amount—in tonics, wines, and soft drinks.[20] Its emergence coincided with a period during which pharmaceutical regulation was relatively lax and druggists could liberally prescribe medications. This lax regulation allowed druggists such as Dull to prescribe habit-forming recreational drugs like cocaine to bolster profits.[21]

On the street, the drug was known as "coke" and its users known as "coke fiends," "whiffers," and "snowbirds." The drug was ingested both hypodermically and through inhalation. In Maryland, the General Assembly made the sale and distribution of unprescribed cocaine a misdemeanor offense in 1904. Thus distribution relied on strong connections between druggists and dealers. Dealers often received the drug from druggists in bulk quantities that they would "whack up" into smaller packets or "decks." These decks were sometimes diluted with yeast or other white powders to increase profits. If druggists wished to eliminate the process of employing dealers, they could sell the drug from their storefront using any number of codes to veil the transaction. For instance, in one *Sun* exposé on drug trafficking, the reporters noted that asking for a "trip to heaven" was code in some druggeries for one deck of cocaine.[22] In other instances, drug users could use specially marked receptacles to signal to the druggist that they were interested in procuring the drug. Druggists might also sell the drug as a seemingly innocuous medicine to treat headaches, congestion, or foot pain. Once drugstores became ensnared in the controversy of the "cocaine evil," some druggists, like Dull, moved their operations to other fronts. Dull's "cigar store" in an overcrowded home on Chestnut Street was a prime example of such a front.

In The Pot, Dull first ran the cocaine trade from his drugstore on Gay and Exeter streets, while his top dealers, Daniel "Big Dan" Waters and Alverta "Sweetie" Bailey, sold coke along Chestnut Street. The lion's share of information about Big Dan and Sweetie Bailey comes from *Sun* reportage, which is less than reliable considering the paper's pronounced political bent and its bold-faced racial prejudice at times. Census information indicates that Big Dan was likely born in Maryland in 1870 and roomed in Dull's cigar store at some point. In the press, Big Dan was described as a saloon-keeper-turned-drug-dealer and a "hoodoo" practitioner who carried a conjure bag filled with quicksilver and rabbit's feet. His "corner" was on Low and Chestnut, and his cocaine sales were made distinct by the pink packaging of his decks. In a piece written in May 1908, the *Sun* detailed, in dramatic fashion, the infiltration of Big Dan's home and the opening of his safe, which was said to hold "$16.90, a package of powder which [was] believed to be cocaine, and a 'conjure bag.'"[23] A mugshot of Big Dan accompanied the story (see Figure 2).

Alverta "Sweetie" Bailey was dubbed the "Cocaine Queen" by the press for her centrality to Will Dull's operation. Though just a petty dealer, Sweetie Bailey was repeatedly included in press accounts of the cocaine drama in The Pot and habitually described as Big Dan's "girl." The recurrent references to Big Dan and Sweetie Bailey's extramarital relationship in the press reinforced prevailing associations between sexual impropriety and black life—particularly as they affected young black women—and the presumed causal link between promiscuity and the deterioration of black communities. Sweetie Bailey was the embodiment of what Helen Pendleton described as the city's "Fighting Mags": young black women whose sexual freedoms and other indulgences could only be curbed by the imposition of a tight moral code.[24]

The press coverage of black drug dealers and users in The Pot dovetailed with Progressive thought concerning the irregular and antisocial lifestyles that were seen as distinct qualities of black people within a Jim Crow context. The reproduction of Big Dan's police sketch provided a literal face with which the *Sun*'s readers could associate the cocaine evil. Thus, the national discourses on black deviance were reproduced, in no uncertain terms, in local representations of black life and vice versa. At both levels, the intensification of police power in poor neighborhoods became seen as warranted and necessary. Big Dan and Sweetie Bailey's arrest in early May for their ties to Dull's cocaine trafficking was heralded by the *Sun* as "the most important capture so far in the crusade against cocaine."[25] That accolade would be tarnished in short order as scandal overtook the city's police department in a show of political theater that spurred the passage of Swann's Cocaine Ordinance.

Potters on Trial

In the summer of 1908 five white police officers of the city's Central District were suspended indefinitely on charges of "neglect of duty" for providing protection to Dull and his cocaine dealers in The Pot. The officers in question were Sergeants William Jenkins and George Hoyle and Patrolmen Robert Porter, Cornelius Roche, and John J. Acker. The Police Board based the charges on several testimonies by incarcerated black men and women who alleged that the officers were complicit in the sale and distribution of cocaine in The Pot. Among the accusers were the recently incarcerated Big Dan Waters and Sweetie Bailey.

The trial began on June 6, 1908. The presiding judge for the Police Board was Colonel Sherlock Swann, the primary author of a proposed ordinance to prohibit the sale and possession of illicit drugs in the city, including eucaine, opium, morphine, heroin, hydrated chloral, and cocaine.[26] The ordinance was

"BIG DAN" WATERS
(Drawn from a photograph.)

FIG. 2 Image of "Big Dan" Waters (drawn from a photograph). Source: *Baltimore Sun*, 1908.

heard and debated in the City Council while the trial was ongoing. On the first day of the trial, more than a dozen witnesses testified, most of whom lived or operated in The Pot. They accused the officers of looking the other way when they bought or sold cocaine, receiving hundreds of dollars from Dull in return for police protection, alerting dealers to police activity in the neighborhood, recruiting dealers for Dull, and even, in one case, steering black voters away from the polls on election days.

The officers' counsel mounted a defense that relied on demonstrating that the witnesses were untrustworthy. The defense's cross-examinations of the Potters were geared toward eliciting admissions of guilt to past criminal offenses, as well as exploiting their unique speech habits and lifestyles to magnify distinctive black cultural idiosyncrasies that whites generally interpreted as dishonest or untrustworthy. Over the course of the trial, the witnesses were obligated to admit to committing acts of larceny, assault, violence against women, perjury, and even the highly contemptible criminal act of "fussing." These admissions displayed for the Police Board what they had always purported to be the case—and what the *Sun* and reformers simultaneously alleged: that black people were unable to live civilly in urban communities without tight regulations.

After three days dominated by the public incrimination of The Pot's black witnesses, the white officers briefly took the stand. The officers were asked one question: Had they seen high-ranking officers in Dull's drugstore? After responding in the negative, the case was brought to an abrupt end. The defense had not even argued its side.[27]

On June 9, Colonel Swann delivered the verdict. All five officers were fully acquitted of the charges, immediately reinstated to active duty, assured they would receive payment for the period of their suspension, and tasked with "cleansing" the immoral conditions of The Pot within thirty days of their acquittals. Commenting on the abrupt nature of the acquittal, Colonel Swann said, "Although we heard the statements of some of the witnesses before the trial, we heard a different side of the case. We didn't know the witnesses were the class of people they proved to be."[28] Colonel Swann refused to hear additional testimony from the Potters unless it was accompanied by supplementary evidence. The defense's strategy worked.

Swann's Cocaine Ordinance

After the officers were acquitted, their defense counsel noted that their task of eliminating cocaine traffic in The Pot remained very challenging because it was difficult to capture parties engaged in the act of selling cocaine.[29] If officers could arrest and charge users who simply *possessed* cocaine, however, they would be much more successful in eradicating the cocaine evil. Fortunately for the police, as the trial unfolded, Colonel Swann's ordinance to criminalize the possession of illegal drugs was rushed through both branches of the City Council.[30] Mayor J. Barry Mahool signed the ordinance into law on June 19, just ten days after the end of the officers' heavily publicized trial. This provision would undoubtedly empower the officers charged with "cleansing" The Pot of the cocaine evil by allowing them to convict drug users on charges of possession, in addition to druggists and dealers on charges of sale and distribution.

Conclusion

It is unclear whether the Police Board intentionally decided to stage the political theater of the five officers' trial to facilitate the criminalization of drug possession at the local level. What is clear, however, is that, in the months leading up to the drug ordinance's passage, The Pot became publicly known as the center of a "cocaine belt." In this way, vice and criminality were affixed to physical space in ways that gave the "cocaine evil" immediate local implications. Moreover, the reporting on Big Dan and Sweetie Bailey put faces (literally, in the case of Big Dan) to the trafficking. The reports concerning the case were skewed heavily against the black witnesses who were compelled to describe in thick detail the goings-on of the cocaine traffic in The Pot. Their testimony corroborated what some of the city's Progressive reformers believed. The discourses on the inherent relationship between blackness and criminality circulated in multiple sites of city life—from the press, to the police, to reform circles. The passage of Swann's Cocaine Ordinance was the crystallization of these discourses—consolidated in a policy that, with the passage of time and in various permutations, would wreak havoc on black neighborhoods where bodies became the sites of potential illegality.

In 1955, the community known as The Pot would disappear forever as Lafayette Courts, a high-rise public housing complex, was erected in its place. Throughout the 1980s and 1990s, however, Lafayette Courts would be cast similarly to The Pot in the urban imaginary. Raids, overdoses, and violence associated with the sale of crack cocaine peppered the pages of the *Sun* and the local television news until, in 1995, the once-revered high-rise, described then as "a bleak symbol of urban decay," came tumbling down in a twenty-second demolition.[31] In both the nineteenth century's drug crusade in The Pot and the War on Drug's effects on the people of Lafayette Courts, we see eerily similar dynamics. These parallels lend credence to the notion that the intentional regulation of narcotics as a means of social and political repression has much deeper roots than is popularly understood.

Even more eerie is the fact that, as I revised this chapter, the Baltimore Police Department (BPD) made national headlines when eight of its officers were implicated in a corruption scandal in which the members of a taskforce were accused of robbing drug dealers, taking cash and drugs, and recirculating the latter in the underground market. In a city awash with news of police brutality and scandal, Baltimore's police activity within black communities has been and continues to be marked by violent repression, opportunism, and scapegoating.

The Pot, like many other black neighborhoods in the United States during Jim Crow, was just one site of such scapegoating as black Baltimoreans were forced to endure intense scrutiny, political opportunism, and criminalization justified by cultural critiques that cast the blame on blackness itself. Blackness and criminality met at the site of the black woman cocaine "whiffer" and the black cocaine "dealer," images that exist with us to this day. The neighborhood was built, torn down, built, and torn down over the course of a century. The voices of the neighborhood's inhabitants, like Henrietta Woods, Sweetie Bailey, and Big Dan Waters, echo unreliably in the archive. From there, we must piece The Pot and neighborhoods like it back together if we are to understand how to prevent the further destruction of today's urban neighborhoods.

Notes

1 Chestnut Street is now Colvin Street, and "The Pot" existed in the area where the U.S. Postal Service Building on East Fayette Street is currently located.
2 "Cocaine & Beer Cause Trouble," *Baltimore Sun*, June 21, 1902.
3 This chapter relies exclusively on *Baltimore Sun* coverage that exhaustively documented the goings-on of drug use and enforcement within The Pot in the first decade of the twentieth century. During this same period, the city's most prominent black newspaper, the *Afro-American*, published very few stories on cocaine that I could find. Though there was some mention of cocaine's negative social effects, the *Afro* did not publish massive investigative pieces detailing sensationalized drug use within the city's black communities like the *Sun* did. Of the stories they did publish, many focused on the use of the drug within a pharmaceutical or medical context. They also joined many newspapers in dubiously reporting on famed sharpshooter Annie Oakley's alleged arrest for "stealing the trousers of a negro in order to get money with which to buy cocaine." The prevalence of sensationalized stories of black drug users in the *Sun*, the city's most prominent white newspaper, and their glaring absence in the city's most prominent black newspaper serve as further evidence to suggest that white constructions of black drug users were politically motivated by white desires for social control within a Jim Crow context. See "Housekeepers Are Not Angels," *Afro-American*, July 25, 1903; "Annie Oakley's Fall," *Afro-American*, August 15, 1903; "New Anesthetic Discovered," *Afro-American,* July 29, 1905; and "Proclaim New Anesthetic," *Afro-American*, February 17, 1907.
4 For stories on the drug's perceived antisocial effects, see "The Atlanta Riot," *Baltimore Sun*, September 26, 1906; "The Police Board and the Charges against Members of the Force," *Baltimore Sun*, May 27, 1908; and "Dope," *Baltimore Sun*, July 23, 1906. For more historical context on the origins and prohibitions against cocaine over time, see David F. Musto, *The American Disease: Origins of Narcotic Control* (Oxford: University of Oxford Press, 1998). Notably, Musto outlines the

ways that cocaine use was activated by southern whites, whose fears about a black uprising were intensified by imprecise attributions about the effects of the drug on physical and mental faculties, to institute more intensive policing. See also Paul Gootenberg, ed., *Cocaine: Global Histories* (New York, Routledge, 1999). In his introduction to this edited collection, Gootenberg details how cocaine, which was first synthesized in 1860 in Germany, underwent rapid regulation and criminalization between 1900 and the 1920s. Before its criminalization, the drug was used in scientific trials, botanical appraisals, and recreational activities in Germany, Britain, Peru, France, and North America. According to Gootenberg, the drug's use among the working class at the turn of the century provoked a "mania" that caused reformers and police departments to advocate for its illegalization.

5 "Cocaine Evil Grows: Nearly Every Negress Arrested Is a Victim of the Drug," *Baltimore Sun*, December 18, 1905.

6 The concept of "intersectionality" was developed by black feminist scholars like Kimberlé Crenshaw, Patricia Hill Collins, and Bonnie Thornton Dill. It broadly refers to a theoretical framework in which social identities are understood as existing within a hierarchy of interrelated structural oppressions and privileges. According to Crenshaw, "an analysis sensitive to structural intersections explores the lives of those at the bottom of multiple hierarchies to determine how the dynamics of each hierarchy exacerbates and compounds the consequences of another." In my historical application of intersectionality, I am attentive to the ways that social identities were articulated and generalized within popular discursive constructions and how those constructions manifested in institutional contexts. This formation allows us to see how hierarchies of power were produced, institutionalized at the structural level, and reproduced over time. See Kimberlé Crenshaw, "Mapping the Margins: Intersectionality, Identity Politics, and Violence against Women of Color," *Stanford Law Review* 43, no. 6 (1991): 1241–1299; Patricia Hill Collins, *Black Feminist Thought: Knowledge Consciousness, and the Politics of Empowerment* (New York: Routledge, 2000); and Bonnie Thornton Dill and Ruth Enid Zambrana, eds., *Emerging Intersections: Race, Class, and Gender in Theory, Policy and Practice* (New Brunswick, NJ: Rutgers University Press, 2009).

7 Though not specifically about the discursive construction of localities, Benedict Anderson's famous work, *Imagined Communities*, provides insight into the ways that print capitalism abetted the circulation of ideas that, in turn, came to construct, model, adapt, and transform conceptions of space. Pushing the analysis further, this construction, which is textual in nature and can become representationally violent, can also serve to create racialized geographies, as was the case in The Pot. See Benedict Anderson, *Imagined Communities: Reflections on the Origin and Spread of Nationalism*, rev. ed. (New York: Verso, 2006).

8 Clayton Colman Hall, *Baltimore: Biography* (Baltimore: Lewis Historical Publishing Company, 1912).

9 "To War on Baneful Drugs," *Baltimore Sun*, August 5, 1903.

10 Baltimore's unique geographic identity distinguished it from many other northern cities, such as New York, Chicago, and Philadelphia that were scrutinized as part of an increasing Progressive preoccupation with black settlement in the North. Unlike these cities, Baltimore's developmental identity has always been typified by its distinctive mix of southern culture and northern industry. The results of such a mix are numerous. For the purposes of this chapter, the city's lengthy history of

surveilling and policing black neighborhoods had been deeply entrenched long before the Great Migration of the early 1900s, which augmented the black populations of other northern cities. Evidence of this long history of policing emerges in Baltimore's pioneering residential segregation and narcotics regulations, which endeavored to constrict the social mobility of black people. See Joseph L. Arnold, "Baltimore: Southern Culture and a Northern Economy," in *Snowbelt Cities: Metropolitan Politics in the Northeast and Midwest since World War II*, ed. Richard M. Bernard (Bloomington: Indiana University Press, 1990), 25–39.

11 Khalil Gibran Muhammad, *The Condemnation of Blackness: Race, Crime, and the Making of Modern Urban America* (Cambridge, MA: Harvard University Press, 2010).

12 Chad Heap, *Slumming: Sexual and Racial Encounters in American Nightlife, 1885–1940* (Chicago: University of Chicago Press, 2009).

13 Paul Boyer, *Urban Masses and Moral Order in American, 1820–1920* (Cambridge, MA: Harvard University Press, 1997).

14 Baltimore's Progressive reformers were not of one ideological mind by any means, though many did understand blackness as culturally deficient on some level. For instance, members of the city's Charity Organization Society, established in the 1880s, were invested in providing well-intentioned interventions into poor communities to curtail poverty and neighborhood violence. Despite their good intentions, members of the organization, including Helen Pendleton and Janet Kemp, whose report on housing conditions continues to be an oft-cited example of early liberal Progressivism in the city, pathologized black culture by placing their observations of black life in relation to the lives and cultures of ethnic whites, with whom they shared an affinity for whiteness. For instance, in Kemp's famous *Housing Conditions in Baltimore*, the reformer accused black alley dwellers of possessing "low standards," an "absence of ideals," and "irregular life and habits." These characteristics were observed in relation to Polish families whose cleanliness and work ethic seemed almost "heroic" to Kemp. For Kemp and reformers like her, black people's "irregular lifestyles" would make it much more difficult for them to adapt to city life than could white immigrants. This line of reasoning would animate the type and amount of aid extended to each population group. Khalil Muhammad refers to this comparative racialization as the "condemnation of blackness," of which many members of the Charity Organization Society were, intentionally or not, proponents. For more information on the Progressive era reform movement in the city, see James B. Crooks, *Politics & Progress: The Rise of Urban Progressivism in Baltimore, 1895 to 1911* (Baton Rouge: Louisiana State University Press, 1968).

15 J.H.N. Waring, "Some Causes of Criminality," *Charities* 15, no. 1 (1905): 45–49.

16 The concept of "respectability politics" was articulated in 1993 by Evelyn Brooks Higginbotham and refers to the rejection of moral and cultural practices exhibited by a minoritized group that might clash or undermine dominant white ideals of moral life. See Evelyn Brooks Higginbotham, *Righteous Discontent: The Women's Movement in the Black Baptist Church, 1880–1920* (Cambridge, MA: Harvard University Press, 1993).

17 "Quiet Region of Homes, and Later a Resort of Bad Men, 'The Pot' Is Now the Center of the Cocaine Trade," *Baltimore Sun*, May 31, 1908.

18 Garrett Power, "Deconstructing the Slums of Baltimore," in *From Mobtown to Charm City: New Perspectives on Baltimore's Past*, ed. Jessica Elfenbein, John R.

Breihan, and Thomas L. Hollowak (Baltimore: Maryland Historical Society, 2002), 47–63.

19 See Antero Pietila, *Not in My Neighborhood: How Bigotry Shaped a Great American City* (Chicago: Ivan R. Dee, 2010).

20 Joseph F. Spillane, "Making a Modern Drug: The Manufacture, Sale, and Control of Cocaine in the United States, 1880–1920," in Gootenberg, *Cocaine: Global Histories.*

21 The state of Maryland did not officially begin to regulate the sale of cocaine until 1904 when the General Assembly passed a law intended to control the sale of narcotic drugs and curtail the "evils resulting from [their] traffic."

22 "Baltimore's Negroes Are in the Thrall of Cocaine," *Baltimore Sun*, December 16, 1906.

23 "'Big Dan's' Safe Opened," *Baltimore Sun*, May 29, 1908.

24 Helen Pendleton, "Negro Dependence in Baltimore," *Charities* 15, no. 1 (1905): 50–58.

25 "'Big Dan' Sent to Jail," *Baltimore Sun*, May 7, 1908.

26 A local anesthetic and narcotic-like cocaine sometimes used by dentists of the period.

27 "Concluding Testimony: Witnesses Tell of Cocaine Selling in 'The Pot,'" *Baltimore Sun*, June 9, 1908.

28 "Policemen Acquitted: All Declared Not Guilty without Defense Being Heard," *Baltimore Sun*, June 9, 1908.

29 "Policemen Acquitted."

30 The Baltimore City Council was a bicameral body until 1922 when it was replaced with its current unicameral structure.

31 JoAnna Daemmirch, "Lafayette Courts Ends in 20 Seconds of Explosions, Cheers, Tears," *Baltimore Sun*, August 20, 1995. For more information on public housing in Baltimore, see Rhonda Y. Williams, *The Politics of Public Housing: Black Women's Struggles against Urban Inequality* (New York: Oxford University Press, 2005).

4

Vacant Houses and Inequality in Baltimore from the Nineteenth Century to Today

•••••••••••••••••••••

ELI POUSSON

Vacant houses tell a story about how racial and spatial inequality are built and maintained. Baltimore's official count of vacant buildings topped sixteen thousand properties at the outset of the national foreclosure crisis in 2008.[1] These buildings are the physical consequence of decisions by people dedicated to preserving housing segregation, enacting transportation and land use policies that favor automobiles, and taxing and policing buildings in ways that stigmatize poverty.

The concentration of these properties in historically segregated black neighborhoods in East and West Baltimore makes vacant housing an urgent problem for tens of thousands of poor residents. Even more residents share the risks to both individual and collective health and safety created by vacant and abandoned buildings. For the city, vacancy reduces tax revenue needed to support public services, forcing the remaining occupied buildings to bear a greater share of the costs. Ultimately, vacant buildings are a problem that affects everyone, whether or not they live in a neighborhood with a high vacancy rate.[2]

Many see demolition as a fast and cheap solution to the problem.[3] But "vacants," as these abandoned houses are widely known, are not a problem that can be solved with an excavator and a landfill alone. Vacant buildings are a tragedy that has shaped Baltimore for generations, and their legacy remains in place long after buildings come down.

Understanding abandonment and long-term vacancy as conditions produced by uneven, racially discriminatory regional housing markets helps counter the stigma and popular myths surrounding "blighted" and abandoned buildings. In his study of demolition in Flint, Michigan, Andrew Highsmith explained how the nation's "obsession with urban decline and abandonment has always concealed a more ambivalent and complicated reality."[4] A close look at Eastwick in Philadelphia led Amy Cahn, director of the Garden Justice Legal Initiative at the Public Interest Law Center, to conclude, "We are past the time to retire 'blight,' not simply as metaphor, but as a policy and legal framework for rebuilding cities."[5]

In Baltimore, we should listen to the words of people who deal with vacant houses both directly and indirectly: tenants, landlords, neighbors, public workers, and elected officials. Of course, even the sight of a vacant house often prompts questions about people: Who lived in this empty house? Who moved away and left the building behind? Who is heartbroken, scared, or relieved when this vacant house falls down? Who wants to tear down this vacant house? Who will clean the vacant lot after the house is gone?

Effective and equitable solutions to the problems presented by vacant houses are hard to find. In her 2015 report on the city's Vacants to Value program, Joan Jacobson acknowledged the city's work "identifying and cracking down on owners of derelict houses in scarred neighborhoods with plummeting property values." However, Jacobson also called on the city to "do more to address the problems of vacancy in 'distressed' neighborhoods" with weak housing markets. Since 2016, city staff have used the relative strength or weakness of neighborhood housing markets to decide which vacant buildings to demolish under a $700,000,000 program known as Project CORE.[6] But this "market typology" created by the Baltimore City Planning Department in 2004 bears a striking resemblance to the infamous "redlining" map drawn sixty-seven years earlier by the federal Home Owners' Loan Corporation (HOLC).[7] Recent studies confirm that mortgage discrimination remains a major barrier to black and Latino homebuyers, more than fifty years after the passage of the Fair Housing Act in 1968.[8]

Why are vacant buildings such a hard problem to solve? Elected officials have repeatedly proven unable or unwilling to engage with the question of how race, power, and inequality decide what happens to every house in the city, vacant or occupied. Instead, politicians and planners have consistently presented vacant buildings as the outcome of an inevitable, "natural" process, rather than the result of specific actions, choices, and policies shaped by white supremacy and structural inequality.

For example, in December 1932, C. Dana Loomis, a local architect who later worked for the Baltimore Housing Authority, bluntly argued that rowhouse lots had no potential for "modern and reasonably attractive" use. Baltimore's "dying areas," he predicted, would be forced into a "hopeless future competition" with new suburban development at the edges of the metropolitan region.[9] Twenty years later, in 1955, Dr. Abel Wolman, a professor of engineering at Johns Hopkins University, lectured residents in Waverly on "urban blight." He suggested that cars made the city's "'great spill' into outlying areas" possible, but that a "nomadic" American identity made the trend "inevitable."[10]

Even if observers recognize the role of segregation, inequality, and sprawling residential growth in encouraging abandonment, the conversation about how to solve the vacant building problem often starts and ends with demolition. Tearing buildings down is easier than integrating the city's segregated neighborhoods, reforming the tax sale process, or reversing decades of automobile-oriented development. Imagining alternatives—more comprehensive and lasting solutions—requires a broader perspective.

"Each Vacant House Is a Standing Menace to the Rest"

Vacant houses have a much longer history in Baltimore than many people realize. As early as 1831, newspaper publisher Hezekiah Niles wrote about the connection between employment and housing demand in Baltimore, explaining how "the want of employment" after the Panic of 1819 caused a "consequent removal of the people, to the north, south, east and west."[11]

Capital investment from wealthy white men like Niles, together with labor from recent European immigrants, enslaved people of African descent, and free people of color, enabled Baltimore to grow quickly: its population doubled between 1830 and 1850.[12] Beginning in 1844, private companies started running horse-drawn omnibus rail lines to connect the dense city center to growing communities in Baltimore County. After the Civil War, large property owners, builders, and investors took advantage of the new rail lines to build thousands of new suburban houses to sell or rent to affluent white Baltimoreans.

Local builders constructed roughly three thousand houses each year between 1885 and 1887, but this pattern of "over-building" left many houses again standing empty after the Panic of 1893. A writer for the *Sun* complained, "Other cities have endeavored to make capital of reports of the very large number of vacant houses in Baltimore, claiming it as an evidence that this city is falling behind."[13] At the time, vacant houses were a secondary concern for city officials more interested in policing the growing number of occupied houses built in Baltimore and in the large part of Baltimore County annexed by the city in 1888.[14]

In 1893, Baltimore enacted a new building code laying out detailed rules for construction and alterations. The law gave the city's Inspector of Buildings the power "to condemn all unsafe buildings or walls" and to fine property owners if they did not remove an offending structure. Three years later, an amendment gave the inspector the additional power to tear a building down at the property owner's expense if he or she did not comply with a demolition order within ten days.[15]

City officials were slow to use this new authority at first. Inspector of Buildings Benjamin B. Owens condemned just thirty buildings in 1897, and by the end of 1899, Owens's successor Everett J. Dowell condemned only sixty-one more. Then, in early 1900, Mayor Thomas G. Hayes appointed a fifty-six-year-old white builder named Edward D. Preston to the job.

Preston radically expanded enforcement of the building code for both occupied and abandoned buildings.[16] In his first four years leading the Department of Buildings, Preston's office issued more than nine hundred building condemnation notices.[17] Preston declared a "War on Unsafe Buildings" in the summer of 1901, pledging his determination to "clean Baltimore of buildings . . . which are a menace to public safety." The inspector worried about dangerous work by inexperienced builders and noted, "There are many houses in the city which, while not in a condition to condemn are still in a very bad way."[18]

Edward Preston himself lived at 1637 Edmondson Avenue in a segregated white neighborhood in West Baltimore built near Harlem Park in the 1870s. While he often highlighted the necessity of code enforcement for public safety, he used a different standard in his own neighborhood after a nearby property at 604 North Gilmor Street was sold to a church-operated black orphanage in March 1906.

At an "indignation meeting" of outraged white neighbors, Preston promised to "take a stand against" the orphanage and suggested the "laws governing dwellings turned into institutions" may require the building to be "torn down before it can be used for an asylum," perhaps creating an opportunity for Preston to prevent the change. By the end of the meeting, residents established the Harlem Park Protective Association and quickly sent off a letter of protest to the Real Estate Exchange attacking Charles Morton, the agent for the sale. Morton responded, "The house has been idle for more than a year and the owner," a white woman living in Hagerstown, Maryland, was "compelled to sell to meet obligations."[19]

In the year before Preston stepped down as inspector in 1911, his white neighbors in West and Northwest Baltimore seriously considered the threat presented by nearby vacant buildings. Weakening demand among white tenants and homeowners for older houses had left a growing number of buildings in the area empty. On Gilmor Street and elsewhere, property owners seeking to rent or sell houses to black Baltimoreans undermined efforts by the remaining white residents to maintain strict boundaries of racial segregation.

In August 1910, the Baltimore Police Board released a "complete census of the number of houses, both vacant and occupied in the city" at the request of William Martien & Company, a forty-year-old local real estate firm. The survey found more than thirteen hundred vacant dwellings in the northwestern district—about one-quarter of the 5,655 vacant buildings found across the city. James Carey Martien, son of the firm's founder, argued that vacancy was caused by both the "many dwellings being built in the suburbs" and the "dilapidated condition of many [dwellings] in Baltimore."[20] But, in a telling omission, Martien's analysis of supply and demand neglected to acknowledge the growing role of racial segregation in shaping the regional housing market.[21]

A series of letters in 1910 responding to concerns over vacant houses in Northwest Baltimore illustrate the relationship between vacant buildings and racial segregation. One August 25 letter (signed "Pure White") is direct: "When a man works and saves and buys a home thinking it will be his shelter in his old age, and wakes up some morning to find he has a negro neighbor, he feels hurt and aggrieved that he has to give up his home, but he moves. . . . The real estate men—a few of them, not all—are to blame for the vacant houses and with them, lies the remedy."[22] Several days later, another writer echoed this sentiment and demanded that elected officials protect his neighborhood against the threat of black neighbors and vacant houses: "There are several vacant houses in the block, and this fear [of "negro invasion"] may be the potent cause of non-rental or sale. Each vacant house is a standing menace to the rest."[23]

Panicked segregationists in Northwest Baltimore were relieved on December 19, 1910, when Baltimore City's mayor signed into law the nation's first municipal ordinance requiring racially segregated housing on a block-by-block basis. Less than a month later, judges on the Supreme Bench of Baltimore City voided the ordinance on a technicality, but the City Council quickly passed a replacement and then a third version in May 1911.

In June 1913, W. Ashbie Hawkins, a local black lawyer living at 529 Presstman Street, went to court to defend Reverend John H. Gurry, the black pastor of King's Apostle Holy Temple. Gurry faced criminal charges for moving his church to 581 Laurens Street: what the police called a "white block" under the segregation law.[24] In June, Hawkins won Gurry's case and the law was ruled unconstitutional.[25] Four years later, in 1917, the U.S. Supreme Court decision in *Buchanan v. Warley* overturned a similar ordinance in Louisville, Kentucky, ruling municipal segregation laws unconstitutional. In that case, Hawkins submitted an amicus brief on behalf of Warley for the Baltimore chapter of the National Association for the Advancement of Colored People (NAACP).[26]

Unsurprisingly, white residents wasted no time in forming more "protective" associations and adopting racially restrictive housing covenants.[27] But as segregated white suburbs grew in the 1920s, the "color line" at the edges of older segregated black neighborhoods remained unstable. White Baltimoreans continued moving even farther out of the city, leaving vacant buildings behind.[28]

"Vacant Buildings Went from Bad to Worse"

During this same period, affluent white Baltimoreans' increased use of automobiles created new conflicts over spaces occupied by black households and vacant buildings. After the Great Baltimore Fire of 1904, the city condemned properties around the downtown area, taking privately owned land to repair the city docks, widen existing roads, and create a new plaza on Saint Paul Street near the Baltimore City Courthouse.

Historian Samuel Roberts Jr. describes how a "selective practice of official neglect" plagued the historically black neighborhood located in the blocks north of the courthouse. Indeed, "the lack of sanitary services in some areas . . . was so profound and corrupted as to be advertent and systematic," so that, by the early 1910s, "site selection for redevelopment seemed the result of a self-fulfilling prophecy."[29]

By 1914, Mayor James Preston secured the money and authority to condemn and start demolition on ten blocks of houses on Saint Paul, Courtland, Lexington, and Franklin Streets and replace them with a park and a redesigned roadway. Designed by architect Thomas Hastings and completed in 1919, the new Preston Gardens park straightened Saint Paul Street, making it a faster and easier route for white residents driving from segregated northern suburbs to the downtown civic center.

Early road-building projects like Preston Gardens were funded by revenue from local property taxes. Landlords passed the cost of these taxes to tenants in the form of higher rents. In some circumstances, landlords stopped paying taxes, with the confidence they could make more money by collecting rent, neglecting maintenance, wearing out the building, and, eventually, abandoning their property. Consequently, tax sales—auctioning off property liens to recover unpaid property taxes—has been a common practice in Baltimore since at least 1881, when records of auction results first began to be kept.[30]

Widespread unemployment at the start of the Great Depression—especially among black workers subject to intense discrimination—meant that many tenants could not afford to pay rent and property owners could not afford to pay taxes. The number of vacant and occupied buildings sold at tax sale auctions started to climb in 1928, a year before "Black Thursday" on October 24, 1929.

By 1936, the city listed more than one thousand properties at auction. Unfortunately for the city's tax collectors, an overwhelming share of the liens they attempted to sell received no bids at all, forcing Baltimore to become the buyer of last resort. That year's record-setting 1,006-property auction at the Municipal Building on Holliday Street found buyers for just 130 houses. The city was left with the remainder. More than five hundred of the "so-called improved properties were vacant . . . 161 were wrecks, 179 unimproved lots and 285 improved properties in bad condition."[31]

In April 1936, two black workers were hospitalized after the collapse of a city-owned vacant house at 218 North Bethel Street left them buried by debris. In June 1936, two city-owned buildings at 1029 and 1031 McCulloh Street collapsed. Two more at 905 and 907 Ryan Street fell down just days later. In June 1936, the city initiated a haphazard push to "raze scores of dilapidated city-owned houses before they cave in." City engineers planned to fill in the foundations of the houses "after the removal of any valuable building materials," but the *Sun* observed, "What will be done with any large areas cleared has not been determined."[32]

Another terrifying near-miss took place at a vacant house in West Baltimore in the 1000 block of Hillock Alley on April 18, 1937, when a condemned city-owned building "tumbled down" just minutes after a group of black children walked out the door.[33] Esther J. Crooks, a board member for the Baltimore Urban League, responded to the Hillock Alley collapse: "How does it happen that our city authorities permit these ramshackle buildings to remain standing as an eyesore and a menace to the community?"[34]

A few weeks later, Mayor Howard W. Jackson organized a committee of thirty-four "builders, engineers, and real estate men" (only four of whom were black) to come up with a new approach to the "rehabilitation of so-called blighted areas" in which Baltimore had seen "the decay and sometimes virtual abandonment of whole sections, once desirable residential neighborhoods."[35]

In response to the announcement, the *Sun* observed that the housing "problem that confronts Baltimore" was "growing worse ever since the motor vehicle came into general use . . . which enabled people to move away from congested surroundings into the suburbs." The paper saw this "natural" movement as inevitable and grimly concluded that "when districts were largely deserted for residence purposes, real estate values rapidly deteriorated, vacant buildings went from bad to worse and the blight set in."[36]

By the end of 1937, Baltimore had an inventory of around three thousand properties, labeled by the *Sun* as "an embarrassing amount of unwanted real estate."[37]

"I Wish Someone Would Tear It Down or Fix It Up"

The abundance of vacant buildings shaped the site selection and design process for "slum clearance" projects in the 1930s, the development of public housing in the 1940s, and the designation of urban renewal areas in the 1950s.[38] These projects required the traumatic displacement of black tenants, homeowners, churches, businesses, and community institutions from occupied houses, churches, and commercial structures in those urban renewal areas.

Resistance to displacement expressed by both black and white Baltimoreans was most visible around the varied highway proposals planned and built between the 1940s and 1980s. The Baltimore Beltway (I-695) opened in stages around the city between 1955 and 1962 alongside discriminatory zoning and planning patterns in Baltimore County that sparked an investigation by the U.S. Commission on Civil Rights in 1970.[39] The Relocation Action Movement, established in 1966, and the Movement against Destruction delayed realization of the plans for the East–West Expressway but, beginning in 1975, the construction of I-170 (also known as the "Highway to Nowhere") cut a swath of destruction across West Central Baltimore.[40]

The population of Baltimore County and Anne Arundel County more than doubled from 387,665 in 1950 to 918,616 in 1970. In that same twenty years, Baltimore's population fell by more than forty thousand residents. Black residents increased as a share of the city's population from 24 to 46 percent.

By the mid-1960s, housing reform advocates realized that they did not even have a handle on the full scale of the vacancy problem. A 1965 report from the Citizens Planning and Housing Association (CPHA) summarized both the advocates' and the city's ignorance of the problem: "No one person knows how many vacant houses are owned by the city, how many should be razed, how many have a known owner, how many are needed for other uses and how many are involved in some stage of the law enforcement process."[41]

In 1968, the same year the Fair Housing Act became federal law, reform efforts resulted in the formation of the Department of Housing and Community Development—created from the merger of the twelve-year-old Baltimore Urban Renewal and Housing Authority (BURHA) and the long-established Bureau of Building Inspection. Mayor Thomas D'Alesandro III appointed city councilman and CPHA member Robert C. Embry Jr. to be the department's first director.

Regardless of progressive policy changes, the city's official count of vacant buildings grew relentlessly from 4,125 houses in 1964 to 5,457 in 1973.[42] In the 1970s, the Baltimore code enforcement office used a mainframe computer to create and maintain a "Vacant House File" with detailed property information.[43] By December 1981, the file listed 6,142 buildings—an increase of more than six hundred in just eight years.

One vacant rowhouse stood next door to the home of seventy-nine-year-old Rosa Bevins on North Wolfe Street in East Baltimore. At night, noises came through her home's brick party wall: sounds of rats and, at times, the voices of people who had torn plywood boards off windows of the empty house to get inside. Bevins worried about her safety: "I'm afraid I'll wake up and somebody's started a fire.... I wish someone would tear it down or fix it up. It makes me nervous."[44]

Elected officials, public employees, and local residents explored strategies other than demolition to address the glut of vacant housing. Homesteaders rehabilitated hundreds of vacant houses through the famed "Dollar House" program established in 1974.[45] Yet this and other alternatives, notably the scattered-site public housing program, made only a small dent in reducing the vacant housing stock.

Between 1970 and 1990, 17,088 units of vacant housing were torn down. The counties surrounding the city continued to grow as Baltimore's population continued to decline. In 1950, the city's residents made up around 65 percent of the regional population, but by 2010, city residents made up less than 25 percent of the regional population (see Figure 3). The city intermittently attempted to address vacancy on a broader scale but, in 1993, the city counted 6,974 vacant houses: an increase of more than 800 houses since 1981.[46] Maryland's savings and loan crisis in May 1985 and austerity measures for the city, state, and federal government contributed to the city's setting a new record for the number of vacant buildings: 8,600 tax-delinquent properties were up for tax sale auctions in 1987.[47] At the same time, budget cuts in the city code enforcement office resulted in a sharp decline from 43,225 building inspections in 1989 to 33,466 in

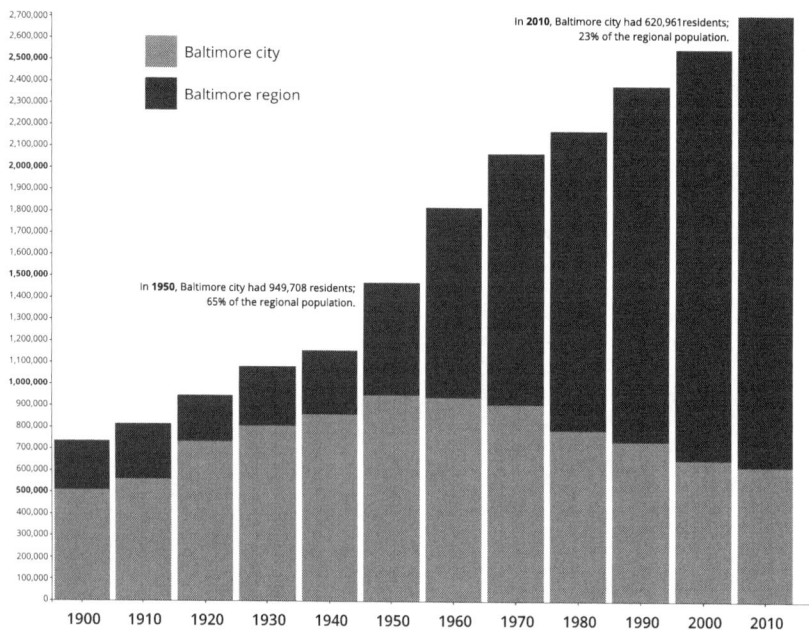

FIG. 3 Growth in the population of the Baltimore Metropolitan Statistical Area, including Baltimore City and the following counties: Anne Arundel, Baltimore, Carroll, Harford, Howard, and Queen Anne's. All the data are from the U.S. Decennial Census, 1900–2010, 1. Chart by Eli Pousson, 2017.

1991, and violation notices dropped from 27,709 to 20,775.[48] Meanwhile, during the decades of the 1970s and 1980s, the city lost nearly 170,000 residents while the metropolitan region gained more than 300,000.[49]

In 1994, Daniel P. Henson III, who served as the commissioner of Housing and Community Development from 1993–1999, offered "communities" a stark choice of "two short-term options—a vacant house or a vacant lot." Given these limited options, residents would "take the latter every day." Mayor Kurt Schmoke shared Henson's view: "If we have vacant houses that are sitting as nuisances in the neighborhood . . . I want to tear them down."[50]

But eight months later, Councilman Lawrence A. Bell III, representing West Baltimore's Fourth District, said the mayor and commissioner promised a solution they never delivered. "I don't think that [demolition] should ever have been put out as a panacea," said Bell. "I think it's very appealing to a lot of people on first blush because they're so frustrated. . . . But I'm concerned that after the demolition takes place, you have another vacant lot."[51]

In 1997, after multiple midblock demolitions resulted in the collapse of adjoining houses, critics asked why Commissioner Henson had not consulted with a structural engineer before taking down the vacant houses. Henson's unsatisfying explanation? "We didn't have problems before."[52]

"Caught beneath a Falling Wall while Playing in the Ruins"

At their worst, vacant houses can be deadly for neighbors and for neighborhoods. In August 1913, seven-year-old Elizabeth Handley was playing with her twin sister Loretta and four-year-old brother Reginald, skipping in and out of a condemned house at 604 Gutman Avenue in the Waverly neighborhood of North Baltimore. Earlier that afternoon, Harry W. Fox and a crew of workers had stopped work on the demolition of the building for the day, leaving an unsupported brick wall still standing. At 6 P.M. that evening, Elizabeth was "caught beneath a falling wall while playing in the ruins." She was "so badly crushed that she died almost instantly."[53]

More than a century later, the risks of living near vacant houses are not shared equally by all Baltimore residents. In the largely white neighborhoods of Hampden, Remington, and Medfield in North Baltimore, less than 1 percent of the houses are vacant—around sixty buildings. In contrast, for the largely black residents of Sandtown-Winchester and Harlem Park in West Baltimore, more than one-third of the houses in their areas are vacant—more than two thousand buildings. A 2014 analysis showed that in areas where less than 50 percent of residents are black, the average vacancy rate is less than 3 percent. In areas where more than 80 percent of residents are black, the average vacancy rate is more than 13 percent.[54]

More than a century after a falling brick wall killed Elizabeth Handley, vacant houses continue to cause tragedy and demand change. On March 28, 2016, Thomas Lemmon, a sixty-nine-year-old retired truck driver, sat in his "prized Cadillac" parked next to a 110-year-old vacant brick rowhouse on Payson Street in the West Baltimore neighborhood of Midtown-Edmondson.

The first owners of the house, Jacob Bauerman and his wife, lived there until they sold it in 1948—the same year the U.S. Supreme Court's decision in *Shelley v. Kramer* made restrictive racial covenants unenforceable. In 1973, the house sold in a tax sale, and it was permanently abandoned by the mid-1990s. The property sold at tax sale again in the 2000s, but the buyer never finalized the purchase, and the building languished.

"Every day, he would come out and sit in that car," relax, and listen to music, said Lemmon's cousin, Robert English. But that afternoon, high winds pushed over the two-story wall of the vacant rowhouse at 900 North Payson Street. A pile of bricks dropped onto Lemmon's car, killing him.[55]

Two years later, on March 27, 2018, Baltimore mayor Catherine Pugh and Maryland governor Larry Hogan held a press conference in front of six boarded-up vacant houses on the 1000 block of North Stockton Street in Sandtown-Winchester. Hogan announced the newest phase of Project CORE: the planned demolition of five hundred abandoned buildings that his press release labeled "a haven for criminal activity in neighborhoods most at risk."[56] The list included seventy-five vacant buildings in the Midtown-Edmondson neighborhood where Thomas Lemmon died.[57]

Other than demolition, however, Hogan offered few solutions for West Baltimore residents struggling to live around vacant buildings. In 2015, Hogan abruptly canceled the Red Line—an east–west light rail project that had secured more than $900 million in federal funding—just a year before construction was scheduled to begin. Hogan then redirected state funding for public transportation to expanding highways in suburban and rural counties. Before the end of 2015, the NAACP Legal Defense Fund and the ACLU of Maryland filed an administrative complaint with the U.S. Department of Transportation Office of Civil Rights on behalf of the Baltimore Regional Initiative Developing Genuine Equality (BRIDGE), citing the long history of inequitable transportation policy in Baltimore and Maryland. In July 2017, the office closed the complaint without any explanation or substantive response.[58] By 2018, when Hogan sat down at the controls of a John Deere excavator and, with help from a contractor, started tearing down those six houses on Stockton Street, the city had shared a proposal to replace the vacant buildings with a new park—but the city had not yet made a plan to pay for it.[59]

The vacant rowhouses on Stockton Street disappeared into trucks and dumpsters within days. The brick walls on Gutman Avenue and Payson Street took just a moment to fall on Elizabeth Handley and Thomas Lemmon, respectively.

A lasting solution to the problem of vacant houses in Baltimore will take much longer. When people with power in the Baltimore region acknowledge the complex history behind every vacant house, new approaches might gain the political and financial support required to address the broader issue of vacancy. Until then, vacant houses remain an ever-present tragedy.

Notes

1 *Vital Signs 8: Housing and Community Development* (Baltimore: Baltimore Neighborhood Indicators Alliance–Jacob France Institute, 2009), https://bniajfi .org/wp-content/uploads/2014/04/VS-8-Housing-and-Community -Development.pdf.

2 Jennifer Leonard and Joe Schilling, *Vacant Properties: The True Cost to Communities* (Washington, DC: National Vacant Properties Campaign, August 2005).

3 Joan Jacobson, *Vacants to Value: Baltimore's Bold Blight-Elimination Effort Is Making Modest Progress despite Limited Renovation Funds and Questionable Accounting* (Baltimore: Abell Foundation, November 2015), https://www.abell.org /publications/vacants-value.

4 Andrew R. Highsmith, *Demolition Means Progress: Flint, Michigan, and the Fate of the American Metropolis* (Chicago: University of Chicago Press, 2015), 280.

5 Amy Laura Cahn, "On Retiring Blight as Policy and Making Eastwick Whole," *Harvard Civil Rights-Civil Liberties Law Review* 49 (2014): 450.

6 Luke Broadwater and Yvonne Wenger, "Baltimore and Maryland Officials Begin Ramped-up Demolition Plan," *Baltimore Sun*, January 7, 2016.

7 HOLC Division of Research & Statistics, *Residential Security Map of Baltimore Md.*, 1 col. map; 69 × 62 cm, c. 1:38,000 (Home Owners' Loan Corporation, May 29, 1937), https://dspace-prod.mse.jhu.edu/handle/1774.2/32621; Baltimore City Department of Planning, *Housing Market Typology*, March 17, 2016, https://planning.baltimorecity.gov/maps-data/housing-market-typology.

8 Jason Richardson, Bruce Mitchell, and Nicole West, *Home Mortgage and Small Business Lending in Baltimore and Surrounding Areas* (Washington, DC: National Community Reinvestment Coalition, November 2015), http://www.ncrc .org/images/ncrc_baltimore_lending_analysis_web.pdf.

9 C. Dana Loomis, "Putting Abandoned City Areas back into Use: A Radical Remedy Is Found to Solve the Difficulty of Installing a Good City Plan Now; The Problems Involved in Shaping Old Haphazard Developments to More Efficient Use," *Baltimore Sun,* December 11, 1932.

10 "Way to Fight Blight Told: Whole Community Must Engage, Dr. Wolman Says," *Baltimore Sun,* January 27, 1955.

11 Hezekiah Niles and William Ogden Niles, *Niles' Weekly Register* (Baltimore: H. Niles, 1831), 426.

12 Seth Rockman, *Scraping By: Wage Labor, Slavery, and Survival in Early Baltimore* (Baltimore: Johns Hopkins University Press, 2010).

13 Sherry H. Olson, "Baltimore Imitates the Spider," *Annals of the Association of American Geographers* 69, no. 4 (December 1, 1979): 559; "Demand for Houses," *Baltimore Sun,* October 26, 1898.

14 Joseph L. Arnold, "Suburban Growth and Municipal Annexation in Baltimore, 1745–1918," *Maryland Historical Magazine* 73, no. 2 (June 1978): 117–119.

15 "Buildings Declared Unsafe: Building Inspector Dowell Cites the Law under which They May Be Pulled Down," *Baltimore Sun,* March 22, 1898; Mayor and City Council of Baltimore, *Building Code of Baltimore: Being Ordinance No. 155 of the Mayor and City Council of Baltimore, Approved July 6, 1908* (Baltimore: Harry W. Willson, 1908), http://archive.org/details/buildingcodebaloopielgoog.

16 "Edward D. Preston Dead," *Baltimore Sun,* May 13, 1919.

17 The count of condemnation notices is recorded in the Department of Buildings' annual reports between 1897 and 1904. *Mayor's Message and Reports of the City Officers* (Baltimore: City of Baltimore, 1905), http://archive.org/details/mayorsmessage19042balt.

18 "War on Unsafe Buildings," *Baltimore Sun,* August 29, 1901.

19 "Sale Raises a Storm," *Baltimore Sun,* March 15, 1906.

20 "5,655 Building Vacant," *Baltimore Sun,* August 21, 1910.

21 Paige Glotzer, "Real Estate and the City: Considering the History of Capitalism and Urban History," *Journal of Urban History* 42, no. 2 (March 1, 2016): 438–445, https://doi.org/10.1177/0096144215623478.

22 Pure White, "Baltimore Is Too Southern to Stand for Whites and Blacks in the Same Street," *Baltimore Sun,* August 27, 1910.

23 "Justice: The Interests of the Many Should Be Considered," *Baltimore Sun,* September 2, 1910.

24 "City Briefs: Attorney Hawkins to Test Segregation Law," *Afro-American,* August 12, 1911; "W. Ashbie Hawkins (1861–1941) MSA SC 3520-12415," Maryland State Archives (Biographical Series), May 15, 2006, https://msa.maryland.gov/msa/speccol/sc3500/sc3520/012400/012415/html/msa12415.html.

25 "Hawkins Makes Masterful Argument: Cites Authority after Authority to Show Segregation Law Unconstitutional," *Afro-American,* June 28, 1913.

26 "Segregation Law Decided Invalid," *Afro-American,* August 9, 1913; Garrett Power, "Apartheid Baltimore Style: The Residential Segregation Ordinances of 1910–1913," *Maryland Law Review* 42 (1983); Dennis P. Halpin, "'The Struggle for Land and Liberty: Segregation, Violence, and African American Resistance in Baltimore, 1898–1918," *Journal of Urban History* (July 2015): 1–22, https://doi.org/10.1177/0096144215589923.

27 Jacques Kelly, "1893 Letter Details Racially Restrictive Covenants in City Neighborhoods," *Baltimore Sun,* March 27, 2015.

28 Olson, "Baltimore Imitates the Spider," 559.

29 Samuel Roberts Jr., *Infectious Fear: Politics, Disease, and the Health Effects of Segregation* (Chapel Hill: University of North Carolina Press, 2009), 205–206; Eli Pousson, *Preston Gardens,* Explore Baltimore Heritage, August 12, 2017, https://explore.baltimoreheritage.org/items/show/71.

30 Joan Jacobson, *The Steep Price of Paying to Stay: Baltimore City's Tax Sale, the Risks to Vulnerable Homeowners, and Strategies to Improve the Process* (Baltimore: Abell Foundation, October 2014), https://www.abell.org/sites/default/files/publications/ec-taxsale1014.pdf.

31 "Tax Sales up 100 Per Cent. in Past Year,'" *Baltimore Sun,* December 29, 1936.

32 "City to Raze Its Buildings Going to Ruin," *Baltimore Sun,* June 14, 1936.

33 "House Caves in just after Children Go," *Baltimore Sun,* April 19, 1937.

34 Esther J. Crooks, "Need for More Attention to Subject of Housing Is Urged," *Baltimore Sun,* April 20, 1937.

35 "To Map Policy on Blighted Areas of the City," *Baltimore Sun,* May 10, 1937.

36 "Big Problem," *Baltimore Sun,* May 11, 1937.

37 "Tax-Sale Properties," *Baltimore Sun,* March 17, 1937.

38 Rhonda Y. Williams, *The Politics of Public Housing: Black Women's Struggles against Urban Inequality* (New York: Oxford University Press, 2004), 21–53.

39 Antero Pietila, *Not in My Neighborhood: How Bigotry Shaped a Great American City* (Chicago: Ivan R. Dee, 2010); *The Zoning and Planning Process in Baltimore County and Its Effect on Minority Group Residents*, Maryland State Advisory Committee to the U.S. Commission on Civil Rights, March 1971, University of Maryland Francis King Carey School of Law, Thurgood Marshall Law Library, https://www.law.umaryland.edu/marshall/usccr/documents/cr12z71971.pdf.

40 Raymond A. Mohl, "The Interstates and the Cities: Highways, Housing, and the Freeway Revolt," *Poverty and Race Research Action Council* 109 (2002): 107; Emily Lieb, "'White Man's Lane': Hollowing out the Highway Ghetto in Baltimore," in *Baltimore '68: Riots and Rebirth in an American City*, ed. Jessica Elfenbein, Thomas Hollowak, and Elizabeth Nix (Philadelphia: Temple University Press, 2011), 51–69.

41 "Abandoned Houses," *Baltimore Sun,* April 19, 1965.

42 "Neglected Homes Here Surveyed," *Baltimore Sun,* March 22, 1964; "Small Decline in Vacant Houses," *Baltimore Sun,* April 11, 1973.

43 Ellen Janes and Sandra Davis, *Vacants to Value: Baltimore's Market-Based Approach to Vacant Property Redevelopment, Putting Data to Work: Data-Driven Approaches to Strengthening Neighborhoods* (Richmond: Federal Reserve Bank of Richmond, April 4, 2012), https://www.federalreserve.gov/publications/putting -data-to-work-vacants-to-value.htm.

44 Pamela Constable, "Vacant Houses an 'Insurmountable' Problem for Neighbors," *Baltimore Sun,* December 6, 1981.

45 Joseph Simpson, "'Urban Homesteading' Begins," *Baltimore Sun,* April 21, 1974; Rufus Wells, "Would You Buy a House," *Afro-American,* September 13, 1975.

46 Shane Scott, "Biography of a Block: Where Families Once Flourished, Addicts, Homeless Move In," *Baltimore Sun,* June 6, 1993.

47 Edward Gunts, "Variety of Properties Set for City's Auction," *Baltimore Sun,* May 3, 1987.

48 "Attacking Housing Blight," *Baltimore Sun,* October 11, 1994.

49 Steven Manson, Jonathan Schroeder, David Van Riper, and Steven Ruggles, *IPUMS National Historical Geographic Information System: Version 12.0* [Database] (Minneapolis: University of Minnesota. 2017), http://doi.org/10.18128 /D050.V12.0.

50 JoAnna Daemmrich, "Schmoke Warns Landlords: Fix It, or City Will Raze It," *Baltimore Sun,* October 7, 1994.

51 JoAnna Daemmrich, "Demolition of Derelict Buildings Gets Slow Start," *Baltimore Sun,* June 21, 1995.

52 "Best Feigned Ignorance: Daniel Henson's Response to Potential Conflicts of Interest," *Baltimore City Paper,* September 17, 1997.

53 "Her Life Crushed Out: Elizabeth Handley, 7 Years Old, Caught under Wall," *Baltimore Sun,* August 10, 1913.

54 Analysis based on data from *Vital Signs 14: Measuring Progress toward a Better Quality of Life in Every Neighborhood* (Baltimore: Baltimore Neighborhood Indicators Alliance–Jacob France Institute, Spring 2016), http://bniajfi.org/wp -content/uploads/2016/04/VitalSigns14_FullOnline.pdf.

55 Tim Prudente, "When Vacant House Fell in West Baltimore, a Retiree Was Crushed in His Prized Cadillac," *Baltimore Sun,* March 30, 2016.

56 "Governor Larry Hogan Announces Latest Phase of Project C.O.R.E. Initiative: Over 500 Properties Targeted for Removal as Part of Efforts to Reduce Violent Crime in Baltimore," Office of Governor Larry Hogan, March 27, 2018, https:// governor.maryland.gov/2018/03/27/governor-larry-hogan-announces-latest-phase -of-project-c-o-r-e-initiative/.

57 Properties selected for demolition under Project CORE and other programs are identified on codeMap, an online map published by Baltimore City. "CodeMap," interactive web map, Baltimore Housing, accessed May 10, 2018, http://cels .baltimorehousing.org/codemap/codeMap.html.

58 Ovetta Wiggins and Bill Turque, "NAACP to Challenge Cancellation of Baltimore Red Line Rail Project," *Washington Post,* December 21, 2015; NAACP Legal Defense Fund, "Baltimore Red Line Complaint," December 21, 2015, 44; Katherine Shaver, "Federal Officials Close Civil Rights Complaint about Baltimore Light-Rail Project," *Washington Post,* July 13, 2017.

59 *Baltimore Green Network Plan: March 2018 DRAFT* (Baltimore: Baltimore City Department of Planning, March 2018), http://greennetwork.civicomment.org/.

5

A Psychology of Place

· · · · · · · · · · · · · · · · · · · ·

Race, Violence, and Community in Baltimore

DANIEL BUCCINO

AND TERESA MÉNDEZ

> The best image to sum up the uncon-
> scious is Baltimore in the early morning.
> —Jacques Lacan, 1966, Baltimore

It is impossible to appreciate life in Baltimore without considering its psychology, though surely psychologizing a city is impossible. Freud cautioned against "wild analysis," efforts at understanding art, culture, history, or a city through a psychological lens.[1] The French Freudian, Jacques Lacan, advised that we should look to art and culture for what they can teach psychoanalysis, rather than using psychoanalysis to interpret society. As psychotherapists with more than thirty years of combined clinical experience, we are still looking to our patients to teach us about their multiple Baltimores, instead of presuming to know what their city may be.[2]

But Baltimore does have a certain psychology: a sublime sensibility at once obvious and ineffable, not unlike the unconscious itself. It is alternately tender and tough, swaggering and fearful, northern and southern, black and white.[3] The resigned resilience that many of our patients embody transcends quirky eccentricities or bleak urban and institutional wastelands: portrayals of our "Charm City" that most resonate in the associations of outsiders.

In the aftermath of the 2015 uprising following the death of Freddie Gray in police custody, perennial issues tumbled forth from the tumult of Baltimore's psyche, settling along the concretized fault lines of violence, race, and class. Our former mayor had already designated Baltimore a "trauma-informed city."[4] An African American male is thirty times more likely to be murdered than the average American, making for a murder rate in black Baltimore that ranks fifth in the world.[5] While the violence disproportionately affects its African American communities, Baltimore remains one of the most violent cities in the world.[6] The bloodshed seldom spills beyond certain "red lines," yet the murders, as well as lesser crimes, contribute to a sense of fear for many.

Perhaps equally violent is what one black psychoanalyst has described as a lifetime spent subsisting on racial microaggressions, racism that one of our black patients noted had gone underground, for a time, only to re-emerge with a vengeance in the wake of the presidential election of 2016.[7] This patient recalled the white woman he saw while walking into the building of one of our offices. She looked startled as he opened the door, as if afraid he might snatch her purse. When asked what he did in response, he said he laughed, refusing to absorb her projection: "Because I knew this, at least, was her crazy, not mine."

Political theorist Michael Walzer describes "the peculiar evil of terrorism" as "not only the killing of innocent people but also the intrusion of fear into everyday life, the violation of private purposes, the insecurity of public spaces."[8] Certainly, the psychologies of many of our residents, black and white, are colonized by this "endless coerciveness of precaution": a hypervigilance that is the hallmark of trauma.

Yet just as trauma fractures, it can also constitute. Our patients, with lives scarred by racism, poverty, abuse, addiction, malnutrition, lead poisoning, substandard education and housing, and rampant violence in and out of prison, take a perverse pride in how rough Baltimore is and how they have survived it. They boast that inmates from Baltimore are known as the toughest across state and federal penitentiary systems. One described Baltimore's own Golden Rule: "Don't start no shit, won't be no shit." The stories our patients tell themselves about themselves are full of suffering, but also of the overcoming of it.

Consistent with Baltimore's traumatic internalization of itself as "Harm City" is its relationship to drugs, especially heroin. Though persistent reports place the rate of heroin addiction in Baltimore at 10 percent of the population, the reality is probably one-third of that.[9] Yet, nearly 25,000 people struggle with heroin and opiate addiction and its associated medical, psychiatric, and psychosocial comorbidities. One elderly patient reports that this has been his family business for five generations. In addition to providing a living history of the drug trade in the 1970s and 1980s ("The kids on the street these days have no respect!"), his ancestry anchors the drug trade in Baltimore to the early twentieth century. Even before that, several prominent Baltimore merchants and merchant ships were involved in trading Turkish opium to China, establishing their fortunes in the nineteenth century. In fact, one of contemporary Baltimore's most coveted neighborhoods, Canton, and its central (John) O'Donnell Square, reflect its profitable roots in the Chinese (Cantonese) opium trade.[10]

Baltimore has also long been a pioneer of racist housing policies in the United States.[11] In 1910, Baltimore city government adopted one of the first residential segregation ordinances in the country, restricting African Americans to designated blocks.[12] Although the Supreme Court invalidated laws requiring residential segregation along racial lines, a century of federal, state, and local housing policies, as well as racial covenants, have essentially quarantined the black population to ghettos and reinforced segregated neighborhoods. The residue of this redlining reverberates today: the riots of 1968 and the uprising of 2015 were concentrated in neighborhoods that have been "ghettoized" for a century.[13]

These neighborhoods are prey to "economies of extraction," where the poor are forced to pay more in rent because home ownership is unduly and prohibitively expensive, while communities starved for income pay exorbitant fees in the form of taxes, unseen court and incarceration costs, and miscellaneous fines.[14] While the economy may remain terrible, "the hustle" is terrific.[15] This double-edged sword, of survival and exploitation, resilience and reinscription, is a veritable Freudian "symptom formation": a conflicted effort to transcend that also reproduces and reinforces the very stressor that is holding one back.[16]

Even as major historical and cultural threads weave a complicated symptom in the Baltimore psyche, there are unique and largely unappreciated histories of psychoanalysis rooted in Baltimore as well: these are narratives of transcendence and transgression. With its reputation as "The City That Bleeds," a eulogy to the way psychic pain becomes memorialized in the body, Baltimore's psychology also includes its locus as the birthplace of psychoanalysis—one might even say of the unconscious—in the United States. In 1911, two years after Freud's only visit to the United States, when it is claimed that Freud said he was "bringing . . . the plague," the American Psychoanalytic Association was established at the Stafford Hotel in Baltimore's Mount Vernon neighborhood.[17]

At that time, Baltimore was the home of Johns Hopkins Hospital and Adolf Meyer, the pre-eminent psychiatrist and father of "psychobiology." Originally from Zurich, Meyer had attended lectures by the Swiss psychoanalyst Carl Jung and was taken by Freud's ideas, then considered the leading edge of science.

Meyer's psychobiological approach was an effort to capture the liminal and unbridgeable brain(bio)/mind(psycho) gap. He was instrumental in formalizing psychiatry as an academic medical discipline, founding the Henry Phipps Psychiatric Clinic at Hopkins in 1913, the first inpatient unit in a general hospital in the United States expressly designed to treat those with mental illness.[18]

Baltimore functioned, once more, as a lure for psychoanalysis when, in 1966, Lacan arrived here on the first stop of his inaugural trip to the United States to speak at the Johns Hopkins University symposium, "The Languages of Criticism and the Sciences of Man." This conference marked the founding of the Hopkins Humanities Center and served to position Hopkins as the gateway for contemporary Continental thought into North America.[19] It was considered so foundational that French literary theorist Jacques Derrida, who was at the conference, later reflected, "What is now called 'theory' in this country may have an essential link with what is said to have happened there in 1966."[20]

Though not well known, the remarks Lacan made in Baltimore in 1966 are memorable. Insisting on speaking in English, Lacan's text reads like one of his seminars:

> When I prepared this little talk for you, it was early in the morning. I could see Baltimore through the window and it was a very interesting moment because it was not quite daylight and a neon sign indicated to me every minute the change of time, and naturally there was heavy traffic, and I remarked to myself that exactly all that I could see, except for some trees in the distance, was the result of thoughts, actively thinking thoughts, where the function played by the subjects was not completely obvious. In any case the so-called *Dasein*, as a definition of the subject, was there in this rather intermittent or fading spectator. *The best image to sum up the unconscious is Baltimore in the early morning* [emphasis added].[21]

Lacan locates the unconscious, the sublime nexus of all our psyches, in Baltimore in the morning. The unconscious, he tells us, is like dawn—that hypnopompic threshold between sleep and waking. It is a pulsating neon sign, ticking time, advertising enjoyment. It is intermittent and fading, present and absent. The unconscious is like Baltimore, with its sublime oscillations between wounded and surviving, swaggering and fearful, northern and southern, black and white.

According to Freud and Lacan, there is no universal "dream book" meant to provide facile interpretations of every dream image. Neither is there an easy decoder ring for the psychology of Baltimore. Every resident must tell his and her own story of the psychology of this place. Yet we all wake each day into the unconscious that is Baltimore in the early morning, a sublime place both horrifying and beautiful.

Notes

1   Sigmund Freud, "'Wild' Psycho-Analysis," in *The Standard Edition of the Complete Psychological Works of Sigmund Freud*, ed. and trans. James Strachey, vol. 6 (London: Hogarth Press, 1957), 221–227.

2   Jacques Lacan, *The Four Fundamental Concepts of Psychoanalysis* (New York: Norton, 1978).

3   Edmund Burke, "A Philosophical Enquiry into the Origin of Our Ideas of the Sublime and Beautiful," in *The Bloomsbury Anthology of Aesthetics*, ed. Joseph J. Tanke et al. (New York: Bloomsbury Academic, 2012), 163–185.

4   Andrea McDaniels, "City Staff Learn New Ways to Help Troubled Residents: Training Sessions Focus on 'Trauma-Informed Care,'" *Baltimore Sun*, August 28, 2015.

5   Edward Ericson Jr., "Three Hundred Murders, and Counting," in "Top Ten Local News Stories of 2015," *Baltimore City Paper*, December 23, 2015.

6   Jess Bidgood, "The Numbers behind Baltimore's Record Year in Homicides," *New York Times*, January 15, 2016.

7   *Black Psychoanalysts Speak*, film directed by Basia Winograd (2014).

8   Michael Walzer, *Arguing about War* (New Haven: Yale University Press, 2004), 51.

9   *Treating Substance Use Disorders in Baltimore; Responding to a Communitywide Challenge*, Behavioral Health System Baltimore, accessed March 30, 2016, http://www.bhsbaltimore.org/site/wp-content/uploads/2015/12/30522-Substance-Abuse.pdf.

10 Van Smith, "Baltimore's Narcotic History Dates back to the 19th-Century Shipping-Driven Boom, Quietly Aided by Bringing Turkish Opium to China," *Baltimore City Paper*, October 21, 2014.

11 Richard Rothstein, "How Government Policies Cemented the Racism That Reigns in Baltimore," *The American Prospect*, April 29, 2015.

12 Antero Pietila, *Not in My Neighborhood: How Bigotry Shaped a Great American City* (Chicago: Ivan R. Dee, 2010).

13 Jessica Elfenbein et al., eds, *Baltimore '68: Riots and Rebirth in an American City* (Philadelphia: Temple University Press, 2011).

14 N.D.B. Connolly, "Black Culture Is Not the Problem," *New York Times*, May 1, 2015.

15 Lester Spence, *Knocking the Hustle: Against the Neoliberal Turn in Black Politics* (New York: Punctum Books, 2015).

16 Sigmund Freud, "The Paths to the Formation of Symptoms," in *The Standard Edition of the Complete Psychological Works of Sigmund Freud*, ed. and trans. James Strachey, vol. 16 (London: Hogarth Press, 1957), 358–377.

17 Jacques Lacan, "The Freudian Thing," in *Écrits: The First Complete Edition in English*, trans. Bruce Fink (New York: W. W. Norton, 1996), 336.

18 S. D. Lamb, *Pathologist of the Mind: Adolf Meyer and the Origins of American Psychiatry* (Baltimore: Johns Hopkins University Press, 2014).

19 Richard Macksey and Eugenio Donato, eds., *The Structuralist Controversy: The Languages of Criticism and the Sciences of Man* (Baltimore: Johns Hopkins University Press, 1970).

20 Jacques Derrida, "Some Statements and Truisms about Neo-Logisms, Newisms, Postisms, Parasitisms, and Other Small Seismisms," in *The States of Theory*, ed. David Carroll (New York: Columbia University Press, 1990), 80.

21 Jacques Lacan, "Of Structure as an Inmixing of an Otherness Prerequisite to Any Subject Whatever," in *The Structuralist Controversy*, ed. Richard Macksey and Eugenio Donato (Baltimore: Johns Hopkins University Press, 1970), 189.

6

Community Health
and Baltimore Apartheid

• •

Revisiting Development,
Inequality, and Tax Policy

LAWRENCE BROWN

> Baltimore is like a set of fraternal twins
> Conceived as one. Birthed into two . . .
> Mansions in Guilford.
> Vacants in Gilmore . . .
> —Lady Brion (Baltimore writer, poet,
> and educator), "Fraternal Twins"

Discriminatory Development in Tax Policy

Since the turn of the twenty-first century, Baltimore's mayors and City Council members have greatly expanded the city's use of inequitable tax policies, driving the stake of inequality into the heart of an already racially hypersegregated city.[1] This recent wave of activity continued the public spending on downtown and harbor redevelopment by mayors in office from 1943–1999, such as Theodore McKeldin, Thomas D'Alesandro Jr., Thomas D'Alesandro III, William Donald Schaefer, and Kurt Schmoke.[2] Urban redevelopment activity during the last half of the twentieth century was funded by a combination of federal community development block grants and local urban renewal, Empowerment Zones, and HOPE VI initiatives. Since 2000, Baltimore's mayors—especially Martin O'Malley and Stephanie Rawlings-Blake, and Sheila Dixon to a lesser degree—have used a bevy of tax-increment financing bonds (TIFs), payments in lieu of taxes (PILOTs), and tax breaks or incentives near the waterfront of the city to spur growth and development. Although in the twenty-first century the percentage of urban redevelopment funding provided by federal subsidies decreased in favor of more funding from local subsidies, much of the city's development logic favoring corporations continued as before: waterfront and downtown neighborhoods received massive investments, while many of the city's core neighborhoods were neglected.

By 2015, the Baltimore Development Corporation (BDC) and city leaders had authorized twelve active PILOTs costing city schools $13 million a year and eleven active TIFs costing city schools at least another $17.4 million annually, according to reporting by the *Baltimore Sun* journalists Luke Broadwater and Natalie Sherman.[3] *City Paper* reporter Edward Ericson Jr. compiled a list of eleven TIFs and thirteen PILOTs between 2000 and 2013.[4] The state funding formula for education provides lower levels of funding for public schools as land values rise, on the assumption that a locality has an increased

Table 1.
Selected Development Projects in Baltimore City

ID	Project Name	Location	Tax mechanism	Property value	Annual taxes paid
1	EBDI	Middle East	$78 million TIF	unknown	taxes diverted to TIF
2	Marriott Waterfront	Harbor East	PILOT	$155 million	$1
3	Lockwood Place	Downtown	tax credits	$58 million	unknown
4	Zenith luxury apartments	W. Pratt St.	tax credits	$40 million	pays 15% of property taxes
5	Canton Crossing	Canton	PILOT	$65 million	unknown
6	Harbor Point	Harbor East	$107 million TIF	unknown	taxes diverted to TIF
7	Amazon warehouse	SE Baltimore	PILOT/tax break	$141 million	$400,000 ($2.3M tax break)
8	Sagamore Development	Port Covington	$660 million TIF	unknown	taxes diverted to TIF

ability to pay for its schools. While the costs to city schools have been calculated to some level of specificity, the costs to public health have been less specified.[5]

Since 2000, the large majority of current development funded by tax policies has occurred near the waterfront, near downtown, or near so-called anchor institutions such as universities and hospitals (see Table 1). These tax policy tools have been barely used in the city's disinvested, redlined, majority African American neighborhoods—unless they are located near predominantly white institutions such as Johns Hopkins Medical Institutions (e.g., $78 million in TIF bonds for the Hopkins proxy called EBDI, the East Baltimore Development Initiative) or the University of Maryland, Baltimore BioPark (a $17.5 million TIF in 2016 to Wexler Science + Technology, a local development firm that caters to universities, academic medical centers, and major research institutions). The one significant example where the city and the BDC have implemented one of these tools in a majority African American neighborhood was the approval of a $15 million TIF in 2008 at Mondawmin Mall. This TIF was issued by the BDC to coincide with the opening of a Target retail store, which closed its doors nearly ten years later in February 2018. Local reporters and researchers have called attention to the city's inequitable and discriminatory tax policies (i.e., TIFs, PILOTs, tax breaks, etc.), especially their deleterious effect on public schools, but this chapter addresses a dimension that remains underexplored: their impact on community and public health.[6]

Baltimore Apartheid

To fully understand community and public health in Baltimore, one must understand the city's history and its spatial geography. From its founding until the Civil War broke out in earnest in a riot on Pratt Street on Friday, April 19, 1861, Baltimore was a port city that served a key role in the American international and domestic slave trades of Africans and their descendants. A number of wealthier white Baltimoreans practiced slavery and benefited from it after the city was founded in 1729. For fifty years preceding the Civil War, slave traders and slavers operated slave jails or pens on or near Pratt Street, and slavery persisted within the city's confines.[7] Immediately after the Civil War, multiple transportation companies segregating passengers by race operated in Baltimore, and in 1867 city leaders funded the first public schools for people then known as Negroes.[8] White Baltimoreans' slave trading, slave auctioning, and enslaving of people of African descent, along with the city's racially segregated public services and accommodations, gave rise to Baltimore Apartheid.

Baltimore Apartheid is the combination of containment (i.e., racial segregation) and clearance (i.e., forced displacement) of African American residents, initially to prevent civil disorder, the devaluation of white homes, miscegenation, and the spread of disease to white communities.[9] Multiple systems, including criminal justice, real estate, public housing, finance, banking, economic and community development, K–12 and higher education, parks and recreation, public works, and public health, helped enforce and expand Baltimore Apartheid. Baltimore's discriminatory tax policies and property tax valuation have helped shape and reinforce the city's spatial landscape of inequality, thereby intensifying the nature of Baltimore Apartheid and exacerbating public health crises and social pathologies in the city.[10] Social pathologies include persistent hyperpolicing and recurring uprisings, along with elevated levels of violent crime, poverty, and substance abuse in deeply redlined communities. For example, Baltimore Apartheid was intensified by the tripling of the city's police budget from $165 million in 1991 to $523 million in 2017, which siphoned off funding from critical city social services.[11] In 2013, Mayor Rawlings-Blake closed or privatized more than twenty recreation centers; earlier mayors had already cut funding for libraries, afterschool programs, and summer jobs.[12] This spending shift made possible a rise in hyperpolicing of disinvested, redlined black neighborhoods and the further weakening of the social fabric holding together many Baltimore communities.

Community and Public Health in the Black Butterfly

Baltimore's neighborhoods are characterized by striking racial segregation and can be roughly divided into two distinctive spatial geographies: a White L and a Black Butterfly. Baltimore's current hypersegregation is the fruit of a long litany of policies and practices deployed and perfected between 1910 and 1950, including the following: racial zoning, racially restrictive covenants, real estate conspiracies that shut African Americans out of housing markets, redlining, racially segregated public housing and public schools, and intense lobbying by white segregationist residents, churches, and protective or improvement neighborhood associations. These racial segregation policies and practices played a powerful role in shaping development choices and health outcomes for decades to come.

The Baltimore City Health Department's 2011 report, *Healthy Baltimore 2015*, documents a variety of diseases and access issues that disproportionately affect African American residents, ranging from cardiovascular disease to sexually transmitted diseases (STDs) to a lack of mental health access to infant mortality.[13] The oft-cited statistics should come as no surprise given the structural greenlining and advantaging of the White L and the simultaneous structural redlining and disadvantaging of the Black Butterfly. Redlining can be defined as the restriction by public and private entities of the capital and resources allocated to a community, while greenlining is the inequitable privileging of a community that allows it to receive higher levels of public–private capital and resources. Subpriming is the predatory offering of loans at high interest rates and unfavorable terms to some borrowers over others. Redlining, greenlining, and subpriming vary based on the predominant race living in a community: African American communities are systemically redlined and subprimed, while white communities are systemically greenlined.

Public health outcomes are often simply a reflection of a community's socioeconomic health and the equity of resource allocation. A community's ability to be healthy is affected by whether it is structurally redlined or greenlined by public and private policies, practices, and investments. The Health Department's neighborhood health profiles—released in 2008, 2011, and 2017—highlight the degree to which health outcomes vary drastically depending on the community in which residents live.

Community health is largely determined by Baltimore Apartheid, the result of the city's aggregate discriminatory economic development, tax policies, and annual budgetary spending. White L neighborhoods are able to secure greater access both to public resources and private lending that help boost the health of their residents. For instance, 35 percent of African Americans in Baltimore live in a food desert characterized by a lack of nutritious food retailers, compared to 8 percent of white Baltimoreans, who live in White L neighborhoods that are closer to higher-quality grocery stores and farmers' markets.[14] Since 2015, White L neighborhoods have obtained significant biking infrastructure, including protected bike lanes and bike rentals from Baltimore Bike Share, while Black Butterfly neighborhoods have been denied access to quality biking infrastructure.[15] In 2016, Mayor Rawlings-Blake and the City Council approved the Sagamore TIF that authorized $139.8 million in park spending for the Port Covington project (at the corner of the White L), which is three times the entire amount to be spent on parks and recreation in FY2018 ($46.27 million) for the entire city. Access to more nutritious foods, biking infrastructure, recreation centers, and equitable spending on public parks would help residents in Black Butterfly neighborhoods lower their comparatively higher rates of obesity, diabetes, hypertension, and heart disease. Instead, the public policies and practices of city officials expand and exacerbate food, transit, park, and recreation deserts.

A 2017 analysis of the capital budget by city planning officials found that the city of Baltimore had allocated nearly twice as many funds to majority-white community statistical areas ($15,048,000) than to majority-black community statistical areas ($8,303,000).[16] This discriminatory public redlining is not a recent phenomenon: it stretches back to the beginning of residential racial segregation in Baltimore. By greenlining and investing in White L neighborhoods via tax policy and not curbing private bank redlining/subpriming, city officials allow economic despair and high unemployment to cascade into crises expressed in crime, violence, and substance abuse in disinvested, redlined black neighborhoods. Subsequently, huge investments are made in policing and incarceration to impose social control and address the social pathologies caused by decades of disinvestment and displacement. Intracommunal homicides and extracommunal hyperpolicing induce urban posttraumatic stress disorder (PTSD), race-based traumatic stress, racial battle fatigue, and chronic stress that elevate the infant mortality rate and lower cognitive function for children born in the Black Butterfly. Compounding the problem is the lead poisoning crisis that still afflicts thousands of Baltimore youth.[17]

Even when economic development does come to the Black Butterfly, it is often accompanied by neighborhood displacement, as in the Middle East community, which is threatened by the biotechnology park to be built by Johns Hopkins Medical Institutions and EBDI; public housing demolition and land disposition by the Housing Authority of Baltimore City also contribute to displacement.[18] A $120 million mixed-use development and tech hub called Innovation Village is currently being built in West Baltimore on the same location where residents in Madison Park North Apartments lived before the complex was torn down because of managerial neglect and neighborhood redlining.[19] In other cases, development in disinvested neighborhoods has resulted in environmental injustice and a threat to community health, as seen in the planned trash incinerator that was to be placed in and near the South Baltimore neighborhoods of Curtis Bay, Brooklyn, and Cherry Hill.[20]

Additionally, Baltimore's discriminatory development means that there are lost opportunities to address pivotal health issues. For example, if more inclusionary and fair housing had been included in the Sagamore TIF deal for Port Covington, another 450 or more African American families could have been moved from lead-ridden homes to lead-free homes. TIFs, PILOTs, and tax breaks have been used almost exclusively for economic development, but not to invest in and expand health-enhancing infrastructure and activities. City leaders have ignored long-standing and escalating public health emergencies and failed to invest in lead abatement, violence prevention, substance abuse treatment, and overdose death prevention, in favor of boosting economic, business, and real estate development for entities such as the Sagamore Development Corporation and Johns Hopkins Medical Institutions.

Since 2015, the number of fatal drug overdoses has more than doubled, and more than 300 Baltimoreans are murdered each year. Yet, violence prevention programs such as the public health intervention Ceasefire and Safe Streets, directed by the criminologist David Kennedy, have either been discontinued or have lost grant funding. Even though Safe Streets' grant funding was restored via a December 2017 budget deal struck by the mayor and City Council for FY2018, it was only operating five sites as of early 2018 when the need requires twenty-five to thirty sites across the city. Little to no public health attention is being directed to large gun distributors and reducing illegal firearm distribution as a preventive measure. The Health Department is working hard to make naloxone widely available to stop people from dying from opioid overdoses, but little attention is given to the critical issues that drive people to despair and substance abuse: the annual seven thousand rental evictions, the roughly four thousand tax lien and mortgage foreclosures, and the lack of affordable housing.[21]

Thus Baltimore's historic and contemporary approach to economic development, tax policy, and budgeting has and continues to result in severe health crises and catastrophes. A drastically different approach is needed to address these crises and catastrophes that threaten the social fabric of the city. Just as city policies, practices, and investments helped create the current situation, so Baltimore can change its course to enhance and bolster the health of residents in the Black Butterfly, not just the White L.

To make possible an alternative health-enhancing approach, the city could issue a $3 billion Racial Equity Social Impact Bond (RESIB) that could work very much like a TIF, with spending to be allocated as follows:

- $1.245 billion to eliminate lead poison as a public health hazard to Baltimore's children ($845 million for lead abatement of homes, $100 million for lead remediation of soil, and $300 million to remove lead pipes from water systems)
- $200 million to hire and train local residents to do the lead abatement and remediation work
- $500 million for permanent housing for people without homes
- $255 million to help eliminate transit, biking, and food deserts in the Black Butterfly
- $100 million for violence prevention: funding a robust and renewed public health Ceasefire program, along with expanding Safe Streets program to twenty-five to thirty neighborhoods
- $100 million for substance abuse treatment, social work, and counseling
- $500 million for the top twenty-five to thirty disinvested, redlined neighborhoods for community-driven redevelopment
- $100 million for administration and management of the bond by the Baltimore Office of Civil Rights

If the RESIB were adopted, it would immediately begin to address the legacy of discriminatory development and tax policies in Baltimore. As a social impact bond, it would be paid for by the savings to the budget that would be derived from lower crime and therefore decreased budgetary spending on policing. Another way to ensure funding for the RESIB is to dedicate the $1.7 billion in net gain that is calculated to result from the Sagamore TIF to help cover any gap not covered by lowering the annual budget of policing to at least $400 million by 2025.

Conclusion

Baltimore's current development and tax policies, along with the annual budget allocations, reinforce the city's long history of Baltimore Apartheid that has manifested in its current hypersegregation: a city conceived as growing along two separate paths, producing two different health landscapes for residents in the White L as compared to the Black Butterfly. The solution is for the city to invest deeply in community and public health in the Black Butterfly at a level equal to investment in white neighborhoods going forward—in other words, to make Black Neighborhoods Matter. A $3 billion Racial Equity Social Impact Bond would help Black Butterfly neighborhoods reach their full potential for holistic development and assist in dismantling Baltimore Apartheid by not only focusing on the construction of buildings but also investing in the healing and wholeness of human beings and the restoration of neighborhoods in which they live.

Notes

1   Douglass Massey and Jonathan Tannen, "A Research Note on Trends in Black Hypersegregation," *Demography* 52, no. 3 (2015): 1025–1034.
2   Marc V. Levine, "'A Third-World City in the First World': Social Exclusion, Racial Inequality, and Sustainable Development in Baltimore," in *The Social Sustainability of Cities: Diversity and the Management of Change*, ed. M. Polese and R. E. Stren (Toronto: University of Toronto Press, 2000), 123–156.
3   Luke Broadwater, "Baltimore Development Boom Leads to Loss of State Funding for Schools," *Baltimore Sun*, February 7, 2015; Natalie Sherman, "City Poised to Approve Second, Larger-Than-Expected Round of Harbor Point TIF Bonds," *Baltimore Sun*, July 12, 2016.
4   Edward Ericson Jr., "Checking up on the Developers Who Get City Tax Breaks," *Baltimore City Paper*, June 19, 2013.
5   Luke Broadwater, "Baltimore's Quick Economic Growth Contributes to Loss in State Aid to Schools," *Baltimore Sun*, February 8, 2016.
6   Luke Broadwater, "Baltimore Leads State in Growth," *Baltimore Sun*, February 4, 2017.
7   Scott Shane, "The Secret History of the City Slave Trade," *Baltimore Sun*, June 20, 1999.
8   David Bogen, "Precursors of Rosa Parks: Maryland Transportation Cases between the Civil War and the Beginning of World War I," *Maryland Law Review* 63 (2004); "A Thorny Path: School Desegregation in Baltimore," *Underbelly*, May 15, 2014, http://www.mdhs.org/underbelly/2014/05/15/a-thorny-path-school-desegregation-in-baltimore/.

9   Garrett Power, "Apartheid Baltimore Style: The Residential Segregation Ordinances of 1910–1913," *Maryland Law Review* 42 (1983): 289, http://digitalcommons.law.umaryland.edu/mlr/vol42/iss2/4.

10 Louis Misrendino, "Baltimore's Property Tax Privileged v. Punished," *Baltimore Sun*, July 4, 2016, and "A Failed Redevelopment and Tax Policy," *Maryland Public Policy Institute*, May 22, 2015; Lawrence Brown, "Two Baltimores: The White L vs. the Black Butterfly," *Baltimore City Paper*, June 28, 2016.

11 Mark Reutter, "Closing Rec Centers and Slashing Youth Programs Were Root Causes of Riot, Councilman Asserts," *Baltimore Brew*, May 4, 2015.

12 Mark Reutter, "Mayor Proposes Rec Center Closings and Transfers in 2013 Budget," *Baltimore Brew*, March 21, 2012.

13 Michelle Spencer, Ryan Petteway, LaVeda Bacetti, and Oxiris Barbot, *Healthy Baltimore 2015: A City Where All Residents Realize Their Full Health Potential* (Baltimore: Baltimore City Health Department, 2011).

14 Amanda Behrens Buczynski, Holly Freishtat, and Sarah Buzogany, *Mapping Baltimore City's Food Environment* (Baltimore: Baltimore Office of Sustainability, 2015).

15 David Dudley, "Enlisting Equity in the Fight against Inequality," *Citylab*, December 19, 2016.

16 Oscar Perry Abello, "Baltimore Reckons with Its Legacy of Redlining," *Next City*, November 22, 2017.

17 M. B. Pell and Joshua Schneyer, "Off the Charts: The Thousands of U.S. Locales Where Lead Poisoning Is Worse Than Flint," *Reuters*, December 19, 2016.

18 Lawrence Brown, "Down to the Wire: Displacement and Disinvestment in Baltimore City," in *The 2015 State of Black Baltimore: Still Separate, Still Unequal* (Baltimore: Greater Baltimore Urban League, 2015), 71–89.

19 Andrew Zaleski, "The Great 'Innovation' Rebrand of West Baltimore," *Next City*, March 20, 2017.

20 Darryl Fears, "This Baltimore 20-Year-Old Just Won a Huge International Award for Taking out a Giant Trash Incinerator," *Washington Post*, April 18, 2016.

21 Public Justice Center, *Justice Diverted: How Renters Are Processed in the Baltimore City Rent Court* (Baltimore: Public Justice Center, December 2015); The Reinvestment Fund, *Mortgage Foreclosures in Baltimore, Maryland* (Baltimore: Goldseker Foundation, September 2006); *Racial Wealth Divide in Baltimore* (Baltimore: Prosperity Now, January 2017).

Part II

Histories of Contestation
and Activism in a
Legacy City

• •

Baltimore City vacillates constantly between renaissance and revolution. Through our environment, our roads, our social services, and even our access to entertainment options, Baltimoreans have pushed back against inequality in its many forms as they sought to create their own landscapes of equality (see Figure 4).

Leif Fredrickson explores how, following the unrest in Baltimore and many other U.S. cities during the 1960s, city officials sought to pacify black residents with new and improved recreation options, parks, and sanitation infrastructure. Shannon Darrow examines how campaigns of multicommunity, collaborative activism and intersectional resistance can succeed, but not always, in defeating highway construction plans poised to destroy city neighborhoods. Her chapter explores movements that stopped the construction of one freeway from destroying a white working-class neighborhood in East Baltimore while failing to prevent another highway from tearing through African American neighborhoods in West Baltimore.

Joshua Clark Davis explores the long history of activists who started businesses in the city dating back to the 1820s. His research pushes the reader to rethink the city's "relationship to capitalism and business and to expand our view beyond the city's better known history of shipping, steelmaking, transportation, and health care." Davis focuses on activists from a wide array of movements—abolitionism, feminism, socialism, labor, and the black freedom

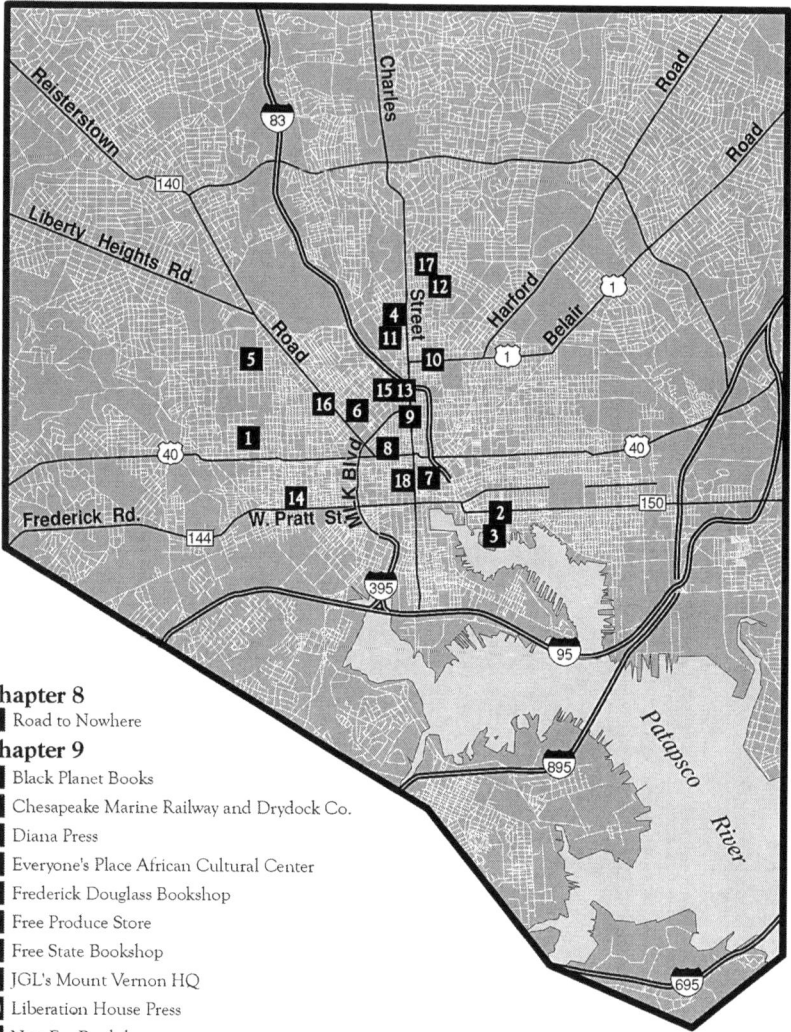

Chapter 8

1 Road to Nowhere

Chapter 9

2 Black Planet Books
3 Chesapeake Marine Railway and Drydock Co.
4 Diana Press
5 Everyone's Place African Cultural Center
6 Frederick Douglass Bookshop
7 Free Produce Store
8 Free State Bookshop
9 JGL's Mount Vernon HQ
10 Liberation House Press
11 New Era Bookshop
12 Pathfinder Bookstore
13 People's Unemployment League
14 Pratt Street Conspiracy
15 Red Emma's Bookstore Coffeehouse
16 The Black Book
17 31st Street Bookstore

Chapter 12

18 Ford Theater

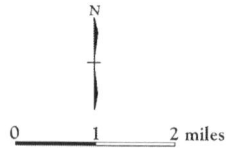

FIG. 4 Map of locations described in Part II. Created by Joe School, 2018.

struggle—all of whom established small businesses in Baltimore with the goals of advancing justice and equality while also making a modest living. Amy Zanoni's chapter investigates the intersectional movement of black women fighting for welfare rights in Baltimore. In the process, she describes activists from the 1960s to the 1980s who offer us a compelling organizing model for our own era in which the state regularly shirks its social responsibilities.

This part's final two chapters explore the social implications of popular entertainment, particularly film, as an arena in which Baltimoreans fought for freedom and equality. Joe Tropea looks at the history of film censorship in Baltimore, carried out by the longest-lasting public censorship board in the country, which determined which movies Marylanders could and could not view in theaters. Jennifer Ferretti's snapshot of the protests to desegregate Baltimore's Ford Theater in the 1940s and 1950s reveals a successful but widely forgotten campaign in Baltimoreans' struggle to achieve a more just city.

Taken together, the chapters in this section remind us that Baltimoreans have carried out political struggle—sometimes successfully, sometimes not—for a wide variety of causes and in a wide range of settings.

7

The Riot Environment

•••••••••••••••••••••

Sanitation, Recreation,
and Pacification in the Wake
of Baltimore's 1968 Uprising

LEIF FREDRICKSON

In the 1960s, African Americans in cities across the United States lashed out against police brutality, segregation, exploitation, and other forms of racist oppression with collective acts of property destruction, violence, and civil disturbance. At the time, people usually referred to these acts as "riots," but they are better conceptualized as "uprisings." They were unorganized and therefore not "insurrections," but nor were they irrational or apolitical, as the term "riot" implies. Large uprisings occurred in Harlem in 1964, Watts in 1965, and Detroit in 1967. But there were hundreds more, especially after Martin Luther King Jr. was assassinated in 1968. Baltimore's April 1968 uprising was one of the biggest.[1]

As cities burned, Americans searched for causes and solutions, all against the backdrop of civil rights protests, escalating environmental concerns, urban problems, and President Lyndon Johnson's "Great Society" liberal reforms. Indeed, the Great Society and the uprisings coevolved. Johnson initiated his first salvo of reforms in late 1964 and early 1965, several years before most of the uprisings, but the implementation and justification of these reforms—especially the Equal Opportunity Act (1964), the linchpin of Johnson's "War on Poverty"—subsequently included the goal of preventing riots, along with reducing poverty and structural racism. Liberals construed the later Model Cities Program of 1966–1974 even more explicitly as an antiriot policy.[2]

While liberals saw the Great Society as responding to and preventing riots, conservatives saw it as the cause of those riots. Radicals had usurped the community-led programs of the Great Society, according to conservatives, and permissive liberalism had fostered lawlessness. Seeing the uprisings as the result of criminals or radical agitators, conservatives emphasized a law-and-order solution: surveillance, punishment and military suppression.[3]

While the conservative emphasis on law and order eventually won out, Johnson's War on Poverty was an extended experiment in implementing programs designed to cultivate economic and social opportunity and tackle poverty, racial inequality, and the "urban crisis"—the deteriorating fiscal, physical, and social aspects of cities, including their liability to uprisings. One tactic of the War on Poverty was to improve the environment of cities, especially of the "inner cities." By "inner city," people at the time meant the older, neighborhoods in the urban core that were mostly poor and African American. These inner-city neighborhoods suffered from disinvestment, traffic congestion, poor city services, and segregated and exploitive housing, all of which made for degraded environments. "Inner city" was, and is, an imperfect term, but there was not, and is not, an alternative that captures these overlapping problems.

This attempt at environmental improvement, like other aspects of the War on Poverty, was implemented with great variability across communities and cities.[4] Some of the most ambitious programs to improve the inner-city environment and to take inner-city youth out of that environment occurred in Baltimore in the years surrounding the city's 1968 uprising.

The Great Society programs to improve the inner-city environment can be seen as early environmental justice programs.[5] They were attempts to mitigate serious health hazards and to improve real disparities in the aesthetic and recreational aspects of the inner-city environment. They reflected broader social concerns about pollution and environmental aesthetics that were also part of the Great Society. At the local level, too, disadvantaged Baltimoreans cared deeply about these issues. But the improvement of life for the disadvantaged was not the sole purpose of these programs. Like other aspects of the Great Society, including attempts to foster economic opportunity and community engagement, politicians, bureaucrats, and the media justified these programs based on how they would benefit society more broadly through reductions in delinquency, crime, riots, and other forms of social disorder. In the strongest interpretation, Great Society programs to improve the urban environment can thus be seen as attempts to contain problems and to control and pacify African Americans and the poor and thus to appease them with superficial changes or preoccupy them with activities.

The history of this uneasy tension between the provision of environmental quality to achieve justice and its provision to maintain order is important for thinking about aspects of environmental justice today, particularly in the wake of the 2015 uprising in Baltimore and the resurgence of interest in the connection between the environment, crime, and other aspects of urban disorder. The double purpose of justice and order can be politically expedient, but in the long run, it can compromise justice.

Long, Hot Summers and the Urban Environment

From nearly its inception, the War on Poverty responded to uprisings and tried to change the physical environment. In 1965, a year after Harlem's uprising, the Office of Economic Opportunity (OEO) funded projects to clean up the neighborhood, plant trees, and provide recreation. The strategy was effective, one OEO administrator later claimed: "Harlem was cooled. . . . There were no riots."[6] More broadly, President Johnson pushed, in 1965, for the creation of a national summer jobs and recreation programs. After a dispute over access to water from fire hydrants catalyzed an uprising in Chicago in 1966, the Johnson administration tried to literally cool off cities by supplying pools and sprinklers.[7] The president's National Advisory Commission on Civil Disorders, created in the wake of huge uprisings in 1967, re-emphasized the importance of environmental factors. The Kerner Commission, as it became known, noted great disparities in the environmental conditions, such as rat infestations, affecting black and white people. Listed among the "deeply held grievances" of African Americans were dilapidated housing, inadequate sanitation, and poor recreational facilities.[8]

In Baltimore, the connection between the environment, black dissatisfaction, and civil disturbance was also evident. African Americans had long agitated for equal access to parks and recreation.[9] The state dubiously charged black protesters in Baltimore attempting to desegregate tennis courts with "inciting a riot" in 1948.[10] But the closest approximations of riots in the city in the 1950s and early 1960s were instigated by organized racists and white crowds who mobbed black Baltimoreans trying to integrate parks and pools.[11] As larger-scale, black uprisings swept the nation in the mid-1960s, however, fears shifted to disturbances emanating from African Americans. Stories in the *Baltimore Afro-American* in 1966 and 1967 warned that disparities in recreational opportunities, lead paint exposure, and rat infestations could stoke riots. One story quoted Senator Edmund Muskie (D-Maine), who called for rent supplements and pollution control programs "to solve community environment problems for all—not just a few—of the people," lest unmet needs lead to riots.[12]

Baltimore did take some measures to improve the city's environment. It was one of ten cities in 1966 to receive federal funding for Operation Champ, a summer recreation program. In the press, Vice President Hubert Humphrey denied that Operation Champ was intended to sideline potential rioters, but he conceded that it could have that effect. Local officials and leaders, in contrast, frequently explicitly stated that Operation Champ and other recreation programs could stave off riots and crime.[13] In response to the Kerner Commission, the city also developed plans to improve employment, housing, schools, black political participation, civil rights, police relations, and recreation. These initiatives would take time, and in March 1968 the mayor stated he hoped dialogue and a "show of good faith" would be enough.[14] But a month later, on April 6, the city was in flames. When the uprising was over, six were dead and seven hundred were injured. While Baltimore's uprising was less deadly than Newark's or Detroit's, it was one of the costliest in terms of property damage, which totaled about $12 million.[15]

Inside the Inner City

Responses to the uprising varied. Maryland governor Spiro Agnew swerved hard into the law-and-order lane, blaming the entire black community for the uprising and calling for police and military crackdowns. His rhetoric garnered him a position as Richard Nixon's running mate and, ultimately, the vice presidency in 1968.[16] But continuing adherence to the Great Society at the city level and the inertia of federal programs meant that many of its programs continued into the early 1970s.

In Baltimore, two Great Society programs, the Baltimore Model Cities Agency (BMCA) and Model Urban Neighborhood Demonstration (MUND), began in 1967 in the shadow of uprisings in other cities and expanded after the city's own uprising. In addition to socioeconomic concerns, these programs emphasized improving the physical environment of the city—improvements that the programs' architects hoped would deliver a higher quality of life and fend off urban disorder.

The Model Cities program combined the emphasis on community control and social issues from the Equal Opportunity Act with the emphasis on the physical environment from urban renewal. It also went much further than urban renewal in addressing environmental health and quality of life. President Johnson, appealing to Congress to pass the Model Cities bill in 1966, claimed the program would be a "total environment" approach, one aimed at creating a "decent" and "harmonious" urban environment. He emphasized not only the need for jobs and social support in the "ghetto" but also for parks, playgrounds, "attractive landscaping," and "open spaces free from pollution." Without these changes, Johnson said, every city center would become "a hive of deprivation, crime, and hopelessness."[17] Congressman Henry Gonzalez of Texas, a champion of the bill, called it "the real antiriot bill of the 89th Congress." When the bill passed, the *Afro-American* hailed its potential to stem riots.[18]

MUND was similar to Model Cities in many ways, but it was administered and created by business elites: the Greater Baltimore Committee (GBC) and the Westinghouse Corporation. MUND was part of a larger reaction from the business community to the riots and the urban crisis. New organizations like the National Alliance of Businessmen were created in "direct response" to the 1968 riots, and business magazines tackled the significance of the uprisings.[19] For example, a pamphlet insert into *Business Week*, titled *Business and the Urban Crisis,* argued that if businesses ignored the crisis, "no one else may be able to cool the anger that boils up in riots" and slums would "siphon off" profits.[20]

Along these lines, the GBC justified MUND both in terms of its benefits to the urban poor and of profit. In its creators' words, it was a project of "enlightened self-interest." The GBC had earlier developed Baltimore's nationally renowned commercial revitalization project, Charles Center. But, as the GBC noted in its proposal to create MUND, downtown revitalization could "become a house of cards unless the physical and social pathologies of the vast deteriorating area" around the downtown were dealt with.[21]

The GBC thus created MUND in response to the general urban crisis, of which uprisings were an acute symptom, and Baltimore's own uprising subsequently shaped the program. On April 3, 1968, GBC's associate executive director, after reading *Business and the Urban Crisis,* resolved that the GBC should "stimulate action now" to prevent a riot "rather than correcting its damage."[22] Just a few days later, Baltimore erupted, and MUND's first major project became a "massive" community cleanup campaign of riot-torn areas (see Figure 5).[23]

MUND's director, Lloyd Davis, connected the environment to urban disorder and uprisings. Davis began his 1970 article titled "Inside the Inner City" with this statement: "The events of the last few years have caused many Americans . . . to come to the profound realization that the problems of poverty and the problems of the cities affect everyone." One problem with cities was the "destruction of the physical environment," which stripped people of "contact with sun and fresh air, clean rivers, grass, and trees, condemning them to a life among stones and concrete, neon lights, and an endless river of automobiles." MUND thus sought to improve the physical environment of the inner city, which included improving city services, recreation, and "cleaning up the air and improving the water supply."[24]

Both MUND and the BMCA initiated environmentally related projects, including sanitation, rat eradication, housing repair, and neighborhood beautification with grass and flowers.[25] These were issues that residents identified

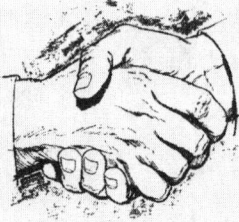

ANNOUNCING

MUND NEIGHBORHOOD CLEAN-UP CAMPAIGN

JUNE 6th thru JUNE 27th

A Partnership in Community Rebuilding

Sponsored by
● Mund Neighborhood Council
● City of Baltimore
● Greater Baltimore Committee
● Westinghouse Corporation

The First Step in An All Out Effort for

✓ CLEAN STREETS   ✓ CLEAN ALLEYS   ✓ RAT CONTROL
✓ BETTER GARBAGE COLLECTION   ✓ CLEAN BACK YARDS
AND VACANT LOTS   ✓ REMOVAL OF ABANDONED CARS

and for

*NEW STREET LIGHTS   REPAIRED STREETS, ALLEYS AND SIDEWALKS
LANDSCAPING (Trees, Flowers, Grass)*

THE CLEAN-UP TARGET DATE FOR YOUR AREA IS

● Calvert-Greenmount Area — June 5, 6, 7   ● Howard-Calvert Area ———— June 19, 20, 21
● Greenmount-Kirk Area ———— June 12, 13, 14   ● Kirk-Hartford Area ———— June 26, 27, 28

YOU CAN HELP BY PLACING YOUR BULKY TRASH OUT ON THE PUBLIC CURBS or ALLEYS FOR COLLECTION ON THOSE DATES LISTED ABOVE. All of these days fall in each target area on a Wednesday, Thursday, or Friday.

COME TO THE CAMPAIGN KICK-OFF RALLY ON SATURDAY JUNE 8

at 10a.m. at the Calvert Education Center (Calvert and North Avenue)

Speakers will include: Mayor Thomas D'Alesandro and
A Representative from the Southern Christian Leadership Conference

Entertainment will be provided by local school bands and other musical units.

A parade will take place before the Rally and will form at 8 a.m. at 24th and Calvert.
The line of march will be South on Calvert to 21st Street.

FIG. 5 Sign advertising MUND's post–1968 "riot" clean-up campaign. Source: MUND Records, Folder 6, Box 6, Series I, University of Baltimore Langsdale Library Special Collections.

as significant and that, as noted earlier, the media and government reports had characterized as points of dissatisfaction that contributed to urban uprisings.[26]

MUND and the BMCA also tried to increase park space and recreation opportunities, their lack being another key source of conflict and dissatisfaction in urban areas. The programs temporarily closed streets for children to play in and pushed for access to vacant lots and unused parcels owned by businesses.

MUND dubbed its signature playground King and Kennedy Park, a name they hoped would help white and black kids play together rather than fight.[27] By 1970, the BMCA claimed that 38,000 residents benefited from their efforts to extend hours of operation for recreational facilities. The BMCA expanded recreation, in part, to "reduce neighborhood tensions and costly conflicts between residents and law enforcement officials."[28]

Another purpose of expanded parks and recreation was to control delinquency. This was an idea with deep roots. Progressive reformers in the late nineteenth and early twentieth centuries believed that parks and playground could provide relief from the ills of the city, resulting in improved moral and mental health and controlling urban unrest.[29] Similarly, social scientists in the 1920s and 1930s believed that recreation could stem juvenile delinquency by providing positive outlets for play and occupying the idle hours of young, unemployed people.[30] Operation Champ, which BMCA took over, was built on many of these ideas. Even its local manager conceded that it "started as program to pacify the blacks in the summer, and in that sense it was a negative program." But by 1969, the manager contended, the program was "embarking on something really constructive," expanding its recreation programs to be year-round. The program had supporters, but like many other Great Society antipoverty programs, residents and politicians criticized its financial management, organizational procedures, purpose, and effectiveness in serving the community.[31]

Outside the Inner City

While MUND and the BMCA sought to improve the environment of the inner city, another program, Camp Concern, looked to take "underprivileged youth" out of Baltimore to a better environment for the summer. Baltimore Colts tight-end John Mackey, Mayor Thomas D'Alessandro III, the U.S. Navy, and other community members created the program in the months after the April 1968 uprising. It was, according to D'Alessandro, the first combination of a "massive summer-camp recreation program . . . with health education and training, plus wholesome recreation, sports, entertainment." Camp Concern's first session, which ran from July 1 to August 31, 1968, was located at Bainbridge Naval Base in northwest Maryland. The Department of Housing, Education, and Welfare and the OEO gave the program $130,000 (about $715,000 in 2017 dollars) in its first year, and the Navy offered its resources for free. The city parks department administered the camp.[32]

The program dwarfed other Baltimore city recreation programs for disadvantaged youth. In peak years, it hauled in 9,100 campers, 12 percent of the disadvantaged children in the city. Ninety percent of the campers were from the inner city, and although both black and white children attended, photos suggest that most of the participants were black.[33] The Office of the President, the

Department of Defense, and legislators praised the program. It gained substantial media coverage, particularly when First Lady Pat Nixon helicoptered in for a visit.[34]

The camp offered job training, health education, and recreation. Promoters emphasized that it would provide new opportunities and a better physical environment for disadvantaged youth. The Navy's promotional film, *A Cause for Concern*, began with images of children in Baltimore wandering alleys and playing with junk. The film then showed the camp's pools, basketball courts, and green grass to play on. The Navy's promotional pamphlet, also called *A Cause for Concern*, concluded with a picture of the bricks-and-concrete inner city and a caption that read, "The 'grass in the ghetto isn't green, a trip is no vacation and there's nothing scenic about the 'scene.'" At Camp Concern, things were "cleaner and greener."[35]

Many children appreciated the change in environment, expressing delight in seeing horses, cows, boats, fish, water, trees and bushes in the *Camp Concern* film. According to a councilman from a predominantly African American part of the city, no recreation program was more loved by children in his district. Since its inception, the demand for the camp outstripped available spots. Members of the community also praised it for the opportunities it gave children. "They come back as different children," one said.[36]

James Smith, who ran the camp, later described it as "like motherhood in the city. No one ever says anything bad about it."[37] But that was not quite true. Some critics, such as civil rights activist Madeline Murphy, saw Camp Concern as a way to pacify African Americans rather than provide substantial benefits.[38] This criticism, as noted earlier, had been leveled at other War on Poverty programs, such as Operation Champ. But Camp Concern was even more distressing for some critics because of the role of the military, especially the camp's connection to the Domestic Action Program (DAP).

In the late 1960s, the military became interested in how it could address domestic issues stemming from poverty and racial conflict. In 1966, the Department of Defense (DOD) launched Project 100,000, Secretary of Defense Robert McNamara's effort to obtain more soldiers to fight in the Vietnam War by lowering recruitment standards. The DOD also justified this initiative as an antipoverty program that allowed the poor to gain skills and benefits from their military service. In the following years, the military made concerted efforts to engage poor and disadvantaged communities in jobs and recreation programs. Secretary of Defense Melvin Laird formalized these efforts as the Domestic Action Program in April 1969.[39]

The DAP and proto-DAP programs were as much about national, internal security as they were about improving the lives of the poor. The programs were, according to John McLucas, the Air Force DAP representative, created in the "face of race riots and growing social unrest."[40] Secretary Laird described the

DAP as an attempt to "overcome some of the serious domestic problems which face the nation today." He envisioned programs ranging from "cleaning the environment to helping the disadvantaged get a fresh start in life." But Air Force lieutenant Carl Carey also traced the idea for the DAP to Laird's predecessor, Clark Clifford, who had called for "total national security" by engaging in domestic programs.[41] The DOD's *Commanders Digest* paraphrased Roger Kelley, chairman of the Domestic Action Council, who said that "some military officers find it difficult to understand how the Domestic Action Programs are part of the military mission." It was easy to identify the "communist threat" outside the United States, Kelley said, but "it is not as easy to identify some of the threats that exist within the American cities." The national security threats at home were "severe," however, and the military needed to address both in Kelley's view.[42]

Although Camp Concern was created a year before the DAP officially started, it became one of its crown jewels. Both the military and local government officials connected the camp to efforts to fend off riots and otherwise pacify inner-city youth, while simultaneously emphasizing its benefits to those youth. Kelley toured the camp in 1969, concluding that "the military should and must be involved in these type programs. . . . This is a vital dimension of national security." He and McLucas, who also toured the camp, argued that the program could and should be expanded to hundreds of places around the nation.[43] The *Cause for Concern* film included a dramatic voiceover proclaiming, "There is a cause for Camp Concern. A cause that is familiar to many in this country today. A cause that is found in every major city. Where the disadvantaged are pushed out of the way for progress. It is caused by big industry. *Riots*. Racism. *Riots*. Poverty. *Riots*."[44]

In Baltimore, community members, the media, and government officials tended to frame Camp Concern as a way to improve disadvantaged children's quality of life and provide education and employment.[45] But the justification for the camp also included its being a bulwark against delinquency and uprisings. The *Afro-American* hailed the program as "critically needed to insure the chance of a peaceful summer," and it noted approvingly the "remarkably timely" start of the camp the day that school ended.[46] Director James Smith wrote that the camp was designed to "direct the energies of Baltimore's disadvantaged youth—many of whom had participated in the riots and the looting—into constructive channels." Another report stated, "Camp Concern began in the realization that although the rioting had stopped, the circumstances that lead to it had not."[47] Mayor D'Alessandro eschewed the antiriot function of the camp, but in one interview he noted the camp's "soothing effect throughout the city," before adding, "We don't operate this program with the idea that . . . we're avoiding any civil disturbance."[48] D'Alessandro and the Navy also emphasized the role of the camp in producing good disciplined citizens. Although life at

Bainbridge was putatively a refuge from the "up-tight pressures of the inner city," the camp was built around discipline and was fully structured to eliminate any downtime.[49]

Critics of the DOD's domestic action programs and of Camp Concern in particular focused on their troubling dual purpose of helping and pacifying the poor. Two students, George Corey and Richard Cohen, wrote an academic article titled "Domestic Pacification," which concluded that the DAP's main goal was not altruism but "control or pacification of ghetto populations." It was trying to divert "potential rioters by removing them from the frustrating and potentially explosive environment." The goal was to "curb ghetto riots," rather than "attacking their roots, the actual problems of poverty." Camp Concern was a prime example, according to the authors, who quoted a Navy press release about the camp that stated, "Something had to be done to direct the energies of the city's disadvantaged youth into constructive channels," away from the "riots that left hundreds of inner city business establishments in smoking ruins."[50]

In her column in the *Afro-American*, Madeline Murphy drew on Corey and Cohen's article, arguing that the government used Camp Concern to control a potentially hostile population through the soft power of doling out resources. She also argued that, like Project 100,000, Camp Concern was a tool to recruit poor, black people into the military. While the camp might appeal to anxious inner-city parents with "obstreperous idle" children, Murphy argued that it could be the "first step toward . . . shoving [black youth] into the military." Murphy and other members of the Community Action Commission had rejected military funding for a recreation program for this reason in 1968. She claimed D'Alessandro intercepted these funds for Camp Concern.[51]

Despite high hopes from the creators and managers of the programs that they would improve the environment of inner-city people, criticisms from both the left and right and waning financial support imperiled their continuation. The election of President Nixon in 1968 brought to power a long-time critic of many Great Society programs, particularly Model Cities. The program suffered continuing funding cuts before it was finally eliminated in 1974. Meanwhile, approaches to crime and disorder shifted heavily to punishment and incarceration. Conservatives strongly embraced the Agnew-style law-and-order rhetoric. And Nixon and later presidents, particularly Ronald Reagan, amplified the law-and-order policies and programs that began under Johnson.[52]

By 1974, the DOD, too, was shifting its domestic engagement away from a focus on poverty.[53] While it outlived the end of the DAP in 1975, Camp Concern faced budget cutbacks as part of the general rollback of Great Society programs under the Nixon and Ford administrations. But the camp had tremendous support from the community, some of whom continued to connect the program to curbing delinquency and riots. One minister, writing on behalf of

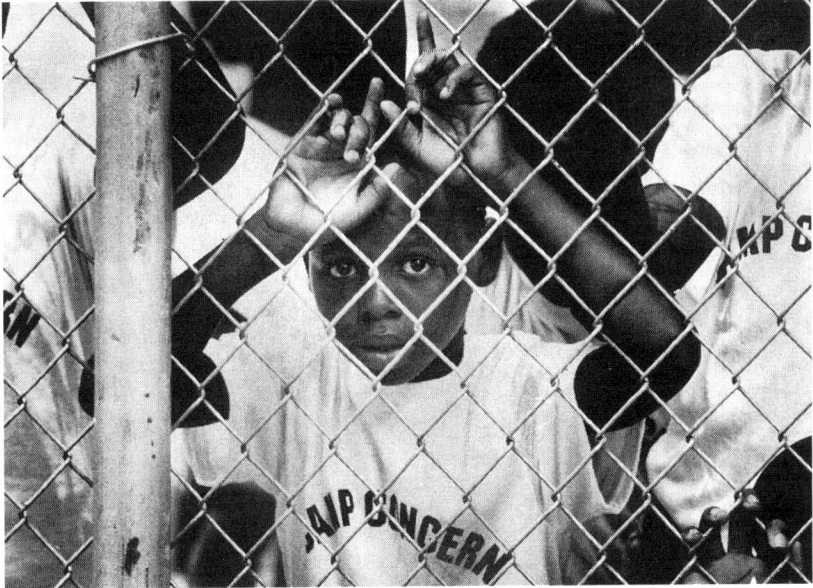

FIG. 6 Boy looking out from behind cyclone fence at Camp Concern, Druid Hill Park, Baltimore. Source: "Camp Concern," *Baltimore Sun*, July 16, 1980, C18. Reprinted with permission from the *Baltimore Sun*.

"sixty thousand" Baptists, claimed that Camp Concern had been "a great factor in us not having long, hot, and violent summers."[54] Mayor Donald Schaefer kept the program, but the cutbacks continued. In 1980, in order to save money, Camp Concern moved back into the city and was relocated at Druid Hill Park.[55]

Twelve years on, the creation story of Camp Concern was still memorable to its long-time manager, James Smith, who noted that the original camp had been designed to "ease tension in the community" after the 1968 uprising. But discourse around the camp was otherwise entirely about giving recreation and respite from the city heat to inner-city children. At the camp, children enjoyed themselves and journalists wondered which concerns the camp's name referenced. Like other local War on Poverty programs, Camp Concern both managed to outlast the assault on the Great Society at the federal level and shed some of the ulterior, pacification motives of those programs. Still, with little or no federal funding, the camp was smaller and more tenuous than it had ever been. The reincarnated camp was not immune to ongoing problems with crime and policing in the inner city. A nine-foot cyclone fence, topped with barbed wire, encircled the camp. At night, a guard sat watch. These measures were designed to keep troublemakers out, not keep children in. Yet the site was nevertheless eerily reminiscent of a prison camp (see Figure 6).[56]

Conclusion

In 2015, Baltimore police violently arrested Freddie Gray, who was fatally injured in the back of a police van. Gray's death ignited protests and an uprising in Baltimore, which, like the uprisings of the 1960s, brought about broader reflection and reactions about urban social problems. These problems included the environment. It came to light, for example, that Freddie Gray had suffered from lead poisoning as a result of living in deteriorating housing as a child, a revelation that brought to the surface Baltimore's long struggle with lead paint poisoning and poor housing among the urban poor.[57]

More broadly, politicians argued for the need to clean up the city and provide green space and recreation to disadvantaged groups. Governor Larry Hogan and Mayor Stephanie Blake-Rawlings called for abandoned, dilapidated buildings to be replaced with "green space and livable new developments."[58] The city also resuscitated an Outward Bound Police Youth Challenge, a program that brought police and disadvantaged Baltimore youth together in parks for team-building exercises aimed at improving police–community relations. In addition to providing a space for recreation, the park's green space, according to the organizer of the program, would reduce stress, anxiety, and depression.[59]

While these projects have been modest compared to the Great Society programs, in no small part because of the long-lasting withdrawal of federal funds from urban projects since the 1960s, they echo the Great Society's concern with the connection between the urban environment, urban disorder, and environmental justice. They also reflect a broader resurgence in the 2010s of interest among social scientists and some activists in the connection between crime, social disorder, and the environment. Baltimore itself has been one of the key sites of study for what has become known as "green criminology," with studies showing that areas with more trees have less crime. Advocates for more green space in cities have thus argued that providing more parks and trees to disadvantaged neighborhoods could help reduce crime and increase safety.[60] But the history of campaigns to improve the environment for the dual purpose of helping the poor and bringing social order—especially reducing crime and curbing uprisings—ought to give us pause.

One problem is that the environment–disorder connection has tended to ignore or downplay problems with the policing of inner-city neighborhoods. Because poverty has not been effectively tackled in many inner-city neighborhoods, crime remains a serious problem. The law-and-order response to that problem has been more surveillance and harsher policing. This approach can look a lot like a military occupation, as the distinctly prison-camp appearance of Camp Concern at Druid Hill signified. Police practices and laws (about loitering and curfews, for example), in addition to crime and poor services, can also reduce inner-city residents' access to parks and recreation.

Another concern is that the provision of environmental amenities can be a way of pacifying disadvantaged communities. Instead of bringing about fundamental changes that would result in good jobs or more political control for low-income African American residents, the government dispenses parks, better sanitation, and camping trips. To be sure, it is hard to tell when pacification is the main or true motive, because programs are often justified on a number of grounds. In part, that is because multiple actors are involved with pushing them through, and those actors have different goals: inner-city parents want playgrounds and the government wants order. Advocates of parks and recreation for the inner city may also try to sell those programs to hostile or indifferent groups, such as suburban whites who do not want to pay for them. This can muddy the underlying motives of programs, since advocates may use the rhetoric of safety and order to sell a program that is genuinely about environmental justice.

To say that efforts to improve the environmental quality of life in the inner city can be forms of pacification or be otherwise problematic, however, is not to say they are superficial. In the history presented here, recreation, parks, sanitation, and beautification were some of the most important issues for city residents. Some saw them as a means of social control, while others advocated for them on the basis of environmental justice—equitable provisions for all people—and basic human needs. As ideas about the connection between riots, crime, and the environment resurface, we should be wary of social control justifications and consider foregrounding urban environmental improvements via justice rather than social control.

Notes

1 Peter Levy, *The Great Uprising* (New York: Cambridge University Press, 2018), 7.
2 Roger Biles, *The Fate of Cities: Urban America and the Federal Government, 1945–2000* (Lawrence: University Press of Kansas, 2011), 112–160.
3 Levy, *Great Uprising*, 3–6.
4 Annelise Orleck and Lisa Hazirjian, *The War on Poverty: A New Grassroots History, 1964–1980* (Athens: University of Georgia Press, 2011).
5 The environmental justice movement is usually traced to the 1980s. Julie Sze, *Noxious New York: The Racial Politics of Urban Health and Environmental Justice* (Cambridge, MA: MIT Press, 2006), 13. But see Jeffrey Sanders, *Seattle and the Roots of Urban Sustainability: Inventing Ecotopia* (Pittsburgh: University of Pittsburgh Press, 2010), 65–98, who argues that Seattle's robust Model Cities program can be seen as an early form of environmental justice.
6 Maurice Carroll, "Project Up-Lift to 'Cool' Harlem," *New York Times*, June 5, 1966; Michael Gillette, *Launching the War on Poverty: An Oral History* (New York: Oxford University Press, 2010), 255.
7 Joseph Sterne, "Jobs and Swimming Pools: U.S. Makes Massive Drive to Ease Summer in Slums," *Baltimore Sun*, May 14, 1967.
8 National Advisory Commission on Civil Disorders, *Report of the National Advisory Committee on Civil Disorders* (New York: E. P. Dutton, 1968).

9　Victoria Wolcott, *Race, Riots, and Roller Coasters: The Struggle over Segregated Recreation in America* (Philadelphia: University of Pennsylvania Press, 2012).

10　"Riot Charged in Tennis Case," *Baltimore Sun*, September 4, 1948.

11　Stephen Nordlinger, "More Violence at Park Feared," *Baltimore Sun*, May 23, 1963.

12　"AJC Warns 5 Major Areas on Drastic Need for Change: Urges Improvements in Housing, Schools, Jobs to Prevent Riot Outbreaks," *Afro-American*, February 5, 1966; "Subtle Violence," *Afro-American*, August 12, 1967; "Those Anti-Riot Bills," *Afro-American*, October 22, 1966; "Needed: Brains Not Bayonets," *Afro-American*, August 12, 1967; "Misery Breeds Riots, Solon Warns Labor," *Afro-American*, August 19, 1967.

13　Donna de Varona, "Operation Champ Aids 200,000 Kids," *Afro-American*, October 8, 1966; "New Recreation Program to Help City's Slum Youth," *Baltimore Sun*, May 19, 1966; "Group to Fight Closing of Pool," *Baltimore Sun*, August 1, 1967; "Mayor Plans Programs to Avert Riots," *Baltimore Sun*, July 26, 1967; "Mayor Vows 300 City Jobs Immediately," *Baltimore Sun*, July 28, 1967; "'Hot Summer' Meeting Held," *Baltimore Sun*, June 17, 1967.

14　David Runkel, "City Developing Program to Soothe Racial Woe," *Evening Sun*, March 1, 1968; Floyd Miller, "How Baltimore Fends off Riots," *Reader's Digest*, March 1968, 109.

15　Maryland Crime Investigation Commission, *A Report of the Baltimore Civil Disturbance of April, 1968* (Annapolis: 1968); Jessica Elfenbein, Thomas Hollowak, and Elizabeth Nix, *Baltimore '68: Riots and Rebirth in an American City* (Philadelphia: Temple University Press, 2011).

16　Levy, *Great Uprising*, 189–221.

17　Lyndon Johnson: "Special Message to the Congress Recommending a Program for Cities and Metropolitan Areas," January 26, 1966, in *The American Presidency Project*, ed. Gerhard Peters and John Woolley, http://www.presidency.ucsb.edu/ws/?pid=27682.

18　"Great Victory for the Cities," *Afro-American*, October 29, 1966.

19　Jim Kotmir, "First Chance," *Substance* 2, no. 3, 3, Folder 5, Box 12, Series II, Model Urban Neighborhood Demonstration Records (hereafter MUND), Langsdale Library Special Collections, University of Baltimore (hereafter LLSP); "Special Issue on Business and the Urban Crisis," *Fortune*, 1968.

20　Joseph Allen, *Business and the Urban Crisis* [insert in *Business Week*, February 3, 1968] in Folder 9, "Correspondence 1968," Community Development Subcommittee, Group 14, Series XIII, Greater Baltimore Committee Records (hereafter GBC), LLSP.

21　GBC, "A Proposal for the Planning and Implementation of a Model Urban Neighborhood Demonstration in Baltimore," May, 1967, Folder 50, Box 1, Series I, MUND.

22　Eugene Petty to Robert Levi, April 3, 1968, Folder 6, Box 6, Series I, MUND.

23　"Clean-Up Campaign Minutes," May 31, 1968, Folder 1, Box 7, Series II, MUND.

24　Lloyd Davis, "Inside the Inner City," *IEEE Transactions on Aerospace and Electronics Systems* 6, no. 3 (May 1970): 360, reprint in Folder 35, Box 29, Series II, MUND.

25　BMCA, "Neighborhood Sanitation Services," Folder 12, Box 12; BMCA, *Comprehensive Demonstration Plan/Summary, 3rd Year* (no date), 11, Folder 9, Box 12; "Survey Shows Trash Service Improved since Clean-Up Campaign," *MUND Newsletter* 2, no. 4 (June 1969): 7, Box 24; all in Series II, MUND. MUND, *First Year Final Report, Volume 1* (December 1968), 6–5, Folder 1, Box 2; Westinghouse, "Rat Control for Baltimore"; Floyd Rogers letter to ES, September 11, 1970, Folder 13, Box 9; in both Series II, MUND.

26 "Tenant Tells Story of Rats to Warn Future Renters," *MUND Newsletter* 4, no. 6 (September 2, 1970): 1, Box 24, Series II; Beautification Survey Responses, circa November 1968, Box 3a, Series II; Axel Jerome, *Model Urban Neighborhood Demonstration Progress Report No. 3*, 4-5, Folder 9, Box 6, Series I; Barbara Gaver to Harry Smith and Lloyd Davis, November 12, 1968, both in Folder 15, Box 3a, Series II; all in MUND.

27 BMCA, *Comprehensive Demonstration Plan*; "Playground Named for King, Kennedy," *Evening Sun*, October 27, 1969, in Folder 13, Box 9; both in Series II, MUND.

28 Barbara Gaver to William Robertson, July 17, 1968, Folder 15, Box 3a, Series II, MUND; MUND, *First Year Final Report*, 6-5.

29 Paul Boyer, *Urban Masses and Moral Order in America, 1820–1920* (Cambridge, MA: Harvard University Press, 2009), 225–232, 243–245.

30 David Wolcott, *Cops and Kids: Policing Juvenile Delinquency in Urban America, 1890–1940* (Columbus: Ohio State University Press, 2005), 136–138.

31 Joseph Nawrozki, "Self Help Housing Unit Dwarfs MUND—Chase," *News American*, March 5, 1969, Folder 13, Box 9, Series II, MUND; "Operation Champ Planning Broad All-Year Program," *Baltimore Sun*, March 13, 1969.

32 Edna Goldberg, "Baltimore's Inner-City Children: Bainbridge Navy Center Opens Gates to Camp Concern," *Baltimore Sun*, August 5, 1969; Statement of D'Alessandro for press conference, June 20, 1968, Folder 26, Box 450, D'Alessandro III Files, BRG9-26-48, Baltimore City Archives (hereafter BCA). The relative cost is the "historic opportunity cost"; see Samuel Williamson, "Seven Ways to Compute the Relative Value of a U.S. Dollar Amount, 1774 to Present," MeasuringWorth, 2018, https://www.measuringworth.com/calculators /uscompare/.

33 James Smith, *Camp Concern 1968 Executive Director's Report*, Folder 337, Box 494, D'Alessandro III Files, BRG9-26-4, BCA. For photos, see U.S. Navy, *A Cause for Concern* [pamphlet] (May 1970), Folder 337, Box 494, D'Alessandro III Files, BRG9-26-4, BCA and Joseph Gordon, Jack Redfern, James Smith, "Camp Concern," *Public Health Reports* 84, no. 6 (June 1969). Health and Welfare Council, "Camperships 1973," Unpublished report, Folder 41, Box 5, Series III, Health and Welfare Council Records (hereafter HWC), LLSP.

34 "Nomination for Harry Greenstein Organization Achievement Award," Unpublished report, March 31, 1975, Folder 19, Box 16, Series III, HWC; Caroline Heck, "Pat Goes to Camp," *Washington Post*, August 14, 1970.

35 U.S. Navy, *A Cause for Concern* [film] (Culpeper, VA: National Audiovisual Center, 1970); U.S. Navy, *A Cause for Concern* [pamphlet], 16.

36 U.S. Navy, *A Cause for Concern* [film] Maryland Department of Human Resources, *Evaluation of Camp Concern* (March 1979), 4, Folder Camp Concern Evaluation, Box 22, Donald Schaefer Files, BRG9-42-22, BCA. Burns to Schaefer, April 8, 1975, Folder Camp Concern, Box 278, Donald Schaefer Files, BRG9-42-276, BCA.

37 Sandy Banisky, "Camp Concern Faces Sharp Cutbacks, City Says," *Baltimore Sun*, June 18, 1981.

38 Madeline Murphy, "Concern, Camp or Potential Garrison?," *Afro-American*, July 22, 1972.

39 John McLucas, *Reflections of a Technocrat: Managing Defense, Air, and Space Programs during the Cold War* (Maxwell Airforce Base, AL: Air University Press, 2006), 234.

40   McLucas, *Reflections of a Technocrat.*

41   "Domestic Action Policy: People Helping People," *Commanders Digest* 13, no. 10 (January 11, 1973): 1–2, at archive.org; Carl Carey, "Domestic Action: A DOD Welfare Program?," *Air University Review*, March–April 1971, http://www.au.af .mil/au/afri/aspj/airchronicles/aureview/1971/mar-apr/Carey.html.

42   "Domestic Action Programs Tied to U.S. Serviceman," *Commanders Digest*, October 11, 1969, 7, at www.archive.org.

43   Department of Defense, "Bainbridge Training Center Is Model for Youth Programs, Secretary Kelley Forecasts Expanded Local Participation," *Commanders Digest*, September 6, 1969, Folder 337, Box 494, D'Alessandro III Files, BRG9-26-4, BCA.

44   U.S. Navy, *A Cause for Concern* [film].

45   Baltimore Department of Recreation and Parks, *Annual Report July 1, 1968 to June 30, 1969*, 33, Folder 24, Box 19, Series X, GBC. D'Alessandro to Maryland Congressional Delegation, February 25, 1970, Folder 337, Box 494, D'Alessandro III Files, BRG9-26-4, BCA.

46   "Camp Concern," *Afro-American*, July 6, 1968.

47   Smith, *Health Components of Camp Concern*; Thomas D'Alessandro III, *The Emerging City: A Report From the Mayor* (1971), Folder 18, Box 24, GBC.

48   U.S. Navy, *A Cause for Concern* [film].

49   Ibid.; Goldberg, "Baltimore's Inner-City Children."

50   George Corey and Richard Cohen, "Domestic Pacification," *Society* 9, no. 9 (July 1972): 17–23.

51   Murphy, "Concern, Camp or Potential Garrison?"

52   Biles, *Fate of Cities*, 170–173; Elizabeth Hinton, *From the War on Poverty to the War on Crime* (Harvard, 2016), 1–18.

53   McLucas, *Reflections*, 236.

54   Vaughn to Mayor, April 5, 1975; Graves to Schaefer, April 7, 1975 and Smith to Schaefer, April 7, 1975; and other letters in Folder Camp Concern, Box 278, Donald Schaefer Files, BRG9-42-276, BCA.

55   Sandy Banisky, "Camp Concern Faces Sharp Cutbacks, City Says," *Baltimore Sun*, June 18, 1981.

56   "Camp Concern," *Baltimore Sun*, July 16, 1980; Rob Kasper, "Urban Camping," *Baltimore Sun*, July 28, 1980; "Happy Faces at Camp Concern," *Baltimore Sun*, July 31, 1981. "Camp Concern," *Afro-American*, July 29, 1980; Orleck and Hazirjian, *The War on Poverty.*

57   Michal Tomasky, "Why Freddie Gray Never Had a Chance: Lead Poisoning Is Killing Inner-City Baltimore," *The Daily Beast*, May 5, 2015, http://www .thedailybeast.com/articles/2015/05/05/why-freddie-gray-never-had-a-chance-lead -poisoning-is-killing-inner-city-baltimore.html.

58   "Baltimore to Raze Thousands of Buildings, Starting Where Freddie Gray Died," *Fox News*, January 5, 2016, http://www.foxnews.com/us/2016/01/05/buildings-to -be-torn-down-to-fight-baltimore-urban-blight.html.

59   Krista Langlois, "Nature Might Hold the Secret to Healing Police-Community Relations," *Outside*, December 5, 2016, https://www.outsideonline.com/2138696 /nature-might-hold-secret-healing-police-community-relations.

60   Morgan Grove and Michell Kondo, "Greening Cities Makes for Safer Neighbor-hoods," *The Conversation*, July 20, 2016, https://theconversation.com/greening -cities-makes-for-safer-neighbourhoods-62093.

8

"The People's Side of the Road"

• •

Movement against Destruction
and Organizing across Lines
of Race, Class,
and Neighborhood

SHANNON DARROW

Movement against Destruction (MAD) was a broad coalition that worked across lines of race, class, and neighborhood in 1968 to fight highway construction in Baltimore. Grassroots organizations that fought against large-scale development exemplified the power of building coalitions across diverse geographic and social boundaries in achieving fair development. MAD was not only against destruction: this coalition of diverse stakeholders was *for* the city and *for* a different kind of planning and urban policy that included more direct citizen participation.

Under urban renewal—frequently referred to as "Negro removal" because of the often racist implications and consequences of highway construction—thousands of poor and working-class neighborhoods were plowed under and paved over with highways and parking lots.[1] This clearing of huge swaths of the city had a devastating impact on both the urban built environment and the people who were displaced.[2] In the 1940s, transportation planner Robert Moses proposed a system of highways he argued would efficiently move people and goods in and out of downtown Baltimore. In speaking of his highway plan Moses said, "We do not propose to tear down familiar and cherished landmarks which cannot be replaced, nor will the Franklin Expressway make the town unrecognizable. Nothing which we propose to remove will constitute any loss to Baltimore."[3] Moses was wrong.

MAD's document "History, Facts, and Opinions on the Expressway" ("History, Facts, and Opinions" hereafter) countered Moses's view of Baltimore by naming the key natural and architectural assets along the proposed highway route. Produced in 1968 and presented at the Expressway Conference, an organizing conference at Baltimore's Catholic Center, "History, Facts, and Opinions" would become the foundational document for MAD's activism.[4] However, MAD, which was founded in 1968, was not the first organization whose mission was to protect neighborhoods from being destroyed by highway construction. In West Baltimore's African American communities, middle-class homeowners in Rosemont had joined working-class homeowners and tenants along the Franklin-Mulberry Corridor to form Relocation Action Movement (RAM) to argue that their homes and communities were not expendable and to fight for just financial compensation for those displaced by highway construction.[5] Founded in 1966 at the height of the civil rights and Black Power movements, RAM viewed displacement by highway construction as a form of structural and economic violence against black communities. In her analysis of RAM, Sherry Olson argued, "There had already been many uproarious highway hearings, exposés, and confrontations, but the new resistance to black removal was a more serious threat because it resonated with nationwide vibrations."[6]

The connection between RAM and national civil rights and Black Power movements is evident in its partnership with the Congress of Racial Equity (CORE). When RAM activists were initially unsuccessful in persuading elected officials to meet their demands, members of the West Baltimore group reached out to CORE for organizing support in 1967. Making explicit the connection between highway opposition and black empowerment, RAM issued a position statement that read, "We will make our stand in the streets and in the doorways of our homes. Unless black people's demands are satisfied the Expressway WILL NOT be built."[7]

Much of the vocal opposition to the East–West Expressway came from the white, working-class, waterfront communities on Baltimore's southeast side, including Fells Point, Canton, and Highlandtown. Like African American communities in Baltimore, these neighborhoods were "redlined" because of their aging housing stock, proximity to industry, and their high poverty rates; as a result, they were also targeted for disinvestment and slum clearance.[8] However, in the 1960s, the historic character and waterfront location of these neighborhoods started to attract educated, middle-class residents who began buying and renovating properties in Fells Point. In 1967, these new residents founded the Society for the Preservation of Federal Hill, Montgomery Street, and Fells Point to protect those neighborhoods from demolition. Despite class-based tensions in the gentrifying neighborhoods, lifelong working-class residents who wanted to save their homes and communities joined forces with preservationists to form the Southeast Committee against the Road (SCAR). SCAR was a single-issue coalition focused on opposition to highway construction; the issue of the road was also taken up by the Southeast Community Organization (SECO), a group devoted to neighborhood empowerment and economic justice that was part of the Industrial Areas Foundation (IAF), a national network of community and faith-based organizations associated with Saul Alinsky's organizing model.[9]

As indicated by the bottom-up cultural geography of Baltimore mapped out by the Expressway Conference Committee in opposition to Robert Moses's top-down view of the city, a city-wide movement such as MAD would be needed to effectively fight "the Road." The proposed highway plan for Baltimore would have affected a diverse set of city neighborhoods outside of the central business district and would have destroyed both public assets and private property. As "History, Facts, and Opinions" points out, the proposed highway plan also carried tremendous financial costs at $324 million. Redirecting the funds reserved for highway construction toward community investment and the construction of a public transportation network was central to MAD's organizing strategy. In a personal essay, MAD activist Carolyn Tyson argued, "National transportation policy for two generations has promoted the decline of the city through an almost exclusive emphasis on highway construction."[10] In the view of MAD, building a network of expressways not only would have destroyed African American and working-class white neighborhoods but would also have benefited suburban commuters and business interests rather than city residents. Investing in public transportation instead of a highway system would benefit the built and natural environment and would also increase the mobility of poor and working-class city residents unable to afford a car.

Although named "Movement against Destruction," it is important to view MAD's goals and demands as advocating for the city and its residents, rather than just advocating against the highway. Defending the city against forces of destruction—including disinvestment and neglect, as well as highway construction—was central to MAD's organizing strategy. A counter vision of a more just, equitable, and sustainable city—especially in relationship to budget priorities—emerges when various documents from the MAD archives are read in conversation with one another. Joseph Wiles from the Rosemont Neighborhood Improvement Association began his 1972 letter to the City Council by stating, "The most important question being should Baltimore City be a place to live?"[11] He explained how residents in his once stable and close-knit African American neighborhood now experienced a much lower quality of life due to the threat of having their properties condemned. Neighborhood activists had been able to convince the city to lift the condemnation ordinance in 1970, but the damage to the neighborhood had already been done, and Rosemont had become plagued with vacant houses and declining property values. Wiles ended his letter with an impassioned plea for "community participation" in planning decisions and the implementation of city programs. He also stated, "It is our feeling that if a major portion of the efforts and money being spent for urban highways were redirected and coordinated into some comprehensive planning for interacting urban programs, such as housing, transportation, education, recreation, and health, this type of planning and resourcefulness would uplift the hearts and lives of all who share the city, and perhaps then we could finally make our city a better place in which to live and to work."[12]

A similar plea to redirect funding allocated for highway construction toward community programming was made by Barbara Mikulski in a campaign speech for her first bid for a City Council seat. Milkuski introduced herself as a social worker and "long time road fighter" with deep roots in Highlandtown's working-class ethnic community. In arguing against the expressway she said, "We're paying for it with our homes, our neighborhoods, and our taxes."[13] As part of her platform as a City Council candidate Mikulski explained that she would use the funds allocated for highway construction to build a new junior high school in Southeast Baltimore, a recreation center and a library, an expanded playfield, a harbor clean-up program, and a senior center and health care clinic. She added, "This would still leave us over $100 million for developing a mass transit system fixing up existing streets and alleys and doing other worthwhile community projects."[14]

This tracing of similar themes across documents in the MAD archives that were written around the same time but came from distinctly different social locations—for example, a middle-class black man writing as a local leader in West Baltimore and a working-class white woman aspiring to make the transition from a neighborhood activist to an elected official in Southeast Baltimore—reveals the ways in which MAD built a coalition across racial, economic, and neighborhood lines. MAD was an umbrella organization that encompassed more than twenty smaller organizations that opposed highway construction.[15] RAM and SCAR were the oldest and most robust of those organizations and are the focus of this chapter. They offer a window into the strategies and tactics used in organizing in opposition to highway construction in Baltimore. RAM and SCAR also provide a way to examine cross-class intraracial organizing in two distinct clusters of neighborhoods slated for demolition: one in West Baltimore and one in Southeast Baltimore. Finally, looking specifically at RAM and SCAR provides a way of thinking through how structural racism would ultimately hinder the ability of activists to achieve long-term goals of equitable revitalization of black and white neighborhoods.

It is also remarkable that MAD was founded in 1968, the year that uprisings in the wake of the assassination of Dr. Martin Luther King Jr. shook Baltimore and other cities.[16] MAD was able to work against this fragmentation by framing opposition to the highway in terms of the interests of the city as a whole, rather than the interests of specific neighborhoods within a racially segregated and economically stratified city. The ability of MAD to unite diverse communities and constituencies around the issue of "the Road" was impressive, but more importantly the citywide coalition against highway construction achieved its aim.

Baltimore was not the only city to experience "Freeway Revolts" in the decades spanning 1950–1980. In his analysis of community opposition to highway construction in the 1960s, historian Raymond Mohl argues, "Successful freeway revolts generally shared several commonalities. Persistent neighborhood activism, committed local leaders, and extensive cross-city, cross-class, and interracial alliances were needed to bring a high level of attention to the freeway problem over a sustained period of time."[17] He cites both the civil rights movement and the New Left/counterculture as important factors influencing the strategies and tactics used by protest movements against highway construction in American cities. The cacophonous public sphere of the 1960s was shaped by debates about citizen participation and community empowerment, which led to the formation of organizations like RAM, SCAR, and ultimately MAD.[18] Many scholars have problematized Habermas's conception of the monolithic bourgeois public sphere devoted to the common good, and when examining the Freeway Revolts of the 1960s it is important to acknowledge that much of this activity was shaped by non-elite or counterpublics.[19] Although Mohl's analysis of grassroots activism against highway construction situates this activity within the context of the social movements of the 1960s, framing the struggle against "the Road" in terms of the people versus powerful interests also evokes older traditions of activism, including the work of Saul Alinsky, considered the founder of modern community organizing.[20] Analyzing MAD within the context of Alinskyism, particularly traditions of cross-class and interracial neighborhood-based organizing during the late 1960s and early 1970s, presents it as a model for grassroots activism across boundaries.[21]

Historian Francesca Gamber argues that residents in Greater Homewood—a cluster of neighborhoods that border the Johns Hopkins campus—made the sense of shared neighborhood belonging, rather than racial identity, the common ground for organizing and in turn "gave GHCC [Greater Homewood Community Corporation] a way to tackle a broad range of racial and economic concerns."[22] This focus on place rather than race was significant because it shifted the locus of organizing from aggrieved identities to neighborhood issues that had the potential to encourage collaboration across racial, ethnic, and socioeconomic lines. The consensus-building and asset-based approach taken by GHCC and similar organizations also was a main distinction between community development and community organizing.[23]

The Southeast Community Organization (SECO) is another community development organization that was formed in the late 1960s. While GHCC was an interracial organization, SECO was largely a white organization because of neighborhood demographics. It focused on organizing neighborhoods along the Eastern Avenue corridor, including Fells Point, Canton, and Highlandtown.[24] In his analysis of white working-class politics and activism in Baltimore during the late 1960s and 1970s, historian Kenneth Durr complicates the idea of the conservative white working-class silent majority by arguing that the politics of these communities was marked by internal contradictions.[25] Durr's essay is largely a case study of SECO, "which became known nationally as one of the more successful of the grassroots, ethnically based community organizations to spring up in the early 1970s."[26] There was both an antiestablishment and an antiassimilationist bent to SECO, and Durr examines the complex relationship between a renewed interest in "ethnic roots" among white and black and brown pride movements of the same era.[27] In examining how tensions between newer and older residents of the neighborhood were negotiated within SECO, Durr argues, "Middle-class liberals valued a politics of ideas and ideals, but white working-class politics was grounded in practice—it derived from, and sought to protect, white working-class community [while improving material conditions]."[28] In a white working-class set of neighborhoods that were undergoing gentrification, class was sometimes as large a source of tension within the organization as race.

This clash between a politics of ideals and a politics of practice rooted in lived experience also played out within the work of the Economic Research Action Project (ERAP), a New Left organization devoted to creating an interracial movement of the poor. Although there was an ERAP chapter in Baltimore, the organization was most successful and had the longest-lasting impact in Chicago, Newark, Boston, and Cleveland. A community-based project of the campus-based Students for a Democratic Society, ERAP saw itself as an urban and northern counterpart to civil rights movement organizing, which was largely rural and southern. In her analysis of the work of ERAP, Jennifer Frost demonstrates that through direct outreach in poor and working-class urban communities, organizers learned that community members, particularly African Americans and low-income white women, were most concerned about housing, urban renewal, education, blight, and policing. In drawing attention to the gendered dimension of these concerns and to the ways in which poor people's concerns challenged (white, male, Marxist) conceptions of "the political," Frost claims that these concerns "generally emerged from inequalities in the areas of economic distribution and consumption and were often defined as private concerns that fell outside the domain of politics and social movements."[29] Frost's scholarship provides a useful framework for thinking about MAD as a coalitional organization both because it provides a national context for understanding multiracial community organizing in the late 1960s and early 1970s and because the community concerns raised by ERAP members are fundamentally problems of the city.

In an urban context these "inequalities of economic distribution and consumption," especially as they relate to housing and displacement, are directly connected to race.[30] This point was made by West Baltimore activists within the MAD coalition, as is evident in the RAM position statement:

> Rivers of concrete are to be pushed through parks, areas of historical significance, and most importantly serve as a source of destruction for many residential areas. It is no coincidence that most of the neighborhoods slated for demolition are black. For too long the history of Urban Renewal and Highway Clearance has been marked by the repeated removal of black citizens. We have been asked to make sacrifice after sacrifice in the name of progress, and then when that progress has been achieved we find it marked "White Only."[31]

As the RAM position statement makes clear, not every organization (much less individual citizens) in MAD had the same concerns in opposing highway construction.

As analysis of SCAR, SECO, and the Society for the Preservation of Federal Hill, Montgomery Street, and Fells Point makes clear, social class shaped not just how people lived in the neighborhood but also their reasons, strategies, and tactics for fighting "the Road." Both Jennifer Frost's study of the ERAP and Francesca Gamber's analysis of the GHCC point out that the neighborhoods where interracial and cross-class community organizing took place were often "in transition."[32] In addition to the pressures of what were the early stages of gentrification, historically white working-class neighborhoods in South and Southeast Baltimore were also being transformed by deindustrialization and the loss of good-paying blue-collar jobs.[33] These same economic forces were also leading to the deterioration of communities in West Baltimore, where they were exacerbated by a process of neighborhood decline that, while based in racism, had different consequences for middle- and working-class black residents.[34]

To make sense of community organizing against highway construction in Baltimore, it is important to understand that RAM, just like SCAR, was a cross-class coalition and that Franklin-Mulberry and Rosemont, although they were both African American neighborhoods in West Baltimore, were very different communities in the late 1960s and 1970s than they are today. Located in the heart of "Old West Baltimore"—a set of neighborhoods along Pennsylvania

Avenue that are closely associated with African American history and culture—Franklin-Mulberry was, by the late 1960s, a largely poor, working-class, and highly distressed neighborhood.[35] Among the factors contributing to growing poverty and deteriorating conditions in central West Baltimore was the outmigration of middle-class African American residents as housing opportunities began to open up in other parts of the city (especially in the far west and northwestern sections of Baltimore) during the 1960s.[36]

Rosemont was among the communities created in Baltimore as the result of what historian Thomas Sugrue has termed the sorting of African American neighborhoods by class during the years of blockbusting and racial transition.[37] In "'White Man's Lane': Hollowing out the Highway Ghetto in Baltimore," Emily Lieb describes how "when road builders looked at Rosemont, they did not see a leafy, middle-class, in-town suburb; they saw a black neighborhood and therefore a slum."[38] And yet as Lieb's research demonstrates, Rosemont residents, in challenging the highway plans, frequently pointed out their status as middle-class homeowners, the pride they took in maintaining their homes, and the stable suburb-like qualities of their neighborhood. As historian Robin D. G. Kelley points out in his comparative analysis of the NAACP and the International Labor Defense (ILD), it is crucial to examine the interracial class politics of black communities and look at how race-based organizations have depended on respectability politics and been focused on advancing the interests of the black middle class.[39] These factors are especially salient in the outcomes of highway politics in Baltimore. MAD's citywide organizing against the highway, bolstered by RAM's crucial role in the coalition, saved many neighborhoods (including Rosemont) from the bulldozer. Unfortunately, it could not prevent the Franklin-Mulberry corridor from being razed for construction of the infamous "Highway to Nowhere," and much of the damage was already done to African American neighborhoods.

Despite the various cleavages around race and class that existed both between and within Baltimore neighborhoods, MAD worked to unite diverse communities around the common message that no community was expendable. In describing her participation in the Baltimore's "Road Wars," MAD's first president Carolyn Tyson writes, "In 1968, people who had been seeing one another protesting at highway hearings organized a coalition of anti-road organizations known as the Movement Against Destruction (by expressways). Present memberships, include twenty-two community organizations ranging from small community groups to city-wide organizations, representing perhaps 10,000 people."[40]

The complexity of both identities and interests that comprised the MAD coalition are embedded in the life story of Carolyn Tyson, its first president. She was a middle-class, middle-aged white woman who taught in Baltimore's schools. Before her involvement in MAD, Tyson was active in the civil rights movement. She did not live either in West or Southeast Baltimore, but in the far west Baltimore neighborhood of Franklintown; she first became involved in protesting the road because of its negative impact on Leakin Park.[41]

MAD's focus on native leadership, drawing on multiple local cultural traditions, and working closely with faith-based organizations characterizes it as a "people's organization" closely associated with the work and community-organizing traditions of Alinsky.[42] Alinsky-style organizing also influenced MAD's tactics and rhetorical strategies by framing the struggle against "the Road" as one between "the people" and powerful interests. Alinsky's approach was conflict based and centered on activating disempowered people around a powerful target. Implicit in Alinsky's method was the understanding that the problems faced by poor communities result from a lack of access to resources and power and that organizing is best understood as the process through which communities build power from within. The role of the organizer was to "serve as a stimulus, a catalytic agent," asking open-ended questions about whose interests are served by a particular policy or project.[43]

A wide range of documents within the MAD archive frame "the Road" as the target and the work of the organization as educating the public about how "the Road" benefits powerful interests located either outside the city or within the central business district, rather than Baltimore City residents. "History, Facts, and Opinions" states, "It is obvious from their actions that the 'road gang,' made up of politicians, highway technocrats and lobbyists for car, oil, concrete, and other special interests, is not concerned with transportation. Their real interest is road-building and what concerns them is not people but profit."[44] Carolyn Tyson also mentions the special interests that comprise "the road gang" in her essay, "The Road: The Expressway War."[45] What is especially significant about Tyson's essay is her discussion of the research MAD activists undertook to uncover the logic and interests behind Baltimore's proposed highway plan. She states, "For two years MAD has done an analysis of the city budget to attempt to calculate the cost of the expressways."[46] This focus on grassroots research in service of an activist agenda also situates MAD within the context of community-based research projects like the ERAP and GHCC.[47]

The grassroots research undertaken by MAD activists uncovered another special interest behind "the Road," and hence another target for the organization: the Greater Baltimore Committee (GBC). The GBC was an organization of business and civic leaders focused on promoting economic growth and stimulating private sector investment in Baltimore City. Tyson notes, "Until recently, the membership of the GBC was difficult to ascertain; recently MAD found a list and published it, noting that two-thirds of its membership lived outside the city and several outside the state! All are wealthy men."[48] In addition to publishing the list, MAD also represented this research visually. Its doubled-sided document "Who Does Want the Road and Where Do They

Live?" lists the names, business connections, and zip codes of the 103 GBC members on one side.[49] On the reverse side is a hand-drawn map of Baltimore encircled by the I-695 beltway, with the route of the proposed highway through the city. The location of the homes of each GBC member is also noted: there is a small cluster of members in the northern "gold coast" zip codes of 21210 and 21212, but the greatest concentration of GBC members is in the Northwest suburbs. What is remarkable about reading these primary sources in conversation with scholarly literature is how closely MAD's analysis of planning for the central business district at the expense of the city as a whole mirrors the findings of the formal planning literature.[50]

The map showing the neighborhoods where GBC members lived accomplished two important organizing objectives. First, it clearly and visually demonstrates that "the Road's" most ardent supporters were not directly affected by the highway route, and for the most part these people's investment in the city was largely financial. Second, and more subtly, the map creates a countergeography of communities affected by highway construction and for whom the city was "where they lived." In his assessment of the organization Robert Mohl says, "The cross-class and multiracial character of MAD took the organization beyond the parochial self-interest of smaller neighborhood groups and conveyed the sense that it spoke for the people against the interests."[51] A common critique of Alinsky-style organizing, one that is often supported by the transformation of his Back of the Yards organization into a white protectionist organization by the 1950s, is that the parochial and the polarizing dynamics of "us" versus "them" can be used in exclusionary ways.[52]

MAD directly linked "the Road" to the health of the city. Much of MAD's activism took the form of advocating for specific programs or better uses for funds currently allocated to highway construction.[53] In addition to making policy arguments, MAD also engaged in cultural work including humor, songs, and festivals that affirmed city life. An interesting example of this cultural work is *The MAD Coloring Book*.[54] Produced by Mary Rosemond in 1972, this children's coloring book juxtaposes images of a city ruined by highway construction and of an idyllic city without the road. On one page, the letter *C* stands for cars, and the image is of a heavily trafficked road against a backdrop of modernist skyscrapers. Rosemond instructs children to "color them fast, color them sharp, color them bold. Color them red, yellow, blue, green. These cars let out exhaust." On the following page, *C* is for city, and the image is of a tree-lined street of Italianate rowhouses with flowerboxes. The text reads, "C is for City, your city, our city. Color it silent in the morning, color the sky clear, color birds singing, color it contented, color it peaceful, color it friendly, the city comes alive with people."

In 1974 the city announced plans to abandon the highway plan. The only piece of Moses's plan for Baltimore that got built was the two-mile stretch along the Franklin-Mulberry corridor. This infamous "Highway to Nowhere," according to Mohl, "sent an inner-city black community into rapid decline and still serves as a reminder of the huge social costs of the interstate era."[55] Mohl cites the work of the MAD coalition as crucial, but also points out other factors including budget constraints and declining support for the highway among both the planning profession and politicians. "Without these other ingredients," Mohl argues, "there was a very good chance that the freeway would get built anyway." He also points out that some of the most effective strategies used by anti-road activists were getting Fells Point listed on the National Register of Historic Places and court cases like Volunteers Opposing Leakin Park Expressway *VOLPE v. Volpe*, which sought protection for Leakin Park. The use of these strategies raises questions about how tactics like legal and legislative advocacy, which by definition depend on the specialized expertise of trained professionals, can coexist and collaborate with more grassroots community organizing. The greater effectiveness of the tactics employed by the Society for the Preservation of Federal Hill, Montgomery Street, and Fells Point versus those of SECO and of VOLPE versus RAM also points to tensions and contradictions within the MAD coalition. These tensions were not only about race and class but also about demands for protecting the amenities associated with urban life (historic buildings and public parks) versus those for affordable housing, transportation access, and the equitable provision of basic city services.

Ultimately MAD was far more successful in stopping "the Road" than in achieving the organization's more expansive vision of a just, equitable, and sustainable city. At the end of "The Road: The Expressway War," Carolyn Tyson warns, "If the flight to the suburbs continues, Baltimore by 1990 will be predominantly old, poor, and black."[56] Today, Tyson's prediction has been realized in some parts of Baltimore. Today the claim "I love city life" has been adopted as the slogan of Live Baltimore, an organization that promotes buying a home in Baltimore by marketing the city as a desirable place to live. Although such marketing campaigns encourage individuals to make emotional and financial investments through home buying that can stabilize city neighborhoods, such efforts avoid the deeper and more contentious terrain of improving material conditions in distressed neighborhoods or distributing resources in a more equitable way along the lines of race, class, and neighborhood.

The uneven outcomes within the neighborhoods saved by MAD have less to do with its goals and tactics than with larger structural factors beyond the scope of a single organization. One consequence of the protracted fight against "the Road," and of the city's decision to vote for condemnation ordinances on a neighborhood-by-neighborhood basis, was a glut of vacant properties in nearly all of the neighborhoods in the original path of the highway. In South and Southeast Baltimore, these houses became part of the famous "dollar house" urban homesteading program, through which many educated professionals renovated houses in the neighborhoods first pioneered by the Society for the Preservation of Federal Hill, Montgomery Street, and Fells Point. Although MAD and RAM were successful in securing $5,000,000 to reinvest in Rosemont, the homesteading program was less successful there. As Emily Lieb notes, the renovation of these properties was often done poorly, and racist real estate practices like flipping and predatory lending undermined neighborhood stabilization efforts.[57]

The Baltimore Book features a transcript of an impassioned speech that Barbara Mikulski delivered to the American Planning Association in 1979.[58] In making her case about the value of community organizing she said, "Just about every part of Baltimore that is being called 'vitalized' is here because of a community organization and a citizen protest movement." What Mikulski's speech does not address is the stark unevenness along racial lines of reinvestment and revitalization in the neighborhoods saved from demolition. In the decades since this address was given to the American Planning Association, the former working-class neighborhoods along Baltimore's waterfront have become a new gold coast, forming the base of a pattern of unequal development that public health scholar Lawrence Brown has termed "the White L" (see chapter 6). To make Baltimore a just and sustainable city, contemporary coalitions in defense of city living that cross the boundaries of race, class, and neighborhood must be coupled with restorative policies and practices that as Brown argues "Make Black Neighborhoods Matter."[59]

Notes

1   The phrase "Negro removal" was first used by James Baldwin in a 1963 televised interview with historian Kenneth B. Clark. See *The Negro Protest: James Baldwin, Malcolm X, and Martin Luther King Talk with Kenneth B. Clark* (Boston: Beacon Press, 1963).

2   For an overview of urban renewal and its racial impacts in Baltimore see Antero Pietila, *Not in My Neighborhood: How Bigotry Shaped a Great American City* (Chicago: Ivan R. Dee, 2010), and Emily Lieb, "'White Man's Lane': Hollowing out the Highway Ghetto in Baltimore," in *Baltimore '68: Riots and Rebirth in an American City*, ed. Jessica I. Elfenbein, Thomas L. Hollowak, and Elizabeth Nix (Philadelphia: Temple University Press, 2011), 51–69.

3   Lieb, "'White Man's Lane,'" 56.

4   Expressway Conference Committee, "History, Facts, and Opinions of Expressway," MAD Organizing Conference: Catholic Center, 1968, University of Baltimore, Langsdale Library, Special Collections Department, MAD Collection, Series 6, Box 1, Folder 2.

5   "A History of Relocation Action Movement," typescript, ca. 1968, University of Baltimore, Langsdale Library, Special Collections Department, MAD Collection, Series 7, Box A1; "Position Statement Relocation Action Movement," typescript, ca. 1968, University of Baltimore, Langsdale Library, Special Collections Department, MAD Collection, Series 7, Box A1.

6   Quoted in Raymond Mohl, "Stop the Road: Freeway Revolts in American Cities,"
    Journal of Urban History 30 (2004): 674–695.

7   "Position Statement Relocation Action Movement."

8   See Linda Shopes, "Fells Point: Community and Conflict in a Working Class
    Neighborhood," in *The Baltimore Book: New Views on Local History*, ed. Elizabeth
    Fee, Linda Shopes, and Linda Zeidman (Philadelphia: Temple University Press,
    1991), 121–143.

9   Kenneth Durr, "The Not So Silent Majority: White Working Class Community,"
    in *From Mobtown to Charm City: New Perspectives on Baltimore's Past*, ed. Jessica
    Elfenbein, John Breihan, and Thomas Hollowack (Baltimore: Maryland Histori-
    cal Society Press, 2002), 225–249.

10 Carolyn Tyson, "The Road: The Expressway War," typescript, ca. 1971, University
    of Baltimore, Langsdale Library, Special Collections Department, MAD
    Collection, Series 7A, Box 1, Folder 1.

11 Joseph Wiles, Letter to the City Council of Baltimore, January 24, 1972, Univer-
    sity of Baltimore, Langsdale Library, Special Collections Department, MAD
    Collection, Series 6, Box 4, Folder 22.

12 Wiles, Letter to the City Council.

13 Barbara Mikulski, "Anti-Expressway Speech," Delivered at a Public Meeting at
    St. Brigid's Hall, June 29, 1971, University of Baltimore, Langsdale Library, Special
    Collections Department, MAD Collection, Box 7, Folder 94.

14 Mikulski, "Anti-Expressway Speech."

15 For details on MAD's founding see Tyson, "The Road," 9.

16 For more on the 1968 riots in Baltimore see *Baltimore '68*.

17 Mohl, "Stop the Road," 676.

18 This chapter is informed by the argument that organizations can only come into
    being because of the way an issue is debated in the public sphere. For a case study
    on how this works, see Francesca Gamber, "The Public Sphere and the End of
    American Abolitionism, 1833–1870," *Slavery and Abolition* 28, no. 3 (Decem-
    ber 2007): 351–368.

19 Craig Calhoun, "Introduction: Habermas and the Public Sphere," and Mary
    Ryan, "Gender and Public Access: Women's Politics in Nineteenth Century
    America," both in *Habermas and the Public Sphere*, ed. Craig Calhoun (Cam-
    bridge, MA: MIT Press, 1997), 1–50, 259–288.

20 Saul Alinsky, *Reveille for Radicals* (New York: Vintage, 1969); Robert Fisher,
    "Radical Neighborhood Organizing, 1929–1946," in *Let the People Decide:
    Neighborhood Organizing in America* (New York: Twayne Publishers, 1994),
    32–65.

21 Francesca Gamber, "Where We Live: Greater Homewood Community Corpora-
    tion, 1967–1976," in *Baltimore '68*, 208–225; Jennifer Frost, *An Interracial
    Movement of the Poor: Community Organizing and the New Left in the 1960s* (New
    York: New York University Press, 2001), 49–93.

22 At its founding in 1967 as the Greater Homewood Community Project the
    organization was focused on neighborhoods "demarcated by Cold Spring Lane to
    the north, Twenty-fifth Street to the south, the Jones Falls Expressway to the west,
    and Greenmount Ave to the east." Gamber, "Where We Live," 210.

23 For an overview of asset-based community development, see John Kretzmann and
    John McKnight, *Building Communities from the Inside Out: A Path toward
    Finding and Mobilizing a Community's Assets* (Chicago: Acta Publications, 1993).

For a history of community development in Baltimore see Kate Davidoff, "From Protest Politics to Granite Countertops: The Shifts in Community Development in Baltimore, Maryland from 1950–2000" (PhD diss., Rutgers University, 2015).

24 The demographics of Southeast Baltimore have shifted considerably since the late 1960s and 1970s. In addition to undergoing gentrification, these neighborhoods have seen a huge influx of immigrants from Mexico and Central America. Today Fells Point and Highlandtown are among the most ethnically diverse neighborhoods in Baltimore and home to the city's Latinx community. The Southeast CDC (formerly SECO) is a bilingual and multicultural organization.

25 Durr, "The Not So Silent Majority."

26 Durr, "The Not So Silent Majority," 225.

27 For a deeper discussion of these dynamics, see work on collaboration between the Young Patriots (working-class whites), Young Lords (Puerto Ricans), and Black Panthers, particularly in Chicago, in Amy Sonnie and James Tracy, *Hillbilly Nationalists, Urban Race Rebels, and Black Power: Community Organizing in Radical Times* (Brooklyn: Mellville House, 2011).

28 Durr, "The Not So Silent Majority," 226.

29 Frost, *An Interracial Movement of the Poor*, 98.

30 See George Lipsitz, *How Racism Takes Place* (Philadelphia: Temple University Press, 2011); Mindy Thompson Fullilove, *Root Shock: How Tearing up City Neighborhoods Hurts America, and What We Can Do about It* (New York: Ballantine, 2005).

31 "Position Statement Relocation Action Movement."

32 Durr, "The Not So Silent Majority; Shopes, "Fells Point"; Gamber, "Where We Live"; Frost, *An Interracial Movement of the Poor*, 49–93.

33 Shopes, "Fells Point," and David Harvey, "A View From Federal Hill," both in *The Baltimore Book*, 227–254.

34 For an overview of deindustrialization, race, and neighborhoods see Thomas Sugrue, *The Origins of the Urban Crisis: Race and Inequality in Postwar Detroit* (Princeton, NJ: Princeton University Press, 1996).

35 Karen Olson, "Old West Baltimore: Segregation, African American Culture, and the Struggle for Equality," in *The Baltimore Book*, 57–84.

36 Pietila, *Not in My Neighborhood*; W. Edward Orser, "Flight to the Suburbs: Suburbanization and Racial Change on Baltimore's West Side," in *The Baltimore Book*., 203–224.

37 Sugrue, *The Origins of the Urban Crisis*.

38 Lieb, "'White Man's Lane,'" 68, 59.

39 Robin D. G. Kelley, *Hammer and Hoe: Alabama Communists during the Great Depression* (Chapel Hill: University of North Carolina Press, 1990).

40 Tyson, "The Road," 9.

41 While some of this background information on Carolyn Tyson is in the public record, much of it comes from an oral history I conducted with Carolyn's widower, George Tyson, as an assignment for Eric Singer's "History of Baltimore" class in the fall of 2013.

42 Alinsky, *Reveille for Radicals*.

43 Alinsky, *Reveille for Radicals*, 74.

44 "History, Facts, and Opinions of Expressway," 7.

45 Tyson, "The Road."

46 Tyson, "The Road," 11.

47 Gamber, "Where We Live," 208–225; Frost, *An Interracial Movement of the Poor*, 49–93.

48 Tyson, "The Road," 6.

49 "Who Does Want the Road and Where Do They Live?," typescript, ca. 1971, University of Baltimore, Langsdale Library, Special Collections Department, MAD Collection.

50 See the discussion of planning to revitalize the central business district in both Lieb, "'White Man's Lane,'" and Mohl, "Stop the Road," 674.

51 Mohl, "Stop the Road," 698.

52 For more on this critique of Alinskyism, see Robert Fisher, "Radical Neighborhood Organizing," 32–65.

53 Wiles, Letter to the City Council of Baltimore; Mikulski, "Anti-Expressway Speech"; Tyson, "The Road."

54 Mary Rosemond, *The MAD Coloring Book* (1972), University of Baltimore, Langsdale Library, Special Collections Department, MAD Collection.

55 Mohl, "Stop the Road," 698.

56 Tyson, "The Road," 13.

57 Lieb, "'White Man's Lane.'" For a fuller discussion of predatory lending and race in Baltimore see also George Lipsitz, "The Crime *The Wire* Never Names," in *How Racism Takes Place* (Philadelphia: Temple University Press, 2011), 95–114.

58 "Barbara Mikulski: The Senator as Community Activist," in *The Baltimore Book*, 147–149.

59 Lawrence Brown, "Fix the City: Make Black Neighborhoods Matter." *Urbanite: Truth, Reconciliation, and Baltimore* 100 (November 2015).

9

More Than a Store

• •

Activist Businesses in
Baltimore

JOSHUA CLARK DAVIS

In 1970, an unusual business opened its doors in Baltimore's Hollins Market neighborhood. The Pratt Street Conspiracy was a "head shop" that sold clothes, rolling papers, incense, and pipes to local hippies and curious community members. Although it was staffed by long-haired teenagers and decorated with psychedelic murals and peace symbols, the Pratt Street Conspiracy aimed to be more than just a countercultural retailer. It was also a nonprofit cooperative that employed local teenagers and offered low-income residents an alternative to shopping at downtown department stores or exploitive neighborhood shops that overcharged them. The store even gave customers from poor neighborhoods and students a discount on purchases. The Pratt Street Conspiracy was funded primarily by Baltimore's Community Action Agency, an organization established through the federal Office of Economic Opportunity as part of President Johnson's War on Poverty and headed by civil rights veteran Lenwood M. Ivey. The Volunteers in Service to America (VISTA) program and a Title I grant administered by an "urban action development committee" at the University of Baltimore paid several people as community organizers to work out of the shop. The Pratt Street Conspiracy channeled any funds remaining after covering its costs back into two local antipoverty community organizations, Project Unite and Hollins, Inc.[1]

At first glance, the Pratt Street Conspiracy may seem like a countercultural curiosity with little connection to the rest of Baltimore's history. Yet this short-lived shop emerged from the city's long tradition of businesses that work directly with social movements. This history of "activist businesses" in Charm City stretches from the 1820s to today. The people who established these enterprises re-envisioned the products, places, and processes of American business in several ways. First, they sought to introduce goods that promoted progressive and radical politics in the marketplace. Second, these entrepreneurs conceived of their storefronts as political places or "free spaces" that incubated cultures of activism and solidarity. Third, many activist enterprises reconceptualized processes of doing business by promoting shared ownership, limited growth, and democratic workplaces. In turn they rejected capitalist norms of limited proprietorship, profit maximization, and hierarchical management.

Although virtually every American city has been home to activist businesses, Baltimore seems to have been particularly conducive to these political enterprises, perhaps because so many social movements have thrived within its borders. Indeed, the range of Baltimore's activist businesses—including abolitionist "free produce" stores, union-owned manufacturers, suffragist pop-up shops, Black Power bookstores, lesbian-feminist printing presses, and even today's worker-owned infoshops and social justice ice cream sellers—provide a window into the history of the city's progressive and radical movements. Most importantly, activist enterprises force us to rethink Baltimore's relationship to capitalism and to expand our view of business in the city beyond its better known history of shipping, steelmaking, and health care.

Activist businesses emerged in Baltimore as early as the 1820s, a decade that historian Michael Kazin identifies as the starting point for the United States' radical social movements.[2] In 1826, antislavery activists Michael Lamb and Benjamin Lundy, the Quaker publisher of the abolitionist newspaper *Genius of Universal Emancipation*, opened a "free produce" store at 61 Calvert Street, only the third of its kind in the United States. Lundy and Lamb sold groceries and other goods produced by paid laborers, and they avoided products made by enslaved workers. Announcing their opening in August 1826, the abolitionist business partners declared that *"free labor is,* invariably, *more profitable than that of slaves.* . . . For this reason and from motives of a conscientious nature, many have resolved to abstain from using the productions of slave-labor, and encourage those who may produce the staple commodities of slaveholding countries by *free hands."*[3] Both this store and another one that Lundy opened in 1830 proved short-lived, but the free produce movement flourished as an arm of the burgeoning antislavery cause in mid-Atlantic cities with sizable populations of Quakers and free blacks. More than anywhere else, free produce stores proliferated in Philadelphia, where abolitionists attending the Unrequited Labor Convention in 1838 established the American Free Produce Association. As the association proclaimed at its founding meeting, any consumer "partaking of goods procured through the unrequited labor of the slave" was complicit in the system of slavery.[4]

The struggle for organized labor stands out as the second member of a trio of key early American radical social movements. In addition to forming unions, early organized labor groups established worker-owned cooperative businesses. In 1866, African American shipbuilders led a collective effort by black laborers, churches, and mutual aid societies in Baltimore to launch the worker-owned Chesapeake Marine Railway and Dry Dock Company in Fells Point. At the helm of this workers' cooperative was Isaac Myers, a man born to free black parents in 1835 who had worked as a skilled ship caulker since he was a teenager. The Company employed three hundred African Americans within a year of its founding, paying them on average a generous wage of three dollars per hour. Myers, whom historian Philip Foner described as "the first important black labor leader in America," soon organized the Colored Caulkers' Trade Union Society of Baltimore, and in 1869 he became the founding president of the Colored National Labor Union (CNLU), an affiliate of the nascent National Labor Union. Although the CNLU folded within several years, the Chesapeake Marine Railway and Dry Dock Company thrived for two decades as a shipbuilding cooperative and a hub for other local black cooperatives and community organizations in Baltimore.[5]

By the 1880s, another organization, the Knights of Labor, had firmly established itself as one of the country's premier backers of cooperatives. The Knights announced its dual objectives in its 1885 constitution: "to associate our own labors; [and] to establish co-operative institutions, such as will tend to supersede the wage system by the introduction of a co-operative industrial system."[6] In Baltimore, the organization operated a small cooperative factory at 107 West Fayette Street where female textile workers produced shirts carrying the Knights label. Other labor groups and union locals in Baltimore joined the Knights in establishing cooperatively owned businesses such as bakeries, a glass-blowing company, a furniture maker, a publishing press, and a barrel maker.[7]

Women's suffrage rounded out the trio of key early American radical movements, and like their peers in the abolition and labor movements, Baltimore suffragists experimented with entrepreneurship. In the 1910s, the city's premier suffrage group, the Just Government League (JGL), held "suffrage bazaars" or movement fundraisers like the ones New England women's groups had organized since the 1880s. These events offered "home economics" goods and pro-suffrage memorabilia for sale, as well as live entertainment and speeches by suffragists. Individual members also mailed boxed goods periodically to JGL headquarters to sell as unopened mystery gifts for ten cents apiece in "parcel post sales." These one-day events—what might be called pop-up shops today—were designed to raise funds for suffrage organizing and to attract potential recruits to the JGL's Mount Vernon headquarters at 817 North Charles Street.[8]

Amid the depression of the 1930s and 1940s, the American Left's increasing affinity for Marxism spurred a growth in businesses with socialist and communist ties. In 1933, affiliates of the socialist League for Industrial Democracy founded a new organization for labor rights and racial equality in Baltimore, the People's Unemployment League (PUL). One of the city's few multiracial political groups, PUL established a "handicraft exchange" operating on a "barter basis" at 1400 North Charles Street, which was later converted into a cooperative grocery open to active PUL members. Operating out of a space leased for free from a local doctor, the cooperative grocery doubled as a venue for weekly meetings and recruiting events.[9]

Members of the Communist Party of the United States of America (CPUSA) also established businesses in Baltimore. By 1937, local communists had launched the Free State Book Shop at 205 West Franklin Street, next door to the Baltimore CPUSA chapter's headquarters. Alexander Munsell, an heir to an industrial fortune who bankrolled communist causes in Baltimore, operated the store along with his wife Louise Ellen Munsell. In 1943, the Munsells and the CPUSA established a second store, the Frederick Douglass Bookshop, at 1422 Druid Hill Avenue. Described by the FBI as the "Communist Party literature distribution point in the Negro section of Baltimore," this bookstore held organizing meetings and "New Members Classes" for the party. Both the Free State and Frederick Douglass bookstores ceased operations by the end of the 1940s, however, as communists and other radicals faced widespread repression across the country.[10]

As the postwar Red Scare ebbed by the 1960s, new radical businesses opened in Baltimore. Two CPUSA members, Robert W. Lee and George Myers, joined with famed atheist Madalyn Murray to launch the New Era Bookshop on the 100 block of West 22nd Street in the fall of 1962. Lee was a former worker at Bethlehem Steel's Sparrows Point plant, as well as an organizer of the Tobacco Workers union, and the House of Representatives' Un-American Activities Committee had investigated him for subversion in the early 1950s. A few years later, Lee and his wife, the Finnish American activist Sirkka Tuomi, became active members of the Congress of Racial Equality (CORE). The New Era made local news in February 1967 when Xavier Edwards, a leader in the Interstate Knights of the Ku Klux Klan, and American Nazi Party member Philip Jenkins announced they would force the bookshop's new location at 408 Park Avenue to close within a month. Over the next few weeks, hooded Klan members protested outside the New Era, and the store faced a series of attacks, including a fire bombing and a physical assault on Lee. The crimes were never solved.

Although Robert Lee died in 1971, the New Era continued to operate as one of Baltimore's most important radical public spaces through the middle of the 1990s.[11]

Despite the attacks on the New Era, other activists involved in the civil rights and Black Power movements established businesses in Baltimore in the late 1960s and early 1970s. CORE organizer Walter Lively operated a black-oriented bookstore and print shop called Liberation House Press at the start of the 1970s at 432 East North Avenue.[12] In 1972, local Black Panther Party captain Paul Coates launched a bookstore, The Black Book, as an auxiliary of the George Jackson Prison Book Movement, a short-lived campaign to provide reading materials to incarcerated individuals. The store struggled at multiple locations until closing in 1978, but that same year Coates launched Black Classic Press, a company that has become one of the country's most successful publishing houses specializing in African American literature and history. It currently operates in nearby Halethorpe in Baltimore County. Coates is also the father of writer Ta-Nehisi Coates, who described his upbringing in his 2009 memoir, *The Beautiful Struggle*, and won the National Book Award for nonfiction in 2015 for *Between the World and Me*.[13]

A number of activists in the women's movement also started businesses in Baltimore. In 1968, Dee Ann Mims, Donna Keck, Vicki Pollard, and Carmen Arbona launched second-wave feminism's first nationally distributed publication, *Women: A Journal of Liberation*. Preceding such feminist publications as *Ms., off our backs,* and *Big Mama Rag* by several years, *Women* quickly became an influential voice in the national women's movement, as well as an incubator for local feminist organizing in Baltimore. Meanwhile, local feminists Francine Brown and Betsy Bean Millman operated the 31st Street Bookstore, a shop specializing in books for women, children, and the LGBT community, from 1973 to 1995 at 425 East 31st Street (now Normal's Books & Records).[14]

In 1972, an antiwar activist and former printer of *Women*, Casey "KC" Czarnik, joined with Coletta Reid, a former *off our backs* staffer and member of the Washington, D.C., lesbian feminist collective The Furies, to establish a print shop in Baltimore. Reid, Czarnik, and several other female staffers originally shared an office with "a group of leftist hippy men"; the men typed and laid out the orders and the women printed them. By October 1972, however, political infighting prompted most women to resign from the collective. Those who stayed asked the men to leave, after which they chose the name Diana Press for their new all-female business.[15]

The fledgling company faced considerable challenges. Diana Press started with just $400 from staffers' personal savings, a donation of another $400 to purchase a twenty-five-year-old Multilith printer, and a loan of $170 to buy an instant plate maker. The women had to teach themselves how to operate the complex printing equipment. Undaunted, Diana Press opened for business at

12 West 25th Street in Charles Village and not far from Waverly, two neighborhoods with sizable communities of radical feminists and antiwar activists. The women received individual monthly salaries of $100, which they then promptly reinvested in the business. All of Diana Press's workers quit their outside jobs, so they depended entirely on the shop to make a living. Despite this combination of high stakes and meager finances, the women of Diana Press "didn't worry about making money, or our profit margin, or whether we were underpricing." As Reid would tell the *Wall Street Journal* for a front-page story on feminist businesses, "men don't touch any job that we do" at Diana Press. "Our goal is to help other women."[16]

In late 1972, the lesbian author and feminist Rita Mae Brown approached Diana Press with an order to produce her second book, a poetry collection titled *Songs to a Handsome Woman*. By early 1973, employees had collated and stapled by hand 2,000 printed copies of the book. As Reid recalled, "We got into publishing with no experience but with a strong feeling that there were women's words that could not be spoken or heard because all publishing companies were owned by men." Within a year, the company would publish a handful of books and pamphlets with titles such as *Class and Feminism* and *Heterosexuality & the Women's Movement*. Diana Press quickly became one of the premier woman-owned publishing houses, joining established movement publishers like The Feminist Press in New York City.[17] After flourishing for several years in Baltimore, Diana Press relocated to Oakland to collaborate with Bay-area feminist businesses in 1977. Sadly, the company was forced to close by the end of the decade due to financial setbacks it suffered following a mysterious act of sabotage in October 1977 that destroyed much of its printing equipment.[18]

Baltimore's activist businesses struggled in the 1980s and 1990s. The decline of second-wave feminism and Black Power hurt movement storefronts, as did competition from chains such as Barnes & Noble that now sold black-authored and feminist books once shunned by conventional booksellers. Yet some new activist stores did open for business. The Socialist Workers Party launched a chapter of its Pathfinder Bookstore network at 2913 Greenmount Avenue in the mid-1980s. Black Planet Books, one of a cohort of anarchist bookstores known as infoshops that emerged around the world in the 1990s, opened at 1621 Fleet Street in Fells Point. By 2003, however, both stores had closed.[19]

Today, Baltimore's longest operating activist business is Everyone's Place African Cultural Center, founded by Nati and Tabia Kamau-Nataki in 1986 at 1356 West North Avenue, near Pennsylvania Avenue. The store's ground floor is devoted to African and black-themed art, jewelry, and clothing, while the upstairs level is filled with books on African American and diasporic topics, including the civil rights movement and black nationalism. A room in the basement level is available for any community members or organizations looking for a place to meet. The Kamau-Natakis also operate a distribution company,

Afrikan World Books, which distributes printed material wholesale to black-owned bookstores across the country.[20]

Another prominent activist business in Baltimore is Red Emma's, a radical bookstore and cafe founded in 2004 by several former members of the Black Planet Books collective. Originally operating out of a modest basement location at 800 St. Paul Street in Mount Vernon, the collective moved to 30 West North Avenue in fall 2013, taking over a space that was more than five times the size of its original store and substantially larger than most other activist businesses, past or present. In the fall of 2018, the collective moved to an even larger, multistory space at the corner of Cathedral and West Preston Streets. Red Emma's offers customers a vegan menu and coffee sourced from environmentally sustainable and democratically organized farms, as well as one of the mid-Atlantic's largest selections of radical books. Named after Emma Goldman, the cooperative is explicitly committed to inclusion, social justice, and workplace democracy. With roots in anarchist infoshops' principles of horizontalism, the store is owned collectively by its workers and has a nonhierarchical management structure. Decisions are made by consensus or by at least three-quarters of members present at collective meetings. Collective members are also affiliated with the long-standing Industrial Workers of the World union.[21]

Red Emma's has become an important incubator for local organizing and a vital meeting place for activists and politically engaged people in Baltimore. In the days after April 27, 2015, as Baltimore City Public Schools closed during the uprising following Freddie Gray's death in police custody, Red Emma's remained open and offered free food and a meeting space to students and protesters. Indeed, the collective welcomes all people into the store regardless of whether they make a purchase, as long as they are respectful of other people in the space and follow a few minimal rules. Red Emma's offers a near-constant series of free public talks and book events by progressive and radical speakers—more than 130 in 2016 alone.[22]

Meanwhile, several of Red Emma's owners work in key positions in regional and national organizations devoted to advancing economic democracy and shared ownership, including the Baltimore Roundtable for Economic Democracy (BRED) and the Democracy Collaborative in Washington, D.C. Both of these organizations promote and assist cooperatives and worker-owned companies, and BRED is developing plans for a national financial cooperative with The Working World, a New York-based organization that provides collateral-free, nonextractive financing to cooperatives and collectives.[23]

One local business that Red Emma's has collaborated with is Taharka Brothers, an ice cream company named after Taharka McCoy, a community mentor in East Baltimore who was shot and killed in 2002. In 2010, Taharka Brothers registered in Maryland as a benefit corporation, a legally recognized business entity that documents its benefits for workers and local communities through annual public reports. Founded by nonprofit manager Sean Smeeton and operated by a collective of young African American men, Taharka seeks, in its own words, "to promote peace, social and economic justice to communities both local and non-local."[24] In 2016, Taharka obtained a $15,000 loan that was jointly approved by The Working World and BRED, which is assisting the business to reincorporate as a worker-owned cooperative.[25]

Baltimore activist businesses' current collaborations with national organizations and with each other distinguish them from their predecessors. For years, individual activist enterprises in Baltimore operated in isolation both from their peers in their own city and in other parts of the country. Many activist businesses in Baltimore have restricted themselves to working within their individual movements. But this isolation has likely contributed to their short lifespans. Today, many movements are embracing an intersectional approach to social justice and organizing; one hopes that activist enterprises' increased willingness to collaborate around basic, shared goals of equality and inclusion can improve their odds of survival.

The history of activist businesses in Baltimore offers us a new way of understanding activism in our city. While Baltimore's movements may be best remembered for marches and mass meetings, local activists eagerly harnessed small businesses as a tool for community organizing and disseminating their ideologies. Indeed, activist enterprises nurtured local movements and challenged the widespread belief that the work of social justice and political dissent is by definition antithetical to all business activity. In the twenty-first century, activist enterprises' efforts to create public spaces where radical politics and organizing thrive may be what most distinguishes them from other businesses. Their products, be they radical literature or artisanal ice cream, can usually be had elsewhere. But in this era of the ever-shrinking public sphere, activist businesses like Red Emma's or Everyone's Place are among the few places in Baltimore where anyone and everyone are welcome, regardless of their economic status or ability to make a purchase.

Notes

1   Jo Ann Harris, "The Pratt Street Conspiracy Is a Boutique," *Baltimore Sun*, February 7, 1971; Clementine Flatbush, "S.W. Baltimore Conspiracy," *Harry*, January 8, 1971; "Pratt Street Conspiracy," *Harry*, April 24–May 7, 1971; Earl Arnett, "Anti-Poverty Funds: Community Action Agency Director Airs Views and Hopes," *Baltimore Sun*, January 26, 1972. On community activists in the War on Poverty, see Annelise Orleck, "'This Government Is with Us': Lyndon Johnson and the Grassroots War on Poverty," and Rhonda Y. Williams, "'To Challenge the Status Quo by Any Means': Community Action and Representational Politics in 1960s Baltimore," both in *The War on Poverty: A New Grassroots History, 1964–1980*,

ed. Annelise Orleck and Lisa Gayle Hazirjian (Athens: University of Georgia Press, 2011), 31–86.

2 Michael Kazin, *American Dreamers: How the Left Changed a Nation* (New York: Vintage Books, 2011), 5.

3 Michael Lamb and Benjamin Lundy, "Produce of Free Labor: Circular to the Farmers, Planters, Merchants, and Others, in the United States, and Elsewhere," *Genius of Universal Emancipation*, August 5, 1826; "Productions of Free Labor," *Genius of Universal Emancipation*, August 1830. On Lundy and free labor stores, see Julie L. Holcomb, *Moral Commerce: Quakers and the Transatlantic Boycott of the Slave Labor Economy* (Ithaca, NY: Cornell University Press, 2016), 75–76, 115, 145–146, 148–149.

4 *Minutes of the Proceedings of the Requited Labor Convention* (Philadelphia: Merrihew and Gunn, 1838), 3; Lawrence B. Glickman, "'Buy for the Sake of the Slave': Abolitionism and the Origins of American Consumer Activism," *American Quarterly* 56, no. 4 (2004): 894–895.

5 Philip S. Foner, *Organized Labor and the Black Worker, 1619–1973* (New York: Praeger, 1974), 21–46; Bettye C. Thomas, "A Nineteenth Century Black Operated Shipyard, 1866–1884: Reflections upon Its Inception," *Journal of Negro History* 59, no. 1 (January 1974): 1–12.

6 *Preamble of the Constitution of the Knights of Labor* (Philadelphia: Knights of Labor, 1885), 4; T. V. Powderly, *Thirty Years of Labor, 1859–1889* (Columbus, OH: Excelsior Printing House, 1889), 453.

7 Daniel R. Randall, *Cooperation in Maryland and the South*, ed. Herbert B. Adams (Baltimore: Publication Agency of the Johns Hopkins University, 1888), 494–501. On Knights of Labor cooperatives, see also Steve Leikin, *The Practical Utopians: American Workers and the Cooperative Movement in the Gilded Age* (Detroit: Wayne State University Press, 2005), 53–88.

8 Margaret Mary Finnegan, *Selling Suffrage: Consumer Culture & Votes for Women* (New York: Columbia University Press, 1999), 118–119; "The Suffrage Bazaar," *Maryland Suffrage News*, October 3, 1914; "Just Government League to Have Parcel-Post Sale," *Maryland Suffrage News*, January 9, 1915.

9 "P.R.R. May Lend More Houses to the City's Idle," *Baltimore Sun*, September 28, 1933.

10 "Baltimore People Shared Munsell's Million Dollars," *Baltimore Afro-American*, December 1, 1934; "Communist Plan Answer to Charges," *Baltimore Sun*, September 1, 1940; "A Great Book by a Great Thinker," *Baltimore Sun*, August 11, 1944. See also Federal Bureau of Investigation, "Alexander Orr Ector Munsell," November 20, 1943, Section 1, 79; "Louise Ellen Munsell," April 18, 1944, Section 1, 127; "Louis Ellen Munsell," November 25, 1943, Section 1, 106; "Alexander Orr Ector Munsell," April 27, 1944, 144; all from FBI files 65-461 and 100-1663, "Munsell, Alexander E. and Louise Ellen," FOIPA request by author.

11 Vernon L. Pedersen, *The Communist Party in Maryland, 1919–1957* (Urbana: University of Illinois Press, 2001), 173, 175, 181–182, 188–190, 192; "New Era Book Shop Is Stoned," *Baltimore Sun*, February 13, 1967.

12 Rudolph Lewis, "Walter Hall Lively," *ChickenBones: A Journal for Literary & Artistic African-American Themes*, http://www.nathanielturner.com/walterlively.htm.

13 Paul Coates, interview with author, digital recording, June 13, 2012; Ta-Nehisi Coates, *The Beautiful Struggle* (New York: Spiegel & Grau, 2009) and *Between the World and Me* (New York: Spiegel & Grau, 2015).

14 Louise Parker Kelley, *LGBT Baltimore* (Charleston, SC: Arcadia Publishing, 2015), 8, 17.

15 Casey Czarnik, interview with author, audio recording, May 12, 2015; Margaret Blanchard, "Speaking the Plural: The Example of *Women: A Journal of Liberation*," *NWSA Journal* 4, no. 1 (Spring 1992): 84–97; *The New Woman's Survival Catalog: A Woman-made Book* (New York: Coward, McCann & Geoghegan, 1973), 9.

16 *New Woman's Survival Catalog*, 9; Handwritten manuscript, "Est. Your Own Printshop," 1979, Box 13, Folder 10, Diana Press Records, 1970–1995, Collection 2135, UCLA Library Special Collections; Bill Hieronymus, "For Some Feminists, Owning a Business Is Real Liberation," *Wall Street Journal*, April 15, 1974.

17 Rita Mae Brown, *Songs to a Handsome Woman* (Baltimore: Diana Press, 1973); Coletta Reid and Kathy Tomyris, "Diana Press: An Overview," written March 9, 1979, 1, Atlanta Lesbian Feminist Alliance (ALFA) collection, Sally Bingham Center for Women's History & Culture, Duke University, Box 11, folder 24; *New Woman's Survival Catalog*, 9; Nancy Myron and Charlotte Bunch, eds., *Class and Feminism: A Collection of Essays on the Furies* (Baltimore: Diana Press, 1974); *Heterosexuality & the Women's Movement* (Baltimore: Diana Press, circa 1973).

18 "Diana Press," 1, circa 1978, ALFA collection, Bingham Center, Duke University, Box 11, folder 24; Mickey Friedman, "A Feminist Publishing House That Refused to Die," *San Francisco Chronicle,* February 26, 1978, Scene-4.

19 On infoshops, see Joel Olson, "The Problem with Infoshops and Insurrection: U.S. Anarchism, Movement Building, and the Racial Order," in *Contemporary Anarchist Studies: An Introductory Anthology of Anarchy in the Academy*, ed. Randall Amster, Abraham DeLeon, Luis Fernandez, Anthony J. Nocella II, and Deric Shannon (New York: Routledge, 2009), 35–45; and Chris Atton, "Infoshops in the Shadow of the State," in *Contesting Media Power: Alternative Media in a Networked World*, ed. Nick Couldry and James Curran (Lanham, Md.: Rowman & Littlefield, 2003), 57–69.

20 Deborah Johns Moir, "Out of Africa," *Baltimore Sun*, December 1, 1991; Jean Marbella, "Controversial Book Selling Big," *Baltimore Sun*, August 2, 1990.

21 Author's email with K Froom, May 4, 2017; "Bylaws," Red Emma's, https://github .com/johm/redemmas/blob/master/bylaws.md; "Thread Coffee," Red Emma's, https://redemmas.org/thread; "Our History," http://redemmas.org/about; Stephen Roblin, "Dovetail: An Interview with Kate Khatib from Red Emma's," *Indypendent Reader*, January 28, 2013, https://indyreader.org/content/dovetail -interview-kate-khatib-red-emmas. On horizontalism, see Marina Sitrin, "Horizontalism and the Occupy Movements," *Dissent* (Spring 2012): 74–75.

22 Judith Rosen, "Red Emma's Offers Free Lunch in Wake of B-More Riots," *Publishers Weekly*, April 28, 2015, http://www.publishersweekly.com/pw/by-topic /industry-news/bookselling/article/66432-red-emma-s-offers-free-lunch-in-wake -of-b-more-riots.html; "Events at Red Emma's," https://redemmas.org/events.

23 Oscar Perry Abello, "Closing the Funding Gap for Worker Cooperatives," *Next City*, https://nextcity.org/daily/entry/red-emmas-working-world-nyc-financial -cooperative; "Network," BRED: The Baltimore Roundtable for Economic Democracy, https://baltimoreroundtable.org/network/.

24 "Taharka Bros. Food for Thought," http://www.taharkabrothers.com.

25 "Taharka Brothers," BRED, https://baltimoreroundtable.org/taharka-brothers/; "Project with Taharka Brothers," The Working World, http://www .theworkingworld.org/us/loans/loans/1186.

10

"Welfare Isn't a Single Issue"

• • • • • • • • • • • • • • • • • • • •

Baltimore's Welfare Rights Movement, 1960s–1980s

AMY ZANONI

"We're fighting to stay alive because we don't have enough to live on," Margaret McCarty told Maryland legislators at a House of Delegates Ways and Means Committee budget meeting in 1969.[1] McCarty was then a mother of seven, a welfare recipient, and the chairwoman of Rescuers from Poverty, an East Baltimore-based welfare rights organization that she had cofounded three years earlier. She had traveled to the state capitol in Annapolis on that cold February day with representatives of several other welfare rights groups to testify against the governor's inadequate welfare budget. From the 1960s to the 1980s, thousands of Baltimore welfare recipients like McCarty joined together and sustained a vigorous and long-lasting welfare rights movement, as Rhonda Y. Williams, the leading scholar of Baltimore's tenant and welfare rights organizing, has shown.[2] Welfare recipients' struggle for dignity and benefits that would allow them to live safe, healthy lives reveals how they envisioned and advocated for an alternative to both budget cuts and the diversion of public monies into development projects.[3] By connecting their struggle to other issues, movements, and the larger political and economic context, welfare rights activists resisted the ever-more pervasive idea that poverty was a failure of personal responsibility.

Punitive and prejudiced policies have long plagued the welfare system in the United States. Historically, "welfare" has referred to Aid to Families with Dependent Children (AFDC), a program established in 1935 to provide assistance to single mothers and their families. From the outset, the means-tested program perpetuated and policed patriarchal ideas about female dependency and racialized notions about work. In the postwar era, as welfare rolls increased with more unmarried mothers, particularly more African American women, seeking aid, the "culture of poverty" discourse raged, and recipients faced heightened surveillance and rising work requirements intended to "rehabilitate" them. Though the War on Poverty injected federal funds into poverty programs around the United States, antiwelfare sentiment spurred policies that eroded such gains during the 1970s–1990s.[4]

In Baltimore, stigma and misinformation fueled the disinvestment from social services and amplified accusations of deceit during the late twentieth century. In 1973, for instance, the state of Maryland hired a "fraud squad" to investigate abuses. The following year, the state started requiring welfare recipients to carry photo IDs to cash welfare checks and created a team of "parent locators" to track down and fine, in the words of *The Sun*, "negligent fathers."[5] Recipients with disabilities and health issues faced particularly steep challenges. On some occasions, the welfare department prohibited recipients whose family members suffered from epilepsy and emphysema from owning telephones.[6] Between 1974 and 1982, taking inflation into account, Baltimore's investment in social services fell by 45 percent, a pattern of reduced spending that paralleled funding slashing at the state and federal levels.[7]

But an organizing fervor paralleled such developments. In Baltimore, like elsewhere in the nation, the War on Poverty's "maximum feasible participation" mandate created space for community involvement and fostered a sense of empowerment in impoverished communities, particularly among African Americans.[8] Recipients formed welfare groups at public housing complexes, building directly on the organizing work of the city's female public housing tenants, or in their neighborhoods. The city's first welfare rights organization, Rescuers from Poverty (RFP), was formed in 1965, a year before recipients and their advocates established the National Welfare Rights Organization (NWRO) to serve as an umbrella organization for local groups emerging across the country. In 1969, eleven local welfare rights groups united to form the Baltimore Welfare Rights Organization (BWRO), which boasted six thousand members by 1976. Most members were black women, though many white women were also involved. Black men participated as well; for example, Bob Cheeks, an East Baltimore-born professional football player turned social welfare worker and activist, who became a leading organizer in the late 1970s. The BWRO outlasted the NWRO and many other welfare groups around the country.[9]

Welfare recipients organized to speak for themselves. They claimed that they "better knew the problems of the disadvantage[d]" and that their intimate experiences with poverty made them welfare experts.[10] At a state welfare board meeting in August 1966, when RFP was just a few months old, McCarty testified that the state should train her to become a welfare worker. She and others like her who had navigated the welfare system were better equipped to identify—and fix—the system's shortcomings than state officials and employees who understood poverty only in academic or abstract terms.[11] Baltimore activists believed that poor people should lead their own movement; at the same time they did not shun alliances with radical activists; some social workers, community organizers, and lawyers employed by War on Poverty programs; and churches.[12]

Welfare rights activists sought to empower fellow recipients by demystifying welfare policies and application processes. Many campaigns focused on their demands on local, state, and federal governments, but activists also developed support systems to assist fellow recipients through the process of applying for and claiming benefits.[13] Welfare rights groups' members were posted inside and outside welfare offices to assist clients, recruiting new members in the process.[14]

Activists mobilized when, in the early 1970s, global financial instability and changing U.S. economic policy intensified struggles around health and nutrition.[15] At that time, the state legislature applied restrictions to food stamp sales and winnowed down special diet grants, allowances provided to those with conditions such as malnutrition or diabetes. Meanwhile, inflation was pushing up the cost of food and other basics. In response, activist recipients disrupted state budgetary meetings and called for "cost-of-living raises." In 1972, they invited then-governor Marvin Mandel to a "welfare breakfast" where they served dry toast, water, and coffee to demonstrate recipients' severe difficulties accessing healthy food on the meager incomes the welfare budget granted them.[16]

The Sherwood United Ladies, a welfare rights organization formed in 1970 on a single block in what is today the East Baltimore Midway neighborhood, complained of rodents and dilapidated houses that let in cold air, forcing them to use gas stoves for heat. They also protested the dangerous conditions created by vacant houses on their block. Welfare rights organizers regularly condemned the war in Vietnam and publicized their message that the government should "spend less money on war and much more money on domestic welfare programs" at rallies against the war and for guaranteed income.[17] "Welfare isn't a single issue," an RFP member declared in a 1972 interview published in the Baltimore-based feminist publication, *Women: A Journal of Liberation*.[18]

As deeper cuts jeopardized the funding on which low-income and especially African American Baltimoreans depended in the late 1970s and early 1980s, welfare activists also aligned themselves with labor movements, identifying with the working-class struggle regardless of employment status. One RFP member pointed to the degraded labor opportunities reserved for black women throughout American history as an explanation for welfare dependency: "We have always had the drudgery work—the jobs no one else wants to do. Because of this we get old very quickly and wind up on welfare." In 1980, the American Federation of State, County, and Municipal Employees (AFSCME) affiliated maintenance workers in Baltimore went on strike. Even though the action left thousands of public housing tenants without hot water, the BWRO supported the city workers. Conversely, as historian Jane Berger has argued, public sector workers played an integral role in defending welfare programs on which low-income residents depended.[19]

With investment in social services continuing to decrease in the 1980s, welfare rights activists experienced Baltimore's massive investment in the Inner Harbor as a cruel offense.[20] For the BWRO, garish tourist-driven urban development initiatives represented one strain of a flawed trickle-down theory of wealth distribution promoted at the municipal, state, and federal levels. The police arrested BWRO director Cheeks at the opening of Harborplace in July 1980, when he refused to move his protest across the street. Cheeks called the project "an obscenity," weighing the new aquarium's "fish that cost a thousand dollars each" against a proposed $1 billion federal cut to food stamps in 1981.[21] The city's skewed investments coincided with the state's implementation of ever more invasive application processes and barriers to social services and a punitive turn in enforcing restrictions.[22]

Over the course of the 1980s and 1990s, Reagan and his successors eviscerated welfare, placing the blame for poverty squarely on the individuals who experienced it. Cuts at the federal level were mirrored by the city's embrace of neoliberal policies, eliminating the safety net in Baltimore.[23] After a long struggle to secure funding and the death of key movement leaders, the BWRO ceased operating in the early 1990s.[24]

But Baltimore activists continued to organize. In the 1990s, Baltimoreans United in Leadership Development (BUILD), a self-described "community power organization," joined with AFSCME to conduct the first successful living wage campaign in the nation; the City Council passed the living wage ordinance in 1994. In recent years, the Right to Housing Alliance, an organization led by low-income activists that emerged from the Occupy movement, has fought evictions and the city's plans to privatize public housing. Founded by a group of homeless day laborers in 2002, the United Workers combine environmental justice, housing, and labor activism as part of their broader struggle for "Fair Development."[25] As the stigma of poverty and the conditions threatening the survival of the poor take on many forms, so does the activism demanding change.

Notes

1 Stephen Lynton, "Welfare Client Blames State Legislators for Juvenile Delinquency," *Baltimore Sun*, February 27, 1969.

2 Rhonda Y. Williams, "'We're Tired of Being Treated like Dogs': Poor Women and Power Politics in Black Baltimore," *The Black Scholar* 31, nos. 3–4 (2001): 31–41; *The Politics of Public Housing: Black Women's Struggles against Urban Inequality* (New York: Oxford University Press, 2004); "Nonviolence and Long Hot Summers: Black Women and Welfare Rights Struggles in the 1960s," *borderlands* 4, no. 3 (2005): 1–12; "Black Women, Urban Politics, and Engendering Black Power," in *The Black Power Movement: Rethinking the Civil Rights-Black Power Era*, ed. Peniel E. Joseph (New York: Routledge, 2006), 79–103; *Concrete Demands: The Search for Black Power in the 20th Century* (New York: Routledge, 2014).

3 On similar demands in the national movement as a form of black feminism, see Premilla Nadasen, *Welfare Warriors: The Welfare Rights Movement in the United States* (New York: Routledge, 2005).

4 Originally called Aid to Dependent Children, the name was changed to Aid to Families with Dependent Children in 1962. On means testing and "deserving" versus "undeserving" poor, see Michael B. Katz, *In the Shadow of the Poor House: A Social History of Welfare in America* (New York: Basic Books, 1986). On the gendered and racialized origins of ADC, see, for example, Linda Gordon, *Pitied but Not Entitled: Single Mothers and the History of Welfare 1890–1935* (Cambridge, MA: Harvard University Press, 1994). On the growth of work requirements, the increasingly rehabilitative aims of AFDC, and the "culture of poverty," see Jennifer Mittelstadt, *From Welfare to Workfare: The Unintended Consequences of Liberal Reform, 1945–1965* (Chapel Hill: University of North Carolina Press, 2005). On the punitive turn in welfare policy, see Julilly Kohler-Hausman, *Getting Tough: Welfare and Imprisonment in 1970s America* (Princeton, NJ: Princeton University Press, 2017). On the limits of the War on Poverty's emphasis on job training and education rather than universal benefits, see Premilla Nadasen, Jennifer Mittelstadt, and Marisa Chappell, *Welfare in the United States: A History with Documents* (New York: Routledge, 2009), 42. On parallel trends in public housing, see Williams, *The Politics of Public Housing*.

5 On the implementation of and resistance to IDs and other surveillance measures, see Mary L. Perry, letter to Mr. Bogier, February 17, 1970, Model Urban Neighborhood Demonstration Records (MUND), Series 2, Box 7, Folder 16, University of Baltimore Special Collections (UB SC), Baltimore, Maryland; Tracie Rozhon, "Relief Frauds Probed," *Baltimore Sun*, September 1, 1974, Envelope #1, Social Welfare, 1970–1979, Maryland Room Vertical File (MD VF), Enoch Pratt Free Library (EPFL), Baltimore, Maryland. On accusations of fraud and inefficiency, see Jerome W. Mondesire, "Welfare Overpayments Exceed 43% in Sample," *Baltimore Sun*, November 23, 1973, Envelope #1, Social Welfare, 1970–1979, MD VF, EPFL; Williams, "'We're Tired of Being Treated like Dogs,'" 33.

6 On being denied telephones, see Michael K. Burns, "Emotions Mixed on Caseworkers," *Baltimore Sun*, June 30, 1969; Mary L. Perry, letter to Mr. Bogier, December 18, 1969, MUND Records, Series 2, Box 11, Folder 1, UB SC.

7 Baltimore City lost more than $500 million in federal funds in its budget between 1982 and 1984. David Harvey, "A View from Federal Hill," in *The*

Baltimore Book: New Views of Local History, ed. Elizabeth Fee, Linda Shopes, and Linda Zeidman (Philadelphia: Temple University Press, 1993), 238. For other statistics on funding cuts, Jane Berger, "When Hard Work Doesn't Pay: Gender and the Origins of the Urban Crisis in Baltimore, 1945–1985" (PhD diss., Ohio State University, 2007), 326.

8   On the War on Poverty's effectiveness in improving material conditions for poor residents and creating jobs for black women in Baltimore, see Berger, "When Hard Work Doesn't Pay," ch. 3. On how the War on Poverty spurred civil rights activism for control over Baltimore's antipoverty programs, including welfare rights activists' struggle for recipient welfare board representation, see Berger, "When Hard Work Doesn't Pay," 96, 100–102, 152. On such activities as a form of Black Power activism, see, for example, Rhonda Y. Williams, "'To Challenge the Status Quo by Any Means:' Community Action and Representational Politics in 1960s Baltimore," in *The War on Poverty: A Grassroots History*, ed. Annelise Orleck and Lisa Gayle Hazirjian (Athens: University of Georgia Press, 2011), 75. On this broader trend, see Orleck and Hazirjian, *The War on Poverty*.

9   On public housing as "an organizational base," see Williams, *Politics of Public Housing*, 212. On the founding of RFP, sometimes called "Mother Rescuers from Poverty," see Williams, "'We're Tired of Being Treated like Dogs,'" 33, and *The Politics of Public Housing*, 203. On the BWRO, see Baltimore Welfare Rights Organization, "Who Are We," n.d., Folder 10, Box 1, Women's Union of Baltimore Collection, UB SC; DeWayne Wickham, "Welfare Rights Body Protests Dropping Aid to Employables," *Baltimore Sun*, February 11, 1976. On the Welfare Rights Coalition that preceded the BWRO, see "Welfare Sit-in Protests Delays: Mothers' All-Night Vigil Aimed at Miss Lazarus," *Baltimore Sun*, May 13, 1969; Williams, *Politics of Public Housing*, 217–218. On Bob Cheeks, see "Poor People's Advocate Taking Fight to the Streets," *Baltimore News-American*, December 17, 1978, Envelope #1, Social Welfare, 1970–1979, MD VF, EPFL; Williams, *Politics of Public Housing*, 221. On interracial organizing in Baltimore, see Nadasen, *Welfare Warriors*, 151. On critiques of male leadership, see Williams, "Black Women and Urban Politics," 99. On the long life of the BWRO, which outlasted the NWRO that was dismantled in 1975, see Nadasen, *Welfare Warriors*, 224–225.

10 Quote from Daniel Drosdoff, "Welfare Board Approves Budget: State Training Schools and Forestry Camps Are Due Sum of $," *Baltimore Sun*, August 20, 1966. See also Michael K. Burns, "Face of Welfare Revealed as Women Wait for Hodges," *Baltimore Sun*, March 9, 1969; Williams, *Politics of Public Housing*, 208.

11 Drosdoff, "Welfare Board Approves Budget"; Lee Lassiter, "'Income, Dignity, Democracy'–Part V Welfare: Reform or Revolt," *Baltimore News-American* (BNA), May 1, 1969, Envelope III, Social Welfare, MD VF, EPFL.

12 On welfare rights' organizers' insistence that the poor represent themselves, see Eboni Alexander, "Tent City Focuses on the Poor," *Baltimore Afro-American*, July 5, 1980. On RFP's cooperation with the militant antipoverty organization Union for Jobs or Income Now, see "U.J.O.I.N. Brings Rats to Landlord," August 2, 1966; Daniel Drosdoff, "Welfare Clients 'Forced' to Cheat, U.J.O.I.N. Says," *Baltimore Sun*, March 11, 1967; Williams, "'We're Tired of Being Treated like Dogs,'" 32–33; Williams, *Politics of Public Housing*, 201. On ties to women's liberation activism, see "Women's Rally Scheduled," *Baltimore Sun*, August 7, 1970; Michele LeFaivre, "Women's Day," *HARRY* 1, no. 21 (August 31, 1970): 10. On Margaret McCarty's involvement with the Red Wagon feminist day care

center, see David Michael Ettlin, "Child Center Looks at Homeless Future," *Baltimore Sun*, January 18, 1982. On welfare rights organizing as a form of militant Black Power politics, see Williams, "'We're Tired of Being Treated like Dogs,'" and "Black Women and Urban Politics." On public sector employees including welfare workers being "some of Baltimore's most vigorous defenders of the welfare state," see Berger, "When Hard Work Doesn't Pay," 121. For more on social workers' support, see, Fred Barbash, "Welfare Workers Tackle a System That Failed Them," *Baltimore Sun,* August 15, 1971; "Many Children from City Expected at Welfare Protest," *Baltimore Sun*, March 22, 1972; Williams, *Politics of Public Housing*, 204–205. On working with legal advocates, see Mary L. Perry, letter to Mr. Bogier, March 24, 1970, MUND Records, Folder 16, Box 7, Series 2, UB SC; Mary L. Petty, letter to Mr. Bogier, April 3, 1970, MUND Records, Folder 16, Box 7, Series 2, UB SC. On churches funding and donating space to groups, see "Nine Groups Granted $82,000 by Archdiocese," *Baltimore Afro-American*, August 3, 1968; "U.S. Welfare Plan Scored: Head of Recipients' League Condemns Nixon Reform," *Baltimore Sun*, September 10, 1969; "Welfare Rights Group Gets $30,000 Grant," *Baltimore Sun*, September 21, 1974.

13 Activists sought to "untangle the mess of federal, state, and local welfare regulations," in Fred Barbash, "Welfare Group Sees Progress," *Baltimore Sun*, February 15, 1971. On activist critiques of revenue sharing, see "Mitchell Scores Nixon Plans," *Baltimore Sun*, February 15, 1971; Henry Scarupa, "Cheeks to Poor: You Can Fight City Hall," *Baltimore Sun*, September 13, 1981. On demystifying the application process, see Lassiter, "'Income, Dignity, Democracy'"; Williams, *Politics of Public Housing*, 219.

14 On the actions taken to access space inside the Department of Social Services, see "Welfare Sit-In Protests Delays;" Williams, "'We're Sick and Tired of Being Treated like Dogs,'" 34; Williams, "Nonviolence and Long Hot Summers." On activists positioning themselves near the Welfare Department, see, for instance, "'I Feel Very Bitter': Jackie Raps," *Peace and Freedom News* 1, no. 7 (June 6, 1968): 4; Mary Perry, letter to Richard Byrd, May 5, 1970, MUND Records, Folder 16, Box 7, Series 2, UB SC; Williams, *Politics of Public Housing*, 200.

15 On President Nixon's embrace of New Federalism, which undermined municipal control of poverty programs and reduced spending, as well as Mayor Schaefer's fiscal conservatism, see Berger, "When Hard Work Doesn't Pay," ch. 5. On the larger political economic context, including the embrace of less generous social spending and the shift from Keynesian economic policy to an emphasis on economic revitalization at the federal level, see Berger, "When Hard Work Doesn't Pay," ch. 6; and "'There Is Tragedy on Both Sides of the Layoffs:' Privatization and the Urban Crisis in Baltimore," *International Labor and Working-Class History* 81 (Spring 2007): 29–49.

16 On special diet grants, see Maryland State Department of Social Services, *Helping People Help Themselves* (Annapolis: Maryland Department of Social Services, 1968). On the successful protests in opposition to cuts to special diet grants, see Stephen J. Lynton, "Cut in Special-Diet Budget for State's Poor under Fire," *Baltimore Sun*, March 22, 1970; "Welfare Recipients Call upon Mandel and Solomon," *Baltimore Sun*, July 1, 1970. On cost-of-living raises, see Jerome W. Mondesire, "Welfare Mothers Ask Grant Increase," *Baltimore Sun*, June 26, 1973. On the "welfare breakfast," see "Mandel Misses 'Welfare Meal,'" *Baltimore Sun*, April 6, 1971. On a similar action in 1966, see Berger, "When Hard Work Doesn't

Pay," 166. On "live-on-a-welfare budget campaigns" in other locales, see Nadasen, *Welfare Warriors*, 117–119.

17 Sherwood United Ladies formed when Mary Perry, MUND employee, found several women who were interested in organizing. For details on the first meeting, see Mary L. Perry, letter to Mr. Bogier, February 20, 1970, MUND Records, Folder 16, Box 7, Series 2, UB SC. On Sherwood United Ladies' efforts to improve conditions, see Mary Perry, letter to Richard Byrd; Megan Shook, "Sherwood United Ladies Present Petition to HCD," *MUND Newsletter* 4, no. 2 (May 27, 1970): 18, 20, MUND Records, Folder 23, Box 24, Series 2, UB SC. Recipients around the city routinely voiced similar complaints. See C. Fraser Smith, "B.G.&E. Proposes Cut-Off Halt," *Baltimore Sun*, February 15, 1978; Amy Goldstein, "Judge Tells 8 Tenants to Halt Rent Strike," *Baltimore Sun*, January 7, 1984; Williams, *Politics of Public Housing*, 222–227. On antiwar protests, see "'I Feel Very Bitter,'" 5; "Anti-War Rally on Tax Day," *Baltimore Sun*, April 19, 1970; Williams, *Politics of Public Housing*, 216–217. Quote from Megan Shook, "Welfare Mothers Join National Sit In at HEW," *MUND Newsletter* 4. no. 2 (May 27, 1970): 5. On that protest, see "Welfare Protesters Arrested after a Sit-In," *New York Times,* May 14, 1970.

18 Wildcat, "It Ain't Easy," *Women: A Journal of Liberation* 2, no. 2 (Winter 1971): 2.

19 Quote from Wildcat, "It Ain't Easy," 2. For more on the connections between race, arduous labor, and welfare, see Annelise Orleck, *Storming Caesars Palace: How Black Mothers Fought Their Own War on Poverty* (Boston: Beacon Press, 2005), 74–75. On the BWRO's support for AFSCME see Helen Winternitz, "15,000 Lack Hot Water as City Workers Strike," *Baltimore Sun*, July 2, 1980. Public sector jobs, most of which were held by African American women, had grown as a result of the War on Poverty in Baltimore, but were later cut when Mayor Schaefer embraced austerity and when Presidents Carter and Reagan implemented deeper cuts. See Berger, "When Hard Work Doesn't Pay"; "'There Is Tragedy on Both Sides of the Layoffs.'"

20 The city paid 90 percent of the costs of developing the Inner Harbor, even though private entities managed the project. For a full account of the changes downtown and, in particular, the development projects that promised to bring jobs but instead benefited "corporate and finance capital," see Harvey, "A View from Federal Hill." On the history of these economic developments in Baltimore, see Berger, "When Hard Work Doesn't Pay," ch. 6.

21 Cheeks was protesting Mayor Schaefer's lack of concern for the poor, specifically referencing the public housing hot water shutoffs caused by the maintenance workers' strike. John Schidlovsky, "Today, Harbor Place and City Are One," *Baltimore Sun*, July 2, 1980; John Schidlovsky, "100,000 Flock to the Opening of Harborplace," *Baltimore Sun*, July 3, 1980; quote from Tom Nugent, "A City Arrives in the 'Bigtime!'" *Baltimore Sun*, July 10, 1981; Berger, "When Hard Work Doesn't Pay," 264.

22 On the punitive turn, which included the arrest of a recipient accused of fraud in 1984, see Eileen Canzian, "School Lunch Cutbacks Criticized: Financial Savings Said to Be Offset by Social Costs," *Baltimore Sun*, January 25, 1982; Eileen Canzian, "Rules Tightened for Welfare Clients: Proof of Family Size Required," *Baltimore Sun*, May 23, 1982; Amy Goldstein, "Jackson Host Here Arrested over Fraud Charge," *Baltimore Sun*, August 21, 1984; Eileen Canzian, "Welfare Tie to Schools Considered: Panel Ponders Aid Cuts in Fighting Absenteeism," *Baltimore*

Sun, May 5, 1986. On the larger punitive turn in welfare policy, see Kohler-Hausmann, *Getting Tough*, part II.

23 Three of the most harmful blows to AFDC were Reagan's 1981 Omnibus Reconciliation Act and the 1988 Family Support Act, and Clinton's 1996 Personal Responsibility and Work Opportunity Act. Mittelstadt, *From Welfare to Workfare*, 169, 170–171. On Reagan's impact on welfare in Baltimore, see Berger, "When Hard Work Doesn't Pay," 325.

24 On struggles with funding, see Helen Winternitz, "Welfare Group Alleges Harassment," *Baltimore Sun*, February 10, 1970; "Stricken by Fiscal Paralysis, City's Welfare Rights Organization Is in Trouble," *Baltimore Sun*, September 1, 1974; Eileen Canzian, "Cuts, Rising Needs Shift Aid Groups' Focus to Funding," *Baltimore Sun*, November 21, 1982. On Cheeks's death and the closing of the BWRO office, see Michael Ollove, "Poor People's Advocate Bobby Cheeks Dies at 48," *Baltimore Sun*, September 16, 1988; Dennis O'Brien, "Maryland Welfare Rights Group Could Close: Agency Threatened by Funding Shortage," *Baltimore Sun*, October 4, 1989.

25 On the Baltimore living wage campaign, see Stephanie Luce, *Fighting for a Living Wage* (Ithaca, NY: Cornell University Press, 2004), 117. For more on BUILD, see their website, http://www.buildiaf.org/. For more on the Right to Housing Alliance, see their website, http://rthabaltimore.org/. For more on the United Workers, see their website, http://www.unitedworkers.org/.

11

The Last Censors

• •

The Life and Slow Death
of Maryland's Board of Motion
Picture Censors, 1916–1981

JOE TROPEA

The act of censoring or the outright banning of films arose soon after the art
form appeared in the 1880s, long before film was ever legally regarded as art.[1]
Baltimore was once home to the longest-running film censor board in the
nation, the Maryland State Board of Motion Picture Censors. Created by the
state legislature in 1916, it was tasked with approving, altering, or banning
feature-length films, short films, newsreels, cartoons, and film advertisements.
The entity commonly referred to as the Maryland Censor Board lasted sixty-
five years. It survived countless attempts by state legislators who sought to shut
it down until it finally succumbed to indifference in 1981. It may seem surprising today that state-sanctioned censors once judged film content based on criteria such as race, sex, religion, politics, and violence in a place, ironically known
in this light, as the Free State. Less surprising perhaps is that evidence shows
that the board did not equally protect all citizens, especially in regard to race
and gender. Examination of records left behind by the censor board, legal cases,
and statements made by censors, politicians, exhibitors, and film producers
shows that the ideological work performed by state censors shaped the sense
of who belongs in Baltimore City and in the state of Maryland. This chapter

does not argue that every call for censorship was unwarranted, but rather that censorship as practiced by the state of Maryland was discriminatory and antithetical to freedom.

From the inception of the Maryland Censor Board, responses to the censoring of movies were not unanimously positive. Along with attacks from the Maryland General Assembly, the board also withstood hundreds of legal challenges in the court system. Local theater owners, distributors, and eventually filmmakers and producers resisted the censors. They not only subverted the state's archaic censorship laws in minor ways but also took extralegal actions that eventually landed before the Supreme Court, had a profound effect on how state censorship was practiced, and even contributed to the closing of censor boards in other states.

The story of movie censorship in America is long, complicated, and messy. It is a story of inequality, trampled rights, litigation, witless arguments, and pyrrhic victories. The first movie censorship laws were passed in cities: Chicago in 1907 and New York City in 1908. In 1911 Pennsylvania became the first state to have its own censor board. Within five years, Ohio, Kansas, and Maryland followed suit. After years of debate, in 1916 state legislators created the Maryland State Board of Motion Picture Censors. In the first report to Governor Emerson Harrington, Chairman Charles Harper explained his mission as protector of the moral welfare of the community, especially that of its lesser educated members: "Your board has made every effort to foster the real educational and artistic ventures of the motion picture producers, while all that is lewd, vulgar, and immoral has been discouraged and . . . prohibited. We believe our work in this regard has met the approval of the best elements of the people."[2] This mission received legal support from a unanimous Supreme Court in its 1915 decision, *Mutual Film Corp. v. Industrial Commission of Ohio*, in which Justice McKenna wrote that films "are mere representations of events, of ideas and sentiments published and known; vivid, useful, and entertaining, no doubt, but, as we have said, capable of evil, having power for it, the greater because of their attractiveness and manner of exhibition."[3]

Reformers of the Progressive era had good reason to scrutinize the rapidly growing film industry. Storefront nickelodeons and makeshift theaters were often poorly ventilated, shabbily constructed fire traps waiting for a nitrate film accident to happen. People dropped food and spit on the floor. Theaters filled up with patrons suffering from any number of communicable diseases. Men sat next to women, middle-class people next to the poor. It was the stuff of Victorian nightmares. However, concern for public physical health and safety was quickly subsumed by concern for the public's mental health. Censors judged moving images through a paternalistic lens of Victorian morality. Movies were generally regarded as a medium aimed at the lower classes, and films judged to convey a harmful moral standpoint had to be weeded out.

In the late Victorian era, depictions of relations between men and women, blacks and whites, and citizens and law enforcement in film caused Progressive white reformers much apprehension and anxiety. Organizations such as the Women's Christian Temperance Union, the General Federation of Women's Clubs, and later the Catholic Legion of Decency made film censorship their cause.[4] In Baltimore before the censor board was created, the censoring of films was a police matter. The common practice in 1908 was for a police sergeant to watch each new movie in the theaters of his district and report his findings to headquarters.[5] When this method was criticized harshly in the press, Marshall Thomas Farnan acted to make all citizens of the city censors. Adding extra telephone operators, Farnan's policy became if you see something, say something—by calling the police.

Midway through the 1910s, Marylanders were still not fully convinced their state needed to intervene in movie exhibition. In May 1912, a censorship bill calling for a five-member board failed to clear the state legislature. But a series of Supreme Court decisions in 1915 provided the legal groundwork for film censorship boards. The Mutual Film Corporation had sued the Industrial Commission of Ohio when it set up a censor board in 1913, claiming that the board interfered with its right to interstate commerce and free speech. Other Mutual Film cases followed in Illinois, Kansas, and Pennsylvania. Finally, in the *Mutual Film* case, the Supreme Court unanimously decided against the company, ruling that movies were a business with a "special capacity for evil." As such, film producers and distributors had no right to free speech.[6] This case set the legal basis for Maryland to form its own board in 1916. In the early days of state and city censorship, exhibitors and distributors had no redress against a censor board.[7]

The Maryland State Board of Motion Picture Censors went into operation on June 1, 1916. Board members were paid a yearly salary of $2,400.[8] They charged $2 per reel examined and were authorized to levy fines ranging from $5 to $100 for various offenses committed by theater operators.[9] The three-member panel of censors comprised a chairman, vice chair, and secretary who were appointed by the governor in a process known as green bag appointments—a ceremony in which preapproved names are literally pulled from a green bag by Maryland's governor and then sent to the State Senate for approval. This practice is still in use today. The board members served at the pleasure of the governor for four-year terms, and the board was bipartisan, with two seats going to members of the governor's party and one going to a member of the opposition. The appointments were usually given to party members to whom the governor owed a favor, often mayors of cities from around the state or wives of political operatives. No other qualifications, not even a high school education, were necessary. According to film historian Robert Headley, the prevailing thought was that women made better censors than men.[10] This view persisted presumably because, as mothers, women were viewed as natural protectors of children. While the total numbers of men and women on the board do not exactly bear out Headley's theory, there was always at least one woman member of the censor board, there were often two women board members, and during the late 1960s, the board was helmed by three women.

Women's reform groups almost immediately criticized the censorship board as inadequate. The board came under attack in its first year when concerned citizens voiced their displeasure with the censors' work. A mere six months in, members of the Daughters of the American Revolution, Mothers' Congress, and the Child Welfare League appeared before the board to complain that immoral movies were still being screened.[11] The following July a group led by Miss Grace Turnbull, a prominent local sculptor and painter, petitioned to have Chairman Charles Harper not reappointed as chair for the next year (see Figure 7). Turnbull and her cosigners disapproved of Harper for having too high a threshold for indecency. She felt that all films passed by the censors should be suitable for children. A minor scandal emerged when it was discovered that John Stone, the brother of board vice chairman William Stone, had added his name to the petition. According to the *Sun*, William Stone "was 'joshed' pretty thoroughly at night by his friends. . . . He took the 'joshing' very good-naturedly."[12] However, Stone was replaced the following year by a new vice chair, Clarendon Gould.

FIG. 7 Grace Turnbull carving a sculpture. Photo by A. Aubrey Bodine, November 1952. Courtesy of the Maryland Historical Society.

One of the most controversial films of all time, D. W. Griffith's *Birth of a Nation*, opened at Ford's Theatre in Baltimore in March 1916.[13] A hugely popular piece of racist historical revision, it glorified the rise of the Ku Klux Klan, depicted African Americans in the most negative light, and was largely responsible for the second rise of the KKK.[14] Griffith's film was cheered by white audiences in Baltimore and around the nation for its racist vitriol. Upton Sinclair called Griffith's photoplay, based on the work of Thomas Dixon Jr., "the most absolute terrifying and poisonous play" and predicted that screenings would result in "a hundred thousand murders."[15] *Birth* just missed the scrutinizing scissors of Maryland's censors, which began operating on June 1, 1916, roughly three months after it opened. However, when the film returned to Ford's the following year, the censor board failed to intervene, despite pleas from the *Afro-American* paper and the black community. Nor did it act in the years surrounding the Red Summer of 1919, when hundreds of African Americans were killed by crazed white mobs. In the following decades revival screenings of the film would pop up regularly and occasionally be challenged, but the censors still took no action: when the board might have intervened and actually protected people—African Americans—from the very real danger of white violence inspired by Griffith's film, it failed to do so.[16] It was not until 1952 when State Police superintendent Elmer Munshower and Baltimore City Police commissioner Beverly Ober viewed the film with board members that the board finally determined that it "was morally bad and crime-inciting."[17]

In its first decade, from 1916 to 1926, the Maryland censor board examined on average 5,258 films per year, including features, newsreels, cartoons, and short films. Of those films, the board rejected on average twenty-two films in their entirety per year, with the most rejections coming from the beleaguered administration of Chairman Harper. Dr. George Heller, the second chair of the board, oversaw the most films rejected in a single year—fifty-seven in 1921—although in the later years of that decade, rejections per year dropped to the single digits.

In its second decade, from 1926 to 1936, the number of films reviewed annually by the board nearly doubled to over 10,000 films viewed per year. This was due to the dramatically increased production of movies, fueled by the advent of sound films in 1927. From 1926 to 1962, the number of films rejected per year always remained in the single digits. But in the period spanning the board's first two decades, the board censored anywhere between 200 and nearly 1,200 films per year by demanding alterations.[18]

By the 1930s and 1940s, censors expressed increasing anxiety over foreign films. This was perhaps best exemplified in the romantic drama *Ecstasy* (1933), a Czech film that made Hedy Lamarr a sensation and also earned condemnation by an unsettling trifecta: the pope, the Nazis, and U.S. censors. The film dared to portray taboos including adultery, intercourse, the female orgasm—the latter

two feats accomplished never showing more than Lamarr's expressive face—
and scenes of the actress swimming and running through the woods naked. It
was not as if artful nudity had not been accepted by American censors in the
past. Audrey Munson, the famous art model who took on roles portraying an
artist's model and was known as the "Venus of America," had appeared nude
in 1915's *Inspiration* and 1916's *Purity* without scandal, but when foreign filmmakers attempted similar scenarios in a context not deemed high art, such as
painting or sculpture, censors' hackles were raised. Foreign filmmakers earned
this scorn by not signing on to Hollywood's 1930 production code. Thus they
often suffered more scrutiny from American censors.

Even as the buildup to war limited European film studios' output, anxiety
about foreign films grew. The tension is apparent in the annual reports the board
made to the governor. In 1939, Germany's powerful UFA production company
submitted seventy-two films to the Maryland market, while Poland offered
thirty-six—six of them Yiddish-language films. Britain, a U.S. ally, offered only
eleven films. The annual report of 1939 was the first time Maryland's censors
began listing films' countries of origin, in response to European filmmakers
bypassing the production code.[19] Presumably because censor board members
did not trust the subtitles, they even sought help in understanding foreign films
from willing community members, often priests and ministers, who spoke foreign languages and translated idioms and explained foreign customs.

After World War II, Cold War and racial tensions were at a peak, and the
censor board reacted by banning films on political as well as moral grounds.
Sydney R. Traub was a censor who brazenly banned or held up films for their
political views. An attorney and former Fourth District City Council member who had served in both world wars, Traub headed the censor board from
1949–1954. He is remembered as a zealous enforcer of morality, but quickly
became a favorite target of the *Sun* papers, which had by the 1950s long grown
weary of the state's censor board.

Many of Traub's rulings were challenged and overturned in court. In 1949,
the board, following the lead of its own Polish Committee, banned the documentary *On Polish Lands* (1949) as communist propaganda. Traub and his colleagues spent an entire page of the 1949 annual report denying that they
banned the film for political reasons: "Our action was in nowise 'a political censorship,' as has been claimed, but was based upon the premise that the picture
was found to be untrue. . . . Certainly the screen is no place for subjects presented without truth and sincerity."[20] The contradiction in Traub's statement
makes his message clear: communists and those with unconventional political
views belonged neither in Maryland nor its theaters.

The following year Chairman Traub was embroiled in more political censorship as the board attempted to ban a film that had been passed by the censors twenty years earlier. An ad for the Hiway Theater in Essex, operated by

Robert Marhenke, touted a revival run of the Academy Award-winning *All Quiet on the Western Front* (1930). The ad claimed that the film was one that "Maryland's Film Censor Failed to Ban."[21] An exchange of letters to the editor in the *Sun* revealed how Chairman Sydney Traub had tried to have the acclaimed war film banned. Traub told the *Sun* reporter Ray Martin that he could not find any statutory grounds to ban the film and so asked the War Department to do it. When they responded that the request was "silly," the board attempted to hold the film up under the pretense that a script had not been submitted with the application. Traub protested the accusation that he had sought to ban the film, countering that he merely "suggested 'deferring' the showing 'until the Korean War crisis had ceased to exist,'" because the film was "unpatriotic" and contained "horrifying views."[22]

By the late 1940s, film producers had earned the right to respond to censors' objections to their work, unless their film was rejected "in toto." But they did not have to respond: they could simply pull their movies from a region. *The Well* (1951) had two Academy Award nominations, but it never screened in Maryland because the producer would not agree to the fifteen deletions called for by state censors. This film, which portrayed an outbreak of racial violence in a small town that occurs after a white man allegedly abducts a black child, was regarded as an honest portrayal of black life in America. Yet it hit too many raw nerves in the Free State. Six of the reported cuts were for the use of the word "nigger." Other cuts included various scenes of white people and black people enacting violence on one another. The Urban League and NAACP called for the elimination of the racial epithets, invoking racial discrimination as grounds for editing the film, in contrast to the board's tendency to cite general immorality in the films it censored. Police officials, who actually called for more cuts than the board demanded, called for the elimination of the mob violence scenes.

By mid-century, in response to competition within the industry and the growing television audience, filmmakers were pushing the limits of decency and morality to keep viewers' attention (see Figure 8). Two court decisions loomed large in the 1950s. In 1952 the Supreme Court dealt censor boards a blow. *Joseph Burstyn Inc. v. Wilson* (1952), a case involving Roberto Rossellini's 1948 short "The Miracle," held that a New York law allowing censors to ban a film for sacrilege was a violation of the First Amendment. By finally recognizing film as an art worthy of protection, the High Court dealt the 1915 *Mutual* decision a massive blow, and many states such as Ohio (in 1954), Massachusetts (in 1955), and Pennsylvania (in 1956) abolished their boards. However, Maryland was not yet prepared to do so.

Then in 1957 *Roth v. United States*, a Supreme Court case involving erotic literature and photos sent by mail, forced film censors to clarify the definition of obscenity. The decision established the Roth-Albert test, which determined that materials—and by extension films—could be deemed obscene if they met

FIG. 8 Maryland State Board of Motion Picture Censors at work. Photo by A. Aubrey Bodine, circa 1967. Courtesy of the Maryland Historical Society.

the following criteria: the dominant theme, as a whole, appeals to a prurient interest in sex; the work is patently offensive because it affronts contemporary community standards in its representation of sex; or the work is utterly without redeeming social value. After *Roth,* censors had to work a lot harder to justify their actions.

The 1960s were the start of a period in which the Maryland censor board had an increasing public profile but declining influence: as it gained more visibility, it consistently lost court decisions. In 1960 Governor Millard Tawes, a Democrat, appointed an Italian American widow named Mary Avara from Southwest Baltimore as secretary to the board. She would stay on as secretary for twenty-one years, until the bitter end. Avara was a devout Catholic, bail bondswoman, and politically connected Democratic ward heeler. She became a national sensation in the 1970s when she began making appearances on TV talk shows such as the *Tonight Show*, *Dick Cavett Show*, and the *Mike Douglas Show*. For better or worse, she raised the profile of Maryland's censor board to a national level.

Many began to notice how ineffectual the censor board had become; some began to see it as a joke. Director and lifelong film enthusiast John Waters recalls that audiences would regularly hiss and boo when the censor's seal appeared on the screen before a film.[23] By 1967 the Maryland Court of Appeals had overturned all but one of the board's film bans for the past twenty years, according to the *Sun*.[24] Though attempts to abolish the board began as early as 1933, attacks became more regular by the 1960s.[25] A state senator or representative took up the cause every year, and often the bills they sponsored came very close to passage. In 1968 Republican governor Spiro Agnew went as far as to leave the censors out of his budget because he was so convinced it would be shut down by the General Assembly.

However, the 1960s also saw the birth of a new defense strategy employed by the censor board: to prove the necessity of its work, it would host annual screenings of risqué features and stag films in Annapolis. In 1963 board members showed the nudist camp "sexer"—censor terminology for a dirty movie— *Career Girls on a Naked Holiday* to the General Assembly. According to the *Sun* the screenings were very well attended. This tactic was an even more effective weapon when the board was facing scrutiny in Annapolis. The threat of pointing elected officials out as being in favor of immoral films gave the censors some leverage in those years. Despite whatever backroom deals had been struck, state legislators consistently buckled to the pressure and voted to fund the censors for another year. In addition to attacks from state legislators, there were also grassroots efforts. Board members also hosted screenings for members of the Kiwanis Club.

Around the same time, theater owners and operators were bringing serious challenges to the censor board. Robert Marhenke operated theaters in the Baltimore area from the 1940s through the 1960s and also had a film distribution company, Cinema Film Exchange. He developed a reputation as the censor board's gadfly. He was a regular writer of letters to the editor at the *Sun* in which he would condemn the board and had a cartoon that lampooned the state censors published by the *Catonsville Times*.[26] In 1961 he, along with other like-minded theater runners Ronald Freedman and William Hewitt, formed a censorship committee within the Maryland Theater Owners Association. They convened in Ocean City and made plans to demand an investigation of the censor board on the grounds that the board did not actually watch many films in a week and so its members were drawing salaries for doing very little work. Additionally they criticized the board's practice of double and triple censoring of old films as a waste of time and taxpayer money.[27]

Marhenke and Freedman were also known for engaging in acts of resistance such as regularly reinserting censor-eliminated scenes back into films before screenings. Freedman was said to have occasionally inserted his own frames with messages that read, "This scene banned by Maryland board of censors," in the place of cut scenes in movies.[28] The censor board therefore employed inspectors to make sure such tricks did not occur. They visited theaters to check running times of films to make sure they matched their records and checked for unbroken seals on the film canisters. But there were only so many inspectors and too many theaters and films to check. These defiant acts served equally the purposes of thwarting the board, pleasing audiences by showing all of what they paid to see, and occasionally educating the movie-going public on how their tax dollars were being spent.

Ronald L. Freedman had been a movie lover since his childhood. By the 1950s his love of film landed him jobs managing movie theaters. He cofounded the Baltimore Film Society with Bill Hewitt and other cineastes. This was a club of like-minded film enthusiasts that started out "four-walling" or renting screens from movie theaters on off-nights to show foreign and unusual films. Initially the society was a clever means for this group to get around the censors.

In 1961 Freedman was ready to run his own theater. He opened the Rex in North Baltimore, intending to show classic and art-house films. This was a proposition at a time and place that was unlikely to make anyone rich. After noticing the success in neighboring Washington, D.C., of Russ Meyer's *Immoral Mr. Teas* (1959), Freedman realized the way to put more bodies in seats was to mix in films by "the King of the nudies" Meyer.[29] Naturally this put him at odds with the censor board. But if Maryland's censors thought Freedman would be content to throw light jabs like Robert Marhenke was accustomed to doing, they were sadly mistaken. What followed was an act of cinematic civil disobedience that would not only land at the Supreme Court but would also end film censorship in many states.

On November 1, 1962, Freedman phoned the censor board to inform them that he planned to show a film without their seal.[30] He picked the innocuous *Revenge at Daybreak*, a 1952 French drama set during the Irish revolution. By all accounts it would have easily passed through Maryland's board unchallenged. The next day Freedman screened the film and was, as planned, arrested—along with his partner Hewitt. The pair were tried in Baltimore Circuit Court and fined $25. They appealed the ruling, which was upheld by the Maryland Court of Appeals on February 10, 1964.

Freedman and his backers, a group that included his partners from the Baltimore Film Society as well as the Times Film Corporation, a New York–based distributor that specialized in importing European films, hoped their case would find its way to the Supreme Court and that a ruling in their favor would put teeth behind the 1952 *Burstyn* ruling by placing a heavier burden of proof on censors to pronounce a film "too dangerous to be seen."[31] The following year they got their wish and managed to do what *Burstyn* and other anticensorship cases had failed to accomplish: *Ronald L. Freedman v. Maryland State Board of Motion Picture Censors* brought all movie censorship in the nation to a halt. Justice Brennan delivered a unanimous decision that essentially ended government-operated censorship boards, ruling that a rating board could only approve a film, but had no power to ban a film. The power to ban movies rested with the courts. Further the ruling concluded that a censor board must either approve a film within five days or go to court to stop a film from being exhibited. This was a huge victory in that it shifted more of the burden of proof from the exhibitor onto the state censor board.

Maryland's attorney general Thomas J. Finan called the case "the armageddon of censorship," and in some ways it was.[32] By 1965 only four state censor boards were still functioning: Kansas, Maryland, New York, and Virginia. The *Freedman* ruling caused New York's and Maryland's boards to temporarily cease operations. A hopeful Robert Marhenke telegrammed the censor board to inform them, "The unemployment office is just two blocks away. You may join it."[33] The Kansas and Virginia boards closed permanently in 1966.

Amazingly, Maryland's General Assembly needed just three days to pass a new law to comply with the Supreme Court's ruling: such was the dedication of Finan and Maryland's pro-censorship faction. After that, the board would have thirteen days to render a decision and have it cleared through the Circuit Court of Baltimore City or it would forfeit a seal to the exhibitor.[34] Despite this victory—a pyrrhic victory according to Freedman's son—the ruling did not really help Ronald Freedman. Although the decision freed states and exhibitors across the nation of the burden of lengthy bureaucratic censorship, Maryland's censors continued to prevent him from showing the movies he wanted to screen. The Baltimore Film Society was bankrupted, and keeping the Rex afloat was more than he could financially bear. Freedman had the satisfaction of a place in the history books, but was not able to turn a profit doing what he loved.[35]

The 1960s ended with a battle over a Swedish film and the appearance of a new form of internal film industry censorship. *I Am Curious (Yellow)* (1967) was a harbinger of pornographic films to come. Given what today seems to have been a relatively mild progression of the expression of sexuality in cinema over the decades, the Maryland censor board had no way of anticipating what the hard-core filmmakers of 1970s were about to unleash. *I Am Curious (Yellow)*, a Swedish drama with some elements of documentary and mild sex scenes thrown in, bothered censors greatly. It failed to pass Maryland's censors the first time it was submitted in 1969 because of seventeen objectionable scenes of a sexual nature, and the case headed to court.[36] In fact. all Marylanders had to do to see the film was drive to Washington, D.C., where theaters reportedly got a bump in attendance every time Maryland's censors made headlines with the film.[37] The Supreme Court case known as *Byrne v. Karalexis* was decided in late 1971 and ended in a deadlocked 4–4 decision. Justice William O. Douglas, a civil libertarian, recused himself from the case because the House of Representatives had launched an impeachment probe against him for conflict of interest in this case; Grove Press, the famed publisher and foe of censorship, was the parent company of the distributor of *I Am Curious (Yellow)* and had published Douglas's recent book. If there was one thing both sides agreed to, it was that the issue of censorship had not been resolved.

In 1970 some members of the Maryland censor board became TV talk show regulars. Rosalyn Shecter (vice chair in 1961 and head of the board in 1969–1970) along with Mary Avara and Margery Shriver appeared on Johnny Carson's *Tonight Show* to discuss the notorious Swedish film. Avara and her cohort also appeared on the *Dick Cavett Show* and the *Mike Douglas Show* where she stole the scene every time with lines such as the following "Sex is beautiful. I come from a family of eighteen. There had to be a lot of sex," and "That's beautiful a naked woman, if she's not in motion."[38]

Meanwhile, in November 1968 the Hays Code was replaced by the MPAA's film industry rating system under the leadership of President Jack Valenti. Maryland's vice chair Rosalyn Shecter was instrumental in advocating for this new system, which rated films with a letter system: G, PG, R, and X. Enacted in reaction to the increasing amount of sex and violence in film and as part of an effort to eradicate state censorship, some directors and producers still viewed the MPAA rating system as the same old censorship. It was a system rife with inequality. Certain filmmakers were allowed to submit their script to the MPAA in advance for pre-censoring. The result, and what Americans have lived with ever since—with a few addendums such as PG-13 and NC-17—is preferential treatment for studio films over independent filmmakers.

The 1970s brought on an unprecedented level of sex and violence in movies. Within just three years of being scandalized by the relatively mild sex scenes in *I Am Curious (Yellow)*, Avara and company were being subjected to the hardcore pornography of *Deep Throat* (1972). In May 1974, a normally shuttered theater on North Avenue was reopened to show *Deep Throat*, but at the film's opening the board converged on the theater and confiscated the print. The theater remained defiant and continued to show the film with what seemed like an unending supply of replacement prints, provided by an organized crime syndicate that was known to back pornographic films at the time, while the board continued to raid its screenings of *Deep Throat*.[39]

Attacks and criticism continued to be hurled at the censor board from all directions. In December 1970, the board was sued for not sufficiently reviewing the peep shows on the Block, Baltimore's red-light district on East Baltimore Street. The suit claimed that inspectors were not entering those establishments, perhaps because many of the inspectors were by this point young women working on a part-time basis.[40] Swedish films continued to push the boundaries of good taste and the censors' buttons. *Sexual Freedom in Denmark* (1970) defeated the censors in court after the exhibitor had shrewdly arranged preliminary screenings at a Johns Hopkins University film series and had obtained comments in support of the film from faculty. Local hero John Waters, whose movies intentionally celebrated bad taste, got around the board by holding screenings in churches such as the First Unitarian where the censors were unlikely to look, much less intervene. Waters hit his censorable peak when he filmed his friend and collaborator Divine eating dog feces in *Pink Flamingos* (1972)—a scene the Maryland censors approved when they finally reviewed the film after it had achieved considerable success on New York City's independent film circuit and returned to Baltimore for showings. Waters recalls Avara later scolding him, "I should've cut that dog doody!"

One of the censor board's final battles with the state legislature occurred in February 1977. According to Senator Howard Denis, "I came to believe they were quasi vigilantes on an ego trip and that Maryland shouldn't be paying people to watch dirty movies. So I put in legislation starting in 1977 to abolish the board."[41] "Celluloid Mary," as Avara came to be known in the pages of the *Sun*, responded after a grueling legislative hearing: "With what I see everyday, I expected to come in here and see everybody nude. If women only knew how ugly they are. As god is my witness the ugliest thing I have ever seen is a gigantic vagina on the screen. When Friday finally comes and I finish for the week, I say thank you, Jesus."[42] An exasperated Avara had long since given up mincing her words: her statement also exposes the gendered terms in which censors had been operating for decades.

The censor board became a joke in newsprint and on television. Acting governor Blair Lee confirmed as much when he told a reporter from the *Sun*, "For my money, putting a man on the censor Board is a sentence not a job."[43] Senator Denis's bill prevailed and a sunset provision was put in motion. Within three years, the State Board of Motion Picture Censors would die a slow, bureaucratic death. The reign of state-sanctioned censorship was over in America, to be fully replaced with the equally flawed MPAA rating system.[44] Henceforth Marylanders could decide for themselves which movies were indecent, objectionable, or offensive, and they could choose to enjoy them or not. The Maryland censor board finally ceased to exist on July 1, 1981. In a poetic twist the last film it passed for audiences was 1981's *For Your Eyes Only*.[45]

Notes

1   The fight to consider movies art or protected speech is long and complex and only briefly explored in this chapter. In *Mutual Film Corp. v. Industrial Commission of Ohio*, 236 U.S. 230 (1915) the Supreme Court declared, "The judicial sense, supporting the common sense of this country, sustains the exercise of the police power of regulation of moving picture exhibitions. The exhibition of moving pictures is a business, pure and simple, originated and conducted for profit like other spectacles, and not to be regarded as part of the press of the country or as organs of public opinion within the meaning of freedom of speech and publication." This decision stood in its entirety until portions of the ruling were overruled by decisions such as *Joseph Burstyn Inc. v. Wilson*, 343 U.S. 495 (1952), *Roth v. United States*, 354 U.S. 476 (1957), and *Ronald L. Freedman v. Maryland State Board of Motion Picture Censors*, 380 U.S. 51 (1965).

2   Jane Addams, *The Spirit of Youth and the City Streets* (Champaign: University of Illinois Press, 1909), 75–76.

3   *Mutual Film Corp. v. Industrial Commission of Ohio*, 236 U.S. 230 (1915).

4   Laura Wittern-Keller, *Freedom of the Screen: Legal Challenges to State Film Censorship, 1915–1981* (Lexington: University Press of Kentucky, 2008), 21.

5   Robert Headley, *Motion Picture Exhibition in Baltimore* (Jefferson, NC: McFarland, 2006), 65–66.

6   Wittern-Keller, *Freedom of the Screen*, 13; Jeremy Geltzer, *Dirty Words & Filthy Pictures* (Austin: University of Texas Press, 2015), 40–53.

7   *Moving Picture World*, June 2, 1917. State Attorney General Albert Ritchie announced in June 1917 that violators had no right to a jury trial.

8   "State Boards Named," *Baltimore Sun*, May 30, 1916. This 1916 salary is equivalent to more than $55,000 per year in 2018.

9   "Censors for the Movies," *Baltimore Sun*, February 1, 1916.

10 Laura Wittern-Keller, interviewed by the author, June 7, 2015.

11 "Women Attack Movie," *Baltimore Sun*, December 16, 1916.

12 "Movie Board Kicks Back," *Baltimore Sun*, July 12, 1917.

13 "'Birth of a Nation' Here," *Baltimore Sun*, March 7, 1916; Untitled, *Baltimore Afro-American*, March 4, 1916.

14 "Colonel" William Joseph Simmons is credited with reviving the Klan after seeing *Birth of a Nation*.

15 Dorian Lynskey, "A Public Menace: How the Fight to Ban *The Birth of a Nation* Shaped the Nascent Civil Rights Movement," *Slate*, March 31, 2015, http://www .slate.com/articles/arts/history/2015/03/the_birth_of_a_nation_how_the_fight _to_censor_d_w_griffith_s_film_shaped.html.

16 David Taft Terry, interviewed by the author, April 26, 2015.

17 "'Birth of a Nation' Banned Because of Fear of Rioting." *Baltimore Sun*, May 24, 1952.

18 Maryland State Board of Motion Picture Censors, *Annual Report*, 1917–1937.

19 Maryland State Board of Motion Picture Censors, *Twenty-Third Annual Report*, 1939.

20 Maryland State Board of Motion Picture Censors, *Thirty-Third Annual Report*, 1949.

21 Display ad, *Baltimore Sun*, September 25, 1950.

22 "Traub Backs Board Record," *Baltimore Sun*, December 31, 1951; Letters to the editor: "Mr. Traub and 'All Quiet,'" *Baltimore Sun*, January 11, 1952.

23 John Waters, interviewed by the author, April 7, 2015.

24 "Censor Reports Gain with Court," *Baltimore Sun*, March 1, 1967.

25 "Move Slated to Abolish Censors," *Baltimore Sun*, February 10, 1964.

26 Ronald Freedman, interviewed by Laura Wittern-Keller, September 11, 2002.

27 "Expenses for Censors," *Baltimore Sun*, June 1, 1961.

28 John Waters, interviewed by author.

29 Laura Wittern-Keller, interviewed by the author.

30 "Film Censorship Test Case Made," *Baltimore Sun*, November 2, 1962.

31 Laura Wittern-Keller, interviewed by the author.

32 "High Court Invalidates Censor Law," *Baltimore Sun*, March 2, 1965.

33 Wittern-Keller, *Freedom of the Screen*, 245.

34 Keller, *Freedom of the Screen*, 246.

35 Ross Freedman, interviewed by the author, April 26, 2015.

36 "*I Am Curious (Yellow)* Still Fails to Pass Maryland Censor's Muster," *Baltimore Sun*, March 2, 1972.

37 "Eroticism Goes to Court," *Baltimore Sun*, April 24, 1970.

38 *The Mike Douglas Show*, July 26, 1974, https://youtu.be/ZCEcs3ZeJVo.

39 John Waters, interviewed by author.

40 "Censor Unit Sued on Peep Shows," *Baltimore Sun,* December 3, 1970.

41 Howard Denis, interviewed by author, December 20, 2016.

42 "Censor Tells Senators of the Trial of Her Job," *Baltimore Sun*, February 24, 1977.

43 "Lee Replaces Harrison in Home Improvement Board," *Baltimore Sun,* October 20, 1978.

44 Kirby Dick's 2006 documentary *This Film Has Not Yet Been Rated* is a well-rounded discussion of the MPAA system.

45 Geltzer, *Dirty Words & Filthy Pictures*, 297.

12

"Temple of the Drama"

• •

The Five-Year Protest at Ford's
Theater, 1947–1952

JENNIFER A. FERRETTI

To its detriment, Baltimore embraced Jim Crow policies that enforced racial segregation in the workplace, public accommodations, and education, among other areas. One such example was in Ford's Theater where black patrons were restricted to the last rows of the second balcony, accessible to them only by a staircase on the side of the building. In 1947 Baltimore's black community declared that the policies at Ford's Theater would no longer be tolerated. The National Association for the Advancement of Colored People (NAACP) launched a protest campaign that would last until the theater finally desegregated five years later. Women in key leadership positions planned the protest, which was carried out by a group of interracial picketers and was supported by well-known actors and activists of the time period. This moral suasion was both inspiring and instructive to social justice activists for decades to come.

Before John T. Ford opened Ford's Grand Opera House—later simply known as Ford's Theater—in his hometown of Baltimore in 1871, he was a notorious figure for his connection to the assassination of President Abraham Lincoln in 1865 and for his friendship with the assassin John Wilkes Booth.[1] After Lincoln was shot at Ford's Theater in Washington, D.C., the War Department seized it. Although he was initially charged with participating in the assassination plot, Ford was exonerated and released after several weeks spent in jail, and he returned to Baltimore soon thereafter.[2] In the decades that followed, Baltimore's Ford's Theater hosted operas, theatrical performances, and film screenings.

Until the 1916 Baltimore premiere of D. W. Griffith's *Birth of a Nation*, Ford's Theater had a reputation of decency among Baltimore's black community.[3] It allowed African American actors to perform on stage, but patrons were restricted to an area with poor sight lines known as "the pit."[4] Black patrons purchased their tickets from the main window and were directed to the alley staircase of the three-story building to reach their seats in the last few rows of the second balcony.[5] The Lyric Opera House, in contrast, maintained the opposite policy, whereby African Americans were prohibited from being on stage, but could sit anywhere in the theater.[6] Ford's Theater's decision to screen the racist propaganda film *Birth of a Nation* sparked an editorial in the *Baltimore Afro-American* newspaper, which condemned the theater for its decision and suggested a boycott.[7]

The Baltimore chapter of the NAACP was four years old when *Birth of a Nation* premiered in Baltimore. The local chapter had been chartered in 1912, just two years after the city had passed a 1910 residential housing segregation law—the first of its kind in the United States—and it initially focused on fighting housing and education segregation laws.[8] Dr. Lillie Carroll Jackson was elected president of this branch in 1935, the first woman in the country to lead a local NAACP chapter.[9] In the mid-1930s, Baltimore's chapter embraced the national organization's campaign that demanded white-owned businesses hire African Americans.[10] The "Buy Where You Can Work" campaign, as it came to be known locally, focused on desegregating businesses along Pennsylvania Avenue and was the jumpstart that Baltimore's NAACP needed to organize other demonstrations.[11] Beginning with only five members when she became president, Dr. Jackson led the charge to increase membership, which swelled to 17,600 in 1946, making the Baltimore chapter one of the largest branches in the country.[12]

In the middle of the twentieth century, push and pull factors motivated African Americans to move out of the South to Baltimore and points northward as part of what became known as the Great Migration. The city's black population more than doubled between 1910 and 1950.[13] During World War II, African American residents were afforded opportunities to work, but discrimination persisted. "Hate-strikes" were organized by white workers to protest the lack of segregation on worksites.[14] Baltimore was more accustomed to picket lines in labor disputes than campaigns against segregated public accommodations such as theaters, parks, and stores.[15]

In 1942, some of the traveling cast members of Gershwin's opera *Porgy and Bess* recounted their experience with Baltimore's "absurd and rotten conditions" brought about by Jim Crow laws.[16] African American cast members were called obscenities on the street and told they could not shop at the May Company department store unless they received a special pass from the manager.[17] Renowned actor, leftist, and civil rights activist Paul Robeson headed the cast of *Porgy and Bess* and threatened to boycott the Ford's Theater's seating policy, but it is suspected that contractual obligation kept him from doing so.[18] In the ensuing years, Robeson returned to Baltimore many more times, not to act but to hold a sign and march outside Ford's Theater demanding action.[19]

After the Maryland and Auditorium Theaters closed in 1943, Ford's Theater was considered the only legitimate theater in Baltimore,[20] and it was frequented by state and local politicians, socialites, and judges.[21] Although partnerships between the NAACP and white allies had previously been focused on legal and legislative goals, the Baltimore NAACP decided to officially sponsor the protest at Ford's Theater in 1947. Beatrice Martin served as protest captain, and Adah Jenkins, piano teacher and the *Afro-American*'s music critic, was the day-to-day organizer.[22] Depending on the theater's programming, the line ranged from a dozen black and white picketers to sometimes just one or two, marching six nights per week, plus during the two weekly matinees (see Figure 9).[23] Students also became involved in the effort.[24] Sixteen-year-old A. Robert Kaufman, president of the Interracial Fellowship, joined the picket line after hearing about it from a classmate.[25] Kaufman credits Jenkins for enabling his increased responsibilities and involvement during the protest.[26] Prominent civil rights activists in the Jackson-Mitchell Family also joined the line, including Parren Mitchell, Dr. Jackson, Juanita Jackson, Clarence Mitchell Jr., and their children.[27]

Kaufman and Jenkins started a letter-writing campaign to individuals in the theater industry across the country, alerting them to their efforts.[28] The Committee for Non-Segregation in Baltimore Theatres, headed by Jenkins, began receiving letters of support from prominent theater producers, directors, and actors, including Oscar Hammerstein II, Eli Wallach, and Olivia de Haviland.[29] Civil rights leader Bayard Rustin joined the picket line in 1949.[30] As the protests went on, it became difficult for elected officials to ignore the picketers "slowly freezing" outside Ford's Theater or the citizens who wrote more than 1,400 letters asking actors and theater unions to support the desegregation campaign.[31]

Baltimore native Theodore R. McKeldin was mayor during the early days of the protest and was largely seen as an ally. After his 1943–1947 term as mayor, he went on to serve as governor of Maryland from 1951–1959. By the time the legislature met in 1951, McKeldin had instituted the Commission on Interracial Problems and Relations. As governor he worked with the black community on integrating accommodations and recreational areas and ending racially segregated lists for state jobs.[32] Nor could he overlook the protestors arranging

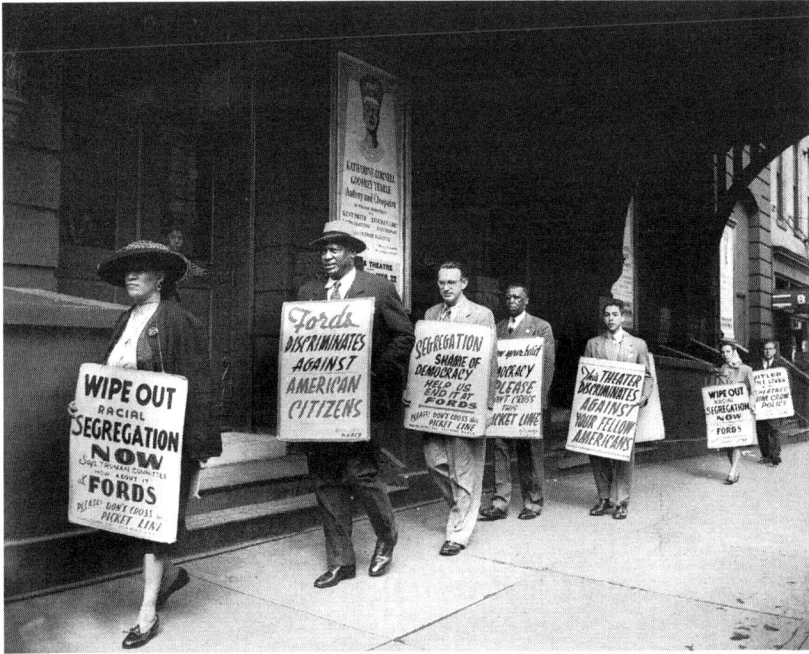

FIG. 9 The picket line protesting the Jim Crow seating policy at Ford's Theater. Mrs. Adah Jenkins is on the far left, and Dr. John E. T. Camper is the fourth from the left. Photo by Paul S. Henderson, March 1948. Courtesy of the Maryland Historical Society.

meetings with the theater's management or those picketing in solidarity, like the Congress of Racial Equality (CORE) members in New York at the office of Marcus Heiman, the Ford lessee in 1950.[33]

The *Afro-American* ran stories throughout the five years of protest. In contrast, the *Baltimore Sun*, the white paper of record, failed to print accounts of the demonstration, only reporting on arrests for disorderly conduct when the police deemed the picket line to be too large.[34] A letter to the editor printed on June 12, 1947, even called out the paper for this embarrassing oversight in reporting.[35] The silent treatment was so obvious and troubling that the protesters organized a meeting of Baltimore citizens with local daily papers in 1950 to discuss their lack of coverage.[36] Even after this meeting, nostalgic editorials about Ford's Theater itself—the "Temple of the Drama," as it was called when it first opened—rarely mentioned the picketing.

As the protest proceeded, Baltimore's civil rights organizations were growing and gaining political traction. In 1950 Dr. Jackson, Juanita Mitchell, and Adah Jenkins went to New York to work with the national NAACP to introduce a nonsegregation clause into the biannual contract between the Actors' Equity labor union and the Guild of Theatres. The segregation policy was denounced by those in the industry as the primary reason for the decline in Baltimore theater.[37] On January 3, 1952, McKeldin wrote a letter to the Commission on Interracial Problems and Relations stating that the policy at Ford's Theater "needlessly affronted" black patrons.[38] He acknowledged that the unjust policy and the resulting picket line may have caused the noticeable decline in attendance.[39] In a resolution on January 16, 1952, the commission implored theaters to lift discriminatory practices, and by January 31, Ford's Theater accepted this recommendation.[40] Ford's Theater remained integrated until it ceased operation in 1964.

It seemed to have been easy for most white Baltimoreans to ignore the protest outside Ford's Theater because the paper of record rarely gave it ink, even though it continued for five years. However, groups such as the Baltimore NAACP, CORE, Interracial Fellowship, and Students for Democratic Action combined their efforts and persevered. Some of Baltimore's white theatergoers hoped that integration of the theater would result in more and better theater offerings, as if that was the biggest loss of the entire five years.[41] Baltimore's black community, in contrast, hoped the result would lead to continued repudiation of the indignity of maneuvering the city's varied Jim Crow policies. Ford's Theater's integration was one step toward the desegregation of schools, pools, parks, and a fusillade of national desegregation legislation.

Notes

1   John Dorsey, "Lights Will Go out Saturday at Theater," *Baltimore Sun*, February 10, 1964.
2   Charles Ford Reese, "I Remember . . . 50 Years of Playgoing at Ford's Theater," *Baltimore Sun*, February 2, 1964.
3   Editorial, *Afro-American*, March 4, 1916.
4   David Taft Terry, "'Tramping for Justice': The Dismantling of Jim Crow in Baltimore, 1942–1954" (PhD diss., Howard University, 2002).
5   Juanita J. Mitchell and Virginia Jackson Kiah, transcript of interview by Charles Wagandt. OH 8097, Governor Theodore McKeldin–Dr. Lillie Mae Carroll Jackson Oral History Project, Maryland Historical Society. (January 10, 1976).
6   "End Race Bias in Theaters: M'Keldin," *Evening Sun*, January 4, 1952.
7   Editorial, *Afro-American*.
8   Lee Sartain, *Borders of Equality: The NAACP and the Baltimore Civil Rights Struggle, 1914–1970* (Jackson: University Press of Mississippi, 2013); Larry Gibson, *Young Thurgood: The Making of a Supreme Court Justice* (New York: Prometheus Books, 2012).
9   John C. Robinson, "Ma Jackson—Fighter from Way Back," *Baltimore News-American*, January 24, 1971.
10 "Leads Baltimore's 'Buy Where You Can Work' Program," \ *Baltimore Afro-American*, December 16, 1933.
11 "Balto. Stores Hire Four New Clerks," *Afro-American*, March 3, 1934.

12 "Balto. Stores Hire"; Carl Schoettler, "Commitment to Nonviolence: Dr. Jackson Still in Negro Rights Fight at 80," *Baltimore Sun*, June 10, 1969.

13 Schoettler, "Commitment to Nonviolence."

14 Schoettler, "Commitment to Nonviolence."

15 Elizabeth Meijer, "The White Viewpoint: As I See It," *Baltimore Afro-American*, March 15, 1947.

16 "'Porgy, Bess' Cast Taste Baltimore J. C.," *Baltimore Afro-American*, October 16, 1943.

17 "'Porgy, Bess' Cast."

18 Terry, "Tramping for Justice.'"

19 Meijer, "The White Viewpoint."

20 Dorsey, "Lights Will Go out Saturday."

21 Juanita J. Mitchell and Virginia Jackson Kiah, interview by Charles Wagandt.

22 Meijer, "The White Viewpoint."

23 Meijer, "The White Viewpoint."

24 "Arrested Pickets Claim Baltimore Theater Bias," *Baltimore Sun*, February 12, 1950.

25 A. Robert Kaufman, "Integrating Ford's," *Baltimore Sun,* September 17, 1993.

26 Kaufman, "Integrating Ford's."

27 Kaufman, "Integrating Ford's."

28 Kaufman, "Integrating Ford's."

29 Adah K. Jenkins, "History of Elimination of Ford's Segregation," *Baltimore Afro-American* January 29, 1952; "Segregation in the Theatre Hit: Hammerstein Joins Stars Disapproving Ford Policy," *Afro-American*, September 29, 1951.

30 "Hit by Jim Crow in MD as Well as NC," *Baltimore Afro-American,* October 29, 1949.

31 Mary C. Camper, "A Fight for Freedom," *Baltimore Afro-American*, January 10, 1948; "After 6-Year Picket Line: Md.'s Ford Theatre Ends Separate Seating Policy," *Baltimore Afro-American*, February 9, 1952.

32 Frederick N. Rasmussen, "Back Story: An Overlooked Civil Rights Legacy," *Baltimore Sun*, February 25, 2006.

33 Jenkins, "History of Elimination of Ford's Segregation."

34 "Arrested Pickets Claim Baltimore Theater Bias."

35 Ella G. Ulman, "Pickets at Ford's Theater. Letter to the Editor," *Baltimore Sun*, June 12, 1947.

36 Jenkins, "History of Elimination of Ford's Segregation."

37 Jenkins, "History of Elimination of Ford's Segregation."

38 "Ford's Drops Its Policy of Segregation," *Baltimore Sun,* February 1, 1952.

39 "Ford's Drops Its Policy of Segregation."

40 "Ford's Drops Its Policy of Segregation."

41 "Ford's Theater Decides to Abandon Segregation," *Baltimore Sun*, February 2, 1952.

Part III

Voices from Here

● ●

Listening to the Past

The chapters in Part III examine Baltimore's history by listening to the people who live and work in the city, a central aim of both social history and community organizing. "Community" is a complicated idea that is often romanticized and oversimplified and thus deserves unpacking. "The community" is an unnamed mass of people, but one that is often invoked (from the outside) to describe working-class people and people of color. Yet all euphemisms aside, community can be a set of lived actions aimed at solidarity, collaboration, and survival, especially for marginalized people. While Baltimore has been a majority–African American city since the 1970s, its racial and ethnic dynamics cannot be reduced to simply black and white. When we think of "the community" in an urban studies context, we must ground our analysis in specific places and listen to the actual voices on the ground.

Jacob Levin's chapter "Because They Were Also Downed People" looks at how African American and Jewish communities in Baltimore not only communicated and collaborated but also conflicted with each other. He focuses on the unrest in Baltimore in the wake of Martin Luther King's assassination in 1968, when many Jewish-owned businesses located in majority–African American neighborhoods were burned and destroyed, perhaps due not so much to anti-Semitism but rather to a desire to strike back against merchants who operated in their neighborhoods but lived outside them. Nearly fifty years later, as unrest unfolded on April 27, 2015, in the wake of Freddie Gray's death, many businesses owned by people of Korean descent suffered similar damage. Aletheia

Hyun-Jin Shin's snapshot of her Onggi art project uses oral history to shed light on Koreans and Korean Americans in Baltimore: she raises questions similar to those raised by Levin about communities that do not fit into the black–white binary that dominates discussions of race in Baltimore.

Ashley Minner, a community artist and scholar, examines the history of another group excluded from dominant narratives of race in Baltimore, the Lumbee people. Minner's chapter "revisits the reservation" at Fells Point, a community that lured waves of immigrants and migrants seeking industrial jobs in the decades around World War II, including members of the Lumbee tribe from eastern North Carolina. In noting the ongoing gentrification in Fells Point, Minner writes, "The neighborhood is currently undergoing a profound transition—one that is not disconnected from the movement and displacement of Lumbee people." It is not merely important to document the transitions of communities but also to understand how residents feel about and negotiate them.

Baltimoreans' perceptions of change often blend together economic and cultural contradictions. Nicole Fabricant's and Michelle Stefano's chapters embrace methods for listening to and amplifying the voices of people struggling to survive the trauma of deindustrialization. In "Overburdened Bodies and Lands: Industrial Development and Environmental Injustice in South Baltimore," Fabricant takes the reader on a "toxic tour" of a neglected area of industrial South Baltimore that encompasses the neighborhoods of Brooklyn and Curtis Bay. The area has long suffered from some of the worst pollution and toxic air in the state of Maryland. Yet the work of young activists publicizing the environmental racism and classism plaguing these neighborhoods gives cause for hope. Stefano explores the human side of deindustrialization with a focus on the collective cultural expressions of steelworkers after the closure of the massive U.S. Steel production facility at Sparrows Point. In "Finding Closure: The Poets of Sparrows Point Steel Mill," she challenges hypermasculine stereotypes of manufacturing work by presenting the creative work of men who have embraced poetry as a means to grapple with the economic and personal pain of being laid off. Through these writings, steelworkers express their pride and dignity, even after losing their union jobs and source of livelihood, which in turn pushes all of us to reconsider the future for cities after deindustrialization.

The search for dignity and community also fueled the dreams of radical feminists and lesbian activists in Baltimore in the 1970s. Elizabeth Morrow Nix, April Kalogeropoulos Householder, and Jodi Kelber-Kaye led a team of students from UMBC and the University of Baltimore in interviewing lesbian feminists who built their own organizations and workplaces in Baltimore's Waverly neighborhood. Their chapter's title "Lessons from Then, Lessons for Now" speaks to the importance of retelling histories of activism as we continue to build networks of solidarity. Here is how the chapter begins: "In the early 1970s,

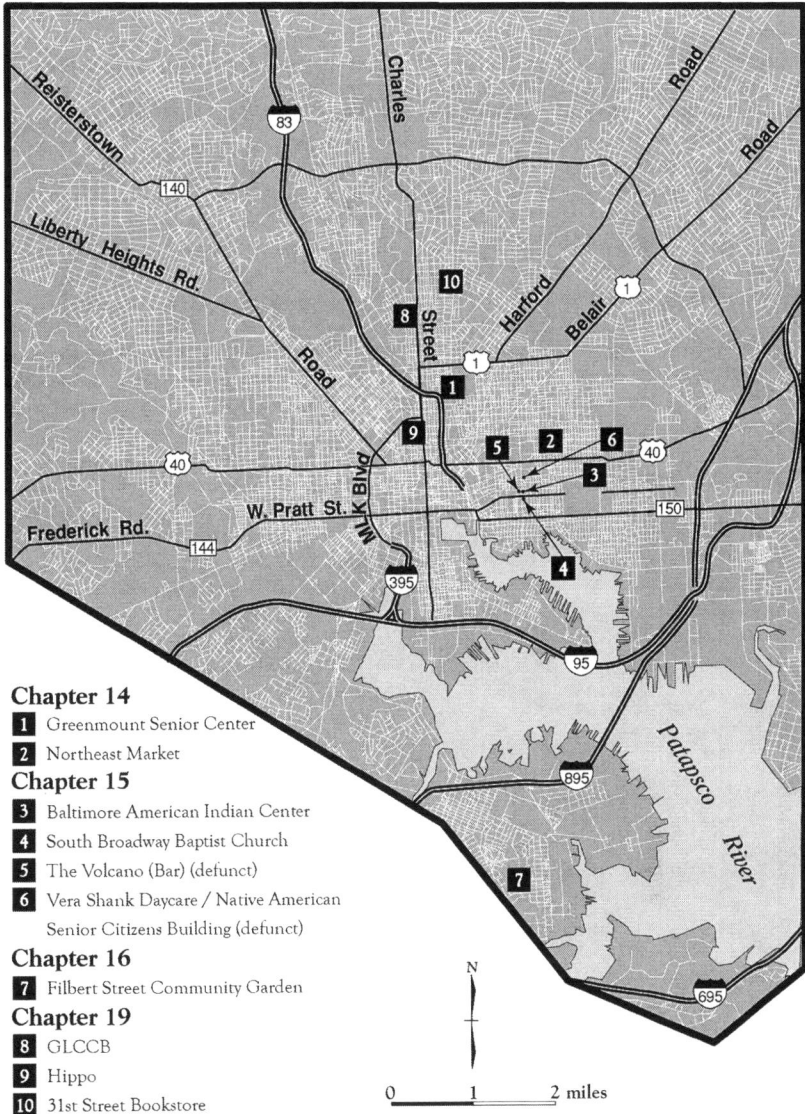

Chapter 14
1 Greenmount Senior Center
2 Northeast Market
Chapter 15
3 Baltimore American Indian Center
4 South Broadway Baptist Church
5 The Volcano (Bar) (defunct)
6 Vera Shank Daycare / Native American
   Senior Citizens Building (defunct)
Chapter 16
7 Filbert Street Community Garden
Chapter 19
8 GLCCB
9 Hippo
10 31st Street Bookstore

FIG. 10 Map of locations described in Part III. Created by Joe School, 2018.

a cadre of young female academics moved to Baltimore to organize what they hoped would be a revolution." In the final chapter of the section, Kate Drabinski interviews lesbian and feminist activist Louise Parker Kelley, who offers her firsthand account as a participant in this inspiring but incomplete revolution.

These chapters illustrate how listening to the voices of the city can be an important and radical act.

13

"Because They Were Also Downed People"

••••••••••••••••••••••

Black-Jewish Relationships in
Baltimore during the 1968
Uprising and Beyond

JACOB R. LEVIN

"Also downed people": that was what African American resident Ruth Stewart saw as shared oppression underlying the perceived camaraderie between the black and Jewish communities, specifically the Jewish merchants in black neighborhoods, in 1950s and 1960s Baltimore. She described a situation where, in contrast to white, non-Jewish store owners, local Jewish merchants would often extend credit to known neighborhood customers and allow them to pay on a biweekly or monthly basis, so they could keep food on the table and afford household supplies. She said in an interview that "in the Jews' stores, they would give you credit that you could pay once a month. . . . You couldn't go into the white stores and say my children need a loaf of bread or a chicken or whatever, or have them give it to you. No way. But in a Jew's store, you could get that." Her belief was that Jewish merchants treated African American customers specially because "they were also downed people" and because "they knew what oppression was."[1]

On April 4, 1968, and in the days following, that solidarity would be tested to its limit. As news of the assassination of Dr. Martin Luther King Jr. spread, outbreaks of violence followed in many cities that would eventually cause dozens of deaths, tens of thousands of arrests, the destruction of thousands of urban businesses, and damages ranging in the tens of millions of dollars across the country. Baltimore was one of those cities.

Much of the scholarship surrounding periods of urban unrest use interchangeably the terms "riots," "rebellions," "uprising," and "unrest," depending on a variety of factors including authorial intentions, audience, and political leanings.[2] This chapter uses the term "riots" because it was the preferred nomenclature in 1968 and is used most commonly in the historical memory of the events decades ago.

In fact, Baltimore's riots were much more severe in intensity than those in most other cities. It was one of just three cities in which federal military troops patrolled the streets to help limit the destruction.[3] It would be the second-most costly of the April 1968 riots, only behind Washington, D.C., in damages incurred.[4] It left a trail of devastation in the city, resulting in 6 dead and more than 700 people injured; 5,500 people arrested; 1,050 businesses looted, vandalized, or obliterated by fire; and an estimated $13.5 million in property damages, or around $80,000,000 to $90,000,000 when adjusted for inflation.[5]

For many in Baltimore's Jewish community, the riots would be the final nail in the coffin of a decades-long "grand alliance" that saw the two groups working symbiotically toward progress on civil rights battles across the nation. In Baltimore, though weakened, the black–Jewish relationship in many ways continued, socially, politically, and economically, because of the determination of leaders and laypersons in both communities. However, in Baltimore as in other urban areas, there were multiple ways in which the groups stood in conflict; the strongest tension related to Jewish business owners' treatment of African Americans, both as customers and employees, in spite of Stewart's rosy depiction of these relationships. In many city centers, Jews disproportionally owned businesses in African American neighborhoods. In his work, *The Store in the Hood*, sociologist Steven J. Gold points out that as early as the late 1800s, black customers complained about Jewish business practices.[6] Often, Jews came to represent exploitive whites in black neighborhoods. Jews also became the face of absentee landlords and the representatives of state and local government services. Jews, after all, were frequently locked out of white-collar private firms, so they flocked to government positions as social workers, teachers, and public officials.[7]

In Baltimore, Jews owned small shops, but in contrast to many other large cities, they also owned the majority of the large downtown department stores. From the 1930s through the late 1960s, department stores represented the height of middle- and upper-class capitalism. Located in a southern town at heart, Baltimore's department stores enacted policies that encompassed a wide range of

Jim Crow restrictions. In hiring, African Americans were blocked from any type of management or sales jobs and were relegated to maintenance and service positions like porters and restroom attendants. African American customers were barred from eating at the stores' lunch counters or using their beauty salons. Additionally, black customers, regardless of personal status or wealth, were not allowed to try on clothing or hats in the stores before buying them and often not allowed to return items once purchased. All of these restrictions were meant to deny the dignity and personhood of the black customer and led to decades of activist efforts and protests.[8]

Jewish business owners, big and small, often existed in a sort of racial middle space, a complex position of relative safety in the United States compared to persecution in Europe, while simultaneously often practicing racist and exploitive business systems in black neighborhoods. The *Afro-American* published dozens of articles throughout the 1930s and early 1940s sympathizing with the plight of European Jews facing Nazi Germany, and Jews garnered some good will for their civil rights efforts against racial discrimination. But the newspaper also challenged Jewish business owners for practicing harsh and humiliating Jim Crow policies. Dan Gardner wrote, "The excuse that the Jew who discriminates is 'not representative' of the 'forward thinking' element among the Jews does not hold water. . . . As minorities, Jews and colored persons must get together and those of the Jews who violate the racial bonds now being established must be publicly denounced."[9] As early as the mid-1930s, the *Afro* was reporting on efforts to confront downtown department stores' racist policies. In one push to change the policies at the Hecht's department store, the speakers at an event in Washington, D.C., noted that even though the store was owned and operated by Jews, the protests should not focus on the Jewish identities of the owners and managers, but rather on the policies themselves, lest their efforts be open to claims of anti-Semitism, rather than anti-Jim Crowism.[10]

The events of April 1968 created more destruction and invoked a stronger institutional state response than the Baltimore uprising of 2015, even though the recent unrest raged on near-constant twenty-four hour cable news cycles. There is no doubt that the pain and grief expressed in both peaceful protests and violence were present in Baltimore during 1968 and 2015 and that the demographics of the city have changed dramatically over the last five decades due to the following: the migration of hundreds of thousands of residents, mostly white, to nearby county suburbs; the collapse of a manufacturing economy and job source; a shrinking tax base and government services; and a declining downtown economic center rebuilt to serve commuters and tourists, not the city's residents. Despite those changes, many of the same institutional and societal problems that in 1968 drove people into the streets, and later inspired their reconciliation and rebuilding, remain the same. Today's activists can look back on these post-1968 efforts as an attempt to reinforce a relationship that has languished in previous decades and as a crucial tool to fight modern-day problems.

The scholarship on the black–Jewish relationship in the United States is both wide in topical scope and deep in its analysis of race, politics, ideology, arts, identity, and activism: it centers on the period from World War II until the generally perceived collapse of the alliance in the late 1960s. Much of the scholarship also leans toward blaming Black Power ideology and movements for this rift, alleviating Jewish communities of blame for their exploitive business practices mentioned earlier.

It is the dominant narrative of black–Jewish relations that four key events caused the bond to weaken to its nadir in the late 1960s and early 1970s. First, in 1966 the Student Nonviolent Coordinating Committee (SNCC) voted to expel its white leadership and then its white members from the organization. The second factor was the June 1967 Israeli–Arab Six-Day War, during and after which many in the Black Power leadership took a decided stand of support for the Arab cause and the elimination of Israeli expansion and military power. Third, many in the Jewish community viewed the New York City teachers' strike of 1968 as pitting a predominantly Jewish teachers' union against a heavily black student population. Last, and the subject of this chapter, the riots that raged across nearly every major U.S. metropolis in the days following King's assassination in April 1968 played a key role in the shift in relations between African Americans and Jewish people. Many Jews, especially Jewish business owners, saw the riots as the "final straw" because they felt that their livelihoods had been targeted and attacked by the customers they had served for decades.[11]

Baltimore is an ideal setting for examining the changing relationship between these two minority communities for several reasons. First, outside of New York, Baltimore had some of the largest proportional populations of each community. At the conclusion of World War II, primarily because of the growth in wartime industries, Baltimore was the sixth largest city in the United States: its population hovered around one million people. During the 1960s, the population began to contract, and by 1970, it had shrunk to 905,000.[12] While the overall white population decreased dramatically during this period, the Jewish and black populations in the city grew both in total number and proportionally. In 1950, the Jewish population was around 75,000, but by 1968 it had grown to approximately 100,000, thereby increasing its proportion of the city's population from approximately 8 percent in 1950 to 11 percent in 1968.[13] Similarly, from 1945 to 1960, the black population in the city grew from 194,000 to 326,000, increasing from approximately 20 percent of the city to a whopping 46 percent by 1970.[14] In 1967, Jews were 4.85 percent of the population of Maryland as a whole.[15] All of these numbers combine to make Baltimore a compelling case study in minority population relations.

The Riots

The violence and destruction that raged in Baltimore City lasted four days and five nights, beginning around sundown on Saturday, April 6, 1968. The unrest caused more than $13 million in damage to small businesses and homes and led to the first federal troops to be deployed within the city since the 1877 B&O Railroad Strike.[16] The great majority of the damage was done in the areas of the city that were heavily populated by African Americans; yet a large portion of the small businesses (liquor stores, markets, pharmacies, small clothing stores, and eateries) that were damaged were owned by Jews who lived above or behind the storefront, or immediately outside the inner city, and commuted downtown to work every day.

During the second day of unrest Mayor Thomas D'Alesandro III toured the city with National Guard general George M. Gelston in the morning, and he was met mostly with either silence or hostility from residents on the streets. The mayor had hoped to get both militant and moderate black leaders onto the streets during the hours after curfew on that second night in the hope that they would be able to reason with the people, but the military leaders rejected the plan for reasons unexplained in the press. The mayor made note of how even windows that had "Soul Brother" written on them had been smashed. He summed up his assessment in one statement: "it's bad, but not as bad as it could have been."[17]

The riots ended in Baltimore by April 12, but before the police and military forces gained control of the city, leaders in the black community on their own had been touring the damage and speaking with residents in an attempt to calm the violence. The most unconventional of these community leaders was Melvin Williams.

Popularly known as "Little Melvin," Williams was a gambling and drug kingpin in West Baltimore. He was out of jail awaiting an appeal when King was shot. Political leaders, whom Williams referred to as "civil defense officials," finally called on him for help, believing that he could have an impact on quelling the unrest.[18] Williams agreed to be driven into the heart of the riots to speak with gatherings of protestors, and when the officials, both white and black, strongly suggested that he wear a bulletproof vest, he refused flatly, saying everyone would know who he was and that he simply did not need one. As Baltimore legend goes, Melvin was driven to an area in West Baltimore where a large crowd of protestors had gathered, stood up on the hood of a car, told the crowd, "That's enough," and they stopped rioting.[19]

Williams recounted what he told the rioters in an oral history interview conducted nearly four decades later:

> You have taken all there is to take out of this Black community. You've taken the heart out of your own area. But more importantly, I've been told by this General that in the event that you cross Howard and Franklin Streets: those two streets that divide the things that belong to the powers that be and white America their [sic] going to kill you wholesale. Their [sic] going to kill you all in a manner that would let it be known that this is something that we will not tolerate. And they tolerated it as long as we were destroying Black things. But they made it clear that you can take Pipe Rack and Cookie's and Rodman's and all those places you can destroy as much of it as you choose. But again, if you cross Franklin and Howard we going to open fire and were going to kill you all wholesale.[20]

The state of emergency declared by Governor Spiro Agnew (and future vice president) lasted from 10 P.M. on April 6 to 10 A.M. on April 15, when the troops were released from active duty.[21] That was when the reality facing the two historically linked communities sunk in, and the real work to repair the damage began.

Where Do We Go from Here?

Before the riots in April 1968, the National Association for the Advancement of Colored People (NAACP) and the American Jewish Congress had met with community leadership to address the relationship between the groups, holding private and public meetings in both January and February of that year to reaffirm the connection. The public meeting hosted by the American Jewish Congress and the Reform Baltimore Hebrew Congregation Associate Rabbi Amiel Wohl at the Jewish Community Center on January 14, 1968, was titled "The State of Colored-Jewish Relations." It was planned to emphasize the importance of the two groups addressing their current tensions, recognizing that the discussion would be a difficult one. As described earlier, the bond had recently strained because of "the big city riots, the emergence of 'black power' advocates and the pro-Arab statements following the Six-Day War in Israel have led to further straining of relations between the two minority groups."[22] Yet, the black organizational partner, the NAACP, was one of the most conservative civil rights organizations, and as such may not have been representative of the larger black community's attitudes toward interfaith relations, and the public meeting was sponsored by just two Jewish organizations.

Black–Jewish relations at that time were more complicated than the brotherhood preached by the leadership of these formal institutions; by the 1960s, these relationships in Baltimore were fraying *before* the "final straws" of 1968. In 1963 while the National Conference of Christians and Jews (NCCJ) was holding its "Brotherhood Week" in Baltimore, nearly 150 college students were arrested and jailed in the city for picketing against local segregated accommodations. In the *Afro-American*, Ralph Matthews Jr. condemned "good Baltimore's silence" on these issues. He wrote, "So far this newspaper has heard no statement from NCCJ or from the great majority of liberal-labeled organizations in this city"; perhaps the students' biggest accomplishment was bringing to light that "Baltimore is nothing like the 'genteel' respectable city it pictures itself as being," when its local political and religious leaders are silent on the jailing of the most respectable and talented of the city's youth.[23]

In January 1968 Har Sinai Congregation, a Baltimore Reform temple, created a synagogue initiative to "improve the social and economic conditions of Negroes in Baltimore's 'inner city.'" It teamed up with Baltimore's Youth Opportunity Program, which worked with the Baltimore business community to create part-time jobs, training, and networking connections. "Domestic work, baby-sitting and similar jobs are not accepted, on the premise that the program must emphasize upgrading of job opportunities," and the Mayor's Office committed to provide full-time, forty-hours-per-week summer programs—including transportation—for students aged eight to twelve at two fully equipped schools directed by professional educators and staffed by Har Sinai adult and youth volunteers.[24]

A meeting in February 1968 celebrating 1968 National Brotherhood Day was sponsored by the NAACP Baltimore branch and held at the Sharp Street Memorial Methodist Church; its featured speaker was Rabbi Israel Goldman of the Conservative Chizuk Amuno Congregation.[25] He was introduced by Rabbi Morris Lieberman of Baltimore Hebrew Congregation and a lifetime member of the NAACP. Juanita Jackson Mitchell, president of the NAACP Baltimore chapter, said at the event, "We must stand together and make clear our principles amidst cries of hate and violence. Black and white together, we shall overcome."[26]

After the assassination of King, religious and secular leaders in both communities worked quickly to reaffirm their shared grief and their desire to maintain good relations between the two groups. Weldon Wallace, the religion editor of the *Sun*, wrote about an interfaith march (a "procession of penance") through Northwest Baltimore led by Catholic, Protestant, and Jewish clergy to decry the racism in white America that led to the assassination of King; it was held on a Saturday a week after King's murder.[27] Around the same time, the Baltimore chapter of the American Jewish Committee, in a telegram to both elected officials and civic leaders, called for a comprehensive effort to attack problems in poor urban centers, specifically through the creation of jobs, overhaul of the welfare system, and increased political representation. While the details of the telegram reflected information from the previous year's report of the National Advisory Commission on Civil Disorders (better known as the Kerner Report), it emphasized the urgent need for change in the face of the ongoing unrest in Baltimore.[28] A discussion on March 6, 1969, by the Panel of American Women, a human relations group consisting of a Catholic, a Protestant, a Jewish woman, and a black woman, was held at the Liberty Jewish Center in Baltimore to discuss how these women had been personally affected by prejudice and discrimination.[29]

In the year that followed the unrest, both government agencies and private groups conducted exhaustive statistical analyses of the violence. The most comprehensive report, *A Report of the Baltimore Civil Disturbance of April 6 to April 11, 1968*, was released on June 10, 1968, by the Maryland Crime Investigating Commission; it included information about impact on Jewish-owned businesses and impact in a section called "Profile of the Victims." This section was the only official statement that suggested that Jews might have been targeted: "Many of these small ghetto merchants are Jewish. The frustrated Negro found this merchant a handy scapegoat. . . . Upon close analysis, this seems to be not only a criminal conspiracy [burning and looting to drive whites or Jews out of urban business] but a step backwards."[30]

Ultimately, research provided no evidence to back this claim. The *Report on Baltimore Civil Disorders April, 1968*, published three months after the Maryland Crime Investigating Commission report, and compiled by Jane Motz in her capacity as a member of the Executive Committee of the National Community Relations Committee of the American Friends Service Committee, noted, "Jewish merchants have claimed that the attacks had an anti-semitic [*sic*] component. Large numbers of ghetto stores are owned by Jews. In some blocks, all the white merchants were Jewish. . . . However, it is clear that vandals and looters attacked their stores not because the owners were Jewish, but because they were the 'nearest exploiters.'"[31] This concept of "nearest exploiters" suggests that the attacks on Jewish-owned businesses had nothing to do with the Jewishness of the owners, but rather were influenced by the proximity of the stores, which were owned by people who happened to be Jewish. Gold addressed this proximity issue in *The Store in the Hood*, writing, "Paradoxically, a major reason for pervasive conflicts between Jewish merchants and black customers was Jews' willingness to associate with blacks."[32] He also reported on some heated exchanges between more radical African American residents in East Baltimore and Jewish merchants, who equated "the approach of their critics with that of the Nazis," but these sentiments were refuted or dismissed by most within the Jewish community.[33]

The Baltimore Jewish Council released a study that was reviewed in the *Baltimore Jewish Times* that attempted to statistically analyze whether the destruction to Jewish-owned businesses was deliberate or not. Several of the statistics and conclusions deserve mention here. Jews owned approximately 64 percent (738 of 1,150) of the businesses affected by the riots: Jewish-owned businesses were more frequently damaged than non-Jewish-owned businesses (64.7 percent versus 46.4 percent). The study claimed that the 18 percentage-point difference between damaged Jewish- and damaged non-Jewish-owned businesses was not sufficient to "warrant a conclusion that Jewish merchants were singled out as the primary targets of the rioters." It concluded that the "senseless vengeance against merchants who happen to be Jewish is quite a different issue than vengeance against merchants because they are Jewish."[34] No major religiously identifiable monuments, such as synagogues or Jewish centers, were damaged or destroyed, furthering the claim from the Motz and Baltimore Jewish Council reports that the rioters seemed to view the Jewish merchants as merchants first, rather than as specific Jewish targets.

Rabbinical students regularly engaged in hands-on advocacy for the poor; in particular, one student rabbi, Roger A. Alper, had seemingly endless energy to drive "mothers on welfare to the office of the mayor of Washington to protest against construction of more housing units in an already crowded neighborhood." During his final month in Washington's black community, "Alper virtually abandoned the 'upper echelon' organizations like church groups and worked instead with grass roots agencies established by the Blacks themselves." He worked to secure funding from Jewish businesses and organizations for social welfare initiatives, but ultimately decided, bringing back this message to his classmates, that "until the Jewish community . . . shift[s] its priorities from heavily publicized establishment back-slapping to quiet grass-roots committed action, it indeed will continue to neither fool nor satisfy anyone but itself."[35] Alper's take on the "real" state of the relations between the two communities was counter to what was being reported in the press, which focused on interfaith events calling for alliances. Alper argued instead that the grassroots advocacy of the previous decades would be what would really move the alliance toward a more concrete bond.

The state and local elections of 1970 proved to be a hallmark moment for both communities, with some neighborhoods still struggling to recover from the destruction of both property and interreligious relationships. Following the election, the pages of the *Afro-American* were filled with editorials praising the combined efforts of the black and Jewish constituents in several districts in electing black politicians. Columnist Max Johnson praised especially the black and Jewish voters in the Seventh Congressional District who united behind Parren Mitchell, enabling him to narrowly defeat Maryland's lone Jewish congressman Samuel Friedel in the primaries and then to beat the "white community's [Republican candidate] Peter Parker."[36] In the same edition, contributor David E. Sloan published a letter, "To a Jewish Neighbor," whom he named Sol: he praised the Jewish community for standing with Parren Mitchell in the hopes that the two-decade-long alliance that had held under elected Jewish politicians would continue. He wrote, "Your people and mine have been in the same bag for so long, it seems ludicrous that we should do anything other than stand shoulder to shoulder in supporting the new black congressman from Baltimore's 7th District."[37]

As the 1970s wore on, further Jewish flight out of the city to the Northwest suburbs and increased strains on the relationship led to the formation of a new organization: the Black and Jewish Forum of Baltimore, or BLEWS. Founded in 1978, the biracial group sponsored lectures, events, trips abroad, and educational programs and encouraged involvement in civil rights protests and political campaigns. Its goal was to "build mutual trust, to advance shared interests, to appreciate each other's uniqueness and perspectives, to enjoy our cultural diversity along with our common humanity, and to develop leadership that can effectively prevent crisis or deal with crises when necessary."[38] Over the lifespan of the organization, its members made frequent appearances on stat sheets of Democratic candidates, running for state and local office and contributing to campaigns.[39] In 1985 they organized protests against South Africa's apartheid policies.[40] BLEWS' religious leadership—rabbis and black clergymen—together challenged Minister Louis Farrakhan's speaking engagement at Morgan State University in 1985, encouraging both the general public and the media to rise above the divisiveness of his message and to not "whip up emotions by taking quotes out of context and blowing them up."[41] BLEWS worked with a coalition of college students to protest another speech by Farrakhan at University of Maryland Baltimore County (UMBC) in 1989.[42] In 1990, BLEWS initiated a program seeking to literally and metaphorically take dialogue to the dinner table and reinvigorate the discussions between the two communities through regular dinner conversations.[43] As of 2018, BLEWS is still active after thirty-five years.

Twenty years after the riots, in 1988, the NAACP led a campaign to create and dedicate the Dorothy Parker Memorial Garden in Baltimore in which her ashes would be interned, at the site of NAACP's national headquarters. Dorothy Parker had left her estate (and remains) to Martin Luther King Jr., with the proviso that, if anything would happen to King, Parker's estate was to be turned over to the NAACP; she was thus interred at the organization's national headquarters in Baltimore, rather than in her beloved New York City.[44] To celebrate the dedication, Rabbi Murray Saltzman of Baltimore Hebrew Congregation and Lois Rosenfield, executive director of the Baltimore chapter of the American Jewish Committee, joined NAACP executive director Benjamin L. Hooks for a ceremony at NAACP headquarters. Hooks expressed the importance of reinvigorating the black-Jewish relationship, recognizing the "traditional bonds of friendship and cooperation that have existed between the black and Jewish communities for such a very long time" and the importance of "renewing our commitment to work hand-in-hand to erase the stain of all forms of racial, religious, sexual, and ethnic injustice and intolerance from our society."[45]

Conclusion

The uprising of 2015 had a different effect on Jewish Baltimoreans than the 1968 riots. Viewers across the United States and world watched live as Baltimore once again exploded into civil unrest following Freddie Gray's death in police custody. Rather than getting information from nightly network news coverage as they had in 1968, Americans learned about the uprising in 2015 from the twenty-four-hour cable news cycle and the endless stream of social media posts. When African Americans took to the streets in the wake of Gray's death, Jewish groups made up of both activists and religious leaders marched along with the protestors. This time, however, practically no Jewish residents or stores were affected, primarily because the majority of small businesses like those owned by Jews in the 1960s were now owned and operated by Korean Americans.[46] By 2010, there were fewer than 5,000 Jewish residents left in central Baltimore and just under 31,000 Jews in the entire city.[47] More than 90,000 live in the immediate Baltimore area, but the majority are in the very northwest corner of the city proper or just outside in areas like Pikesville and Reisterstown in Baltimore County.[48]

As protests began in April 2015, Melissa Gerr of the *Baltimore Jewish Times* interviewed Molly Amster, the Baltimore director of Jews United for Justice (JUFJ), a grassroots organization formed in 1998 to advocate for social, racial, and economic justice. Amster marched in the protests all week and decried the representation of protestors in the media, saying that the news articles continued "to stigmatize and perpetuate the portrayal of people of color in the media."[49] Local interfaith committees signed declarations urging peace, the Baltimore Jewish Council sent volunteers into areas hit by destruction to aid with the clean-up, and local Jewish groups including members of Charm City Tribe, a JCC group for Jewish young adults in their twenties and thirties, worked with volunteer organizations to help repair damaged areas. Similarly, local Jewish organizations joined with African American religious and secular advocacy groups pushing for law enforcement reform.[50]

In an interview with the Israeli newspaper *Haaertz*, Marc Terrill, president of The Associated: Jewish Community Federation of Baltimore, described black–Jewish relations in 2015 after the riots as "collaborative," stating that "not everything is good, but we have the will and desire to work at it." Complicating Terrill's optimistic vision was Baltimore Jewish Council president Arthur Abramson, then executive director of the organization for twenty-five years, who described the situation differently: "Look, Maryland is a southern state. It was a slave state. In general, it's not what I would describe as a place where

African Americans and Jews sit around and sing 'Kumbaya.'"⁵¹ Abramson implied that the relationship since the early 1990s was based on a superficial level of cooperation, rather than an active and positive commitment. JUFJ and other groups have since worked toward that deeper commitment. JUFJ has posted volunteer and donation information from Jewish organizations online, pushing for a united front from all communities fighting injustice guided by Jewish values and text: their signs at the protest simply read "Leviticus 19:16— You shall not stand idly by the blood of your neighbor. #JusticeforFreddie."

Notes

1   Ruth Stewart oral history, Baltimore '68: Riots & Rebirth Collection, University of Baltimore Special Collections, http://archives.ubalt.edu/bsr/oral-histories /transcripts/stewart.pdf, accessed June 25, 2016.

2   See Damien Cave's discussion of the use of these terms in social media following the uprising of 2015, "Defining Baltimore: #Riot, #Uprising or #Disturbance?," *New York Times*, April 28, 2015, online edition, https://www.nytimes.com/live /confrontation-in-baltimore/riot-uprising-or-disturbance/, accessed April 12, 2017.

3   See Jessica I. Elfenbein, Thomas L. Hollowak, and Elizabeth M. Nix, eds., *Baltimore '68: Riots and Rebirth in an American City* (Philadelphia: Temple University Press, 2011).

4   "10 Most-Costly Riots in the U.S.," *Chicago Tribune*, November 24, 2014, http://www.chicagotribune.com/chi-insurance-civil-unrest-riots-bix-gfx-20141126 -htmlstory.html, accessed May 5, 2018.

5   Michael Yockel, "100 Years: The Riots of 1968," *Baltimore Magazine*, May 2007, https://www.baltimoremagazine.com/2007/5/1/100-years-the-riots-of-1968.

6   Steven J. Gold, *The Store in the Hood: A Century of Ethnic Business and Conflict* (Lanham, MD: Rowman & Littlefield, 2010), 62.

7   Gold, *The Store in the Hood*, 74–75.

8   Paul A. Kramer, "White Sales: The Racial Politics of Baltimore's Jewish-Owned Department Stores, 1935–1965," in *Enterprising Emporiums: The Jewish Department Stores of Downtown Baltimore* (Baltimore: Jewish Museum of Maryland, 2001), 40–41.

9   Dan Gardner, "Jews Must Put End to Bias in Southern Stores," *Baltimore Afro-American*, April 28, 1945, 14.

10   "Both Races Unite in Fight against Hecht's Jim Crow," *Baltimore Afro-American*, June 27, 1936, 15.

11   Scholarship on the black–Jewish relationship in America includes Maurianne Adams and John Bracey, eds., *Strangers and Neighbors: Relations between Blacks and Jews in the United States* (Amherst: University of Massachusetts Press, 1999); Mark K. Bauman and Berkeley Kalin, eds., *Quiet Voices: Southern Rabbis and the Black Civil Rights Movement. 1880s to 1990s* (Tuscaloosa: University of Alabama Press, 1997); Paul Berman, ed., *Blacks and Jews: Alliances and Arguments* (New York: Delacorte Press, 1994); Hasia Diner, *In the Almost Promised Land: American Jews and Blacks: 1915–1935* (Baltimore: John Hopkins University Press, 1995); V. P. Franklin, Nancy L. Grant, Harold M. Kelnick, and Genna Rae McNeil, eds., *African Americans and Jews in the Twentieth Century* (Columbia: University of

Missouri Press, 1998); Jonathan Kaufman, *Broken Alliance: The Turbulent Times between Blacks and Jews* (New York: Touchstone Books, 1995); Jack Salzman, ed., *Bridges and Boundaries: African Americans and American Jews* (New York: George Braziller and the Jewish Museum, 1992); Stuart Svokin, *Jews against Prejudice: American Jews and the Fight for Civil Liberties* (New York: Columbia University Press, 1997); and Cornel West and Jack Salzman, eds., *Struggles in the Promised Land: Toward a History of Black-Jewish Relations in the United States* (New York: Oxford University Press, 1997).

12 U.S. Census Statistics, "Maryland: Population of Counties by Decennial Census: 1900 to 1990," http://www.census.gov/population/cencounts/md190090.txt. By 1970, the city's population had declined further, to approximately 905,000.

13 *American Jewish Year Book*, vol. 71 (New York: American Jewish Committee, 1970), 17–21, 347, 349. To place Baltimore's Jewish population in national context, the total American Jewish population in 1968 was estimated to be 5,869,000, out of a total U.S. population of approximately 201,166,000, representing just under 3 percent. http://www.jewishdatabank.org/AJYB/AJY-1970.pdf.

14 Judson Jeffries, "Revising Panther History in Baltimore," in *Comrades: A Local History of the Black Panther Party* (Bloomington: Indiana University Press, 2007), 14.

15 *American Jewish Year Book*, vol. 69 (1968), 282, http://www.ajcarchives.org/AJC_DATA/Files/1968_6_USDemographic.pdf, accessed June 28, 2016.

16 Robert J. Brugger, *Maryland: A Middle Temperament 1634–1980* (Baltimore: Johns Hopkins University Press, 1988), 626.

17 "Mayor Tours a Scarred City, Seeking to Avert a Second Night," *Baltimore Sun*, April 8, 1968.

18 Williams's connection to the Jewish community requires mention here and deserves much more extensive research. His mentor and personal godfather was the undisputed Baltimore crime boss, Julius "Lord" Salsbury, a lieutenant in Jewish gangster Meyer Lansky's national criminal empire. Salsbury recognized Williams's leadership abilities and began tutoring him to control the city's "numbers" and drug enterprises.

19 BPD Detective Ed Burns, ret. Interview in "Melvin Williams," from *American Gangster* BET Network, Season 2, Episode 3, original air date, October 17, 2007.

20 Melvin Williams oral history, Baltimore '68: Riots & Rebirth Collection, University of Baltimore Special Collections, http://archives.ubalt.edu/bsr/oral-histories/transcripts/williams.pdf, accessed June 29, 2016. Nothing like this was ever reported in the newspapers, but in this interview Williams declaratively states that this was the policy told to him by the military and law enforcement leadership.

21 "Emergency Is Declared at End: Agnew's Proclamation Releases Guardsmen from Active Duty," *Baltimore Sun*, April 15, 1968.

22 "Colored-Jewish Relations Topic of Jan. 14 Meeting," *Baltimore Afro-American*, January 6, 1968.

23 Ralph Matthews Jr., "Good Baltimore Silent on Northwood Picketing," *Baltimore Afro-American*, March 2, 1963.

24 "Reform Congregation Working in Inner City," *Baltimore Jewish Times*, January 3, 1969.

25 Pam Widgeon, "In Our Churches," *Baltimore Afro-American*, February 3, 1968.

26 "NAACP Marks Brotherhood," *Baltimore Afro-American*, February 10, 1968.

27 Weldon Wallace, "Walk Set up for Penance: Interfaith Procession Will Take Place Saturday," *Baltimore Sun*, April 11, 1968.

28 "Jews Ask Fight on Ghetto Woe: Group Wires McKeldin to Call Emergency Meeting," *Baltimore Sun*, April 7, 1968.

29 "Panel to Discuss Prejudice from Personal Viewpoints," *Baltimore Jewish Times*, February 28, 1969.

30 *A Report of the Baltimore Civil Disturbance*, 6.

31 Jane Motz, *Report on Baltimore Civil Disorders April, 1968* (Baltimore: American Friends Service Committee, September 1968), 16.

32 Gold, *The Store in the Hood*, 73.

33 Gold, *The Store in the Hood*, 26.

34 M. Hirsh Goldberg, "Statistical Analysis of the Riot," *Baltimore Jewish Times*, May 2, 1969.

35 Ben Gallob, "Rabbinic Students Deplore Jewish Inaction in Slums," *Baltimore Jewish Times*, April 18, 1969.

36 Max Johnson, "Political Notebook: Baltimore Elections Showed Racial Unity," *Baltimore Afro-American*, November 14, 1970.

37 David E. Sloan, "Perspective: To a Jewish Neighbor," *Baltimore Afro-American*, November 14, 1970.

38 Jewish Museum of Maryland, "MS 189 The Black/Jewish Forum of Baltimore (BLEWS) Archive," posted March 31, 2011, http://jewishmuseummd.org/2011/03/ms-189-the-blackjewish-forum-of-baltimore-blews-archive/, accessed June 24, 2016.

39 "Vera P. Hall for City Council in 1987," *Baltimore Sun*, September 17, 1987; C. Fraser Smith, "Barbara Hoffman in 1983 State Senatorial Bid"; "Democratic Panel Wields Kingmaking Power," *Baltimore Sun*, October 24, 1983; "Iris G. Reeves and Rochelle Spector in 1991 City Council Bids," *Baltimore Sun*, September 8, 1991.

40 G. James Fleming, "Blacks-Jews United against S. Africa," *Baltimore Afro-American*, January 12, 1985.

41 Mike Bowler, "Farrakhan Booking Surprises Morgan," *Baltimore Sun*, September 20, 1985. See also Frank P. L. Somerville, "Clergy Defend, Deplore Invitation to Farrakhan," *Baltimore Sun*, September 25, 1985.

42 Patricia Meisol, "Students Plan Low-Key Protest of Farrakhan Visit to UMBC," *Baltimore Sun*, December 9, 1989.

43 Randi Henderson, "'BLEWS' Work to Break down Barriers That Divide People: Dialogues Help Unite Blacks and Jews," *Baltimore Sun*, June 3 1990.

44 Nell Greenfield Boyce, "How Dorothy Parker's Ashes Ended up in Baltimore," National Public Radio, August 19, 2015, Morning Edition, https://www.npr.org/2015/08/19/432830913/how-dorothy-parkers-ashes-ended-up-in-baltimore, accessed May 6, 2018.

45 James Williams, "NAACP Focus," *The Crisis*, October 1988, 38.

46 Jean Marbella, "Korean-American Merchants Face Hurdles in Rebuilding after Baltimore Riot," *Baltimore Sun*, Jun 13, 2015.

47 The Associated: Jewish Community Federation of Baltimore, *What Does Your Future Hold? The 2010 Greater Baltimore Jewish Community Study* (Bronx, NY: Ukeles Associates, 2010), ii–iii, 10.

48 *American Jewish Year Book*, vol. 108 (2008), 194. The latest numbers were calculated in 1999, and the *AJYB* counts the 22,500 Jewish residents of Howard County in the "Greater Washington Total in Maryland," rather than the

"Baltimore Total," even though Howard County is geographically closer to Baltimore than Washington, DC. Available at http://www.ajcarchives.org/AJC _DATA/Files/AJYB806_USPopulation.pdf.

49   Melissa Gerr, "The Jewish Community and Freddie Gray Protests," *Baltimore Jewish Times*, April 27, 2015.

50   Marc Shapiro, *Baltimore Jewish Times*, December 22, 2015, http://jewishtimes .com/43657/a-call-for-reform/news/, accessed June 28, 2016.

51   Rachel Cohen, "Baltimore Jews Join Freddie Gray Protests but It's Complicated," *Haaretz*, May 5, 2015, http://www.haaretz.com/jewish/features/.premium-1 .655032, accessed June 29, 2016.

14

Korean Communities in Baltimore

• • • • • • • • • • • • • • • • • • • •

ALETHEIA HYUN-JIN SHIN

Shin is a Korean community artist who received her Master of Fine Arts degree in Community Arts at the Maryland Institute College of Arts (MICA) in 2015. Below are selections from her art project, The Onggi Project: The Korean Immigrant Communities of Baltimore, *which debuted in spring 2015 in the Station North area of Baltimore and was also displayed at City Hall in September 2015. Shin helped organize* Bmore Seoul to Soul, *a performance-based project also in Station North that blended Korean traditional music, song, and dance with dynamic Baltimore Club performances.[1] The event brought Korean and African American artists together in September 2015 to build community just months after the Baltimore Uprising. Art and culture are key ways of sharing stories and bridging gaps among the diverse people who live and work in a city.*

The Onggi Project

The Onggi Project displays a series of traditional Korean vessels created by or in collaboration with various Korean communities in Baltimore. Because Onggi is a significant vessel form used by Koreans for more than five thousand years to store everyday foods, it serves as a metaphor for the history and wisdom in the untold story of the Korean community in Baltimore. Through the Onggi Project, Korean community partners, including first-generation Korean immigrants at the Greenmount Senior Center, Korean vendors at the Northeast Market, and current Korean students at the Maryland Institute College of Art (MICA), came together to educate and raise awareness of the long-standing yet untold presences of the Korean community in Baltimore. In collaboration, we explored our past and present journeys living as Koreans in America, wrestled with the dual consciousness of being both a Korean and becoming part of the palate of the United States, and explored stories that will ground and connect us to the world that surrounds us.

Oh Kyoung Hwan

Mr. Oh is the facilities manager of the Greenmount Senior Center. To make his vessel, he chose solid contrasting colors to embody the vibrancy and strong will of the Korean community. He also sought to depict peace in the botanical forms he painted on his vessel (see Figure 11).

FIG. 11 Onggi Project: Oh Kyoung Hwan. Photo by Aletheia Shin, 2015.

FIG. 12 Onggi Project: Jung Ki Hwa. Photo by Aletheia Shin, 2015.

Jung Ki Hwa

Jung Ki Hwa's Onggi reflects the light within the shot in the dark of the immigrant's lived experiences (see Figure 12). The words "let us live well" are highlighted in bright colors on the darkly colored Onggi. Ms. Jung also embedded sparkles of bright colors and stars in the interior of the Onggi to represent the sparks and celebrations of her life in the United States.

A Curated Conversation

It has been an honor to record the long-standing yet untold stories of the Korean community in Baltimore. The interview series was motivated by a desire to understand and explore what it means to live in a city that most people seem to understand as being strictly divided between blacks and whites. As an individual who does not identify as either black or white and as a transplant in the local community, I felt compelled to reach out to the people with whom I identified myself: residents and workers who embody and live the past and present history of the Korean community in Baltimore. The following curated dialogue is an exploration undertaken with an array of individuals: young and old, from multiple generations of immigrants who have worked as vendors of public markets, small business owners, artists, lawyers, and so on—all of whom are people of Korean descent living or working in Baltimore today. I attempted to include both the familiar and unfamiliar narratives of immigrant stories, which brought new insight to my assumptions and understanding throughout this journey.

ALETHEIA: How did you end up immigrating to the United States and working as a small business owner?

Oh Kyong Hwan, manager at Greenmount Senior Center: I came to U.S. in 1971. In 1971 Korea, at that time there was nothing in Korea. No factories, no jobs. The first immigrants, who came to U.S. often as contracted workers, realized that their jobs were no less better than people who were working in delis and corner stores. So one by one people began to throw off their contract work to work in small businesses.[2]

A: What was your experience running a small business with your family?

Chris Kim, public defender, son of a retired market vendor: My parents woke up at 5:30 or 6 in the morning, and they did manual labor until they closed. Everything from taking orders, answering the phone, stocking inventory, cleaning, food prep . . . it's just brutal work. I had to do it throughout my childhood even sometime in college, and I really hated it with a passion. So I told my parents that I was never ever going to do that kind of work when I got older.[3]

Sonia, retired vendor at Northeast Market: Our children often grew up thinking that we are workaholics, loving the work we do. But this work, we are doing it so our children can have a better life. It's a duty and sacrifice my generation is making to build up the next generation. We don't work in these businesses to pass it on, but to build on.[4]

A: Baltimore City named immigration as an "entrepreneurial act," based on data that reveal that 7 percent of the immigrant population in Baltimore holds ownership of 21 percent of the businesses, thereby contributing great economic benefits to the city.[5] How do these data speak to you?

Mr. Suh, Papi's Tacos at Broadway Market: I believe the data. I think what we don't realize is that we actually have a lot of power. Korean people are money-making machines. We reap and sow from the hard work we put in. We pay taxes and that gives us a lot of political power we do not recognize for ourselves.[6]

Mr. Kim, owner of Nakwon, a Korean restaurant: I understand that there are many of us. What we need is leadership within our community. We would benefit from gathering and learning from one another, but the problem is everyone is so busy and caught up in living, no one has the time to be the leader and do the extra work to organize ourselves.[7]

A: As a business owner, what was your experience/relationship with your customers who tend to be non-Korean?

Yoon-sun Shin, artist, worker/son of vendor at Northeast Market: I heard, "What's worse than a Jew, is Korean"; "All you guys want to do is make money off of us"; and I wonder . . . well if we weren't here, who's going to be [selling food here]? I try not to say that anything is different because I am Korean. We are all human, we have the same mindsets, the same temptations, we all are guilty for something.[8]

Choi Eun Soon, senior at Greenmount Senior Center: I had a friend named Hama. He was from Baltimore, African American, very good person. Hama always sat in front of our store. . . . He will always greet with a handshake, and hang out. He protected us in a lot of ways. If someone stole from our store, he will say to them, they better not come back if they were thinking to steal again. "This is my ma," he will say. I cannot say enough of how much gratitude I have toward him. In return, I made sure he always has plenty of rice and Kimchi to eat.[9]

A: How do you, as a second-generation immigrant, feel about your identity and coexistence in the United States?

Chris Kim, public defender, son of a retired market vendor: In terms of Korean culture, I love it, but I feel disconnected. Even though there are so many Korean people in America, our culture isn't surviving here.[10]

Jamiee Shim, artist: The history of tension between the black and Korean communities in Baltimore reflects how the struggle to survive under a white-dominant oppressive system misdirects anger in a nonproductive way. Horizontal hostility is designed to distract and dispel our deep-seated frustration so that the people in power can keep winning at the game that they made all the rules for. If there are less competitive players, then of course you'll always end up on top. A red herring! How do we shift our focus from surviving to thriving? How can we come together as heavy-hitting and challenging players to this oppressive game? How do we stop hating each other and direct all that fire and passion toward something that will change how we live together on this earth? I think starting collaborations on a personal level, as artists, musicians, poets, filmmakers, chefs, whatever, is a significant way to start this conversation. To communicate and to channel all our passions, struggles, and stories into something that could have never existed without each of our unique experiences and histories. To realize the similarities and differences of our histories in Baltimore in an open and creative way. To uplift each other rather than killing each other, that is real and productive.[11]

Conclusion

The shared dialogues in this brief chapter do not represent every voice in Baltimore's Korean community. These few of the many stories are shared in hopes they can serve as an entry point toward deeper explorations of historical, cultural, social, generational, and systemic layers that continue to shape the narratives of the "we" and the "I" of the Korean community in Baltimore.

What is clear is that our existence and realities are not made alone. War does not happen alone. Migration does not happen alone. Race, class, gender: our differences do not exist alone. Our realities are intricately connected to others' realities. Within the complex relationships between "us" our realities are made. This short essay presents a perspective of Baltimore through the eyes of Korean immigrants. May it also shed light on the shared realities we live in and draw us closer to one another.

Notes

1 *Bmore Seoul to Soul* was supported by MICA's Office of Community Engagement and with state funds from the Maryland Heritage Area Authority.

2 Kyong Hwan Oh, interviewed by Aletheia Hyun-Jin Shin, Greenmount Senior Center, 2014.

3 Chris Kim, interviewed by Aletheia Hyun-Jin Shin, Maryland Institute College of Art, 2014.

4 Sonia, interviewed by Aletheia Hyun-Jin Shin, Northeast Market, 2014.

5 Mayor's Office of Immigrant and Multicultural Affairs, *The Role of Immigrants in Growing Baltimore* (Baltimore: Abell Foundation, September 2014).

6   Mr. Suh, interviewed by Aletheia Hyun-Jin Shin, Broadway Market, 2014.
7   Mr. Kim, interviewed by Aletheia Hyun-Jin Shin, Nakwon, Korean Restaurant, 2014.
8   Yoon-sun Shin, interviewed by Aletheia Hyun-Jin Shin, Northeast Market, 2014.
9   Choi Eun Soon, interviewed by Aletheia Hyun-Jin Shin, Greenmount Senior Center, 2014.
10 Chris Kim, interviewed by Aletheia Hyun-Jin Shin.
11 Jamiee Shin, interviewed by Aletheia Hyun-Jin Shin, Baltimore, April 25, 2017.

15

The Lumbee Community

• • • • • • • • • • • • • • • • • • • •

Revisiting the Reservation
of Baltimore's Fells Point

ASHLEY MINNER

Even the most familiar places sometimes hold secrets.

In late 2016, I invited Museum Studies graduate students from the University of Maryland, College Park to visit the historic Lumbee Indian community in East Baltimore. Their visit was to include a first attempt at a walking tour of sites important to our people in the neighborhoods where Lumbee first settled.

Our day began at the Baltimore American Indian Center, which is a three-story brick row house in Upper Fells Point, so the Museum Studies students could visit an actual museum. But when it was time to take our walk, our first stop was a Baptist church, one block south, where the Indian Center got its start over fifty years ago.[1]

Sister Linda Cox, an elder of the community and one of the most long-standing, enthusiastic members of both the Indian Center and the church, was the real guide. The tour was our idea—hers and mine—but I was there in more of a support capacity. Sister Linda was very excited to be leading the first tour and perhaps even more excited to share the history of the church: we spent more time in front of South Broadway Baptist than any other stop. Known for her gospel singing, at one point Sister Linda even sang a little bit of a favorite hymn, much to the delight of the students and other folks who had joined us

FIG. 13 Sister Linda Cox singing in front of the South Broadway Baptist Church. Photo by Sean Scheidt for Maryland Traditions, 2012.

in the street (see Figure 13). Moved by her recollections of the life our people had left behind in North Carolina and the myriad accomplishments of our community in Baltimore, she sang,

Through many dangers, toils and snares
I have already come:
'tis grace that brought me safe thus far,
and grace will lead me home.[2]

As time passed, lunchtime loomed, and it seemed that the rest of our tour stops would go unvisited. I encouraged the group to head back "up" the street, toward the next site of significance we had discussed: the former Indian Center day care and senior citizens building on Lombard. But we did not make it more than a few feet before Sister Linda yelled, "Wait! Don't you want to tell them about the store?"

I was dumbfounded. "What store?" I asked. We were in front of a Central American restaurant and an alleyway. Well, Sister Linda had to tell all of us about an Indian store that once was in that location; it was either gone before my time or had faded from my childhood memories.

I am a first-generation Baltimore Lumbee. As a community-based visual artist and a folklorist, I have been a lifelong student of the histories of our people, but I have only been alive since 1983. This moment was a good reminder that I did not know everything there is to know about my own community.

Baltimore's historic Lumbee community has few written records. Many of our places have changed owners, inhabitants, and purpose. Some have been demolished and built over—literally and deliberately erased—so no building is left to visit or preserve; there is nothing left to see. Sometimes the only way to learn is to listen to the stories of those who were here before.

Popular narratives of the Great Migration, the mass movement of southern African Americans to northern cities, do not generally include stories of the multitude of southern American Indians who also migrated north around the same time. After World War II, Lumbee Indians from rural North Carolina moved to Baltimore City in droves, eventually forming a large satellite community on the east side.[3] Anthropologist Abraham Makofsky, who conducted fieldwork in the community from 1969 to 1970, noted that it was "perhaps the single largest grouping of Indians from the same tribe in an American urban area."[4] Even today, this Lumbee community remains the largest outside of North Carolina.

Though Baltimore's Lumbee community is absent from popular narratives about the city and has even been referred to as "invisible," its presence has marked both the cultural landscape and built environment. This is particularly true in the adjoining neighborhoods of Upper Fells Point and Washington Hill, where the Lumbee first settled. These neighborhoods are currently undergoing a profound transition, one that is not disconnected from the movement and displacement of our people from the area. To be fair, perhaps the area has always been in transition. Yet it seems especially important for the most recent generation of Baltimore Lumbee to know the places and spaces important to their forbears, as our presence there steadily dwindles.

As I have explained elsewhere, "The Lumbee Tribe of North Carolina is the largest tribe east of the Mississippi River, and the ninth largest tribe within the United States. Our homeland is a southern part of eastern North Carolina. We take our tribal name from the Lumbee River, which winds through the homeland otherwise characterized by pines, farmland, and swamps. We are the present-day descendants of the Cheraw and other Siouan-speaking groups from the same region, and have African American and European ancestry as well."[5] Lumbee escaped Indian Removal through early assimilation and, to some extent, through geographic isolation.[6] Lumbee people became Christian, English-speaking landowners soon after contact with European colonists.[7] Our culture is living and continues to evolve in Baltimore, as in North Carolina.[8]

Lumbee, as a rule, tend to confound popular stereotypes of American Indian people, which contributes to our supposed invisibility, especially in Baltimore. As Omi and Winant so eloquently write in their classic "Racial Formation in the United States," "Our compass for navigating race relations depends on preconceived notions of what each specific racial group looks like. . . . The content of such stereotypes reveals a series of unsubstantiated beliefs about who these groups are and what 'they' are like."[9]

Being Indian can be complicated. We are living in the legacy of settler colonialism, which perpetually denies the existence of people indigenous to this land; as a result, many "Americans" never expect to encounter an American Indian person. Indians, in the national imagination, have been relegated to history books and hermetically sealed museum cases. Mainstream culture denies Indians contemporary personhood. More than five hundred distinct cultures have been lumped into one constructed race. Monolithic portraits and caricatures of Native America—which is, in fact, extremely diverse—have been promoted ad nauseam by Hollywood and the culture industry. In effect, American Indian people must embody a certain phenotype, or stereotype, to be recognized as such by the general public.

Lumbee "run the gamut of physical characteristics concerning skin color and hair color and hair texture. Nevertheless, we have a characteristic 'look' that is understood and recognized among us."[10] In a diverse place like East Baltimore, where our community makes up only a small fraction of the general population, we are seldom recognized by members of the general population as being American Indian because we do not fit a stereotype.[11]

Yet our community is not insular. The first waves of Lumbee to move to Baltimore did so during the time of Jim Crow, when racial intermarriage in the Deep South was not only socially discouraged but also legally prohibited. In some cases, this prohibition was part of the impetus for leaving. Once in Baltimore, many Lumbee started families with non-Lumbee. This trend has continued through first, second, third, and even fourth generations. Today, many of our young people have only one Lumbee grandparent or great-grandparent, which raises other questions about the future of our community.

Southeast Baltimore was predominantly white until "urban renewal" transformed it in the post–World War II years around the time the Lumbee settled there.[12] In his analysis linking racial disparities in Baltimore City to the most recent uprising of April 2015, reporter Jake Flanigan writes,

> The city lost more than 100,000 manufacturing jobs in the latter half of the
> 20th century—depleting its industrial workforce by 75%. There could not have
> been a worse time for an influx of newcomers. Nevertheless, they came.
> Between 1950 and 1970, Baltimore's African American population nearly
> doubled. Historically in the northeast and northwest of the city, black
> communities began overlapping with historically white neighborhoods [as in
> southeast]. Middle- and upper-class whites, already in flight as a result of
> industrial job-loss, sped for the suburbs.[13]

This white flight was the beginning of a long period of divestment and racial tension in the city, which had only ever been known (and is still mostly known) as being black and white. Enter the Lumbee Indians. Identifying as neither black nor white, our people were bound to be consistently "misread" and misunderstood on the Baltimore landscape.

Minnie S. Maynor, a dark-skinned Lumbee woman who arrived in 1957, recalls the difficulty she encountered in getting a job: "I came to Baltimore and applied for jobs, and of course I didn't get one. It was really difficult because I would call and make an appointment for an interview, and I would sound one way on the telephone [not black] . . . and I looked a different way when I went to the office [presumed to be black]. And they would say to me, 'Oh, that job has been filled.' And of course I followed the newspaper, and I would see that job in there from week to week."[14]

Despite such struggles, there was a sizable Lumbee population in the city by the late 1950s. Brother Hal Hunt Sr., now in his eighties, moved to Baltimore in 1956 when he was a young man. He recalls, "When these Indians come from North Carolina, they looked for Baltimore Street. That was 'the reservation.' When we come to Baltimore, that's what we looked for."[15] Of course, "reservation," in this deployment, is intended to refer to an area populated by Indians and not an officially designated area "reserved" through treaty with the U.S. government. Lumbee Indians in Baltimore designated their own area, with sheer numbers. Sister Linda, who came to Baltimore "to stay" in 1968, remembers, "All the Indians was in East Baltimore. . . . The majority of people that you knew was in East Baltimore . . . [on] Baltimore Street. And we were on Ann Street. So yeah, it looked like people that you could relate with, that looked like you and was part of you."[16]

That same year, following the assassination of Rev. Dr. Martin Luther King Jr., Baltimore experienced the original uprising, which is often characterized as a "race riot." By that time, Minnie S. Maynor was living on the unit block of North Milton Avenue, just north of Patterson Park. She remembers, "I tried to stay in the house because I was frightened to death. And I kept peepin' out the windows to see what was happening. I was always afraid of that stray bullet getting me."[17]

East Baltimore's infrastructure had already deteriorated significantly by 1969, when urban geographer David Harvey moved to Baltimore to work at Johns Hopkins University. He described "terrifying rat-infested inner-city living conditions in the areas wracked by the uprisings in the wake of the assassination": of course, these poor living conditions were not caused by King's assassination or the uprisings, but by institutional racism and divestment.[18] Enter crack in the 1980s and 1990s and you have a real-life version of one of the most widely known, yet fictitious, narratives about Baltimore, *The Wire.*[19] (By the way, there were no Lumbee Indians in *The Wire.*)

Suffice it to say, the neighborhoods in which my own generation grew up in the 1990s and 2000s were and are markedly different from the neighborhood that Sister Minnie, Brother Hal, and Sister Linda first encountered decades before. I once asked Sister Linda's son, Dean "Tonto" Cox Sr., who is close to my age, what it means to him to be Lumbee from Baltimore. He said, "It means that [in] a place like this you have to find yourself. Find your own type of people to hang with.... For me and what I been [through], I almost became a product of my own environment. Would have rather grown up down [North Carolina]. But bein' from [Baltimore] makes you a little slicker."[20]

Our generation was at least fortunate enough to grow up with two enduring cornerstones established by the Lumbee community: South Broadway Baptist Church and the Baltimore American Indian Center. By the late 1960s, Lumbees in Baltimore were already holding annual "Homecomings" in what would become South Broadway Baptist at 211 S. Broadway, in the heart of what had by then become Baltimore's Indian community. Some of the same community members rented space within that same building to establish the "American Indian Study Center" in 1968, the first incarnation of what would be the Baltimore American Indian Center. The Indian Center, a safe place for Indian cultural expressions and a "one-stop social service shop" for those in need, eventually moved from the church to its current location at 113 South Broadway.[21] In the Indian Center's heyday, one could visit there and find assistance with housing, employment, child care, and paying utility bills and, most importantly, fellowship with other Indian people.[22]

Until 2016, the Indian Center owned a mixed-use commercial property on East Lombard Street, which housed the Vera Shank Daycare Center on one side and the Native American Senior Citizens program on the other. It also owned several other properties in the neighborhood, including row houses where visiting artists and culture bearers could stay while in town, workshops were taught, and art was displayed. There were also several Indian-owned stores (in addition to the aforementioned store) and even a Lumbee restaurant.

Makofsky noted the strong relationship between the South Broadway Baptist Church and the Indian Center: "From its inception, the Center's membership... had been drawn primarily from the ranks of the church-going and better educated."[23] But there were apparently many other important—and less formal—community institutions, most of which now only survive in the form of stories.

Coming from the Jim Crow South, some Lumbee were able to sit down and eat inside a restaurant for the first time when they arrived in Baltimore. For many, the particular restaurant where this first happened was a Greek-owned diner, the Moonlight, on the corner of South Broadway and East Baltimore

Street.[24] In fact, much of the planning for South Broadway Baptist Church took place in the Moonlight, though apparently more than that was going on. Lumbee elders recall endless cups of coffee, quiet conversation, *and* fistfights—even knife fights—at the Moonlight.

George Vasiliades worked in the Moonlight as a young dishwasher in 1968; his uncle was the owner. Of the former Moonlight, Mr. George (a great favorite of mine and of many Lumbee people) once hesitantly shared with me, "Now it's a house . . . because the city. . . . It was lot of troubles there by Indians and they close the Moonlight and they make a house."[25] Indeed, there is now no indication at the site of the former Moonlight that there had ever even been a diner there.

There are more stories of "trouble by Indians" at some of the neighborhood bars frequented by Lumbee during the community's peak. Of those, the Volcano, a bar formerly located at the corner of North Ann Street and East Fairmont Avenue, is probably the most famous. I asked a lifelong neighbor and friend to the Lumbee community, Francis Stokes, if he had ever gone to the Volcano when it was open. He answered, "Probably once. It was a troubled bar. A lot of people got shot and stabbed in there, busted upside the head. Lot of Indians went in there. It was a wild, wild bar and if they didn't know you, you knew where you belonged. Not in there."[26]

Much like the Moonlight, there is now no indication at the former site of the Volcano that a bar was ever there. One could not even begin to guess which of the four corners the Volcano used to occupy. Could it be that these places really were literally wiped from the city landscape because of "trouble by Indians"?

I once shared some of this lore with a visiting scholar from Washington, D.C., who is also Indian, though not Lumbee. "Wow! That's sad," he said. "They took on the stereotype of the savage Indian." Maybe. But perhaps these stories point more to what has been called a Lumbee "meanness." Anthropologist Karen Blu once wrote that "meanness," to Lumbee, is "a term suggesting not a miserliness or pettiness, but a sensitivity to insult coupled with a tendency to react to insults quickly, violently, and implacably. It does not signify, for [Lumbee], 'small' or 'base' but rather 'touchiness' and a willingness to 'stand up for oneself' against others."[27] The Lumbee "tend to see their options as dual—be ready to fight or be walked over."[28]

Being able to designate space for oneself in an environment that does not understand or recognize one racially, culturally, or otherwise must require some "meanness." The environment itself is "mean" (this time used in the conventional sense of the word, as a synonym for "unpleasant," "unfair," "cruel"). State-sponsored processes of erasure, cloaked by words like "renewal," "development," and even "beautification," are no less mean.

Over the course of the last two decades, there has been significant reinvestment in the infrastructure of Southeast Baltimore. Young, affluent professionals—colloquially known as yuppies—have flocked to this part of the city, especially to Canton, Butcher's Hill, Patterson Park and Fells Point.[29] Truly, the desired path to these neighborhoods was drawn for this demographic long ago.[30] After all, Fells Point is literally a textbook example of gentrification used in scholarly analyses.[31]

Yuppies are not the only group to move to Southeast Baltimore en masse in recent years. There has also been significant immigration from various parts of Latin America. Today it is more common to hear "Upper Fells Point" referred to as "Spanish Town" or "Little Mexico" than "the reservation"—both racist misnomers that collapse a diverse community of Latinx people—inasmuch as it is an invitation to the remaining members of the "Indian" community to expand their own understandings of indigeneity and of the right to the city.[32] Like the Lumbee in their time, these folks have come seeking jobs and a better quality of life in Baltimore.

Surprisingly, it seems that the sustained presence of nonwhite, working-class populations in Southeast Baltimore has done little to slow the now rampant process of gentrification that was set in motion decades before. According to several scholars who study such phenomena, diversity is actually the main draw for would-be city dwellers and is a prerequisite for gentrification.[33] "As Jane Jacobs[34] wrote long ago, truly great cities are federations of neighborhoods that are made up of all kinds of people."[35] East Baltimore is nothing if not diverse.

Meanwhile, there has been a steady stream of Lumbee moving from Baltimore City to Baltimore County since at least the early 2000s. It would be inaccurate and perhaps unfair to suggest that this secondary migration to working-class suburban neighborhoods like Dundalk, Essex, Rosedale, and other areas outside of the city is entirely a consequence of displacement. It was a goal of many Lumbee families to leave the city, which was achieved by the "success" of our people and their upward mobility. However, many of these families were also "bought out" of their homes (by Johns Hopkins or other developers), which illustrates that the issues at play are complex.[36]

In early 2018, I convened a group of Lumbee elders to map the historic Lumbee Indian community of East Baltimore in an effort to further develop our walking tour. To begin the meeting, I presented each of the elders with a copy of a map that I had come across, titled "Lumbee Community in Baltimore."[37] This map was hand drawn by a researcher in 1969 for a final report of the National Study of American Indian Education, published by the University of Chicago. It is presumably the only existing map of Baltimore's Lumbee Indian community. I thought I had struck gold.

FIG. 14 Howard Redell Hunt Sr. (seated), Jeanette W. Jones (standing), and other Lumbee elders map the historic Lumbee community of East Baltimore for the walking tour. Photo by Sean Scheidt, 2018.

The elders were delighted to see the names of some of their old hangouts on the map—among them, the Moonlight and the Volcano—but soon, they started to grumble. "All this is wrong!" they exclaimed.[38] "And [there's] a whole lot missing!"[39] The map was so "wrong," in fact, that some of the elders took out their pens and set to creating their own maps, rather than attempting to correct the one set before them (see Figure 14).

I learned about so many more of our places on that day. Truly, sometimes the only way to learn is to listen to the stories of those who were there before. And to get things "right," our people have to be able to tell our own stories, on our own terms.

Our walking tour is a way to map, for recent generations of Baltimore Lumbee and the generations to come, the places and spaces important to their forbears. This project requires the reconvening of Lumbee elders in the neighborhood they used to inhabit. By walking and listening to those who remember, we can learn their stories. Those stories connect us to our places. Our stories and our places connect us to ourselves and each other.

Our community is losing something here. This old adage holds true: if you lose something, sometimes retracing your steps is the best way to find it.

Notes

1 Present-day South Broadway Baptist Church is located at 211 South Broadway, Baltimore, Maryland 21231. In 1968, this historic church building was owned by the Methodist Missionary and Church Extension Society of the Baltimore Districts. Space within was rented by leaders of the American Indian community to establish the American Indian Study Center. Members of a growing Indian church were also permitted to hold their annual "Homecomings," or large gatherings when people return to their "home church," at 211 S. Broadway. It was in 1978 that these members purchased the building, formally occupied it, and officially changed its name to South Broadway Baptist Church.

2 John Newton, *Amazing Grace,* 1779, http://www.hymnary.org/text/amazing _grace_how_sweet_the_sound, accessed February 28, 2017.

3 There was representation from other tribes as well, including fellow Carolina tribes like the Coharie and the Haliwa Saponi; however, the majority of Indian migrants to Baltimore City were Lumbee.

4 Abraham Makofsky, "Struggling to Maintain Identity: Lumbee Indians in Baltimore," *Anthropological Quarterly* 55, no. 2 (April 1982): 76.

5 Ashley Minner, "Standing in the Gap: Lumbee Cultural Preservation at the Baltimore American Indian Center," in *The Routledge Companion to Intangible Cultural Heritage*, ed. M. Stefano and P. Davis (London: Routledge, 2016), 387.

6 The Indian Removal Act was signed into law by President Andrew Jackson in 1830, authorizing the president to grant unsettled lands west of the Mississippi in exchange for Indian lands within existing state borders. A few tribes went peacefully, but many resisted the relocation policy and were forcibly removed.

7 Minner, "Standing in the Gap," 387.

8 See Lumbeetribe.com.

9 Michael Omi and Howard Winant, "Racial Formation in the United States," in *Rethinking Society in the 21st Century: Critical Readings in Sociology*, ed. Kate Benzanson and Michelle Webber (Toronto: Canadian Scholars' Press, 2016), 77.

10 Minner, "Standing in the Gap," 387.

11 It is believed that there are currently approximately 5,000 Lumbee in Baltimore, based on a combined 2010 U.S. Census count for American Indian populations in Baltimore City and Baltimore County, and a community-based estimate of additional persons who did not participate in the 2010 Census.

12 Marisela B. Gomez, *Race, Class, Power and Organizing in East Baltimore: Rebuilding Abandoned Communities in America* (New York: Lexington Books, 2013), 18.

13 Jake Flanagin, "White Flight Decimated Baltimore Businesses Long before Rioters Showed Up," *Quartz*, April 28, 2015, https://qz.com/393128/white-flight -decimated-baltimore-businesses-long-before-rioters-showed-up/.

14 Minnie S. Maynor, interview with Ashley Minner and Sean Scheidt, February 11, 2016, transcript.

15 Hal Hunt Sr., interview with Ashley Minner, 2011. Available at http:// ashleyminnerart.com/histories/brohal.

16 Linda Cox, interview with Ashley Minner, 2011. Available at http:// ashleyminnerart.com/histories/sislinda/.

17 Minnie S. Maynor, interview.

18 David Harvey, *Rebel Cities: From the Right to the City to the Urban Revolution* (London: Verso, 2012), 55.

19 *The Wire* is a popular American television series set and produced in Baltimore. It aired on HBO from June 2, 2002, to March 9, 2008. Major themes included crime, gangs, gangsters, and the illegal drug market.

20 Dean Tonto Cox Sr., interview with Ashley Minner for the *Exquisite Lumbee* project, 2011, Baltimore, Maryland.

21 Although members of the Lumbee Tribe of North Carolina founded the Center, it has always been the mission of the organization to serve "American Indian and Alaskan Native families" inclusively. Members of other nations have served in leadership positions at the Center over the years as well. The current mission statement is as follows: "The Baltimore American Indian Center (BAIC) is an Urban American Indian Community Center established to assist and support American Indian and Alaskan Native families with moving into an urban environment and adjusting to the culture change they will experience. The BAIC also serves as a focal point for the Indian community for social and cultural activities and to educate non-native people about the cultures of the North American Indian and Alaskan Native communities."

22 In 2018, the Center struggles to remain open because of a lack of funding and other kinds of support. Yet, it still houses a Heritage Museum, which is open during somewhat regular hours and which features rotating exhibitions and a permanent collection of artifacts from across the Americas. The Center also has a gathering space intended to serve our community's meeting needs.

23 Abraham Makofsky, "Tradition and Change in the Lumbee Indian Community of Baltimore," *Maryland Historical Magazine* 75, no. 1 (March 1980): 68–69.

24 Stemming from this historic relationship, Lumbee people continue to patronize another Baltimore restaurant owned by the same family, the famous Sip & Bite on Boston Street. Mr. George Vasiliades owned, managed, and cooked in Sip & Bite for many years until he retired.

25 George Vasiliades, interview with Ashley Minner and Sean Scheidt, February 12, 2016, Baltimore, Maryland, transcript.

26 Francis Stokes, interview with Ashley Minner, February 24, 2016, transcript.

27 Karen Blu, *The Lumbee Problem: The Making of An American Indian People* (Lincoln: University of Nebraska Press, 1980), 144.

28 Blu, *The Lumbee Problem*, 35.

29 See Natalie Sherman, "City Sees Jump in Young, College-Educated Residents," *Baltimore Sun*, October 26, 2014; Jacques Kelly, "In East Baltimore, A Once-Barren Neighborhood Starts to Bloom," *Baltimore Sun*, May 5, 2017.

30 "Desire path" is a planning term used to describe unofficial routes through physical spaces that are marked (worn) by frequent usage.

31 See Robert Beauregard, "The Chaos and Complexity of Gentrification," in *The Gentrification Reader*, ed. L. Lees, T. Slater, and E. Wyly (New York: Routledge, 2010), 13; Fred Siegel, "The Death and Life of America's Cities," *The Public Interest* 148 (2002): 3–22; and Charles C. Bohl, "New Urbanism and the City: Potential Applications and Implications for Distressed Inner-City Neighborhoods," *Housing Policy Debate* 11 (2000): 761–801.

32 Andrew Scherr, "Spanish Town," *Urbanite*, May 1, 2005, https://web.archive.org /web/20120916231823/http://www.urbanitebaltimore.com/baltimore/spanish -town/Content?oid=1245650. Some members of Baltimore's Lumbee community view immigrants from Latin America as competitors for work and other resources. They do not recognize the newcomers as fellow indigenous people. The "right to

the city"—or a "demand ... [for] a transformed and renewed access to urban life"—is a concept and term originally coined by French philosopher and sociologist Henri Lefebvre, in his book *Le Droit à la ville* (Paris: Anthropos, 1968).

33 See Jane Jacobs, *The Death and Life of Great American Cities* (New York: Vintage Books, 1961), 208; Richard Florida, *The Rise of the Creative Class, Revisited* (New York: Basic Books, 2011, 2012), 293–294; and Sharon Zukin, *Naked City: The Death and Life of Authentic Urban Places* (New York: Oxford University Press, 2016), 15–16.

34 It should be noted that the words of Jane Jacobs are frequently co-opted by both proponents and opponents of gentrification.

35 "The Re-Education of Richard Florida," *Houston Chronicle*, http://www .houstonchronicle.com/business/texanomics/article/The-Reeducation-of-Richard -Florida-10165064.php, accessed December 13, 2016.

36 Johns Hopkins Hospital is the teaching hospital and biomedical research facility of the Johns Hopkins School of Medicine. Located in East Baltimore, Hopkins is the largest employer within the city, and it has rapidly expanded its real estate holdings in recent years.

37 Map of the "Lumbee Community in Baltimore," drawn by John Peck, 1969. Originally published in J. G. Peck, *Education of Urban Indians: Lumbee Indians in Baltimore*, Final Report of the National Study of American Indian Education (Chicago: University of Chicago Press, 1969).

38 Howard Redell Hunt Sr., et al., Lumbee Elders Luncheon hosted by Ashley Minner, March 22, 2018, Baltimore, Maryland, transcript.

39 Sarah Arnold, et al., Lumbee Elders Luncheon.

16

Overburdened Bodies
and Lands

●●●●●●●●●●●●●●●●●●●●●●

Industrial Development
and Environmental Injustice
in South Baltimore

NICOLE FABRICANT

Destiny Watford—a founding member of Free Your Voice, a youth-led activist group focused on human rights—faced a group of fifteen undergraduate students from my anthropology course at Towson University who had traveled to South Baltimore on July 16, 2015.[1] Pointing to the postindustrial landscape, she told them that this community used to be called Fairfield. During her speech, she shared a report from the *Baltimore Sun* that described the 1984 chemical explosion on the Fairfield peninsula that sent fourteen people—ten from a nearby elementary school—to the hospital. Principal Anne C. Fuller of Victory Elementary School described a mushroom-cloud-like explosion near the school that she indicated looked like "Hiroshima." "This blast," Destiny told the group of students, "was the second major incident at the Essex industrial facility in less than a year." Thirty years later, similar catastrophes are still taking place. On Christmas Eve in 2015, at the Solvay Industry Plant on Fairfield Road, a storage tank containing 400,000 gallons of sulfuric acid collapsed, sending a wave of corrosive pollutants into a creek that abuts a densely populated area.[2] During the "Toxic Tour of Curtis Bay," my students and I walked from Fairfield Road on the industrial peninsula, popularly referred to as "Vinegar Road" because of its putrid smells; to Curtis Bay's Pennington Avenue, which is lined with small mom-and-pop grocery, gas, and liquor stores; and then to the Filbert Street Community Garden in Curtis Bay.

On the industrial peninsula, the students saw the eighty acres of land that the multinational FMC Corporation, which ran an agricultural chemical plant on the site until 2007, leased to Energy Answers International, a multinational corporation planning to build one of the largest trash-to-energy incinerators in the United States.[3] A small sign read "Energizing, Revitalizing and Growing Baltimore's Industrial Base: Fairfield Renewable Energy Project." The clear promise of the project was to bring jobs and industry back to Baltimore, while simultaneously creating a source of "clean and green" energy. Watford, our "toxic tour" guide, told us that the proposed incinerator would burn 4,000 tons of waste daily and emit 240 pounds of mercury and 1,000 pounds of lead per year into the air, along with dioxins and ultrafine particulate matter.[4] Between 15 and 25 percent of the ash incinerated trash would be disposed of in landfills.

The putrid air—a mixture of dust and dirt, garbage, and coal dust from a local dock—got caught in our throats as we lingered at the site. Some students breathed through handkerchiefs; others without a way of filtering the air pollution felt nauseated. Fairfield Road is a major artery for tractor trailers delivering cars for automotive export-import businesses and crude oil to refineries. This traffic combines with the other air pollutants to produce labored breathing. In the distance, we saw one of the largest coal piers in the Northeast. The mountains of open-air coal from Southwestern Virginia in Appalachia, piling up on the dock, were vividly clear and visible from a Curtis Bay park and playground.[5] Across the water, Watford pointed to one of the largest landfills in Baltimore in a community once called Wagner's Point, a formerly Eastern European working-class neighborhood, where late nineteenth-century Polish immigrants worked in a thriving canning plant.

As we walked from site to site, Watford who was an undergraduate at Towson University majoring in Communications and English, mapped the lessons she and other youth from Curtis Bay learned in their political struggle to stop a trash incinerator from being built in their neighborhood. Watford grew up in Curtis Bay, and while she was a teenager at Benjamin Franklin High School she worked with United Workers, a human rights organization, to found a youth movement called Free Your Voice, which focuses on issues of environmental justice in Curtis Bay. She highlighted three critical lessons: (1) the importance of understanding the history of large-scale industrial capitalism and its "burden" or "cost" in terms of residents' health, (2) the history of structural racism that shapes dynamics in South Baltimore today, and (3) the importance of art and creativity in building a local movement. Watford's insights about historical and global trends put into context the present industrial development in the region. From the late nineteenth century, when the peninsula became a major importer of guano fertilizer from Peru, to the World War II years when it was home to shipbuilding, to the postwar decay of those industries, these waves of industrialization have cumulatively wreaked havoc on lands, soils, and bodies.

Environmental scholar Rob Nixon's concept of slow violence is a useful framework for understanding the environmental and bodily violence of industrial capitalism in Curtis Bay: it is "a violence that occurs gradually and out of sight, a violence of delayed destruction that is dispersed across time and space, an attritional violence that is typically not viewed as violence at all."[6] This framework requires us to rethink conventional assumptions about violence as highly visible, time bound, and body bound. Slow violence is inherently not immediate, but rather "its calamitous repercussions play out across a range of temporal scales."[7] How can we then use Baltimore's long history of industrial development—dating back to its guano production—to think about its industries' residual effects on bodies, communities, and environment? Environmental justice is central to understanding economic history, which prompts two critical questions: Who pays the price for industrial development and resulting pollution? In what ways does this history of violence inform movement building and collective imagining of a more sustainable (both economic and ecologically) future?

Youth groups like Free Your Voice that are resisting the most recent iteration of toxicity have used art, music, and popular culture to make visible these historic inequities and bring attention to what is hidden from public view, including overburdened bodies and lands. In turn, they are now pressuring state legislators to hold corporations like Energy Answers accountable and to support local efforts struggling to achieve a more sustainable future.

Watford's focus on history is a critical lens for viewing "toxicity" in relationship to a place over time. She mentioned on the tour how Curtis Bay had been a site for the import of some of the most toxic fertilizers, such as guano. To gain a fuller understanding of the cumulative impact of various forms of toxic industrial production processes on the land, air, and health of Curtis Bay, it is necessary to examine industrialization in the nineteenth century.[8] Guano fertilizer from Peru was then a prized commodity for gunpowder and for agricultural needs, particularly for farmland around the Chesapeake Bay where both cotton and tobacco had drained the soil of its nutrients. As pressure on the land increased because of immigration and population growth, it became less and less feasible to reverse nutrient depletion simply by allowing the land to remain fallow.

The importation of guano, which was shipped to and often remained in Curtis Bay, initiated a long period of dangerous and inequitable disposal of hazardous and/or toxic materials in the soils, air, and bodies of residents. By the early twentieth century, Monumental Acid Works at Fairfield, which produced fertilizer, had developed and manufactured an artificial equivalent to guano—superphosphate—a highly corrosive and strong mineral acid that can cause severe burns and is similarly toxic.[9] Guano was so hazardous that merchants considered it as a cargo of last resort for captains and shipowners, in large part because yellowish dust covered every part of the ship during loading and the noxious odor dried out noses and irritated eyes.[10] Conditions were worse in Peru where Chinese laborers produced guano under hazardous circumstances. The Navassa Phosphate Company, based in Fairfield, used African American and Haitian workers and white supervisors from Baltimore to work on Navassa Island in the Caribbean where conditions were even more exploitive.[11] Black workers, who were often undernourished and treated with extreme brutality, rebelled in 1889 and killed five of their white supervisors.[12]

The global guano trade illustrated not only the early division of labor along race and class lines but also what Wayne Ellwood calls "Old Globalization": the interconnectedness of economies in the nineteenth century and the super-exploitation of African American workers as part and parcel of expanding capitalism.[13] Workers from Baltimore were shipped to work in Peru as toxic fertilizer was imported through our ports. African American bodies and lands became both sites of control, management, and exploitation. The experience of laborers in Curtis Bay during this period was also adversely affected by the poor quality and limited availability of basic amenities such as housing. Historian Sherry Olson describes how African American migration from rural Maryland in the 1890s created a housing shortage.[14] Simultaneously, racist policies restricted all development of new housing for African Americans.[15] Consequently, shantytowns were built by the owners and managers of the chemical factories in Fairfield up through World War II. These company towns were built on patriarchal and paternalist patron-client relationships, in which housing and/or food was given to maintain tight control over laborers.[16] Today vestiges of this approach are found in Curtis Bay where major chemical companies like Grace Chemical continue to have great influence in the community.[17]

As we walked down some of the side streets of Curtis Bay, Watford told the group about early forms of labor control in the canning industry. The tight control over labor continued as the industrial base of Curtis Bay shifted from fertilizer production to canning in the late nineteenth century. Martin Wagner built a large and successful oyster and fruit packing plant in 1883 at the southern tip of the Fairfield peninsula in an area that became known as Wagner's Point. Child labor and exploitive working conditions in Baltimore's canning industry are well documented. Sociologist and photographer Lewis Hine reported on his visit to Baltimore, "On every hand, one can see little tots toting boxes or pans full of berries/tomatoes, and it is evident the work is too hard. Then there are machines which no small person should be working around."[18] Importantly, in the early twentieth century, intense industrial fires ravaged much of the area. One of the worst fires occurred during the summer of 1920 in Curtis Bay. As Nicole King documents, there was widespread panic: "Flaming oil flooded the streets and thirty-two homes were destroyed, leaving one hundred people homeless."[19] The presumption of the disposability of laborers was consistently reflected in the working conditions of the canneries, where unhealthy and unsafe workplaces—particularly for children—were defining experiences for workers. The dominance of the owners over the factory workers was reinforced through paternalistic relations in housing, transportation, and food, which workers bought in the company store, often at exorbitant prices.

Watford walked confidently down Pennington Avenue and onto Filbert Street as she narrated some of the historic dangers of oil refineries and more recent fears of transporting crude oil by rail. When cannery owner Martin Wagner died in 1903, his family sold the land to various oil companies, including the Prudential Oil Corporation, which established a refinery in the middle of the peninsula in 1914. The Texas Oil Company of Delaware (later known as Texaco) was established before the end of World War I. By the time the city of Baltimore annexed the industrial peninsula in 1918, Fairfield was home to at least three petroleum refineries and several fertilizer plants.[20] By 1932, Continental Oil established a large refinery and the Baltimore & Ohio Railroad built the world's largest mechanized coal pier on the industrial peninsula. These two industries combined to pose many health hazards for residents: oil refining exposes the surrounding community to the risk of intense explosions, while coal dust exacerbates lung and cardiovascular disease.

Blatant disregard for the quality of life of both workers and residents of Curtis Bay continues to this day. Recent proposals—passed without input from community residents—to use South Baltimore as a gateway for the processing and shipping of crude oil, which have grown because of increased oil fracking in North Dakota and tar sands oil extraction in northern Alberta, illustrate the disposability of impoverished populations. Not only are the contents of toxic oil dangerous to community residents but also the oil trains themselves are outdated and pose safety risks. A study by the National Transportation Safety Board found that crude oil trains have a high incidence of failure.[21] The oldest model trains, DOT-111, derailed dozens of times in 2015, causing serious negative consequences. For example, in April 2014, ten fairly new tank cars carrying crude oil derailed and exploded in Lynchburg, Virginia, spilling about thirty thousand gallons of Bakken crude oil and setting the James River on fire. In South Baltimore, CSX trains run right through the heart of the community. Oil companies—along with CSX—have concealed the actual routes, frequency, and volume of crude oil traveling through Curtis Bay. As Watford and other members of the Free Your Voice human rights group have articulated on numerous occasions, "such back-deal politicking is about a lack of transparency."[22] Part of the Free Your Voice leadership development model has been about holding corporate entities like Energy Answers and CSX accountable for such undemocratic practices.[23]

As we headed toward Filbert Street on our tour, Watford mentioned the importance of shipbuilding during the World War II era and how it shifted neighborhood dynamics. The wartime effort in the 1940s to manufacture materials needed to fortify American troops affected Curtis Bay. During this period, thousands of workers from West Virginia and elsewhere in Appalachia, as well as African Americans from the South, migrated to the Fairfield peninsula for jobs in shipbuilding and other emergent wartime industries.[24] White workers received decent government-subsidized housing, while African American workers continued to be exiled to "Old Fairfield," having access only to substandard housing in increasingly undesirable areas.[25] Elected city-level officials and business leaders made no attempt to hide their biases: "They are going to bring Negro workers. They are going to send us scum," a city official stated at a public meeting. "If more Negroes are brought here, then, they should be housed in trailers so they can be easily moved out after the war is over."[26]

After the war, the entire area became a mix of polluting industries. For example, after World War II many Liberty ships—massive cargo ships built on the industrial peninsula during the war effort—had to be broken down, and in the process heavy metals polluted the water and the soil.[27] In the 1960s, residents continued to experience the effects of city, state, and federal government disinvestment from their neighborhood; increasing pollution from oil and chemical companies; and growing mounds of trash and toxins accumulating from shipbreaking, salvage yards, and dumps.[28] Fairfield residents were predominantly African American and lived in substandard housing without basic services or a sewage system until the late 1970s. After a series of fires in the 1980s, Baltimore City began to relocate residents of both Wagner's Point and Fairfield as part of the demolition of public housing and dispersal of residents (particularly African American ones) in areas across the city. The entire area is now designated M-3—zoned solely for heavy industry—and the last residents were relocated in 2011. The memories of destructive capitalism, exploitive laboring relations, race- and class-based discrimination, and toxicity do not simply linger as historic artifacts, but rather continue to define how this landscape is viewed in Baltimore today.

The Towson students who accompanied me on the "Toxic Tour of Curtis Bay"—many of whom live in the suburbs—had a hard time grasping what it means to live amidst such polluting industries; they had a hard time comprehending fears of an oil train derailing and exploding or of breathing coal dust like a miner in Appalachia. Their sense of safety was very much tied to how their middle-class and predominantly white bodies remain protected from toxic industrial production. What we saw in Curtis Bay was a classic example of environmental racism or environmental classism, whereby environmental hazards are disproportionately located in low-income, predominantly black and Latino communities. Their genuine disorientation during the tour was in large part a consequence of living in places that are far removed from those spaces bearing the costs of industrial expansion and from postindustrial wastelands that have been dumping grounds for many decades. However, as the students were thrust into Watford's world and directly experienced the intensity of industrial pollution, they raised many questions about the intersection of race, class, and environmental justice.

Standing on the proposed site of the trash-to-energy incinerator, Watford told us,

> Curtis Bay has always been a frontline community, forced to bear the costs in our health to satisfy the demands of the market . . . we have learned that the incinerator and the fact of its location fits into a historical pattern . . . of meeting the demands of the economy, regardless of cost. . . . The incinerator project was a routine development in my community, another market-driven project extracting wealth. Maybe not this time from the agricultural products like Wagner's cannery or . . . the big agricultural pesticide companies, this time wealth extraction was rooted in the service economy and trash.[29]

In 2009, Energy Answers announced it would build the nation's largest trash-to-energy incinerator in Fairfield, presenting the project as a solution to two crises: the waste crisis and the energy crisis. The idea of converting waste into energy became popular in the United States during the global energy crisis of the 1970s; by the 1990s this concept had become significant within energy investment circles. Federal and state legislation created market incentives to revalue waste materials, and the policy environment encouraged technological innovation.[30] In November 2011, then-Governor Martin O'Malley signed a bill making trash incineration a tier-1 renewable energy like wind, solar, and geothermal. Energy Answers International cut a $100,000 check to the O'Malley-led Democratic Governors Association on the very same day that Governor O'Malley indicated he would sign the state legislation.[31]

Energy Answers International promoted the project as a power plant that would provide schools and other facilities with "green energy." The incinerator was originally slated to be sited less than a mile from Benjamin Franklin High School and Curtis Bay Elementary, which violated state environmental regulations. However, when the Public Service Commission approved the incinerator as an energy plant, it granted an exemption because the "tire rubber, vinyl, plastic, and metals would be processed into fuel elsewhere."[32]

Curtis Bay already had the highest level in the state of toxic air pollutants released by stationary mobile facilities, including mercury, lead, and fine particulate matter.[33] Despite this record, the incinerator project would introduce additional pollutant stressors. It is important to reiterate that Curtis Bay represents a kind of palimpsest containing layer after layer of historic epochs that polluted the land, air, and people. Local bodies were a primary repository for toxicity.

The oil and coal industry have worked very hard to conceal or obfuscate these outcomes: endless amounts of money have been funneled into covering up the impacts of their industries, particularly the links between nonrenewable fossil fuels and climate change denialism.[34] Frantz Fanon wrote about the role an army of "cultural bewilderers" plays under capitalism.[35] Rob Nixon argues that this lavishly funded and expansive army of bewilderers creates discourses that promote levels of uncertainty that often guarantee inaction.[36] This form of slow violence allows the bewilderers to buy time, and doubt becomes a "bankable product."[37] Yet young activists inside these "environmental" war zones are refusing to accept those claims or to be bewildered by such tactics of subterfuge. They understand their experiences of environmental toxicity and reject the notion that Curtis Bay is merely a bankable product. Their continuing agenda has been to learn about Curtis Bay's history of toxicity, to understand how structural racism has contributed to past and present uses of the community, and to develop a platform and campaign for alternative forms of development. The experiences of this group of young people have impelled them to pressure public entities such as Baltimore City and Baltimore County school boards, public libraries, and even some public museums to divest from Energy Answers' "dirty" incineration practices.

Free Your Voice has used art, culture, and music to make visible the "slow violence" of incineration and to envision alternative landscapes, raising the consciousness of "disasters that are long in the making and slow moving."[38] Through the urgency of their art, they rouse public sentiment and drive political intervention. They have used photography and videography to tell local stories of injustice and environmental degradation. Through social media, they have launched these stories into critical seats of power at the local and regional level. In fall 2016, they hosted a month-long art exhibit, "Development without Displacement," to which local artists, poets, musicians submitted work that told stories of community and struggle. This work challenges mainstream media representations of the neighborhood and its people as disposable. As Nixon articulates, "our media bias toward spectacular violence exacerbates the vulnerability of ecosystems treated as disposable by capitalism while exacerbating the vulnerability of what Kevin Bale calls 'disposable people.'"[39] As Watford told the student tour group, "We looked within and relied on the strengths and the tools we had to combat the dumping ground mentality. We were artists, poets, musicians, and writers."

On May 27, 2014, two sisters who are members of Free Your Voice performed their rap song about contaminated air and the incinerator to the Baltimore City School Board to encourage them to cancel their contract to buy energy from the incinerator. Their music tells a story not only about environmental degradation but also about resistance. Audrey Rozier sings,

> 18 year-old girl living in the world . . . where no one cares about the safety of the girl. Money, money, money. That seems to be the anthem destroying the world and always taking it for granted. No more greed. All I can see is landfills. I'm disgusted. I can't believe we trusted the world. But it's not too late to be adjusted we have our rights according to the amendments. But why do we feel like we have been so resented? Shoved to the side where opinions don't matter, where opinions only die. It's time to stand up and let our voices be heard. Incinerator move because you are not preferred. It's time to stand up and free your voice.[40]

Free Your Voice also organized a sunflower parade through the streets of Curtis Bay in April 2015, featuring the Christian Warriors Marching Band and marchers carrying hundreds of hand-painted sunflowers. Their vision is a city that embraces fair development and sustainable futures.[41] Reinforcing the work of Free Your Voice, local performers and artists such as Valeska Populoh and Ellen Cherry have written plays like *The Holy Land* that have been performed at community events such as the Fairfield Reunion, where members of Old Fairfield gather at the Curtis Bay Recreation Center to socialize, and at the Human Rights Dinner, a fundraising event for United Workers.[42] Performance and art thus have been used to tell stories about communal forms of displacement in South Baltimore and as a vehicle to project and amplify community voices into places of affluence across the city. If the incinerator proposed creating value out of waste, Free Your Voice turned art, music, and performance into true "social value."

After a series of protests and demonstrations that used art as a way to articulate alternative visions of change, Baltimore City Public Schools agreed to end its agreement with the Energy Answers Incinerator Project in March 2015. This remarkable victory removed an important source of revenue for the incinerator project. After a major protest in front of the Maryland Department of the Environment (MDE), where seven members of the Stop the Incinerator campaign were arrested for civil disobedience in March 2016, the MDE pulled the permit and the Energy Answers incinerator project was defeated, for the moment.[43] However, the story and the fight do not end with the demise of the incinerator project.

There are discussions about how to reclaim the land from the FMC Corporation to build a community land trust. Curtis Bay resident Amanda Maminski said, "We believe there are other alternatives to the proposed incinerator, alternatives that will not involve poisoning the already-toxic environment within and around Curtis Bay."[44] Free Your Voice—working alongside United Workers—has mobilized residents to translate some of the community narratives of "injustice" into sustainable socioeconomic alternatives. Maminski imaginatively traced what a collectively owned, collectively run solar plan might look like for the eighty acres of land leased by Energy Answers. She argued, "Stopping the incinerator isn't enough. We understand that Baltimore needs electricity and that the incinerator was to create jobs and stimulate the local economy. However, we believe there are other alternatives, which will not involve poisoning the already-toxic environment within and around Curtis Bay. One of those is a solar facility on the tract of land currently owned by FMC Corporation."[45] She has presented this solar plan at several community association meetings in South Baltimore and formally has taken these plans to city government officials like Baltimore's former mayor Stephanie Rawlings-Blake. Unfortunately, this plan has not moved forward. However, other plans for cooperative economies (tied to urban agriculture) are currently being developed. Rodette Jones, the Filbert Street community garden manager, is building a local network to promote both urban agriculture as a solution to food deserts and curbside composting and recycling programs as more sustainable solutions to waste disposal.

Despite strong community resistance, Fairfield's industrial peninsula and the residential neighborhoods of Brooklyn and Curtis Bay remain locations for crude oil transport and chemical and open-air coal storage. The community has neither developed the power nor the economic alternatives to radically alter this dynamic. Consequently, the practices of these corporations continue to burden the bodies of residents as leachate from landfills seeps into waterways, chemicals are dumped into rivers, and layers of heavy metals are deposited into the soil. The slow process of building a communal movement to protect working-class bodies and spaces in the face of global economic dynamics is both arduous and frustrating. And yet it is necessary to continue this struggle to alter the historic trajectory that has defined Curtis Bay and its inhabitants as disposable. Outcomes are not assured, only the need for struggle. This slow violence of capitalism is not spectacular; it is often hidden from the public view; it can only be slowed and reversed through local fights that over time cohere into a larger resistance.

As hard as it is to rejuvenate soils and "bring back monarch butterflies into the community garden," as Rodette Jones tells our group, it is just as hard to reconnect residents to one another.[46] Documenting this slow violence is the first step in changing the fate of this historic community. But the hard work of creating alternative development models, building sustainable communities, and collectivizing labor will have to be the responsibility of young people for generations to come.

Notes

1 Free Your Voice is a youth-led movement that evolved out of an afterschool human rights club at Benjamin Franklin High School sponsored by United Workers (UW), a Baltimore low-wage workers' organization (see unitedworkers.org). Students learned about the plan to build the nation's largest incinerator in their community as part of the UW-designed curriculum on capitalism, poverty, and politics. Students had previously read about the social and environmental history of the Peninsula. Destiny Watford won the Goldman Environmental Prize in 2016 for her work on behalf of environmental justice in her community.

2 Destiny Watford, speech at United Workers Human Rights Dinner, June 2015.

3 Energy Answers, which markets itself as a green company, was founded in 1981 with a focus on the "environmental sustainability" of incineration. See http://www .energyanswers.com/ and http://www.fmc.com. Trash-to-energy incineration is a growing industrial sector that sees exchange value in municipal solid waste. However, there are significant social, economic, and environmental implications of turning trash into a source of energy. See Lindsey Dillan, "Waste to Energy, The Discard Studies Compendium," *Discard Studies*, 2013, https://discardstudies.com /discard-studies-compendium/#WTE, accessed on July 31, 2017.

4 Curtis Bay is one of the most polluted zip codes in Maryland. See Alex De Metrick, "Curtis Bay and Brooklyn Are Maryland's Most Polluted Zipcodes," WJZ-TV/CBS Baltimore, http://baltimore.cbslocal.com/2012/03/16/study-curtis-bay-brooklyn-are -marylands-most-polluted-communities/, accessed August 3, 2017.

5 The CRX export coal terminal handled 13.8 million tons of coal in 2010. China received 25% of the coal, while the rest went to South Korea and the Netherlands. https://www.csx.com/index.cfm/customers/commodities/coal/terminals/curtis -bay-coal-piers-in-baltimore-md/, accessed August 3, 2017.

6 Rob Nixon, *Slow Violence and the Environmentalism of the Poor* (Cambridge, MA: Harvard University Press, 2011), 2–3.

7 Nixon, *Slow Violence*, 2.

8 With the "guano mania" of the 1840s and the 1850s, Baltimore became the national leader in the fertilizer industry. Baltimore's port received an estimated 58% of the 66,000 tons of guano entering the United States from Peru between 1844 and 1851. Philip Diamond, *An Environmental History of Fairfield/Wagner Point* (Baltimore: Digital Commons at University of Maryland Carey School of Law, 1998), http://digitalcommons.law.umaryland.edu/mlh_pubs/31/.

9 Diamond, "An Environmental History of Fairfield/Wagner Point."

10 Peter Lesher, "A Load of Guano: Baltimore and the Fertilizer Trade in the Nineteenth Century," *Northern Mariner/Le Marin du Nord* 18, nos. 3–4 (July–October 2008): 121–128.

11 Lesher, "A Load of Guano."

12 At the subsequent trial before an all-white jury in Baltimore, three of the workers were condemned to hanging. The company was not compelled to change its work conditions. See Diamond, *An Environmental History*, 28–30.

13 Wayne Ellwood, *No Nonsense Guide to Globalization* (Oxford: New Internationalist Press, 2010), 5–10.

14 Sherry Olson, *Baltimore: Building of an American City* (Baltimore: Johns Hopkins University Press, 1980), 275–276.

15 Antero Pietila, *Not in My Neighborhood: How Bigotry Shaped a Great American City* (Chicago: Ivan R. Dee, 2010), 30.

16 Nicole King, "Preserving Places, Making Spaces in Baltimore: Seeing the Connections of Research, Teaching, Service as Justice," *Journal of Urban History* 40, no. 3 (2014): 425–449.

17 Manufacturing at this location began in 1910 with the production of sulfuric acid, a building block of the early chemical industry. During World War I, sulfuric acid was used in the fabrication of munitions and as the basis for producing silica gel, which was largely used to keep supply shipments dry throughout World War II. Grace Chemical continues to have a production site in Curtis Bay, and it is alleged to have experimented with thorium nitrate to build chemical weapons during the Cold War era. Chloe Ahman, "Waste to Energy: On Toxicity and Historicity in Curtis Bay" (PhD diss., George Washington University, 2018).

18 Lewis W. Hine, *Child Labor in the Canning Industry of Maryland*, July 1909, https://www.loc.gov/pictures/static/data/nclc/resources/images/canneries3.pdf, accessed July 30, 2017.

19 King, "Preserving Places," 435.

20 The Annexation Act of 1918 gave the people of Brooklyn and Curtis Bay who were annexed by the city no voting power or voice on the issue of annexation.

21 Chesapeake Climate Action Network, "Oil Trains in Baltimore: Too Dangerous for the Road," February 2016, http://chesapeakeclimate.org/wp/wp-content/uploads/2015/01/Crude-by-Rail-Factsheet_February-2016.pdf, accessed January 1, 2016.

22 Watford, Speech at United Workers Human Rights Dinner.

23 Watford, Speech at United Workers Human Rights Dinner.

24 Diamond, *An Environmental History*; King, "Preserving Places."

25 King, "Preserving Places," 425–449.

26 Pietila, *Not in My Neighborhood*, 80.

27 King, "Preserving Places," 437.

28 In December 1965, a nine-alarm fire erupted at Continental Oil Company, the area's third fire of the year. It injured thirty-two people and produced a mushroom cloud visible from downtown Baltimore. Diamond, *An Environmental History*, 99; King, "Preserving Places," 425–449.

29 Watford, Speech for United Workers Human Rights Dinner.

30 Watford, Speech for United Workers Human Rights Dinner.

31 Opinion, "O'Malley Should Trash the Waste-to-Energy," *Baltimore Sun*, May 9, 2011, http://www.baltimoresun.com/news/opinion/editorial/bs-ed-waste-energy-20110509-story, accessed July 30, 2017.

32 Darryl Fears, "This Baltimore 20-Year Old Just Won a Huge International Award for Taking out a Giant Trash Incinerator," *Washington Post*, April 18, 2016.

33 Environmental Integrity Project, "Air Quality Profile of Curtis Bay, Brooklyn and Hawkins Point, Maryland," https://www.environmentalintegrity.org/wp-content/uploads/2016/11/2012-06_Final_Curtis_Bay.pdf, accessed July 1, 2017.

34 Douglas Fischer, "'Dark Money' Funds Climate Change Denial Efforts," *Scientific American*, December 23, 2013.

35   Franz Fanon, *The Wretched of the Earth* (New York: Grove Press, 1963).

36   Nixon, *Slow Violence*, 8.

37   Fanon, *The Wretched of the Earth*, 40.

38   Nixon, *Slow Violence*, 3.

39   Nixon, *Slow Violence*, 5.

40   See http://stoptheincinerator.wordpress.com, accessed July 1, 2017.

41   For Free Your Voice, fair development must improve the well-being of all city residents and communities and advance dignity and equality (see unitedworkers .org).

42   The artists use a crankie (a hand-cranked storytelling device) to tell an environmental allegory about the connection among people, land, and community. Storybook images scroll by as the entire peninsula is eaten up by industry. The story ends with a hopeful message of the power of the community to determine its own fate.

43   The Energy Answers permit had actually expired on October 31, 2013, but there were numerous extensions granted by MDE. Fern Shen, "Maryland Declares Energy Answers' Fairfield Incinerator Permit Expired," *Baltimore Brew*, March 17, 2016, accessed July 1, 2017.

44   See http://stoptheincinerator.wordpress.com, accessed July 1, 2017.

45   Amanda Maminski, informal conversation with the author, November 3, 2015.

46   Rodette Jones, informal conversation with the author during the walking tour with Destiny Watford, July 16, 2015.

17

Finding Closure

● ● ● ● ● ● ● ● ● ● ● ● ● ● ● ● ● ● ● ●

The Poets of the Sparrows Point Steel Mill

MICHELLE L. STEFANO

SILENT STEEL

The furnace is cold, and steel no longer flowed. Silence enveloped the land that had not heard silence for over a hundred years. He stood in the parking lot not knowing what to do next. Four generations of his family gave their lives to the mill. When the boss passed him in the parking lot he yelled out, "Where do I go?" The boss replied, "You go home." He nodded in recognition; however, he did not understand. I am home he thought.

—Troy W. Pritt

On a Wednesday morning in December 2012, Troy W. Pritt read his prose poem, "Silent Steel," to a meeting of hundreds of retired steelworkers at the United Steelworkers union hall on Dundalk Avenue. Six months earlier, it was

FIG. 15 The implosion of the iconic Sparrows Point L-Furnace on January 28, 2015. Photos by William Shewbridge, 2015.

announced that the Sparrows Point Steel Mill was to close, and the process of laying off the remaining 1,975 workers began that June (see Figure 15).[1]

For well over a century, the mill had shaped the lives of hundreds of thousands of steelworkers, associated personnel, and their families and communities. During its peak years in the post–World War II industrial boom, Sparrows Point had almost 33,000 employees, and nearly everyone in Baltimore knew someone who worked there.[2] Owned by Bethlehem Steel from the late nineteenth century to the turn of the twenty-first, the mill saw a succession of owners in its last decade; the last owner, RG Steel, filed for bankruptcy in 2011, signaling the plant's eventual closure in the fall of 2012.

Pritt started working at Sparrows Point in 1997 in the coated products division, on the galvanizing line. He recalls, "I did multiple jobs, from crane operator to quality control. As things went on there, jobs were combined to cut costs, so we pretty much learned to do everything."[3] He was one of the workers laid off in 2012, and as his poem conveys, he did not just lose a job but also a "home" and by extension, a family. He explains,

> It was like a family, and I don't think that people really get that about what we did, because it was such a part of our identity. It wasn't a job; it was who you were. People now get a job and it's to put on their resume. . . . But [at the mill] it was, you went in and you had a job for forty years. This was your family. And

for a lot of guys, their fathers, their grandfathers, their uncles, their aunts—so it was, you were going home. This was your home, as well as your career, as well as your job, and that's what I think a lot of people really don't understand about the experience of working at Sparrows Point.[4]

Indeed, Pritt's father worked at the mill, as did three generations of his wife's family. In the lead-up to its eventual closure, he remembers his wife "reading the writing on the wall" and telling him, "I've been here before; things are gonna get bad."[5] Nonetheless, Pritt felt prepared. Thanks to his involvement in the union and taking advantage of ten-week voluntary layoffs offered by one of the last mill owners, Severstal, he took classes at a local college. In 2013, he enrolled in business classes at the University of Baltimore and, at the time, noted, "This is nothing that my family's ever done; I'm the first one to go to college, so I've been in contact with the professors, and it's like, 'Um, I'm 44 and I need to figure out what I want to be when I grow up.'"

In June 2016, Pritt was working toward his MBA degree and serving as the Senior Employee and Labor Relations Consultant for LifeBridge Health in Baltimore. He spoke of his pride in the fact that that "my little poem has spoken to so many, and has helped tell the story of loss that so many of us felt at that time."[6]

THE STAR
In the distance, behind a sign advertising 3,300 acres for lease,
A steel mill is meeting what free market economists call
Creative destruction.

Two years after the shutdown, the searing pain of those who tended fiery
    furnaces and raging machines is still raw.

Some have comforted themselves with clichéd memes about new doors opening
when others close. But everyone knows even they would go back in a heartbeat.

Back to coworkers who had their backs, shared their pride as the hardened
Industrial Soldiers of Sparrows Point . . .

. . . But what about the Star, ask the workers?

The Star,
Proudly erected by the plant's ironworkers,
Topping the furnace each Christmas.

The Star,
Towering.

Powerful.
Proclaiming.
To gritty neighbors and
Passing strangers in their BMWs and Porsches:
Sparrows Point is alive!
Open for business!
Undefeated!
Still strong!

What will happen to the star, they ask?

The star that hallowed this special place,

Before the Salvage firm came.

—Len Shindel

Len Shindel worked at the mill from 1973 until 2002, when Bethlehem Steel went bankrupt. He served for decades as an elected union official and at one point represented roughly 700 members, with between 16–20 shop stewards under his direction. His love of writing stems back to the early 1970s when, after moving to Baltimore, he and other "left labor activists" produced newspapers and newsletters "linking labor and social justice struggles, domestic and global."[7]

At Sparrows Point, he found that there was just enough "dead time" to read and write. Early on, he submitted a poem anonymously to the local union newspaper and won an award from the United Steelworkers Press Association. Over the years, Shindel has published his writing in numerous outlets, such as the *Baltimore Sun*, *The Pearl and Pig Iron*, and his own blog *This Old Anvil*, which is on the *Baltimore Post-Examiner*'s website.

Written in 2014, "The Star" focuses on the actual star that was placed atop the iconic L-furnace and lit during each holiday season; yet in the words of Shindel, it also represents the following:

> The parallels between the destruction of such a powerful place and how, even in the midst of such devastation, people yearn to go back and follow the star that brought them there. I don't practice any religion. But I always had great respect for the serenity and spiritualism of coworkers in the mill who truly devoted themselves to others. As the blame game accelerated and hopelessness increased among a section of those who had lost their jobs, these spiritual leaders deserved a poem.[8]

The mill's 2012 shutdown was a devastating blow to its community—economically, socioculturally, and emotionally. While the sadness of "Silent

Steel" and "The Star" may still ring true for countless people who once worked at the Point, the poems also reveal a certain resilience that has emerged in the wake of the mill's death. Pritt chooses to frame the Sparrows Point story as one of family and home—notions that can live on in the hearts and minds of its workers, despite the demolition of its physical traces. Shindel is motivated by a sense of camaraderie—nearly spiritual in nature—that helped many survive challenging transitions, shining a light of hope, in the shape of the beloved holiday star, on the impacts of industrial decline.

ODE TO SPARROWS POINT

I won't lie. I hated you nearly as much as I loved you. The problem is that I didn't know that I loved you until it was too late. Until you were taken out of my life, stolen from me, and given away to another I didn't realize the passion you created in me. You were loved more than you'll ever know. You provided to me, carried me, and made me the man I am today. You were my family and yet my enemy, the woman that moved me and the woman that inspired me.

I didn't mind that you cheated on me. I didn't mind that there were other men, other women, which you loved like me. A hundred thousand men and women knew your love, your embrace, your unending desire to please and provide. You had needs beyond which I could fulfill.

. . . I know it's not to be. The sky will remain clear; the smoke of your soul won't darken the sky any longer. No longer will your silhouette stand tall against the fading of the sun, as if daring the very night sky to darken your flame of life. No longer will the Mighty L produce, no longer will the "Beast of the East" challenge her rivals on the field of battle, and no longer will troops of Steelworkers man the mills and coax liquid metal from your belly. No longer will Steelworkers nurse you through the night, through blizzards and floods, through the brutal summer heat.

You were more than a woman, more than a friend, more than a companion. You were also more than a job, more than a way to make a living, more than a place I went to in order to feed my children. You weren't just a mill or a factory, you were Sparrows Point. I wake up every day and think of you, I go to sleep and I think of you. I know the anguish, the resentment, sadness, despair and rage will fade with time . . . but not today.

. . . So when tomorrow comes I'll say goodbye for good. I'll mourn and I'll remember, I'll reminisce and tell stories, but I'll say goodbye. Tomorrow I'll let go.[9]

—Chris MacLarion

Chris MacLarion, who started working in the plate mill in 1996, also experienced a sense of family, home, and resilience. "Reading the writing on the wall," MacLarion knew that the plate mill was in decline, so he transferred into the cold sheet mill a year later, remaining there until 2012.[10] Like both Pritt and Shindel, MacLarion was deeply proud of his union involvement; he eventually became its vice president in Sparrows Point's final years.

Around the same time as Pritt penned "Silent Steel," MacLarion wrote "Ode to Sparrows Point" and posted it on Facebook: this spur-of-the-moment, social media post-cum-poem went viral in hours, being shared on blogs and other related websites, including by the United Steelworkers District Directors as an example of what, as MacLarion states, "a shutdown does to the members." More than 1,000 words long, it brings the reader into the emotional process he engaged in of coping with the mill's death, finding a place for his deep love of it to live for years to come.

When these poems were written, the wounds were raw, and a deep processing of the shutdown, its causes and results, was still needed. These poets of Sparrows Point have helped document and interpret the grim reality of the *bust* that comes after the industrial boom, a time when one of the most well-known and productive steel mills in the world died. An acceptance, albeit reluctant, of this fate is present in their words, yet the emotions of anger, sadness, and regret still linger. Today, it could be argued that the passage of time has helped heal, in part, the senses of loss so powerfully described in "Silent Steel," "The Star," and "Ode to Sparrows Point." Each poem expresses the men's deep connection to the other workers and to its spaces that together became a family and home for so many. Even though the mill's landscape is hardly recognizable, with almost all of its features demolished, its significance, which is built on innumerable memories and stories and comprises a deep-rooted intangible cultural heritage, remains.

Notes

1   Hannah Cho, "Sparrows Point Steel Mill Will Close in June," *Baltimore Sun*, May 24, 2012. For more of Stefano's work documenting the stories of Sparrows Point Steel Mill, see Mill Stories, https://millstories.umbc.edu/, and Baltimore Traces: Mapping Dialogues, https://baltimoretraces.umbc.edu/mapping-dialogues/.
2   Deborah Rudacille, *Roots of Steel: Boom and Bust in an American Mill Town* (New York: Pantheon, 2010), 110–114.
3   Interview with Troy Pritt, March 27, 2013, University of Baltimore, Baltimore, Maryland.
4   Interview with Troy Pritt.
5   Interview with Troy Pritt.
6   Email correspondence with Troy Pritt, June 26, 2016.
7   Email correspondence with Len Shindel, March 1, 2017.
8   Email correspondence with Len Shindel.
9   This is an excerpt from "Ode to Sparrows Point."
10 Interview with Chris MacLarion, July 17, 2013, Belcamp, Maryland.

18

Baltimore's Socialist Feminists—Lessons from Then, Lessons for Now

● ● ● ● ● ● ● ● ● ● ● ● ● ● ● ● ● ● ● ●

Community Empowerment and Urban Collectives in the 1970s

ELIZABETH MORROW NIX, APRIL KALOGEROPOULOS HOUSE-HOLDER, AND JODI KELBER-KAYE

In the early 1970s, a cadre of young white female academics moved to Baltimore to organize what they hoped would be a revolution. In the city they found peace activists, labor organizers, feminist therapists, students, and young wives eager to connect with women in the varied activities of second-wave feminism. Many of these newcomers gravitated to the cheap rentals in the neighborhoods of Charles Village, Abell, and Waverly, which were majority-white neighborhoods in a city that would become majority black by 1980. There they established institutions of a vibrant counterculture: urban communes and collectives, women's therapy groups, a feminist bookstore, a child care center, a food co-op, a coffee house, and *Women: A Journal of Liberation,* a national feminist publication that flourished for the next fourteen years. They crossed some racial boundaries—the *Journal* published the work of black feminists, and they part-nered with the Black Panthers to establish the People's Free Medical Clinic—but their efforts remained mostly separate from those of African American activists working in the city. These white radical and socialist feminists created a revolutionary community centered on 31st Street. Many of these women who were still active in Baltimore agreed to be interviewed decades later for collab-orative oral history projects at the University of Maryland, Baltimore County (UMBC) and the University of Baltimore (UB). They explained how they col-lectively challenged the systems of oppressive patriarchal power structures and shared their deep commitment to and abiding support for empowerment, which they produced and received within the movement.

Baltimore's socialist feminist community had its roots in the local antiwar movement, which gained national attention in May 1968 when the Catonsville Nine, an antiwar group including women, burned draft records in a suburb just west of the city. Together men and women protested what they saw as the impe-rialism of the Vietnam War, extending their activism to other causes like the civil rights movement. However, many men in the movement were oblivious to the patriarchal structure of their own activism. Jessica Heriot remembers that she and other antiwar women "just got tired of making coffee and mimeograph-ing things. And when they tried to participate in policy making, men wouldn't let them, so they got really pissed off, and so the women started meeting in small groups and they began seeing how the political was in fact personal."[1] Histo-rian Nancy MacLean describes the national phenomenon as follows: "Sharing their experiences and feelings with other women in an atmosphere of mutual support, participants realized that they faced society-wide problems that were rooted in power relationships and could be changed through collective action."[2] While second-wave feminism is often rightly criticized for emphasizing the problems of upper-middle-class white women, the socialist feminists in Balti-more used their consciousness-raising groups to intentionally challenge the sys-tems of capitalism and imperialism, connecting their antiwar work with labor organizations.

The local feminists found so much value in their consciousness-raising groups that in 1969 they established *Women: A Journal of Liberation*, which they referred to as the *"Journal."* This ground-breaking publication formed part of what would eventually be called the Women-in-Print movement. The movement's goal was to create "a liberatory superstructure—a writing and cul-ture that would represent, interpellate, and liberate *all* women."[3] Donna Keck, Dee Ann Pappas, Vicki Pollard, and Carmen Arbona began the collective socialist and feminist quarterly in a Baltimore basement, aimed at "women who are isolated in pockets all over the country."[4] They described the mission of their publication in explicitly socialist feminist terms: "to be of use to women engaged in the struggle: struggle for greater awareness and struggle to change conditions.... We want everyone to have her say. That is what the whole upheaval today is about: people have not had their say about what is happening to them. We are dedicated to that end."[5] While they did publish works by single authors, including poems by an up-and-coming poet named Audre Lorde, most articles and editorials were attributed to groups of authors, reflecting the collaborative ethos of the effort.

Unlike its better-known counterpart *Ms. Magazine,* the *Journal* did not accept advertisements, but instead depended on volunteer labor and a dedicated subscription base: it was a direct challenge to the capitalistic corporate structure in publishing. In 1972, one of the premier socialist feminist organizations in the country, the Chicago Women's Liberation Union, echoed this approach: "We see capitalism as an institutionalized form of oppression based on profit for private owners of publicly-worked-for wealth. It sets into motion hostile social relations in classes.... We share the socialist vision of a humanist world made possible through a redistribution of wealth and an end to the distinction between the ruling class and those who are ruled."[6] In this spirit the *Journal* implemented a nonhierarchical model where there was no designated editor or publisher who made final decisions. Instead, the women reached editorial and business decisions by consensus. All participants rotated through all the necessary tasks: reviewing the submissions, developing the graphic design, typing the copy, cutting and pasting, and bundling the printed editions for distribution. In an editorial, three women described this process as essential to the integrity of the publication, because the experience of publishing in this way reinforced the importance of "work solidarity, or that feeling of having significant, indivisible ties with one's co-workers."[7] Thus the *Journal* became a model of socialist feminist cultural and material production.

The *Journal* had strong psychological benefits for its creators as well. Beth Dellow remembers, "The collective was a very disciplined group. We were very clearly socialist and pulling together this magazine was a mission.... We met regularly. Probably weekly. We'd read the articles, we'd discuss all of them, we'd figure out which ones we were going to use.... It was one of the most cooperative collectives that I'd ever participated in. And it was so focused, and the women were very disciplined and very serious about wanting to do this."[8] Decades after Dellow described this experience, sociologists Stephanie DeLuca, Susan Clampet-Lundquist, and Kathryn Edin, writing about young adults who had grown up in poverty in Baltimore City, coined the term *identity project* to describe "a source of meaning that provides a strong sense of self and is linked to concrete activities to which youth commit themselves."[9] Through the *Journal,* women committed themselves to the physical activities that publication required and to the demanding work of reaching consensus and, in the process, strengthened their identity as a collective of socialist feminists.

At its height, the *Journal* had 25,000 subscribers from around the nation and the world. Beth Dellow remembers that they even made deliveries to women's prisons. Subscribers describe the importance of both the individual and collective experiences of reading and the connections it provided for women across the country. Mary Sunshine, who lived in the San Francisco Bay Area in the 1970s, recalls, "I loved [WJL]! It was on sale at newsstands in San Francisco, if you can believe that. I bought every issue. I felt as if it came out [of] a magical women's dimension. It was one of the many brilliant early '70s things that transformed my life."[10]

The articles provided the "ah-ha" moment for many women. These feminist "clicks" often marked women's initial understanding that their personal struggles were connected to larger patriarchal systems of oppression. Even forty years later, Jessica Heriot vividly remembers her first encounter with the publication. Heriot had moved to Baltimore with her husband in 1965, and after they divorced, she saw a tiny note on a bulletin board at the University of Maryland School of Social Work that said "women's liberation." In a private and intimate gesture, she wrote down the time and place of the meeting on the back of her hand. When she attended the gathering, the women there handed her two issues of the *Journal*. Decades later she still remembers the subheadline of one of the issue's main article written by Sandra and Daryl Bems: "The Power of a Nonconscious Ideology."[11] Heriot says she learned from the article that "we're like the fish who swim in the water that don't know the water is wet. As soon as I saw that, I said 'That is me.' I had a master's degree, I had a college degree, I had no clue of what I wanted to do. No one ever told me I should have a career."[12] The collective writing of groups of women helped women readers make connections with other similarly minded women across the country and to make individual life choices, including what careers to pursue.

Some of the careers that Baltimore's socialist feminists pursued had, until the early 1970s, been available only to men. The 1973 Comprehensive Employment Training Act (CETA) gave women access to fields like construction and auto repair for the first time, and Baltimore's feminists were eager to exert their new rights. One woman enrolled in a CETA auto repair program and, to conveniently practice her skills, moved a large carburetor into her shared living room in Ida Brayman House, the feminist collective house in Waverly (see Figure 16).[13] The community helped a mother lobby for her daughter to take a junior-high woodworking class.[14] Barbara Moore became a bricklayer and eventually was elected as the president of Baltimore's bricklayers' union.[15] The women supported each other as they undertook the difficult task of making CETA work for the people.

The activists also challenged traditional ways of delivering health care. Instead of accepting the model of a single doctor serving a single patient, they, in conjunction with the Baltimore Black Panther Party, proposed establishing

FIG. 16 The former Ida Brayman House. Photo by April Householder, 2017.

a People's Free Medical Clinic, staffed by volunteer doctors and patient advocates. Although the Panthers pulled out of the project early on because of concerns that the FBI had infiltrated it, residents of Waverly, Charles Village, and Abell established a weeknight clinic that eventually grew into the People's Community Health Center and operated for forty years.[16] The *Journal* offices were above the clinic at 3028 Greenmount Avenue, and feminist influence on the health care delivery effort was unmistakable. The clinic established a Women's Night at which all the patients and most of the practitioners were women. The services covered basic medical care, as well as reproductive and mental health, and its organizers saw consciousness-raising opportunities in the weekly women's clinics. The editors wrote in the *Journal*:

> Many women who would not feel comfortable seeking out a women's discussion group or rap session will come to a clinic for their medical needs. Once there, they can talk with staff members and other women around them and are casually invited to a rap session (which involves no commitment) while waiting for the doctor. Through these experiences, we all have the opportunity to hear and discuss many important aspects of our lives and situations as women. It is this sharing process which is so important to the growth of the women's liberation movement.[17]

Many women who would neither have considered themselves socialists nor feminists were receptive to these radical ideas when they encountered them in a setting where they could readily see the advantages of organizing at least one aspect of society in a different way.

The success of the collective experiences of the *Journal*, the People's Free Medical Clinic, and the antiwar movement led some feminists to extend the collective ideal into their most private spaces. Experimentation with collective living arrangements not only included single roommates sharing wooden Victorians in Waverly but also extended to families co-investing in shared living spaces. In 1971 Donna Keck told the *Baltimore Sun* about the workings of the Guilford Avenue row house in Charles Village she and her husband bought with another couple they had met through the *Journal*: "We share housekeeping and childcare. Karen [Whitman] is getting a master's degree in history. She can leave her son with me. I go to work and leave my baby with her. It frees us. In the future I really see possibilities. We see a day when I may go to work; and my husband may stay home."[18]

Other Baltimore feminists further challenged the traditional family structure by establishing lesbian collectives in the Waverly neighborhood where lesbian organizations had sprouted. Beth Dellow was a founder of the Lesbian Community Center and rented an office for the organization in the People's Free Medical Clinic building. She remembers that her claim to fame was getting "the telephone company to put the word 'lesbian' into the phone book."[19] The Lesbian Community Center held dances in the building once a month to raise money for the organization.[20]

Although many remember with fondness the supportive community they built in Baltimore, many lesbians nonetheless still faced painful rejection. Ann Gordon, who was taking automotive classes and had not come out to her family, remembers when her mother came to visit her at the Ida Brayman House. "There was a poster in the kitchen that was something like, I don't know, 'All Women are Lesbians,' or 'Feminism is the ideology; Lesbianism is the practice.' And my mother looked at it and laughed and she said, 'Is anyone here a lesbian?' And so, um, I took it to be very literally, because there were only three of us there at the time, and everybody there was, so I said . . . 'Yes, everybody.' So she said . . . 'You've killed the grandchild I've never had.'"[21] Faced with such hostility from their families of origin, Baltimore's radical feminists supported each other. Shirley Parry states, "It was important for all of us to have some kind of support when we were coming out. I mean, I don't think I would have come out if I hadn't been in the middle of the women's movement and there weren't all these people coming out all around me."[22]

Many Baltimoreans explored lesbian and feminist literature for the first time at a women's and children's bookstore in Waverly. In 1974 Betsy Bean and Francine Brown, two young wives who had moved with their husbands to Baltimore, met at a consciousness-raising meeting, worked on the *Journal* together, and then took out ten thousand dollars in loans to establish the 31st Street

FIG. 17 The former 31st Street Bookstore. Photo by April Householder, 2017.

Bookstore (see Figure 17). Bean recalls, "The community was ready for us."[23] They located their store on the same block as other alternative businesses such as Sam's Belly Food Co-Op (named after Uncle Sam) and the Bread and Roses Cafe, around the corner from the People's Free Medical Clinic and the *Journal* offices. Bean remembers that they selected the location because of the "incredible strength of the community, flowing on this one street, creative resources, Alternative Free Press [Alternative Press Center], antiwar movement, energy, vibrancy, creativity."[24] She had never seen a community that was so "same-spirit minded."[25] Bean remembers that "everybody would publish their own books; we loved having that stuff in there, lesbian politics, feminist politics; anybody who wanted to bring in a publication, we would just be thrilled and put it there."[26]

The *Sun* described the store in 1977 in a feature article:

The place looks bright, clean and fresh. The air is filled with sunlight and intelligence. It is all very quiet and soothing. . . . In the aisles devoted to feminism, instead of political tracts, we found the likes of Austen, Colette and Virginia Woolf. . . . Just in passing we noticed titles as different as "Passages" by Gail Sheehy and the "Earthsea Trilogy" by the now-very-much-in-vogue sci fi writer Ursula LeGuin. . . . The same attention to quality as well as political orientation is evident throughout the bookstore. The area devoted to childbearing and rearing is unusually well-stocked, as is the section for children's books. Most of the latter are beautifully illustrated, and we couldn't find a single one that was sappy.[27]

The bookstore provided a place for both exploration and the familiarity of community. The children's section attracted young families and generated the "occasional playpen effect."[28] Shirley Parry says that everyone was there on Saturday mornings.[29] While it served its immediate neighbors, it also had broader appeal. The bookstore took advantage of its proximity to the Johns Hopkins University campus and attracted authors with national reputations. A reporter from the *Baltimore Sun* included this account in his 1978 article about the store: "Adrienne Rich, coming last April before giving a reading from her poetry at Waverly Presbyterian Church, paused raptly before a window full of Suzanne Juhasz, Margaret Atwood, Maya Angelou and Louise Bogan, as well as Adrienne Rich; and remarked to her audience of women that evening how fortunate they are to live in a community with a first-rate feminist bookstore."[30]

The bookstore changed hands over the years, and in 1987, then-owner Amy Gaver decided to sell it. The community was desperate to keep the beloved bookstore from commercialization, and so the lesbian community provided the bulk of the financing to keep the store in the community's hands: "With great zeal some 450 customers and supporters banded together to keep the enterprise open, raising nearly $27,000 and converting the operation to a consumer cooperative."[31]

Conclusion

Socialist feminism was one of the most influential currents in the women's liberation movement in the 1970s because it revealed how capitalism and male dominance combined to the detriment of women and how gender, class, race, and sexuality overlap to shape experience, consciousness, and politics, an understanding we would now call "intersectionality."[32] Women in Charles Village and the Abell and Waverly neighborhoods together created new transactional practices, fostered nontraditional interpersonal relationships, and established wider feminist, liberatory networks. In these neighborhoods they found supportive gathering spots, fulfilling identity projects, and each other. In the *Journal* women wrote, "Most of us have treasured these opportunities to share resources, to nurture others outside of our most intimate relationships, to depend on others whom we may not know well to come through for us because they share our values and beliefs."[33] However, work like this brings its own challenges, and alternative enclaves cannot overturn the entire capitalist system. As writers for the *Journal* stated in 1979, "The nuclear boxes enforced by capitalistic manipulation of our social needs, the isolated cells, the splits between workplace and home, between roots and fruits, between labor and creation, make it almost impossible to sustain and empower community."[34] Today, there are few brick-and-mortar feminist bookstores. Food co-ops have developed into pricey organic food markets. However, the connections that these women established in their neighborhoods were not only realized in both physical places like the bookstore and in tangible productions like the *Journal* but also served useful roles as methods to share ideas about social change. Today's online feminist social networks build on this legacy. Websites like Etsy, Feministing, the Crunk Feminist Collective, the Feminist Wire, Women and Hollywood, Hollaback, the Ryan Gosling Feminist Tumblr, the Binders Full of Women Tumblr, and #BlackLivesMatter are all built on a model of feminism that values deconstructing hierarchies, flattening power structures, owning and controlling the means of cultural and material production, and raising a collective and diverse voice on behalf of women and minorities.

Today, local groups like the BaltiGurls art collective, the Feminist Art Project Baltimore, and Hollaback! Baltimore also continue the rich traditions of feminist community organizing by fusing art, performance, oral histories, and the internet as spaces for empowering personal expression and collective activism. Given the deeply embedded structural inequalities of today's Baltimore, this type of critical work can enable us to see how Baltimore is a vibrant city capable of building radical and intersectional social movements and a collective consciousness based on the concept of equity.

Notes

With great appreciation to Samantha Whittemore, UMBC undergraduate student and research assistant to the Baltimore Collectives and Communes Project, who assisted with the research and writing of this chapter.

1 Jessica Heriot, interview by Hannah Patarini and Emma Matthews, April 20, 2016.
2 Nancy MacLean. *The American Women's Movement, 1945–2000: A Brief History with Documents* (New York: Bedford/St. Martin's, 2009), 17.
3 Trysh Travis, "The Women in Print Movement: History and Implications," *Book History* 11 (2008): 282.
4 "Editorial," *Women: A Journal of Liberation* 1, no. 1 (Fall 1969).
5 "Editorial."
6 MacLean, *American Women's Movement*, 111.
7 Jean Turner, Pat Sullivan, and Margaret Blanchard for the Collective, "Editorial: The Ties That Bind," *Women: A Journal of Liberation* 6, no. 3 (1979): 36–39.
8 Beth Dellow, interview by Samantha Whittemore and Sarah Pollock, April 26, 2016.
9 Stephanie DeLuca, Susan Clampet-Lundquist, and Kathryn Edin, *Coming of Age in the Other America* (New York: Russell Sage Foundation, 2016), 66.
10 Written communication with Mary Sunshine by Jodi Kelber-Kaye, June 1, 2016.
11 Sandra L. Bem and Daryl J. Bem, "training the woman to know her place: The Power of a Nonconscious Ideology," *Women: A Journal of Liberation* 1, no. 1 (Fall 1969): 8. This article was published in the first issue of the *Journal*. The authors add a note at the bottom of the page: "The order of authorship determined by the flip of a coin." The lower case is present in the original title.

12 Jessica Heriot, interview.

13 Ann Gordon, interview by Amelia Meman and Robert Barrett, April 6, 2015.

14 Jo-Ann Pilardi, interview by Eleanor Colmers, Michael Bealefeld, and Davi Chkhartishvili, October 7, 2011.

15 Marc Steiner, interview by Christina Smith, Corey Rudolph, Jordan Gray, and Alyssa Florwick, May 1, 2015.

16 Jim Keck, interview by Lee Kenny with Brandi Jones and James Lyle, October 12, 2011. People's Free Medical Clinic/ People's Community Health Center Oral History Collection, Langsdale Library Special Collections, University of Baltimore, http://cdm16352.contentdm.oclc.org/cdm/singleitem/collection /p16352coll14/id/4/rec/6.

17 Kathy Campbell, Terry Dalsemer, and Judy Waldman, "Women's Night at the Free Clinic," *Women: A Journal of Liberation* 2, no. 4 (1972). Sandra Morgen describes the power of emotional discourses for health activists within the feminist health clinic setting in her "'It Was the Best of Times, It Was the Worst of Times': Emotional Discourse in the Work Cultures of Feminist Health Clinics," in *Feminist Organizations: Harvest of the New Women's Movement*, ed. Myra Marx Ferree and Patricia Yancey Martin (Philadelphia: Temple University Press, 1995), 234–247.

18 Barbara Gold, "A Different Kind of Women's Magazine: Baltimore Journal Substitutes Collectivity and Liberation for Romance and Recipes," *Baltimore Sun*, February 21, 1971.

19 Beth Dellow, interview.

20 See Kate Drabinski's interview with Louise Parker Kelly in chapter 19.

21 Ann Gordon, interview.

22 Shirley Parry, interview by Nishay Raja, Meage Clements, and Alexis Scholtes, April 23, 2015.

23 Betsy Bean and Francine Brown, interview by Elizabeth Nix, July 17, 2014.

24 Betsy Bean and Francine Brown, interview.

25 Betsy Bean and Francine Brown, interview. For more information about the Alternative Press Center, see http://www.altpress.org/mod/pages/display/11 /index.php?menu=about.

26 Betsy Bean and Francine Brown, interview.

27 Chaplin and Chaplin, "Good Sign in Waverly," *Baltimore Sun*, March 4, 1977.

28 Betsy Bean and Francine Brown, interview.

29 Shirley Parry, interview.

30 James H. Bready, "Books and Authors: A Store with a Message Makes Good," *Baltimore Sun*, July 23, 1978.

31 Nora Frenkiel, "Five Rooms of Their Own: Feminist Community Makes Bookstore a Part of Themselves," *Baltimore Sun*, Aug 20, 1987. See also Kristen Hogan, *The Feminist Bookstore Movement: Lesbian Antiracism and Feminist Accountability* (Durham, NC: Duke University Press, 2016) and Joshua Clark Davis, *From Head Shops to Whole Foods: The Rise and Fall of Activist Entrepreneurs* (New York: Columbia University Press, 2017).

32 Kimberlé Crenshaw, "Mapping the Margins: Intersectionality, Identity Politics, and Violence against Women of Color," *Stanford Law Review* 43, no. 6 (1991): 1241–1299.

33 Crenshaw, "Mapping the Margins."

34 Turner et al., "Editorial: The Ties that Bind."

19

Relentlessly Gay

● ●

A Conversation on LGBTQ
Stories in Baltimore

KATE DRABINSKI AND LOUISE
PARKER KELLEY

The 1970s were a happening time for Baltimore's queer communities. Balti-more's first Gay Pride parade hit the streets in 1975. In the following spring the first meeting of what would be called the Baltimore Gay Alliance was held, and on March 28, 1977 the articles of incorporation of the Gay Community Center of Baltimore (GCCB) were signed.[1] The GCCB did not have a dedicated space and instead ran on the basement spaces and volunteer work of gay people all over the city. Different branches of activism popped up all over: a gay switchboard took calls on issues ranging from where to get a drink, or what to do when the woman at the deli counter touches your hand a few seconds longer than you think is normal, to how to manage suicidal ideation in a world that often seemed to want you to die. The *Baltimore Gay Paper* started as a newsletter in 1979 and many iterations later is still in distribution as *OutLoud*.[2] In 1978 activists started a health clinic for gay men that would eventually become Chase Brexton, today one of Baltimore's major health care providers.

This organizing happened in the context of feminist, socialist, and black lib-eration movements that sometimes intersected, but often did not. How to organize across differences and seeing others' issues as one's own was every bit the question then as now. Recent efforts to preserve the history of queer organizing in Baltimore have centered on preserving the archives of the Gay and Lesbian Community Center of Baltimore (GLCCB), yet they risk saving only one small part of the story: that of the predominantly white, cisgender men who often dominated official organizing. To tell only that story is to miss the myriad ways other people at other intersections of identity lived, loved, and organized in Baltimore. For just one small example, it was not until 1985 that the word "Lesbian" even made it into the center's name; before that women were often organizing elsewhere.

What follows is a transcribed and edited conversation with activist, historian, and lesbian gadfly Louise Parker Kelley. Kelley has been an active part of LGBTQ life in Baltimore since long before we had that many letters to list. She moved to Baltimore from Silver Spring in 1977 to follow a girl—an old story that explains how many of us end up where we are. In Baltimore Kelley found a community of gay and lesbian people in the early stages of organizing themselves to be a social and political force. Kelley worked on the Gay Switchboard, sold advertisements for the *Baltimore Gay Paper*, wrote and produced plays about lesbian life, fought for domestic partnership rights, and was active in education and politics in the wake of the HIV/AIDS epidemic in the 1980s and 1990s. Kelley has more stories than could possibly fit in the few thousand words that follow, and hers are just one set of memories from what were incredibly diverse and active LGBTQ populations in Baltimore in the earliest days of the movement. In what follows, Kelley discusses her experiences of the early "gayborhoods" of Baltimore and her insights into the past, present, and future of organizing. Hers is one story of many, and presenting it in this chapter is part of a larger project to preserve this history before it is lost. This task is particularly urgent as scholars have yet to undertake a full and robust history of LGBTQ life in Baltimore, even as smaller-scale projects are getting underway. We look forward to many more publications that preserve these histories.

K: So, why did you move to Baltimore?

L: Well, I met Patti Grossman, and we ended up falling in love, and Patti was finishing at University of Maryland and going to the Maryland Institute College of Art (MICA).[3] So, she needed to move back to Baltimore to go to school, and I was going anywhere she was going.

K: That is a familiar story to me. [laughs] And where did you move to?

L: We actually moved to, oh gosh, it was this apartment next to the Abbey Hotel; now it's called the Schaefer, which I think is hysterical.[4] It's on Saint Paul, and I can't remember the cross street—Calvert, maybe. You can take it straight down to the Harbor. Anyway, we lived within, you know, the "gayborhood."[5]

K: Did you know it was the gayborhood before you moved there?

L: No. We just wanted a cheap apartment near MICA.

K: And that's where all the gays were?

L: Well yeah, the gays were there, but they were gay men mostly. The lesbians were up in Charles Village, Greenmount, all that, Waverly [collectively known as Lesbihood in the 1970s].[6]

K: Yeah, I live up there now. I was at a history event last night with [foreword author] Linda Shopes, who used to live at 31st and Abell, and she was telling me they used to call Abell something like the Magic Mile because there were so many swingers on those blocks, you wouldn't know who was sleeping with whom.

L: It was better to not track too closely. [laughs]

K: So, did you ever move up to the Lesbihood?

L: Oh yeah, but we started there [in the "gayborhood"]. Oh god, that apartment, these high beautiful ceilings, and terrible, terrible upkeep. We had fun, I mean, we had a lot of fun. And the gay bars were nearby. It was actually harder to get to the lesbian bars; they were on the other side of town. But we weren't much for bars. When we first started going, we just wanted to dance.

K: One of the early issues of the *Gay Paper* had a map of bars, and the gay bars seemed to be clustered while the lesbian bars seemed to be in Jonestown but also spread over the city.

L: [Jonestown] was Little Italy then. Little Italy, and then over in Greektown, in these outskirt areas. And the other side of Butch Hill. I still love that name.

K: Why did they call it Butch Hill?

L: Butcher's Hill. Abbreviating it was closer to the mark. it was interesting. Men renovated houses more in Mount Vernon and Charles Village and areas around there. Lesbians had a tendency to go for houses in Fells Point or farther out, in Waverly and places like that.

K: Is that because there were already lesbians there, or they were cheaper?

L: I have a feeling that it was as simple as there were a couple of homeowners who were lesbians. But I also think it had to do with colleges in both cases. MICA attracted college students who were interested in art, and a higher percentage than usual would be lesbian or gay, and Johns Hopkins was, you know, really a pioneer, out there in front, with accepting lesbian and gay people. I think it was no accident that the more educated people became, the less issue they had with it. Unless you're talking about Liberty University, which we're not, thank god. Let's *not* talk about it.

So what happened is you have these two magnets, and the University of Baltimore and other universities, and people move in, and then they break up. They don't move that far away because this is where you can find the women, so they don't leave. They go rent or buy something else, and there was a second wave of women with a little more money for whatever reason, and they could afford to buy the row houses on Abell Avenue or wherever. Housing has not gone nuts like it has in some other places.

K: What let you be out? Were you just always out? Or did you have the kind of job that made it OK?

L: When I first got to Baltimore I just got crap jobs. I worked at a retail outlet and at Lexington Market selling cookies, different things like that. But I was hired by the people who hired Gail Vivino, and she was our typesetter for the *Gay Paper*. She had a house off St. Paul Street [in Charles Village], and she introduced me to the folks where she worked as a proofreader. I was by then going to Towson. It took me six months to a year in Baltimore before I enrolled in Towson University [then Towson State] to finish my degree—I had two years at Montgomery College—so when that happened I needed a job I could do around my school schedule. Gail was the one who recommended me for the job, and they got work from [Johns] Hopkins University Press. They were called Brushwood Graphics. So I had a job where they already knew [I was gay]. And Gail worked for [City Councilwoman] Mary Pat Clarke, and I don't remember if she was volunteer, or paid—I don't think she was paid—and she could be out there at City Hall.

K: Is Gail Vivino from Baltimore?

L: I think she lived on the outskirts. She was going to Hopkins, like Gertrude Stein, to become a doctor. Her father was a doctor. And she decided that was not for her, and instead she became very interested in astrology—let's go to the other end—"screw this science"—and let's, you know, think about how our lives are based on where the stars were a couple of hundred years ago at least. [laughs] Oh boy, it's funny to me. I don't have a lot of respect for astrology. I have a lot of respect for my friends who are into astrology because they make it work, but I think it's some dumb shit.

K: Is Gail still around the city?

L: She is in Albuquerque, New Mexico. We heard from her when we were doing the book, because I wanted a picture of her for the book.[7] And instead she sent Richard Oloizia this wonderful, full-color copied certificate that she had gotten from Bill Newhall similar to the one I have in here, but she wasn't going to give up the original, and neither was I.[8] We would have used it, but it really didn't reproduce well. The picture of the house was more important because so much stuff happened there. I mean, Gail would be part of any story about Baltimore, in my mind.

K: Yes, her house is on the walking tour route because so much happened there.[9]

L: Yeah, she was the momma of the movement. She really was.

K: So, did you meet her just by chance?

L: Yeah, I met her at the bar, and she recruited Patti and me to work for the Center. And I was writing and doing layout for the paper, which had been a newsletter up to that point. And Patti did some of the layout but more the cartoons. She was an artist, so she did the cartoons. She did these hilarious cartoons. Sometimes I'd come up with the ideas; sometimes she would. And if you had to explain the cartoon, then this person should not be reading the paper. I'm not sure you're actually gay. It would usually happen around one in the morning, we'd just done a lot of layout, and we were punchy. [laughs]

But anyway, Harvey and Gail were both clear about recruiting people for the Center.[10] And they had to [recruit]. I mean, it was a small organization, and, you know, it was kind of like trying to get a date at last call. You asked everybody until you got a yes. It was fun.

K: Were there a lot of women involved, or was it mostly men?

L: Well, Gail did her best, you know. Women were involved primarily in the paper and in the switchboard to some extent. I think the big drawback for women was that many women were working for women's organizations of one kind or another already. They were the volunteers saying I'm going to do this stuff, or sometimes they worked for 31st Street Bookstore. But for the most part it was hard for them to believe that they would see other women at the Center. And this isn't even necessarily for cruising purposes, just in terms of OK, it says Gay Community Center, and when I see the pictures in the paper it's mostly men.

K: I mean, this is still an issue.

L: And then it becomes the case that you're there, and you're a woman, um, are you really a dyke? Or are you just somebody who likes to hang out with fags? I mean, I got called fag hag more than once. It wasn't super ugly, but it was just a lack of trust, which is understandable because there definitely were some women who were involved with the Center who, if they were lesbians, it never showed up in terms of dating women. Which is fine, it's not required that everybody, you know, but cripes, I enjoyed my lust. I wasn't going to be celibate, jeez.

K: Was it racially mixed?

L: Sometimes, most of the time not. From time to time it would be and everybody goes on and on about how the first president was black and so on; Silas White was part of it in different ways, but it became, um, it became this odd standoff because the men would say to me, we don't have enough women involved, we don't have enough black people involved, would you please go find us some so we don't have to feel so bad, is what they wouldn't say [but actually meant].[11] And sometimes I would, since I had black friends, but after awhile I got fed up. The thing that would happen is whenever a black person came and got involved and ended up staying, everyone would say great, we're OK, because our Treasurer is black or our delegate at large is black. I remember a conversation with John Love,[12] who was saying this to me again, recruit more black members, and I remember getting pissed off at John and finally saying if you want to find black gay people, John, why don't you go look in your living room. And if they're not there, what does that say about you?

So there were black people involved all along. There was no period when I was involved with the Center that there weren't African Americans in leadership positions. But I would not call it really integrated, and I think if it had been it would have been sustained over time.

The other thing that happened from time to time was the expectation that whoever is in that leadership role on the Center Board is prepared to take the shit that was going to come down. And if it was someone in that position who was African American—from my point of view ONLY [because they were African American]—there was sometimes a higher level of criticism and less trust. Not always, it depended on the personality. Nobody ever was, you know, suspicious of certain people, but other folks, if they made mistakes or didn't do "enough," whatever that meant, sometimes there would be a different standard, and that was true of women on the board as well.

K: Was there crossover between the feminist organizing and the lesbian organizing? I mean, obviously there was crossover, but were there people organizing regularly with both?

L: Well, the Women's Growth Center, the bookstore, they had plenty of socializing going on, but the purpose was more revolutionary.[13] The purpose of the Center was revolution. As it began, yes, we wanted gay and lesbian liberation and equality, and people did plenty of work speaking out, going to public places, talking to the cops about entrapment, but the Center was a nonprofit and it was very clear we weren't supposed to be doing lobbying and things like that. And people didn't want to jeopardize that status. Some of them just wanted a clubhouse. And that's why I preferred the *Gay Paper*. There were always political things being said and done around the paper. I didn't always agree with it, but at least it was there. It was a dialogue, as opposed to, go in a room until midnight and argue about the freaking bylaws. Oh my god.

I made a joke once and people just didn't get it. "Is this another bylaws meeting? because I'm not bi." They didn't get it. They took Center meetings very seriously. It was minutiae, and there was stuff going on underneath it that even I didn't know about. Harvey wanted to run the place; there was no doubt about that. It was Harvey's place, and because of him we had a place, and in the view of some, he was, you know, the savior. He gave us an alternative to the bars.

Well, yes, but also it was gonna be his way. What he was really good at was parties and, uh, meetings. He enjoyed the fuss and the fighting. He'd sometimes stir it up.

K: Did you still go to bars when you were at the clubhouse?

L: I went to the bars more when I became ad rep for the paper. I didn't have a lot of money, so going to the bars did not appeal. I didn't want to pay a cover; I didn't drink. Um, I wasn't going out on a date to a bar. And I had plenty of queers in my life without going to any of them. But I got them as sanctuaries, and I had a lot of respect for them. *And* I needed their ad copy.

There were events at the bars we needed to cover, especially in the winter.

K: I noticed in the *Gay Paper* there were a lot of ads for, say, fundraisers where everyone got a haircut. And the party boats, the cruises.

L: Oh my god, those were so great. We only did a couple of those. It was called the Harbor Queen or something. We did a couple of those. The problem was that we didn't know what the hell we were doing and we did these fundraisers and sometimes they made money and sometimes they didn't. And you know the needs went up because we got this building, and now we were basically homeowners. We'd all been meeting in apartments and Gail's basement and free spaces and churches and church basements and church sub-basements—wherever we could find a place—to do something about the revolution. And now we had this four-story warehouse that once held a lot of pinball machines that we had to pay to have hauled away, and before that it was a car warehouse, which you could tell from the oil stains, unless there was some kind of forgery operation going on upstairs or something.

K: How did you get the capital to buy it?

L: Harvey. Harvey went around to the bar owners and other guys he knew in the community, but mostly the bar owners, and he said, "We really need this." It's hard to explain because Harvey could be a real jerk in many ways, but he was a persuasive, bedazzling salesman. He could get people to buy ads for a bar that didn't even have, didn't really want a whole lot of new people coming. They were having a drag show that was already filling up half the bar, but they would take an ad from Harvey; they would pay for an ad from Harvey. He was just good at schmoozing people, and anyway, within a couple of weeks he collected the down payment in cash from these folks. Sure, they could write it off as a charitable contribution, but it was still amazing. And then they got a mortgage from some bank that I don't know, somebody's lover worked for, I don't know how they got the mortgage. I know that, you know, the building had not been in use, so maybe they were just like "Great, somebody will finally do something with this; we don't really care what it is." And then there were other thriving businesses nearby, not just Leon's, but other places like the Drinkery on Read Street.

And the other thing that happened was that it was in the up-and-coming arts district. I don't remember when the Meyerhoff was built, but I don't think it was there when we moved. It could have been. But that did it, and Maryland Institute of Art [MICA], Maryland government offices were across the street, the Hippo was down the street, Theater Project was there at that point, so there were lots of things in the immediate area that were arts related. Some galleries, too. And Read Street. So all those things came together, but it was Harvey who got them to give money.

And what he negotiated was a balloon mortgage, which came up and almost bit us in the ass later because it ballooned. And then five or six guys including John Love, who was president at that point, who had houses in Bolton Hill put up their homes as collateral.

K: Wow.

L: They renegotiated the mortgage, but at that point the mortgage company was like yeah, we get that you guys are in this for justice, freedom, and the American Way, but this is a mortgage and we don't understand how you get your income that you can point to and say yes, you can definitely count on us for this much every month. We need collateral. So that's what they did, they put up their homes. It was very gutsy of them.

And some of them had money, and some of them did not. They were just like, we gotta do something.

K: Did everything move [into] the Center—the switchboard, the paper?

L: Yes, but it took time to renovate. The only thing that moved in to begin with was the after-hours party, which we shouldn't have been having because we didn't have it to code or anything, but the gay youth group did some of their after-hours parties and then, after that, there was a big push to get the clinic in there.[14] And then Gail ended up moving to Albuquerque so we moved into the basement on Chase Street, the paper did, and the switchboard was probably in every floor of the building. I think they were on the first floor; I know they were on the second, the third, and finally the fourth floor. The switchboard and the clinic were the vital services. They needed to have space, and we had gotten into trouble with the landlord at the original location on Maryland Ave. because we were having these parties with drunk teenagers late at night, and other guys who liked the drunk teenagers—and of course they weren't drunk, because that wasn't allowed [because they were underage], but somehow some of them were drunk, it's just curious how that happens; I'm sure it's blood chemistry, not anything anyone supplied booze or anything.

And truly, most of them could not get into bars. Some of them were the boys from Patterson Park, so this was it for them. And Harvey didn't want to give up the after-hours party, because it was the most popular thing we'd done. Sure, we had these nice meetings, and these support groups, the gay married men's group (GAMA), and some of the guys met and became lovers that way, but not all of them were prepared to leave their families. And some of them were out to their families and some of them were not. And some wives were like, "Oh, OK, at least you're not dressing in stockings . . . oh you *do* like stockings, OK, anyway." Other women were like "Ahhhhhhhhh! But we have children! You can't be this way!"

More things in heaven than earth, Horatio. Especially the sex, my god! Human beings are amazing, what they get up to!

K: I know, we really are!

L: The stuff that people find sexy! I thought I knew a lot. And then I went to work with the AIDS administration. Oh my god! The lists that the prostitutes gave us of the kinky stuff people wanted that they'd normally pay a hooker for, because they couldn't get it from anybody else. Shrimping didn't weird me out, first you're into feet, then you're into toes, ok, not so bad. But I will not tell you some of the others, because we are eating.

Anyway, I found out a lot about extremes, and kinks, and we'd have to decide how much of that was going to go in the paper. We had a huge cathartic months-long discussion about whether we were going to take personal ads.

K: You decided not to?

L: Yes, but later we did. Oh my god, we took so many personals. Many of us who were opposed were so righteous about it. "That's not what we're about. It just makes people objects." If you put in no fats and no femmes, and I'm like, that leaves out my two favorite categories, so we can't do that. "Can I just say I want someone who's kinky about books? I just want a bibliophile. Can you spell that? One letter at a time?" [laughs]

K: Did the personal ads pay, is that why you decided to take them?

L: Yeah. The money came with the ad. It was interesting, because we went through cycles with the ads, but the ad rates didn't always change, and then we had to collect on the display ads. And there were some little businesses in particular who would let an ad run for a long time, and then sometimes they could pay it and sometimes they couldn't. And there were some bars that opened and closed in a couple months, and they took out big splashy ads, "Here we are!" And then sometimes the bars came to the Center. Like Girard's came and volunteered a portion of their cover charge to the Center to help pay for the building. Girard's wasn't even completely a gay bar. It was a happening, hotspot. Sometimes it was just to show support, like people take out a page in a yearbook or something: it was like that.

It was great, but every once in awhile we'd be sitting there thinking, can we take this ad or not. There were only two really extreme bars. One was the Gallery. And I say extreme meaning visually, because they were the leather bar. And then there was, oh my god, what the hell was the name of it. The stripper bar, male strippers, and it was underneath the bridge over by the jail. The Atlantis. And it was sleaze. The Gallery was actually kind of nice, just a bar that happened to have a lot of leathermen in a back room that I did not explore but I knew was there. This other place was just like, it had guys dancing on the bar wearing very little, and they had porn shows running constantly. This was before bars had TVs everywhere. Running porn films on the bar, and I realized I had no idea what strip bars were like anyway; this just happened to be the gay male version. I thought oh, OK, the things I'm learning as I go around collecting ad copy. Oh my gosh.

K: There used to be so many gay bars. Why aren't there anymore, do you think?

L: The biggest thing that hurt them is that we won. So there's a whole lot of people that are more out than ever. I mean, people can date in high school now. Not everywhere, but some places. You couldn't be out then. It wasn't safe. It was dangerous. When I came out my aunt wanted to put me in a mental hospital, because lesbian meant mental illness. Um, no, sorry, it isn't the same.

K: Does it blow your mind how much things have changed?

L: I would dream of this because that kept me going. Yes, my mind is officially blown, and I'm enjoying it.

In many ways the dream that kept Louise Parker Kelley going is still a dream. In the rest of our conversation Kelley talked about the way HIV/AIDS changed the community, devastating lives and focusing political activism across gender lines. We talked about the eight-year battle to pass Baltimore's gay rights ordinance in 1988, domestic partnership benefits, and the rise and fall of bars all over the city. As of this writing, the *Gay Paper* is still published weekly as *Outloud*, the GLCCB continues to organize Pride every year from its new digs at 2530 N. Charles Street, less than two miles north of the building Kelley and friends purchased as its first permanent home, and the health clinic is now Chase Brexton, one of the leading health care providers in the city for people of all sexualities and genders.

At the same time, bars continue to close, the Justice Department's consent decree demonstrates a history of police violence against LGBTQ citizens, and while Baltimore and the state of Maryland offer protections against discrimination to trans and gender-nonconforming people, they do so in the context of national attempts to roll back protections and put more of us at risk.[15] Baltimore's LGBTQ activists can learn from the history of this organizing to organize in the present.

Notes

1 "Our History," GLCCB.org, http://glccb.org/?page_id=100, accessed July 7, 2017.

2 "About the Gay Paper," Library of Congress, http://chroniclingamerica.loc.gov /lccn/sn89060364/, accessed July 7, 2017.

3 Maryland Institute College of Art (MICA), founded in 1826, is one of the oldest arts colleges in the United States and an anchor institution in Baltimore.

4 Located in the Mount Vernon neighborhood, which still considered by many to be Baltimore's "gayborhood," the Abbey Schaefer Hotel operated as a rooming house until burning down in 1997. William Schaefer was the mayor of Baltimore from 1971–1987 when he was elected to serve as governor of Maryland until 1995. He was rumored by many to be gay, likely the source of Kelley's laughs here. Peter Rosenstein, "Was William Donald Schaefer Gay?," *Washington Blade*, April 27, 2011, http://www.washingtonblade.com/2011/04/27/was-william-donald-schaefer -gay/, accessed July 19, 2017.

5 Kelley is referring here to Mount Vernon, a neighborhood just north of downtown and in the center of the city. It has long been the center of gay life in Baltimore. It was home to the Hippo, a gay nightclub that operated from 1972–2015 when its owner, Charles L. "Chuck" Bowers, retired and the space became a CVS pharmacy. Leon's, another bar in the neighborhood, has operated as a gay establishment since 1957. Mount Vernon was also home to the Gay and Lesbian Community Center (GLCCB) from 1980–2016, the gay health clinic that would become Chase Brexton; this neighborhood was the setting for many John Waters films and other touchstones of LGBTQ life in Baltimore.

6 Kelley is describing several adjacent north Baltimore neighborhoods near Johns Hopkins University's Homewood campus.

7 Louise Parker Kelley, *LGBT Baltimore* (Mount Pleasant, SC: Arcadia Publishing, 2015).

8 Oloizia is a retired librarian who was an active organizer in Baltimore's LGBT community from the 1980s to the present. A member of Baltimore's LGBT History Committee, he organizes and leads historical walking tours of Baltimore's gay neighborhoods.

9 I am referring here to a walking tour I help lead with other members of the LGBT History Committee at Baltimore Heritage, a local history and preservation group. Other members include Richard Oloizia, Louis Hughes, and Shirley Parry.

10 Harvey Schwartz was a leader and organizer with both the Baltimore Gay Alliance and raised the funds to made it possible for the GCCB to publish a newspaper and buy the building on Chase Street in 1979.

11 Silas White worked as a volunteer and as an employee of the GCCB; he was also an activist and performer with Theatre Closet, the first gay-affirmative theater company in Baltimore.

12 John Love was a president of the GLCCB who personally kept it from financial ruin in the 1980s.

13 The Women's Growth Center was a feminist therapy collective that continues to operate in Baltimore. Kelley is referring to the 31st Street Bookstore, another locus of feminist organizing. Both were located in the Waverly neighborhood of Baltimore.

14 Now the Chase Brexton Clinic, an independent AIDS services organization.

15   The consent decree addresses long-standing issues of unfair stops, searches, and
     seizures; police violence; and misconduct during arrests. It specifically addresses
     this misconduct against LGBT people on pp. 20, 31, and 141 where police are
     required to stop doing unnecessary frisks and to use proper gender and name
     identifications with citizens. See https://www.justice.gov/opa/file/925056
     /download for more information. Maryland added protection on the basis of
     sexual orientation to its antidiscrimination law in 2001, and protection on the
     basis of gender identity in 2014 with the passage of the Fairness for All Mary-
     landers Act. Baltimore City added this protection in 2002.

Part IV

Surviving
in the Neoliberal City

• •

Redevelopment in Baltimore

Waves of new arrivals and shifts in labor patterns have ensured that Baltimore's neighborhoods are always, in one sense or another, in transition. Gentrification is a particularly troubling form of change that many Baltimoreans are currently confronting. Although difficult to define, gentrification often occurs when enough middle-class and affluent people move into a neighborhood so that they trigger a raise in rents, forcing many longtime residents with deep roots but little money and power to move. The real estate investors and elected officials who make decisions fueling gentrification and the residents who suffer the consequences of those changes are rarely the same groups of people. We hope that these chapters will begin some conversations and spur new research into how neighborhoods might change *without* inequitable displacement. One of the earliest writings that inspired scholars to scrutinize gentrification in Baltimore was the final chapter in *The Baltimore Book*, David Harvey's "A View from Federal Hill," an analysis of the inequitable redevelopment of the Inner Harbor and downtown.

Marisela Gomez explores how African American residents in East Baltimore have confronted decades of "urban renewal," gentrification, and inequity as the immensely powerful Johns Hopkins Medical Institute has developed and expanded around its hospital complex. Gomez writes as a health care worker and activist who has been on the ground challenging inequitable development

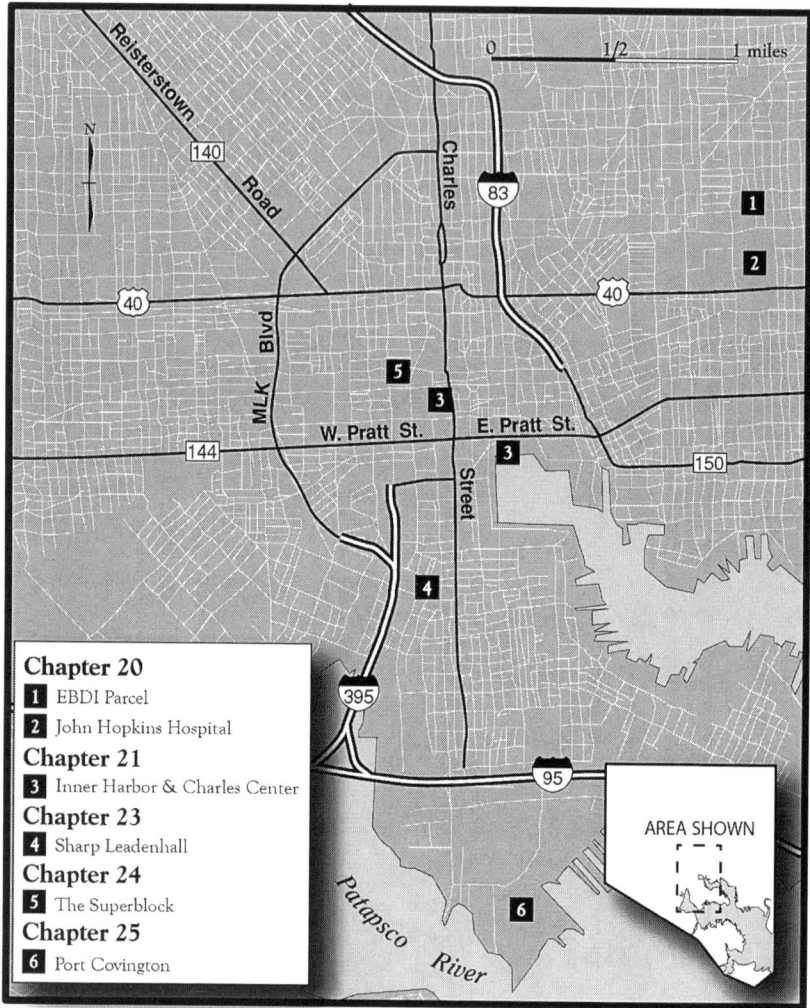

FIG. 18 Map of locations described in Part IV. Created by Joe School, 2018.

that poses its own form of hazards to community members' health and stability. Mary Rizzo's chapter traces how Baltimore refashioned its "infrastructure and image" to transform a city with a diverse manufacturing base into a hub for urban tourism. The city's harbor, once a space of industrial work, was rechristened the Inner Harbor, a site of recreation and play but also service work. Public-private partnerships were largely responsible for reimagining Baltimore's landscape and economy. Unfortunately the city's transformation into a tourist hub has benefited wealthy corporations more than the actual residents. Fred Scharmen shows how skywalks—another form of infrastructure designed with suburbanites and out-of-towners in mind—were supposed to elevate visitors in Baltimore's central business district far above the ground so that they might "shop, dine, and stay at a hotel, all without touching an actual city street at grade." Yet Scharmen's analysis also explains skywalks' underappreciated duality: they were escapist in their design while also allowing, if not forcing, their users to witness an array of often overlooked urban realities such as poverty, homelessness, and police misconduct.

Showing the negative repercussions of downtown development for African American residents, Matt Durrington and Samuel Collins provide a snapshot of gentrification in Sharp-Leadenhall, one of the city's oldest African American neighborhoods, which is located near Baltimore's Inner Harbor. In a commercial case study of redevelopment gone wrong, Nicole King focuses on the so-called Superblock, a project on the west side of downtown that was ultimately canceled in 2015 after more than a decade of planning. The long, slow failure of the project shows the potential harm and waste of development disconnected from the very streets where it is taking place. In addition, the "too big to fail" development model has shown again and again in Baltimore and other cities that big ideas and budgets do not necessarily produce results for all citizens. These insights are urgently needed, as Richard Otten points out in his snapshot about Under Armor's Port Covington development, which is supported by hundreds of millions of dollars in tax-increment financing (TIFs) from the city of Baltimore. If the project moves forward as planned, it would be the largest urban redevelopment project in the city's history. Just a few years after the 2015 uprising, many in Baltimore are left wondering who will benefit from and foot the bill for this upscale development located far from most of the city's neighborhoods.

20

Johns Hopkins University and the History of Developing East Baltimore

● ●

MARISELA B. GOMEZ

After arriving in East Baltimore in 1990 to attend graduate school at the Johns Hopkins Medical Institutions (JHMI), I volunteered in several community organizations and slowly came to know the community surrounding the institution, both as a community organizer and a researcher. The majority of the history that follows is informed by research and community organizing, including participant observation, focus groups, key-informant/one-on-one interviews, listening sessions, and door knocking performed in East Baltimore over more than twenty years. What follows is an account of the experiences of people living and working in East Baltimore as JHMI has sought to displace residents to enable its own growth.

The Big Developer in East Baltimore

In the midst of East Baltimore sits the Johns Hopkins Medical Institutions (JHMI). Johns Hopkins Hospital was established in 1889 on approximately fourteen acres of land. Since then it has expanded into more than sixty acres with an additional eighty-eight acres currently being developed as the Johns Hopkins Science + Technology Park. Ironically, it could be argued that this institution known around the world for curing diseases has in its past and current expansions contributed negatively to its own neighbors' health outcomes through urban renewal tactics and serial forced displacement over the past century.[1] This chronic displacement results in root shock: the disruption of family bonds and fragmentation of communities resulting from urban renewal.[2]

Throughout its history in the East Baltimore community, JHMI has gradually bought individual row houses from existing residents. The late Lucille Gorham was a lifelong organizer for fair housing in the Middle East Baltimore community. She related to me many stories of her time in numerous community associations fighting consistently for affordable housing, against displacement, and for community benefits. She related stories about JHMI's continuous development in both small and large ways.[3]

These practices continued through 2016, as reported by one family living in the 500 block of Castle Street.[4] The family had lived in their home for more than thirty years. JHMI had purchased most of the block, but still needed to acquire a few houses to consolidate the property. While facilities management staff of the institution persisted in trying to acquire properties on this block, the elderly residents became afraid to answer their doors in fear that it was another person from JHMI. They reported to me feeling harassed and were seeking advice from friends and advocates on how to stop such harassment, fearing that the powerful institution could succeed in taking their property even though they had owned it for many years.[5] The fear of losing one's property is warranted in this community, which has witnessed instances when, even after owners refused to sell their properties, JHMI was able to get the land necessary for expansion by partnering with city government.[6] For example, in 2001, for JHMI's largest public–private development to date—the Science + Technology Park—the city acquired and then sold or leased eighty-eight acres bordered on the north by train tracks, the east by Patterson Park Avenue, the south by Madison Street, and the west by Broadway to JHMI for a bioscience park. The development has resulted in the displacement of approximately 800 majority African American households.[7]

Land speculation in East Baltimore has contributed to its current state of disinvestment and abandonment. Many investors, including JHMI, bought property for low prices as the area deteriorated; they then boarded up the houses and provided little maintenance or needed repairs. Over the decades Baltimore's Housing and Community Development Department failed to carry out an effective program of housing inspections; it meted out inadequate penalties for housing code violations, thus allowing landlords and speculators to neglect their houses and leave them in a state of disrepair.[8] Many of these houses were recognized as environmental hazards, as federal legislation sought to ban lead paint and phase out many asbestos products starting in 1970. Vacant houses became sites for illegal dumping, drug use, hiding drugs, and illegal squatting.

This speculation and ineffective housing inspection program contributed to blight directly through the deterioration of the area and indirectly as other real estate speculators bought cheap and sold high when gentrification of an area, anchored by JHMI, began.[9]

In a recent door-knocking project in the neighborhoods adjacent to the eighty-eight-acre JHMI development, several residents reported living in substandard housing that the landlord refused to repair, echoing past strategies of disinvestment. One resident told me that his house "should not have passed inspection."[10] Another reported moving from her East Baltimore home after learning that her child's blood lead level had become elevated while renting there. This type of derelict landlord practice is prevalent in low-income and neglected communities adjacent to JHMI. As the university develops in large and small ways in these under-resourced areas that often lack the social capital to demand equitable development, gentrification follows: landlords renovate housing and increase rents to accommodate affluent arrivals, most of them white, who gradually replace the previous residents, the vast majority of whom are black (see Figure 19).[11] This geographic change can be easily seen when comparing a map of the original landmass of 14.5 acres in 1885 to its expanded footprint of approximately 130 acres in 2018 (including all the amenities and housing that serve the JHMI population).

FIG. 19 Nether, "Urban Renewal," corner of North Washington and East Preston Streets. Photograph by Marisela Gomez, 2016.

Large-Scale Uneven Development in East Baltimore: 1950–1970

The passage of the American Housing Act in 1949 kicked off a long phase of urban renewal. In Baltimore, urban renewal targeted the same African American neighborhoods created by Jim Crow segregation and redlining, as well as some white immigrant neighborhoods. These hypersegregated places had been the sites of extensive disinvestment that resulted in concentrated poverty and were now designated "slums" and "blight" by the federal government.[12] Initially Baltimore had six such designated areas, including one in East Baltimore.[13] In East Baltimore, the Broadway Redevelopment Project exemplifies the way public–private partnerships resulted in uneven development that primarily benefited wealthy and predominantly white institutions like JHMI.

In the 1950s the Broadway Redevelopment project—approximately bordered to the east by Broadway, by Caroline Street to the west, by Monument Street to the north, and by Orleans Street to the south—was initiated by the city of Baltimore to clear blight and provide land for JHMI. It was funded by the federal program of urban renewal. Initially presented for City Council approval as a thirty-nine-acre plan, the project expanded to fifty-four acres by the time it was completed in 1961.[14] The additional acres were provided by the city to JHMI for more parking and future expansion. The state contributed $5.4 million for relocation, acquisition, demolition, and infrastructure repair, even though approximately 60 percent of the redevelopment served the JHMI. The land was leased to JHMI and other developers for 4 percent of its value, essentially a transfer of public wealth to private hands. In the process, more than 1,100 poor and working-poor families, a majority of whom were African American, were displaced. Though two hundred affordable housing units were promised in the first master plan for the development, after a delay of four years, the revised plan provided no affordable housing or amenities for the original residents.[15] The opportunity or right to return quickly became a dream of the past: despite the residents' protests, none of the original residents were able to return. The outcome of one of Baltimore's earliest urban renewal projects was criticized by the U.S. Civil Rights Commission, which stated, "Efforts to provide open or racially-mixed occupancies in redeveloped areas have been largely unsuccessful."[16] During this same period, there were other expansions to JHMI's campus; for the most part they were publicly funded, even as the revenue went to JHMI.[17]

Those spearheading the Broadway Redevelopment Project did not seek input from those already living in the neighborhood. Instead, they surveyed the JHMI community, and their preferences provided direction for the Knott Development Company as it proceeded to rebuild the area. Existing retail shops were replaced by a shopping center on Orleans Street, and part of the land, once inhabited by local residents and now displaced, was walled off; these same residents were physically prohibited from accessing the rebuilt area. Local residents referred to these JHMI protected areas as "the compound." Today residents still tell stories about having to walk around this walled-off compound that encloses the neighborhoods where they used to live and play.[18]

The initial plan for the Broadway Redevelopment project passed by the City Council was thus changed to accommodate JHMI. In response, business leaders, community residents, and civic organizations demanded a hearing at the City Council, where they testified about the lack of affordable apartments and how the new stores would take business away from existing merchants.[19] One resident boycotted the project by sitting in his house, the only one left standing on a block that had been completely demolished. His case went before the Maryland Court of Appeals, which ruled against him.[20]

Urban renewal projects in East Baltimore for the benefit of JHMI supported the private and uneven development of existing neighborhoods. This form of development undermined functional community networks and cohesiveness because it bulldozed large areas of land, dispersed residents without adequate plans for rehousing, and destroyed neighborhood organizations, businesses, cultural institutions, and, as a result, African American political power and social capital.[21]

In contrast, another large-scale development, the Gay Street I project (1965–1967), which was built just across the street from the Broadway Redevelopment project, worked closely with residents: they were surveyed to learn what type of housing they preferred, the city engaged them in forty meetings to finalize a master plan, and residents formed a community development corporation to construct and manage a housing complex within the development. Some of the residents in the Gay Street I project area had been displaced from the Broadway Project and were determined that the same lack of attention to their needs would not happen again. The Gay Street I project resulted in the construction of affordable housing for existing residents, as well as the construction of a new building for Dunbar High School, and residents actively participated in these projects' design and planning. Residents were also hired to provide security for the development, businesses, and playgrounds. There was also minimal relocation of existing residents who were able to return to the rebuilt area. This development benefited the existing African American and low-income residents of the area largely because of its inclusive approach from the start. While this more people-centered development approach addressed the needs of the residents, it was the fact that JHMI actually did not want this land that enabled the public officials to treat residents more fairly—especially compared to the civil rights abuses of the earlier Broadway Redevelopment project.[22]

Uneven Development in East Baltimore Continues: 2001

The turn of the twenty-first century saw a new iteration of JHMI's development in East Baltimore, and with it a new round of displacement of African American residents. In 2001 JHMI announced its master plan for rebuilding an eighty-eight-acre parcel north of the campus, in the neighborhood known as Middle East Baltimore, to create a biotech park. The Science + Technology Park, Hopkins officials claimed, would provide residential housing, eight thousand jobs, and benefits to the adjacent community.[23] As in the announcement for the 1950s Broadway Redevelopment expansion, the area targeted for acquisition was characterized as blighted and in need of redevelopment. This rhetoric—a process of so-called creative destruction—supported the mass displacement of the majority African American and low-income residents who lived in Middle East.[24] Most of these residents only learned about this plan through the newspaper after JHMI, the city, and several philanthropic organizations, including the Annie E. Casey and Abell Foundations, had determined that the mass removal of people and the complete demolition of all houses were necessary for JHMI's expansion.[25]

The original master plan had no provisions for designated affordable housing, no guarantee of local hiring, no offer of relocation assistance as plans had offered in the 1970s, no right of return for existing residents, and no local entrepreneurial opportunities.[26] The city used its power of eminent domain to acquire private homes and then turned the property over to Forest City Enterprise, the developers hired by the newly constituted public–private corporation known as East Baltimore Development Inc. (EBDI). Created in 2002 by the Baltimore City Office of the Mayor to implement the JHMI expansion, EBDI was controlled by JHMI, the Annie E. Casey Foundation, and the city and state government through a board of directors with little community participation. Its mission was "to successfully attract market-oriented investment, development, population, and enterprise to the East Baltimore community."[27]

More than 750 low-income, African American families were displaced to make room for this most recent JHMI expansion.[28] The community fought for legislation to assure that one-third of the housing built would be reserved for low-income residents, but these demands have not yet been met. In 2012, Nathaniel McFadden, the state senator representing the EBDI area, publicly denounced the project as failing to fulfill its promise to the citizens of the area: "Ten years have passed and promises to the Citizens of Baltimore have not been kept. . . . Ladies and Gentlemen, we cannot tolerate this level of performance by EBDI."[29] In 2016, less than 20 percent of the approximately 780 newly constructed rental units, including more than 550 market-rate student-housing units, were designated as low-income housing. EBDI recently announced a plan to construct an additional 246 market-rate units, which is another sign that affordable housing will not return to what was Middle East.[30] One resident of the neighborhood noted the lack of community participation and decision making in this rebuilding project in a conversation with me: "They didn't say anything about these new apartments at the meeting . . . and we asked about other construction. . . . [The executive director] said nothing . . . they just keep lying to us . . . if they tell you one thing you know they have six other things they already doing and not telling you . . . we asked about where the affordable housing was going and he said somewhere outside the EBDI footprint."[31]

Even though the EBDI is violating the ordinance requiring it to build at least 30 percent low-income housing,[32] the Baltimore Development Corporation (BDC) voted in favor of tax incentives (a tax abatement for fifteen years in the amount of $6.75 million) for the new 246 market units. A nonprofit that operates as the economic development proxy for the city, the BDC evolved from earlier economic development boards such as the Greater Baltimore Committee. The BDC is also known for its lack of transparency to the public and was found to have violated Maryland's open meeting law as recently as 2016.[33]

This 2016 tax benefit to Forest City Enterprise, JHMI/EBDI's corporate developer, extended the history of state-subsidized development and serial forced displacement in East Baltimore from the twentieth into the twenty-first century. Today in Baltimore, "Negro removal" is alive and well.[34] Government subsidies to this project exemplify neoliberal community rebuilding in the form of greater government support of corporate wealth accumulation and less oversight for the benefit of the public.[35] Bringing about a substantial benefit to the public is a requirement when government bodies use eminent domain to purchase private property: private interests should not be the main beneficiaries of this practice. For example, the tax-increment financing (TIF) benefit provided to JHMI/EBDI for construction of a biotech building in this project delays the payment of taxes by the developer for fifteen to twenty years.[36] These and other tax subsidies to private developers recently resulted in a cut in state aid for public education of $35 million (because property tax revenues are the basis for public school funding) and a threat of job loss for 393 teachers in 2015.[37] This was despite the fact that the city had experienced a development boom of $1.3 billion and an increase in property values in the previous year. However, extensive subsidies to developers, in the form of TIFs and payments in lieu of taxes (PILOTs), resulted in a decrease in tax revenues for public benefit, even as public funds enabled the development in the first place.

Since the inception of the Science + Technology Park at JHMI, the benefits to African American residents of Middle East have been minimal and secondary to a trajectory enhancing the private corporation of JHMI. For example, residents consistently report that EBDI will not hire them because of their incarceration histories: "They don't want us working for them; this was never about us." The eight thousand jobs promised in the original plan have not materialized. Fifteen years after construction began, only 1,246 permanent workers have been hired; of these only 8.1 percent were living in East Baltimore (minorities). While a total of 6,207 (permanent and temporary) workers were hired during construction, in a city that is 66 percent African American, only 14 percent of those jobs went to African Americans living in Baltimore. The majority of the jobs benefited affluent professionals and new arrivals—not the mostly black and lower-income people who historically lived in the city's Middle East neighborhood.[38]

Changes in the master plan (now in its third iteration) have been made without input from existing residents. The first plan emphasized employment for residents and the local community. After residents were displaced, the second and third plans included a 5.5-acre park, with space for a dog park. The failure to hold public meetings for more than two years between 2012 and 2015 suggests a lack of transparency, accountability, and a bait-and-switch approach by EBDI and JHMI.[39] Though more than ten years have passed since the first resident was displaced, there is still no systematic plan to help those choosing to return; as of May 2018 affordable ownership housing to accommodate those wanting to return has still not been designated in the eighty-eight-acre footprint. Residents displaced into peripheral neighborhoods such as Clifton-Berea, CARE, and Greenmount East report that once relocation benefits such as supplemental rental assistance expired, they had to move into rentals worse than the ones they were forced to move from. More than half the residents of these same neighborhoods are housing burdened, paying more than 30 percent of their income for rent.[40]

A systematic process to assess the benefits of public support for private developments has not occurred to date. What is apparent is that neighborhoods adjacent to the projects undertaken in both the 1950s and 2000s have continued to deteriorate as JHMI has expanded and forced more and more people into those areas to accommodate its expansion. The residents in neighborhoods peripheral to the Johns Hopkins Medical Institutions can expect to live at least ten years less than those residing in majority-white neighborhoods of moderate and greater median income located in other parts of the city.[41]

Residents of Middle East foresaw these results. From the beginning, the 2001 EBDI/Science + Biotech Park was met with protest. Residents created an organization, Save Middle East Action Committee (SMEAC), to challenge the use of eminent domain to remove them: "They finally got what they wanted, they're getting rid of us."[42] After the City Council approved the demolition of the entire eighty-eight acres, SMEAC rallied residents to demand fair relocation packages, safe demolition of the properties and the preservation of others, the construction of affordable housing, and a right of return for residents. As in the 1950s Broadway Redevelopment project, in 2014, after a three-year battle, the Maryland Courts of Appeals ruled against a plaintiff who refused to give up his house to the EBDI project.[43]

Residents and activists have continued to protest the large tax subsidies that the EBDI and the developer Forest City are receiving. As the development removes any trace of the original residents or their culture by rebranding the neighborhood as Eager Park, activists are painting murals on the remaining houses, protesting the continued private wealth accumulation by the corporations and bureaucrats spearheading redevelopment in East Baltimore. Many in the Baltimore area and beyond continue to critique this current redevelopment as one of the worst gentrification projects to date. Baltimore's alternative weekly *City Paper*, for instance, strongly objected to how the neighborhood "has been radically remade to serve the self-interests of local power."[44]

The government policies and programs driving this type of redevelopment in East Baltimore include eminent domain, the Rental Assistance Demonstration (RAD) program that converts public housing to privately owned Section 8 properties, and Homeownership and Opportunity for People Everywhere (HOPE VI), a federally funded program that demolishes public housing sites and replaces them with mixed-income dwellings. Such programs assure uneven development and continued health and wealth disparities through the nonparticipatory rebuilding of African American neighborhoods. Chronic upheaval and forced displacement of residents results in root-shock-style rupturing of the bonds essential to the survival of communities.[45]

Community and housing development in East Baltimore and beyond have occurred in the context of a racialized political economy where corporate wealth accumulation is embedded within and strengthens a white supremacist and classist system. This racialized neoliberal political economy has long favored white wealth accumulation in Baltimore. It is in this context of a long history of racial discrimination in city redevelopment reinforced by neoliberal policies that Johns Hopkins has acted to remake its surroundings under the guise of providing benefit to the community (see Figure 20). A recent quote by the vice president of JHMI exemplifies this approach: "What this project has done is present us a unique opportunity to demonstrate to the community our commitment to be good neighbors. This really is a chance for us to be thoughtful partners on the renewal of this community."[46]

FIG. 20 Houses on Chase Street demolished for a 5.5-acre park. Photo by Marisela Gomez, 2016.

Continued Uneven Development in Baltimore Today

The history of uneven development in Middle East Baltimore has set the stage for increasing public support of private development across all of Baltimore. Over the decades, land condemned by city government has been turned over to elite white developers for projects that have led to gentrification and its negative impacts—increasing property taxes and costs of housing and amenities—resulting in a lack of affordability that forces out existing residents and businesses. These redeveloped areas continue to separate those with resources from those without, thereby further segregating Baltimore. Currently gentrification is facilitated by federally funded programs and policies leading to the displacement of existing low-income and African American communities and the introduction of a growing young professional class and the so-called creative class.[47]

These types of uneven developments are spread across the city. They include the twenty-seven-acre Harbor Point development project, with its business tower, residential apartment complex, parking garage, and park, which began construction in South Baltimore in 2014.[48] The developers of this project requested and received subsidies from the government even after community members protested that such large subsidies should be targeted to improve historically disinvested neighborhoods, like the one just adjacent to the proposed project: the public housing complex of Perkins Homes. Less than two years later, the Baltimore City Housing Department announced that Perkins Homes' 629 units would be sold to a private developer for demolition and redevelopment into a mixed-income housing community. A community engagement plan for a right of return for current residents has not been initiated, and residents and activists fear displacement.[49] Like the Middle East community, the socioeconomic characteristics of the neighborhood adjacent to the Harbor Point development include high unemployment, low educational achievement, low life expectancy, and health inequities. Residents, businesses, civic organization, and activists protested the Harbor Point project.[50] They rallied at City Hall hearings to testify in large numbers about the unfair way the city government was distributing their tax dollars. The Taxation, Finance, and Economic Development Committee ignored the views and opinions of their constituents and voted in favor of the tax subsidies to the developer.

On the heels of Harbor Point came the 260-acre proposed development in South Baltimore in 2015 known as Port Covington. The developer of Port Covington, Sagamore LLC, requested and received one of the largest development subsidies in U.S. history: almost $600 million in TIF for a $5.5 billion development project.[51] Like the Harbor Point project, the subsidies make it much more likely that the project will earn significant profits. These tax subsidies from the city deplete the general funds needed to rebuild other parts of Baltimore. The city government is subsidizing the construction of 14,000 new units of housing for those with an average income of $100,000, in a city where almost tens of thousands of houses remain vacant in low-income and majority African American communities. As with earlier projects, residents, businesses, community groups, and social justice organizations demanded that the proposed subsidies should have been leveraged in communities that have been unevenly developed across Baltimore to begin to close the gap between the rich and the poor.[52]

As with JHMI's development projects in East Baltimore in the 1950s and 2001, the city argued that subsidizing private development in these recent projects was necessary to ensure their feasibility. The incentives provided to JHMI and developers support private wealth accumulation over public benefit because in each case the benefit to the public in affordable housing, local hiring, living wages, and entrepreneurial opportunities has not been adequate, while wealthy developers have been able to leverage capital and receive public subsidies to increase their private wealth.

Conclusion

Baltimore's government continues to tell its citizens that some of them are worthy of investment and others are not, thereby continuing the legacy of uneven development. The 1950s Broadway Development that expanded JHMI by fifty-nine acres was the first example of massive development subsidized by government dollars. The 2001 development followed this same pattern of government-subsidized development and made it the norm, fueling continued inequality and segregation. Changing this pattern requires understanding its history so we know what parts to keep and what parts to change. Will Baltimore's government continue to yield to the white and wealthy class, absorbing their risk and guaranteeing their profit while building unsustainable and inequitable communities? Or will the knowledge of this history of injustice awake in us the intention and action to organize and fight for more equitable development?

Notes

1 For more context, see Marisela B. Gomez, *Race, Class, Power, and Organizing in East Baltimore: Rebuilding Abandoned Communities in America* (Lanham, MD: Lexington Books, 2012).

2 Mindy Thompson Fullilove, "Root Shock: The Consequences of African American Dispossession," *Journal of Urban Health* 78, no. 1 (2001): 72–80; and *Root Shock: How Tearing up City Neighborhoods Hurts America and What We Can Do about It* (New York: Ballantine Books, 2009).

3 John Strausbaugh, "She Gave the Middle East Neighborhood a Name and a Dream," *Baltimore Sun*, August 15, 1982; YouTube video, "Ms. Lucille Gorham on Baltimore's Urban Renewal," https://www.youtube.com/watch?v =hPJLCMav2u8, accessed November 29, 2012.

4 This family, like many of my sources, chose to remain anonymous for fear of repercussions. These communications are cited as "personal communications with the author."

5 This information was gathered during 2016 through door knocking and a listening project in the CARE community in East Baltimore. Marisela B. Gomez, Clara Adjani-Aldrin, and Sabriya L. Linton, "Perspectives and Experiences of Redevelopment and Gentrification: 'This Was Never about Us,'" *Critical Public Health* (forthcoming).

6 Alec Klein, "Homeowners Angered by Hopkins Bids," *Baltimore Sun*, April 26, 1998.

7 Gomez, *Race, Class, Power*, 58.

8 These claims still circulate among residents of the neighborhood who remember the decline in housing stock and their own virtual abandonment over the course of decades. Media reports corroborate these memories. For just a few examples, see James D. Dilts, "Inner-City Landlord Is Found Guilty of 66 Code Violations, Fined $3,375," *Baltimore Sun*, May 24, 1972; Mark Reutter, "Deterioration of Rental Housing Feared as City Alters Inspection Program," *Baltimore Sun*, May 11, 1975; John Schidlovsky, "CPHA Issues Report," *Baltimore Sun*, May 18, 1980; and Melody Simmons, "City's Blight Outpaces Housing Inspectors," *Baltimore Sun*, August 9, 1992.

9 Mark Reutter, "Homeowner Plan Ends in Blight," *Baltimore Sun*, February 26, 1978.

10 Clara Adjani-Aldrin, Sabriya Linton, and Marisela Gomez, "East Baltimore and the Neoliberal Impacts of Gentrification on Health," presentation to the American Public Health Association Annual Meeting, November 2015.

11 Marisela B. Gomez and Carles Muntaner, "Urban Redevelopment and Neighborhood Health in East Baltimore, Maryland: The Role of Communitarian and Institutional Social Capital," *Critical Public Health* 15, no. 2 (2010): 83–102.

12   Wendell E. Pritchett, "The 'Public Menace' of Blight: Urban Renewal and the Private Uses of Eminent Domain," *Faculty Scholarship* 1199 (2003).

13   Baltimore Urban Renewal and Housing Agency, "Outline of Urban Renewal Baltimore 1961," Used with Permission of the University of Baltimore, http://cdm16352.contentdm.oclc.org/cdm/ref/collection/p16352coll8/id/13, accessed October 1, 2016; Digital Scholarship Lab, "Renewing Inequality," in *American Panorama*, ed. Robert K. Nelson and Edward L. Ayers, http://dsl.richmond.edu/panorama/renewal/#view=0/0/1&viz=cartogram&city=baltimoreMD&loc=13/39.3020/-76.6170, accessed January 3, 2019.

14   "The Broadway Pig in a Poke," *Baltimore Sun*, January 20, 1955.

15   See, for example, "Unit Defends Relocation of Broadway Families," April 6, 1958, and "Broadway Slum Housing Plan Unsettled," *Baltimore Sun*, January 18, 1955.

16   "City Renewal Program Is Hit," *Baltimore Sun*, October 6, 1961.

17   See, for example, "Johns Hopkins Hospital Hampton House," *Baltimore Sun*, July 16, 1943, and "Hospital Plans Include Motel, Shopping Unit," *Baltimore Sun*, September 6, 1957.

18   "Renewal with a Difference," *Baltimore Sun*, December 16, 1968; Gomez, *Race, Class, Power*, 52.

19   Jess Glasgow, "Redevelopment Protests Slated: Groups to Appeal to U.S. Officials in Broadway Issue," *Baltimore Sun*, March 17, 1955.

20   "Man, 88, Gives up His House: Moves from Home That Held up Housing Project," *Baltimore Sun*, April 1, 1954.

21   For a general account of these patterns of displacement, see Fullilove, *Root Shock*. For specific examples, see O. M. Smith, "Renewal Fight Won by Council," *Baltimore Sun*, April 29 1958, 32, and "Court Backs City Housing Projects," *Baltimore Sun*, November 22, 1950, 12.

22   "City Renewal Program Is Hit."

23   Gomez, *Race, Class, Power*, 98.

24   Marisela B. Gomez, "Neoliberalization's Propagation of Health Inequity in Urban Rebuilding Processes: The Dependence on Context and Path," *International Journal of Health Services* 47, no. 4 (October 1, 2017): 655–689.

25   Gady Epstein and Eric Seigel, "City, Hopkins Weigh Plans for East-Side Development," *Baltimore Sun*, January 11, 2001; Siddhartha Mitter, "Gentrify or Die? Inside a University's Controversial Plan for Baltimore," *The Guardian*, April 18, 2018.

26   Urban Renewal Plan, Middle East Baltimore, Amendment 6, 2000.

27   EBDI's mission is discussed in its organizational profile at https://www.guidestar.org/profile/27-0037508, accessed March 6, 2017.

28   Gomez, *Race, Class, Power*, 58.

29   Full Transcript of State Sen. Nathaniel McFadden's Official Statement: EDO vs. EBDI, May 2012, http://archive.bmorenews.com/politics/full-transcript-of-state-sen-nathaniel-mcfaddens-o~print.shtml, accessed October 1, 2016.

30   Melody Simmons, "BDC Approves 15-Year PILOT for Market-Rate Apartment Project at EBDI," *Baltimore Business Journal*, June 23, 2016, https://www.bizjournals.com/baltimore/blog/real-estate/2016/06/bdc-approves-15-year-pilot-for-market-rate.html, accessed October 1, 2016.

31   Personal communications with the author.

32   City of Baltimore Ordinance, Council Bill 05-0043, Urban Renewal—Middle East, February 14, 2005, 3.

33   Urban Renewal Plan, Middle East Baltimore, Amendment 8. 2005; Natalie

Sherman, "BDC Violated Open Meetings Act," *Baltimore Sun*, May 23, 2016; "BDC Violated Open Meetings Law by Shutting out Reporters, Board Rules," *Baltimore Brew*, May 3, 2016, https://www.baltimorebrew.com/2016/05/23/bdc-violated-open-meetings-law-by-shutting-out-reporters-board-rules, accessed October 1, 2016.

34 James Baldwin is widely recognized for coining this term for urban renewal, reflecting its tendency to displace African American communities.

35 Joan Jacobson and Melody Simmons, "The Muddled Money Trail," *Maryland Daily Record*, February 1, 2011; Melody Simmons, "EBDI Secures $1M Grant to Demolish 49 More Houses, Buildings," *Baltimore Business Journal*, June 15, 2016.

36 Public subsidies to private developers such as JHMI/EBDI in the form of TIFs and PILOTs, often do not have to be paid back for fifteen to twenty-five years. The tax abatement for construction of new residences in June 2016 was granted for fifteen years and contradicts the previous tax-incentive agreement, which requires the taxes from residential construction to pay back the TIFs for construction of a biotech building.

37 Luke Broadwater, "Baltimore's Development Boom Leads to Loss in School Aid," *Baltimore Sun*, February 7, 2015.

38 "Economic Inclusion: East Baltimore Development Inc. 2017," http://www.ebdi.org/economic_inclusion.

39 Personal communications with the author.

40 Baltimore Neighborhood Indicators Alliance, "Affordability Index Rent 2010–2014," http://bniajfi.org/wp-content/uploads/2016/04/Affordr14map.jpg, accessed June 25, 2016.

41 Madeleine Deason, "In West Baltimore, Life Expectancy the Same as in North Korea," *Capital News Service*, February 16, 2016.

42 Personal communications with the author.

43 Steve Lash, "EBDI Holdout Loses Quick-Take Battle," *Maryland Daily Record*, June 24, 2014.

44 "Best Reminder of What Gentrification Really Looks Like," *City Paper*, September 15, 2015.

45 Mindy Fullilove and Robert Wallace, "Serial Forced Displacement in American Cities: 1916–2010," *Journal of Urban Health* 88 (2011): 381–389.

46 Greg Rienzi, "The Changing Face of East Baltimore: New Mixed-Use Neighborhood Rises just North of University's Medical Campus," *Gazette*, January 2013.

47 Jamie Peck, "Struggling with the Creative Class," *International Journal of Urban Regional Research* 29 (2005): 740–770.

48 Mark Reutter, "Finance Board Approves Big Influx of TIF Bonds for Harbor Point," *Baltimore Brew*, June 17, 2016, https://www.baltimorebrew.com/2016/06/17/finance-board-approves-big-influx-of-tif-bonds-for-harbor-point/, accessed July 1, 2016.

49 Ivonne Wenger, "Perkins Homes to Be Redeveloped under Latest Demo of Baltimore Public Housing," *Baltimore Sun*, June 25, 2016.

50 Kevin Litten, "Harbor Point $107M Tax Deal Draws Support, Criticism at Lengthy Public Hearing," *Baltimore Business Journal*, July 17, 2013.

51 Natalie Sherman, "17 Things to Know about the Port Covington TIF," *Baltimore Sun*, April 29, 2016.

52 Fern Shen, "Blunt Talk about Race as Port Covington Master Plan Is Approved," *Baltimore Brew*, June 24 2016, https://www.baltimorebrew.com/2016/06/24/blunt-talk-about-race-as-port-covington-master-plan-is-approved/, accessed June 25, 2016.

21

Image and Infrastructure

● ● ● ● ● ● ● ● ● ● ● ● ● ● ● ● ● ● ● ●

Making Baltimore a
Tourist City

MARY RIZZO

There are no songs entitled "Way Down
upon the Patapsco," nor "The Baltimore
Blues;" the city has inspired no outstand-
ing novels; it is not planning a world's
fair; it does not boast of the biggest, the
newest, or the fastest anything. This does
not indicate lack of city pride; it merely
means that Baltimoreans are too sure of
themselves and their city to feel the need
of advertising its virtues.
—*Maryland: A Guide to the Old Line
State*, 1940

Baltimore—The Greatest City in
America
—Baltimore city slogan, 2000

In the six decades that elapsed between these two epigraphs, much had changed for Baltimore. Not only had it inspired great novels along with movies, songs, and television shows but it also built a number of large-scale projects that allowed it to compete with other cities around the nation and the world to draw tourists, businesses, and upwardly mobile new residents. These efforts did not occur by accident. Baltimore, like many other cities, experienced severe economic dislocations from the 1950s to the 1970s. Suburbs siphoned off the middle class given federally guaranteed home mortgage loans, while redlining, discrimination in lending, and unethical practices like contract selling led to the deterioration of the city's African American neighborhoods. Shopping malls lured consumers out of the downtown. Baltimore's industrial foundation crumbled. The city was once a major center for manufacturing, canning, steel production, and shipping, but by the 1970s many large employers had closed, moving their operations to locations with cheaper labor costs. Political, business, and civic leaders scrambled to stem the hemorrhaging of people, jobs, and money. Beginning in the 1960s but coming to fruition in the 1970s, they turned to tourism as an antidote to Baltimore's economic woes. Eric I. Weile, chair of the Legislative Council Committee on Tourism, made clear these leaders' hopes in a 1970 speech to the Maryland Hotel & Motor Inn Association. "The travel industry is one of the biggest, if not the biggest business in the United States and it is growing by leaps and bounds . . . we are talking about a sector of the economy that provides a vast number of jobs, and pays enormous sums in federal, state and local taxes."[1] As its promoters repeatedly contended, tourism, unlike manufacturing or shipping, was a clean industry that produced no pollution, but pumped money into shops, hotels, and restaurants. Vacationing families or convention attendees required little in the way of social services since their stays were brief. And tourism would replace jobs lost to deindustrialization—though, as critics would point out, they would be lower-paid, non-unionized service jobs.

By the 1980s, Baltimore had become a national leader in using tourism, arts, and culture to revitalize urban areas: it was cited in the national media and studied by planners and others.[2] The Inner Harbor, in particular, made it "the envy of places like Cleveland and Philadelphia," which competed for the middle-class traveler market.[3] By incorporating a narrative of urban renaissance through branding, marketing, and promotion while simultaneously building an infrastructure of hotels, convention centers, stadiums, and attractions for visitors, Baltimore became a tourist destination. Image and infrastructure worked in tandem. A promotional campaign could not bring visitors to a city with no amenities, but amenities needed to be married to a narrative of the city's uniqueness. Understanding who controls this narrative and who is included—or left out—is critical to seeing who has benefited from the shift to a tourism economy.

The story of how Baltimore became a city that made tourism a central part of its economic development is important for two reasons. First, Baltimore created a template for other cities to follow, shaping how cities around the country responded to postindustrial economic changes by adopting neoliberal strategies. This template included an enlarged role for private investment in municipal affairs. Baltimore's infrastructural achievements, like the Inner Harbor, were public–private partnerships that, many argued, benefited developers more than the city or its residents.[4] Second, certain geographic areas received more resources than others. As I show, Baltimore's narrative of itself as Charm City emphasized its southern roots and whiteness, ignoring the majority African American population. Similarly, capital investment in infrastructure mostly occurred in a contained geographic area around the waterfront, seen as Baltimore's most valuable asset in drawing visitors. The resulting uneven development occurred in both symbolic and real spaces. As neighborhoods where people of color and the working classes lived deteriorated because of state disinvestment, the people who lived there took buses to jobs in hotels and restaurants around the waterfront to serve the tourists whose interest in the city was sparked by aggressive marketing campaigns paid for by municipal agencies. In Baltimore, as in other places, government recalibrated to serve the interests of private investors, developers, and the tourist class, rather than the majority of residents. These strategies continue to shape Baltimore today.

This chapter begins by tracing tourism to Baltimore from the nineteenth century into the mid-twentieth, an era before there was state or municipal investment in attracting visitors. By the 1960s, however, it had become clear that downtown Baltimore was faltering because of suburbanization. The Greater Baltimore Committee, an organization of business and civic leaders, pushed for urban renewal downtown to bring shoppers back into the city. Through its massive building projects and attempts to change the image of the city, urban renewal, while not focused on tourism, set the stage for the tourism push in the 1970s. The ascension of William Donald Schaefer to mayor in 1971 boosted these efforts substantially. Schaefer led both massive development projects, like the Convention Center and the Inner Harbor, and public relations campaigns (his outsized personality drew even more media coverage for the city). Beyond convention centers and the Inner Harbor, sports, history, and heritage were also incorporated as part of the tourism economy. The mayors who followed him, especially Martin O'Malley, built on the foundation Schaefer created. However, tourism has not gone uncriticized. Scholars, activists, and residents argue that public investment in tourism has not had the intended trickle-down effect for the majority of Baltimore's residents, who still contend with high rates of poverty, disinvestment, incarceration, and crime.

For the nineteenth-century elite, railroads and steamships made travel for pleasure to cities like Baltimore possible. By the 1890s, northern travelers visited the South in hopes of finding a quiet place that offered rest and leisure instead of the frenzied pace of life in the industrial North. Writers like Mildred Cram assured them that Baltimore was an appropriately southern city in that regard.[5] While much tourism in this era focused on naturally picturesque areas, Baltimore's attractions included the cathedral, "the most splendid in the United States"; the monument to the 1814 attack by the British, and the Washington Monument and the Shot Tower whose views offered a "bird's-eye glance over the city" that "should receive a visit."[6] Although these attractions were not built with tourists in mind, they helped make Baltimore a place to visit.

While its southern ways appealed to whites, African American travelers had to be highly aware of where they went in the city. The *Negro Motorist Green Book*, a guide published by Victor H. Green & Co. from 1936 to 1964, informed black people which hotels and restaurants would serve them, sparing them humiliation or worse from racist owners or patrons. As this suggests, travel and tourism were not equally available to all Americans. While whites could move relatively easily, for African Americans and other people of color, travel could be an extremely risky venture. The 1938 *Green Book* mentions ten lodging places in Baltimore, including the YMCA and YWCA.[7] By 1956, a few restaurants were sprinkled in with the hotels, all of which were clustered in West Baltimore, a predominantly African American area.[8] Like many southern cities, Baltimore businesses remained segregated into the early 1960s. Protests by student activists finally desegregated the Northwood Theater and Gwynn Oaks Amusement Park in 1963, though the popular local teen TV dance show, *The Buddy Deane Show* (the inspiration for John Waters' film *Hairspray*), was canceled in January 1964, rather than be integrated.[9] Civil rights activists in the city of Cambridge, Maryland, on the state's Eastern Shore, fought a pitched battle for basic civil rights until the passage of the federal Civil Rights Act of 1964, which barred discrimination in public accommodations. By the end of the twentieth century, however, black people were being appealed to as their own market niche among heritage tourists through attractions like the National Great Blacks in Wax Museum.

Two world wars and the Great Depression decreased, though they did not eliminate, tourism, as hotels, airlines, and cruises promoted their services and, by extension, the places they served, to consumers.[10] Baltimore's tourism industry would begin to change in the years after World War II. Federal government support of suburban home ownership through the GI Bill ensured an outmigration of white people and those with middle-class incomes from Baltimore. The widespread use of Homeowner's Loan Corporation's redlining maps by public and private lenders meant that people of color were unable to purchase homes in many areas of the city, forcing them to stay in crowded, deteriorating areas. The construction of the interstate highway system fostered migration to the suburbs while also creating opportunities for tourist travel around the United States. Downtown department stores reported decreasing revenues as competition from suburban shopping centers heated up. Concerned about economic losses and searching for a way to convince people to come back to the city to live and shop, a group of business leaders formed the Greater Baltimore Committee (GBC) in 1955.

Two early GBC projects, Charles Center and the Civic Center, demonstrate the connections between urban renewal and tourism. The business leaders wanted to change the image of the city from seedy to modern and believed that infrastructure development was key. Urban renewal projects, often with substantial federal support, razed and rebuilt urban areas that had been deemed as blighted or slums. Charles Center was begun in 1959 as Baltimore's first urban renewal project. Instead of razing the entire project area, as was common at the time, extant buildings were incorporated into the plans, which created a suite of office buildings as well as amenities for leisure users. Planners envisioned city residents walking from the parking garage through a public plaza on their way to an evening at the Mechanic Theatre. In later years, Charles Center became the site of large city-sponsored public events, like the City Fair, which sought to change the image of downtown from a potentially dangerous place to a fun space for families. As Sandy Hillman, head of the Baltimore Office of Tourism and Promotion, explained in 1979, "the success of the Fair laid the groundwork for all the activities to follow, because it proved that what everybody said could *not* be done could be done—that you could bring people to downtown Baltimore.... Our goal was to make downtown everyone's second neighborhood."[11]

The project's most innovative aspect, however, was its use of public–private partnerships for financing, which then became the way to pay for infrastructure development in Baltimore. Quasi-public organizations, like the Charles Center-Inner Harbor Management Company, managed the project. It worked with the city to condemn properties to be resold as tax write-offs to developers. It also received city funds, all with little to no oversight by the voters, from a revolving loan fund.[12] While this approach was first used in the late 1950s, its use would grow under Mayor William Donald Schaefer, who neoliberalized the city by making it more entrepreneurial. Charles Center's impact was substantial: it offered "something for everyone—a spectrum of downtown uses ranging from commercial to cultural to residential—and therefore may illustrate the problems and the potentialities anticipated by almost every city attempting downtown renewal today."[13]

Connected to Charles Center and built in the same time period, the Civic Center was envisioned as the city's "new auditorium and exhibition hall" that would together create "a vast new convention center with an unprecedented variety of facilities both indoors and out."[14] Baltimore debated whether to build the Civic Center downtown or in the suburbs. The downtown location was chosen as a way to improve economic activity in the area by attracting business travelers. Hosting a convention in a city guaranteed filled hotels and restaurants, but required management and facilities. A few years after the opening of the Civic Center, the GBC created a Convention and Visitor's Council (1968). While conventions brought revenue, convention centers required improvements and upkeep to stay competitive, especially as cities vied for the market of business travelers with ever-improving amenities. In 1979, less than two decades after building the Civic Center, Baltimore replaced it with a new Convention Center in the Inner Harbor, further solidifying the waterfront as the center of the tourist city.

Charles Center was the precursor to the crown jewel of Baltimore's redevelopment, the Inner Harbor. The success of Charles Center proved that Baltimore could create a large-scale downtown urban renewal project. The GBC swiftly shifted its sights to its new target, the harbor: a 250-acre expanse of warehouses and piers that had peaked earlier in the twentieth century with the shipping and canning industries and now housed such déclassé businesses as a fish-oil refinery and the city's wholesale produce market. The Inner Harbor earned national accolades for its two most vocal cheerleaders, William Donald Schaefer and James Rouse—developer, native son, and founder of the Greater Baltimore Committee—making Baltimore a model for postindustrial cities everywhere. Over the course of two decades, the Inner Harbor brought together the two strands of tourist development: the creation of new infrastructure married to an image-making campaign designed to change how people thought about the waterfront and the city as a whole.

Tourism was not envisioned as the major purpose of the Inner Harbor redevelopment at its inception in the 1960s, but as another Charles Center—although the state government was becoming more interested in tourism. Newspaper articles reported on bills being debated in the legislature about supporting tourism, and tourism was the topic of the Governor's Conference on Economic Development in 1965.[15] The Inner Harbor project began with the acquisition of one thousand properties by the Charles Center-Inner Harbor Management company. Seven hundred businesses relocated to make space for the new office buildings that would anchor the area.[16]

Economic development was the overarching purpose of these projects, though Schaefer understood that Baltimore, like other cities that had experienced unrest during the 1960s, had to prove to people that its downtown streets were safe and that there were fun things to do there. Schaefer's Office of Promotion pushed for more amenities and activities to bring visitors to the area. The City Fair was moved from Charles Center to the Inner Harbor in 1973. The Tall Ships that docked in Baltimore harbor during the bicentennial celebration in 1976 attracted droves of tourists, suggesting the area's future potential. Rouse, who had built historically themed shopping and entertainment centers like Faneuil Hall in Boston, suggested a similar plan for the Inner Harbor, which would trade on the waterfront's history to bring tourists and visitors looking for fun, unusual consumer experiences.[17] Residents who lived near the Harbor organized as Citizens for Preservation of the Inner Harbor to resist the plan, wanting to maintain the open space that had been created. In 1978, the forces of development won a public referendum. Harborplace opened in 1980, while the National Aquarium and a Hyatt hotel did so in 1981. "Profit," James Rouse stated, "is the thing that hauls dreams into focus."[18] The Inner Harbor was the profit machine that clarified the dream of a tourism-centered Baltimore that would bring new economic opportunities.

While locals still used the space, including black youth involved in early hip hop, its main purpose was tourism, as suggested by its layout.[19] Harborplace is separated from downtown by the multi-laned Pratt Street, yet a walkway from the Renaissance Baltimore Harborplace Hotel allows its guests direct access without stepping foot on the street. Indeed, all the major tourist attractions are aligned on one side, with Pratt Street acting as a moat separating it from the downtown. The culmination of decades of planning, millions of dollars of investment, and acres of demolition, the Inner Harbor fulfilled the promises of the GBC and Mayor Schaefer. The former industrial heart of the city was now a tourist haven that produced no tangible goods, but instead employed people in service sector jobs to cater to visitors drawn by the much-promoted story of Baltimore's renaissance from blight to brand new. Thanks to the Inner Harbor, the *New York Times* called 1981 "the year of Baltimore."[20]

Tourism in Baltimore extended beyond the Inner Harbor and included arts and culture, sports, and historical and heritage tourism. Great cities competed with each other on the strength of their arts and cultural offerings. Baltimore's included the Baltimore Museum of Art, the Walters Art Gallery, the Morris Mechanic Theatre, Center Stage, and the Joseph Meyerhoff Symphony Hall, among others. While such institutions were originally seen primarily as civic assets, the arts' role in attracting visitors to cities with unique resources became clearer throughout the twentieth century. From 1976 to 1979, Baltimore hosted an international theater festival that drew performers and audiences from around the world, and in 1986, it was the site of the International Theatre Institute's Theatre of Nations Festival. Such activities were promoted by City Hall as they brought economic benefits while supporting the image of the city as a world-class arts hub. Schaefer created the Mayor's Advisory Committee on Arts and Culture in 1974, which financially supported arts activities in the neighborhoods while also taking "advantage of the opportunities provided by the revitalization of downtown Baltimore for introducing a wider range of cultural activities."[21] O'Malley followed suit, creating the Mayor's Cultural Tourism Council and making the Office of Promotion and the Arts a cabinet-level agency that focused on arts and culture.[22] Arts tourism in Baltimore now includes long-standing programs, such as Artscape, and new ones, like Light City Baltimore, which began in 2016.

One of the biggest blows to Baltimore's image as a renaissance city was the loss of the Colts football team in 1984. While there may not have been fans as committed as the character who made his fiancée take a Colts trivia quiz before marrying her in Baltimore native Barry Levinson's film *Diner* (1982), many residents felt a deep love for their local team. But starting in the 1970s, football became more than a national pastime: it was big business deeply tied to urban image-making.[23] Important cities had good teams. Knowing this, team owners, like the Colts' Robert Irsay, extorted money from city and state governments for new stadiums, low-interest loans, and other benefits by threatening to take their team to the city of the highest bidder. After Schaefer and the state legislature attempted to meet his demands, they took a different approach, which emphasized the deep relationship between sports and urban economic development. They claimed that the team was a public amenity and, therefore, could be seized under eminent domain, the same laws that had been used to take ownership of land for urban renewal. When the State Senate agreed, Irsay moved the team to Indianapolis that night.[24] Such a blow to Baltimore's pride motivated city and state legislators to build not one, but two stadiums. Oriole Park at Camden Yards, a retro baseball stadium, opened in 1992, while M&T Bank Stadium, a football stadium also at Camden Yards, opened in 1998. As Edward Bennett Williams, the owner of the Baltimore Orioles, argued in a press conference announcing the stadiums, "It isn't the immediate dollars" that each would bring that was important. It would be the prestige that would make "this city and this state stand tall with publicity they couldn't buy . . . the visibility is so much more dramatic than the economic impact that it's indescribable."[25]

While visitors had been traveling to see Baltimore's historically significant sites since the late nineteenth century, historical and heritage tourism grew after 1945. In 1969, the Baltimore Area Convention and Visitors Council created a summer boat tour of Baltimore's harbor, which was the fourth largest in the nation in terms of international tonnage. An article in the *New York Times* described its highlights, including a view of the nation's oldest warship, the frigate *Constellation*, and Fort McHenry, where Francis Scott Key wrote "The Star-Spangled Banner."[26] History was a commodity, even in the midst of an active port. The 1976 bicentennial brought even more attention to national history, at the same time that many Americans became fascinated by their own family history. For African Americans, the civil rights and Black Power movements made history political. Claiming new names, researching genealogy, and even watching or reading *Roots* were acts that demonstrated a politicized African American identity. The African American Exposition of 1976 celebrated black accomplishments under the banner of the bicentennial with a planning committee made up of city leaders.[27] The National Great Blacks in Wax Museum, founded in Baltimore in 1983, drew from this wave of interest in black history. Extremely successful, the museum's attendance grew even when other African American museums' visitor numbers dwindled nationally in the 1990s and 2000s. But unlike other museums, when asked to move to the Inner Harbor to be more appealing to tourists, it declined, preferring to stay close to its East Baltimore community roots.[28] Starting in the 1970s, white ethnic Americans also became interested in their histories, moving from a desire to dissolve into the melting pot into becoming hyphenated Americans.[29] In Baltimore, as in many places, both ethnic white communities and people of color created heritage festivals that celebrated their distinctive cultures. Once sources of local community solidarity, these events were increasingly geared to tourists who sought out exotic cultural experiences like ethnic foods.[30]

Potential visitors' perception of the city was as important as its infrastructure. Harnessing the power of representation has long been a goal of policy makers. By the end of the nineteenth century "generally speaking, the concern of urban boosters was to replace negative perceptions of their product—whether New York, Houston or another city—with an enticing, all-encompassing, and carefully edited image of the city-in-miniature" in response to the anti-urbanism of the era.[31] Baltimore officials repeatedly created slogan and branding campaigns to define the city, both to instill pride in residents and woo tourists. In 1914, the Merchant and Manufacturers Association of Baltimore assured its readers that "Baltimore has long been known as *The* Convention City—not *a* Convention City" because of its unique attributes, including "that indefinable quality called character; charm."[32] As competition between cities for conventioneers and tourists heated up in the second half of the twentieth century, cities were sold like products, differentiated from each other by characteristics packaged together as unique.

The notion of charm became part of Baltimore's arguably most successful branding campaign, Charm City USA, though it was regarded as a failure at the time by city officials. The 1974 campaign created by the Baltimore Promotional Council revolved around the charm bracelet fad of the era. Visitors could collect various charms representing different aspects of the city to complete their bracelets. The word "charm" had a triple meaning, evoking Baltimore's southern hospitality, lingering ethnic and class-based cultural practices that seemed quaint to outsiders, and architecture from earlier eras. As a press release noted, the campaign's message "expresses Baltimore's commitment to preserve and enhance its history, charm and tradition while giving itself a progressive, modern appearance."[33] Although Schaefer had been a proponent of urban renewal, he agreed with historic preservationists and anti-urban renewal activists that the narrow Baltimore rowhouse with its marble steps attracted visitors and new residents drawn by its charm, as well as the city's aggressive urban homesteading efforts at the end of the 1970s. While the business community did not support the campaign financially and it was soon canceled, the phrase is still used in everything from the name of a local mass transit payment system (CharmCard) to a bakery that was the subject of a reality TV show (*Charm City Cakes*) to a roller derby team (Charm City Roller Girls). As these varying uses suggest, "charm" has been a flexible concept that appeals to varying constituencies both in and out of the city. Welcoming to tourists, it identifies a vague but evocative cultural, historical, and architectural uniqueness that differentiates Baltimore from colder or more modern cities. But "charm" is also racialized, with white ethnic neighborhoods and cultural activities defining it, ignoring the majority African American population of the city, as with the annual HonFest in the Hampden neighborhood. This event, which has grown in popularity to a multiday affair, uses the image of the Baltimore Hon—a white working-class woman from the early 1960s with a particular style and personality—as the image of the neighborhood and, by extension, the city.[34]

Baltimore's tourism officials have experienced as many gaffes as successes in their branding efforts. After Charm City, the city rolled out other campaigns, including "Baltimore Is Best" and "Baltimore: The Greatest City in America." Not everyone supported the sloganeering, which seemed an attempt to gloss over the social and economic problems faced by many working-class Baltimoreans. Hiring advertising agencies to create the campaigns also consumed funding that could have been used for social services. A writer in the grassroots poetry magazine *Chicory*, referenced a slogan only to counter it. He argued, "Baltimore won't be best until societal inadequacies" are solved.[35] Perhaps the most anodyne slogan of all, "The City That Reads," spurred a plethora of parodies, becoming, for example, "Baltimore: The City That Bleeds," referencing the city's high murder rate. Such acts were commentaries on the larger processes of image-making. While tourism officials developed narratives like Charm City that emphasized whiteness and portrayed the city as a playground for visitors, residents and activists tried to leverage the slogans to make their own claims on the state.

Creating a renaissance narrative necessitated controlling the image of the city. Not all images of the city were deemed appropriate by officials. The critical success of the television show *The Wire* exemplified this issue. Based on nonfiction books written by journalist David Simon and former police detective Ed Burns, the show was filmed in Baltimore over the course of five seasons. The city had begun experimenting with a film commission to draw more film and television projects in the late 1970s, after seeing the success of local filmmakers John Waters and Barry Levinson in using the city as a location. But when this bore fruit in the form of a long-running major television series that employed scores of locals, there was concern from Mayor Martin O'Malley and members of the City Council that the portrayal was solely focused on poverty, drugs, criminality, and corruption, which could hurt Baltimore's future economic prospects.[36] According to Simon, O'Malley threatened to hold up their filming permits and told him that "Baltimore wanted to be 'out of *The Wire* business.'"[37] Much safer was the vision of the city posited in controlled environments like the Inner Harbor, which would be expanded under O'Malley and his successors. In 2001 and 2002, for example, $550 million in "new offices, hotels, residences, and entertainment venues" were "being completed or under construction in the Inner Harbor area."[38] Similarly, the 2016 plan to build Port Covington in South Baltimore along the harbor includes 1.5 million square feet for attractions, entertainment, and specialty retail and more than two hundred hotel rooms alongside the 3.9-million square foot global headquarters of Under Armour.[39] In the city but not entirely of them, these projects remove troubling aspects of urban life to provide tourists a clean, safe, and sterile experience.

Sociologists, cultural critics, policy analysts, and community activists have critiqued the centrality of tourism to Baltimore's economic development since the 1970s, arguing that it has enriched corporations and developers more than residents, created only low-paying service sector jobs, deepened racial and class divisions in the city, and privatized and commodified public space to appeal to upwardly mobile visitors and gentrifying residents. Funding for the infrastructure projects that were used as evidence of Baltimore's renaissance by its promoters came from public–private partnerships. For the Inner Harbor, for example, the vast majority of the funding came from public coffers, while management of the site—and its profits—stayed in private corporate hands.[40] According to the Bureau of Labor Statistics, 29,100 people in Baltimore were employed in the tourism and hospitality industries in March 2016, nearly three times the number employed in manufacturing, making it is the fifth largest industry in Baltimore.[41] As Marc Levine has argued, "jobs in the tourism-convention trade are mainly low-wage, subsistence jobs—hardly adequate replacements for lost manufacturing employment. Moreover, the tourism-convention trade is highly cyclical, and thus an unstable basis on which to build a city economy."[42]

One of the most trenchant critiques is that the focus on downtown has neglected the majority of Baltimore's population, which lives in its neighborhoods. Investment has flowed to downtown cultural and tourist institutions, which serve visitors from the wealthy metropolitan region. In between these two rings, however, live people, mainly African American, who contend with high rates of unemployment, poverty, and crime. This "double doughnut" divides the city by race and class, as was powerfully shown in the protests following the death of Freddie Gray while in police custody in April 2015.[43] Not only has tourism ignored these social issues but it has also exacerbated them by privatizing and commodifying public space, as private ownership and control have increased in the era of government austerity. It has also led to the gentrification of certain neighborhoods, especially those near the Inner Harbor. As housing prices have shot up, older and poorer residents have been pushed out by more upwardly mobile ones.[44]

Baltimore is just one of many cities pursuing tourism as a major replacement for lost industrial jobs, making the question of whether the tourist economy benefits cities overall particularly significant. Tourism requires huge investments in buildings and amenities and for branding, advertising, and marketing. For Baltimore, these investments have centered on the downtown and waterfront. Over the last several decades, the story of Baltimore as Charm City has also focused on this area, excluding the majority of its population. Meanwhile, neighborhoods struggle with violence, poverty, and unemployment. The so-called renaissance of the 1980s, built on this marriage of image and infrastructure, has determined Baltimore's trajectory. That it continues to be a city divided by class and race is its most pressing problem. Tourism, while it benefits developers, business owners, and politicians, cannot fix these social issues.

Notes

Epigraph 1: Writers' Program of the Work Projects Administration in the State of Maryland. *Maryland: A Guide to the Old Line State* (New York: Oxford University Press, 1940 [1973]), 205.

1 Speech of Eric I. Weile, Chair, Legislative Council Committee on Tourism to the Maryland Hotel & Motor Inn Association, Linden Hill Hotel, Bethesda, MD, July 24, 1970, Department of Business and Economic Development, Division of Tourism and Promotion, 1960–1975, Box 2, Maryland State Archives.
2 Richard Ben Cramer, "Can the Best Mayor Win?," *Esquire* (October 1984): 57–72; Roberto Brambilla, and Gianni Longo, *Learning from Baltimore: What Makes Cities Liveable?* (New York: Institute for Environmental Action, 1979). National publications from the *New York Times* to *Smithsonian* magazine have covered Baltimore as a tourist destination. See, for example, "52 Places to Go in 2018," *New York Times*, February 12, 2018; Frank Deford, "My Kind of Town: Baltimore, Maryland," *Smithsonian* (January 2007): 18, 20, 22.
3 Jon Teaford, *The Rough Road to Renaissance: Urban Revitalization in America, 1940–1985* (Baltimore: Johns Hopkins University Press, 1990), 299.
4 David Harvey, "A View from Federal Hill," in *The Baltimore Book: New Views of Local History*, ed. Elizabeth Fee, Linda Shopes, and Linda Zeidman (Philadelphia: Temple University Press, 1991), 227–242; Marc Levine, "Downtown Redevelopment as an Urban Growth Strategy: A Critical Appraisal of the Baltimore Renaissance," *Journal of Urban Affairs* 9, no. 2 (1987): 116–117.
5 Rebecca Cawood McIntyre, *Souvenirs of the Old South: Northern Tourism and Southern Mythology* (Gainesville: University Press of Florida, 2011), 145.
6 *The North American Tourist* (New York: A. T. Goodrich, 1839), 404.
7 "The Negro Motorist Green Book: 1938," The New York Public Library Digital Collections, Schomburg Center for Research in Black Culture, Jean Blackwell

Hutson Research and Reference Division, http://digitalcollections.nypl.org/items /f56e0d60-847a-0132-8e19-58d385a7bbd0, accessed June 9, 2016.

8 "The Negro Motorist Green Book: 1956," *The Negro Traveler's Green Book,* University Libraries Digital Collections, University of South Carolina, http:// library.sc.edu/digital/collections/greenbook.html, accessed June 9, 2016.

9 Robert M. Palumbos, "Student Involvement in the Baltimore Civil Rights Movement, 1953–1963," *Maryland Historical Magazine* 94, no. 4 (1999): 449–492; August Meier, *White Scholar and the Black Community, 1945–1965* (Amherst: University of Massachusetts Press, 1992), and "Balto Disk Jock Sez He Was Fired because of an 'Integration Battle,'" *Variety,* December 18, 1963, 24.

10 "Travel America Year Finds a Wide Variety of Ocean Cruises Scheduled from Baltimore," *Washington Post,* June 23, 1940.

11 Brambilla and Longo, *Learning from Baltimore,* 139.

12 C. Fraser Smith, "Two Trustees and a $100 Million 'Bank' Skirt the Restrictions of City Government," *Baltimore Sun,* April 13, 1980.

13 Martin Millspaugh, *Baltimore's Charles Center: A Case Study of Downtown Renewal* (Washington, DC: Urban Land Institute, 1964), 9.

14 Millspaugh, *Baltimore's Charles Center,* 29.

15 "Tourism Fund Bills Readied in Maryland," *Washington Post,* September 5, 1963; and "Md Tourism Post Filled," *Washington Post,* September 9, 1965.

16 Martin Millspaugh, "The Inner Harbor Story," *Urban Land* (April 2003): 38.

17 Alison Isenberg, *Downtown America: A History of the Place and the People Who Made It* (Chicago: University of Chicago Press, 2004), 291.

18 Michael Demarest, "He Digs Downtown," *Time,* August 24, 1981.

19 Aaron Cowan, *A Nice Place to Visit: Tourism and Urban Revitalization in the Postwar Rustbelt* (Philadelphia: Temple University Press, 2016), ch. 5.

20 Paul Goldberger, "Baltimore Marketplace: An Urban Success," *New York Times,* February 18, 1981.

21 Press release, March 2, 1974, Formation of MACAC Folder, Box 886, William Donald Schaefer Papers, Baltimore City Archives.

22 Mayor Martin O'Malley, Americans for the Arts, http://www .americansforthearts.org/by-program/promotion-and-recognition/awards-for-arts -achievement/annual-awards/public-leadership-in-the-arts/mayor-martin-omalley -d-baltimore-md.

23 Teaford, *The Rough Road to Renaissance,* 254.

24 C. Fraser Smith, *William Donald Schaefer: A Political Biography* (Baltimore: Johns Hopkins University Press, 1999), 235–245.

25 Smith, *William Donald Schaefer,* 287.

26 Victor Block, "Baltimore Harbor Boat Tour a Star-Spangled Attraction," *New York Times,* August 17, 1969.

27 Afram Expo 76, Langsdale Library, Special Collections Department, University of Baltimore, http://archives.ubalt.edu/rbc/pdf/rbcae76d1_web.pdf.

28 Andrea Burns, *From Storefront to Monument: Tracing the Public History of the Black Museum Movement* (Amherst: University of Massachusetts Press, 2013), 183.

29 Michael Novak, *The Rise of the Unmeltable Ethnics: Politics and Culture in the Seventies* (New York: Macmillan, 1972).

30 Kenneth D. Durr, *Behind the Backlash: White Working-Class Politics in Baltimore, 1940–1980* (Chapel Hill: University of North Carolina Press, 2003), 162.

31 Miriam Greenberg, *Branding New York: How a City in Crisis Was Sold to the World* (New York: Routledge, 2008), 21.

32 Baltimore, Chamber of Commerce of Metropolitan. *Annual Report*, 1914, 13.

33 Press release, Baltimore Promotion Council Folder, Box 108, William Donald Schaefer papers, Baltimore City Archives.

34 Mary Rizzo, "The Café Hon: Working-Class White Femininity and Commodified Nostalgia in Postindustrial Baltimore," in *Dixie Emporium: Tourism, Foodways, and Consumer Culture in the American South*, ed. Anthony J. Stanonis (Athens: University of Georgia Press, 2008), 264–286.

35 Hasan Mobutu Ngozi, "Poor, Black, and in Real Trouble: A Book Review," *Chicory* 113 (March 1981), http://collections.digitalmaryland.org/cdm /compoundobject/collection/mdcy/id/2655/rec/4.

36 Bret McCabe, "Under the Wire," *Baltimore City Paper*, May 28, 2003, http://www .citypaper.com/news/thewire/bcpnews-under-the-wire-20150520-story.html.

37 Rafael Alvarez, *The Wire: Truth Be Told* (New York: Grove Press, 2009), 392.

38 Millspaugh, "The Inner Harbor Story," 36.

39 Kevin Lynch, "Port Covington Master Plan Receives Unanimous Approval," *SouthBaltimore.com*, June 24, 2016, http://southbmore.com/2016/06/24/port -covington-master-plan-receives-unanimous-approval-from-planning-commission/.

40 Harvey, "A View from Federal Hill," 239.

41 Baltimore Area Employment—March 2016, Bureau of Labor Statistics, http:// www.bls.gov/regions/mid-atlantic/news-release/areaemployment_baltimore.htm.

42 Levine, "Downtown Redevelopment as an Urban Growth Strategy," 116–117.

43 Peter L. Szanton, *Baltimore 2000: A Choice of Futures* (Baltimore: Morris Goldseker Foundation, 1986), 21.

44 Linda Shopes, "Fells Point: Community and Conflict in a Working-Class Neighborhood," in *The Baltimore Book*, 121–154.

22

Skywalk

● ● ● ● ● ● ● ● ● ● ● ● ● ● ● ● ● ● ● ●

The Life and Death
of Multilevel Urbanism
in Downtown Baltimore

FRED SCHARMEN

"In recent years, citizens of Baltimore have watched the deterioration of the Downtown area." So begins a pamphlet circulated in 1958 by a group calling itself the "Citizen's Committee for Charles Center and Civic Center Loans."[1] As its name indicated, this group was in favor of approving loans totaling $42 million, which were up for a vote as bond issues that year in Baltimore City. "Streets choked by cars and busses," the pamphlet text continued, "buildings run down . . . property values tumbling to new depths . . . loss of tax revenues to the City. Something had to be done. Something was done!"[2]

That something was the creation of a new master plan for nine blocks of downtown, clearing out older buildings to make way for new modern office towers and open space, which would be "a compact focal point for commerce as well as for cultural, recreational, and sports activities."[3] A key part of this plan would be the creation of a system of pedestrian walkways—skywalks— to allow people to circulate freely above those car- and bus-choked streets (see Figure 21). "Users of downtown know very well that downtown needs not fewer streets, but more, especially for pedestrians," urbanist Jane Jacobs wrote in *Fortune* magazine that year, describing the growing trend of pedestrian-oriented,

FIG. 21 A skywalk connection to Lexington Market, as envisioned in a Greater Baltimore Council press release, 1958.

density-producing urban renewal in American cities.[4] More than a half–century later, cities like Baltimore are again worried about deterioration, property values, tax revenues, and activity downtown, but current plans are aimed at dismantling the kind of multilevel, pedestrian-oriented "modern" urban design of the recent past. "The retail shop on the street is the key to a multi-use downtown," architect and planner Jaquelin Robertson told *Time* magazine architecture and design writer Kurt Andersen in 1988, "No one goes to Europe to walk along skywalks."[5]

Assessments of the value of skywalks seem to circulate around questions about what the key to a "multi-use" downtown is. But often, this stated desire for multiple uses and multiple users collapses into a discussion about who and what is best for retail and commerce. Even still, as Jacobs wrote in *Fortune*, "a promenade needs promenaders"; that is, people who are there just to *be there*. Attempts to address deterioration and the lack of activity in urban places foreground distinctions about what cities are for in the first place.[6] They also raise questions about who is invited to participate and exist within them. For Baltimore, and the writers like Jane Jacobs who examined the speculative and real development here, the users and the spaces have responded to each other in ways that are much more multidimensional than a simple promenade would imply.

When the Charles Center plan was released, Jane Jacobs was excited about its skywalks. "The sloping site was used to get two separate 'street levels' at certain strategic points, with the cars passing under the pedestrians," she wrote in a review of the project proposal in the June 1958 issue of *Architectural Forum*.[7]

"This arrangement makes possible, over the entire site, truly urban, concentrated, lively design."[8] Her enthusiasm for skywalks in Baltimore might be surprising to the writers who like to cite her influential work in favor of their removal. "Freeways, skybridges follow a similar principle: we should separate uses. . . . Separate the cars from the people so the cars can go fast and the people stay safe," urbanist and blogger David Alpert wrote in 2008 for the advocacy group Greater Greater Washington, "But as we now know thanks to Jane Jacobs and others, separation is dangerous."[9] In 2016 another blogger, writing about Los Angeles for *Curbed*, speculated that a partially finished skybridge project there had been intentionally burned down by "disgruntled Jane Jacobs acolytes."[10]

In Baltimore, the skywalk system that began at Charles Center in the 1960s was extended to the Inner Harbor and Convention Center in the 1980s, but planning groups began removing the skywalks from downtown in the late 1990s. This process has accelerated in the 2010s, led by the business advocacy nonprofit Downtown Partnership of Baltimore (DPB). Kirby Fowler, DPB's president, told the *Baltimore Sun* in 2013 that the goal of this systematic removal, funded by public and private monies, was to increase foot traffic for retail establishments.[11]

If skywalk skeptics cite anything specific about Jacobs's work that might indicate an antipathy to multilevel urban pedestrianism, they say that it breaks up two organizational schemas that Jacobs was famous for celebrating: "eyes on the street," and the "sidewalk ballet." "The stretch of Hudson Street where I live is each day the scene of an intricate sidewalk ballet," begins a long passage from Jacobs's 1961 *Death and Life of Great American Cities*, describing the twenty-four-hour activity cycle of her street in Greenwich Village.[12] From littering middle schoolers in the morning, day-drinking longshoremen and lunching shopkeepers in the afternoon, and the last-minute application of emergency tourniquets, late-night walks with cranky babies, and calls to the paramedics after midnight, multiple cycles of user groups move through the street. This passage comes to a close with the recognition that all of this heterogeneous activity has at least one consistent, omnipresent result: mutual visibility. "We are the lucky possessors of a city order that makes it relatively simple to keep the peace because there are plenty of eyes on the street."[13] Jacobs's street and sidewalk is, in the taxonomy of sociologist Susan Leigh Star, a "boundary object."[14] These are places where "interpretive flexibility" allows many different groups to use the same object or space in different ways or for different reasons. People on Jacobs's street have many backgrounds and many agendas, but no matter why they are there, the effect of their presence is to increase safety and activity. These are the things that make a place as "truly urban, concentrated, lively" as she expected Charles Center to be.

The "fundamental principles" of the plan for Charles Center in Baltimore, as reported in the March 1959 issue of the *Journal of the American Institute of*

Architects, were also oriented toward the experience of people onsite: "1. The separation of pedestrian and vehicular access which permits the existing site to be freely traversed by pedestrians without interference from vehicular traffic. 2. The emphasis on the economic and esthetic need of public open space represented by the parks within the project."[15] The multilevel-grade separation of cars from the public realm was not limited to the design of skywalks above the surface streets; it included several levels of underground parking beneath the plazas and a connection to the Baltimore Metro system. The suppression of automobile traffic at grade and the subsequent handover of the ground surface to public open space and parks in which buildings exist as freestanding objects in space are trademarks of Le Corbusier's "Radiant City" Modernist urban design model. This model was outlined in his "Contemporary City for 3 Million" in 1922 and further elaborated in his "Voisin Plan" of 1925, funded by the French aviation and automobile company of the same name.[16] In this scheme, central Paris would be razed and rebuilt into skyscrapers on a planted ground plane, with three levels of traffic above and below. "Our fast car takes the special elevated motor track between the majestic sky-scrapers. . . . Then suddenly we find ourselves at the feet of the first sky-scrapers," Le Corbusier conjured the vision. "But here we have, not the meagre shaft of sunlight which so faintly illumines the dismal streets of New York, but an immensity of space. The whole city is a Park."[17]

Jacobs had harsh words for the Radiant City in her most famous book, and harsher words for the most prominent proponent of Corbusian urbanism in postwar New York City, planner Robert Moses: "It is understandable that men who were young in the 1920s were captivated by the vision of the freeway Radiant City, with the specious promise that it would be appropriate to an automobile age. At least it was then a new idea; to men of the generation of New York's Robert Moses, for example, it was radical and exciting in the days when their minds were growing and their ideas forming."[18] Jacobs first clashed with Moses in 1955, when she began organizing local opposition against his plan to run a highway and off-ramp through her Greenwich Village neighborhood in Manhattan. Jacobs's advocacy and writing culminated in her 1961 book, which Moses characterized as "intemperate and inaccurate, it is also libelous."[19] Moses's plans for the Lower Manhattan Expressway were officially abandoned a year after Jacobs moved to Toronto, where she spent the rest of her career.

In Baltimore, the expressway system proposed around the same time as Charles Center was also getting pushback. Here the opposition was partially led by community organizer and social worker Barbara Mikulski. Mikulski, later a U.S. senator for Maryland, recalls why she helped lead the fight against the expressway:

I was busy trying to decentralize the local welfare department. Then I got a call about a highway project that was going to destroy the neighborhood where my family settled when they first came to this country. I also knew that there was an expressway coming through the west side of Baltimore that was going to take the first black homeownership neighborhood in Baltimore City. It seemed that highway was going to take the homes of a lot of people in a couple of neighborhoods—the Poles, the Italians, the Greeks, the blacks—and give them nothing in return. It would even have leveled Federal Hill.[20]

In *Architecture Forum*, however, Jane Jacobs praised this expressway plan as a necessary part of the urban design scheme that would make Charles Center successful: "Nor would Charles Center be possible if the city were not dealing with the main reason that brought about the deterioration of this site in the first place. . . . Baltimore's new ring road system, which is now under construction, makes possible at last the reclamation of the traffic-blighted core."[21] For Jacobs, who knew less about the ground truth of Baltimore's fabric and social history than Mikulski, the removal of car and truck through traffic from the downtown core was more important than the preservation of these neighborhoods. If she had been able to observe firsthand the sidewalk ballet in largely black Harlem Park, which did not succeed in fighting off the proposed expressway, or in predominantly white Little Italy, which did, she might have felt differently about the matter.

The authors of the edited volume *The Architecture of Baltimore* link the design of Charles Center to the Corbusian Radiant City paradigm that was popular all over the United States during this era of urban renewal. Indeed Le Corbusier was the first architect invited by the planners to design the complex's theater, although the commission later went to functional expressionist architect John Johansen.[22] With its slabs of glass, steel, and concrete arranged dynamically around open space, Charles Center is certainly an urban composition in the Modernist mode.

Jacobs's enthusiasm for the project—with its attendant skywalks and elevated highways—does not so much reveal a contradiction in *her* thinking, but in that of those who would interpret her legacy instead. Jacobs was no anti-Modernist. Her objection to the freeways in Manhattan was not a wholesale rejection of Modernism as an aesthetic mode; rather it was a rejection of certain organizational principles that were harmful to the urban patterns she had observed. Where the highway off-ramps in Greenwich Village would have obliterated the sidewalk ballet, she believed that the skywalks of Charles Center would have nurtured and encouraged that same intricate interaction. In Jacobs's original sidewalk ballet passage, the only motor vehicles mentioned are taxis and city busses. There are motor scooters, baby carriages, fire engines, roller

skates, tricycles, and even stilts, but there are no private cars in her urban utopia. This is clear in her review of Charles Center, when she refers to the condition that enables the existence of its potential "truly urban, concentrated, lively
design" not to be a system of pedestrian skywalks over automobile roads, but
rather two strategically organized "street levels."[23] The skybridge, for Jacobs, is
not the destroyer of street life: it is itself also a street, with all of the potential
for eyes on its ballet intact, if the heterogeneous composition of public life that
Jacobs observed could come together.

In the early twenty-first century, most of the skywalk system in Baltimore
has been removed, and most of the proposed freeway system was never built.
In a 2008 article about Charles Center for the modernist preservationist group
Docomomo, writer Olivia Klose quoted Charles Center designer David Wallace as acknowledging that the skywalks were "circuitous and hard to find."[24]
The open spaces at Charles Center were being renovated that year, in response
to falling tenancy numbers and competition from new development farther east
along Baltimore's waterfront. The Downtown Partnership's mandate to remove
the skywalks stems from a new plan created in 2008 for Pratt Street. DPB president Fowler stated that his group's priorities for Charles Street in addition to
encouraging more retail foot traffic, are "opening up the view corridors" and
"creating a better plaza to make it more marketable."[25] In 2014, the group cham-
pioned the removal of the skywalks at Hopkins Plaza in Charles Center, and
demolition began on Johansen's Morris Mechanic Theatre, a key node on the
skywalk network, which had sat empty since 2004. Since then, a plan to erect
a mixed-use tower on the site of the theater has not materialized, and this connection point between Hopkins Plaza—the "center" of Charles Center—and
Charles Street remains a hole in the ground.

In 1991 in *The Baltimore Book*, geographer David Harvey argues that
Charles Center and its skywalks had not fulfilled their promise to create a
new public street life downtown for the people of Baltimore. For Harvey,
Charles Center was born from the city elite's fears that they had abandoned
"the symbolic and political center of the metropolitan region to an underclass
of impoverished blacks and marginalized whites"; the point of the project was
to "revive property development and corporate power in the downtown
core."[26] Harvey's critique centers the issue, which is also peripheral in Jacobs's
work, of just who this space was for. The users of the space that Harvey identifies are not the heterogeneous participants in a sidewalk ballet; instead they
are the real estate investors who financed the property and see a return on its
value, the corporations like Sun Life and the Mercantile Bank & Trust Company (both housed in buildings designed by the Baltimore architecture firm,
Peterson Brickbauer), and their employees and tourists commuting in from
the suburbs. The expressways and parking garages allow a different kind of
urban user from the one envisioned by Jacobs, and the cycle of use for the

spaces would not spread to the twenty-four hours necessary to keep eyes on these elevated plazas and streets.

In the 1970s and 1980s, the skywalks were extended from the corporate office buildings and theater at Charles Center to the Inner Harbor. They eventually connected to the two shopping pavilions there, as well as several hotels, a multilevel shopping mall, the arena sports and music venue, and Baltimore's convention center. In theory, at the system's height, it would have been possible to visit Baltimore—for a conference or as a tourist—and to shop, dine, and stay at a hotel, all without touching an actual city street at grade. A proposal to extend the skywalk system westward to the historic Lexington Market, a place where, as noted by the *Baltimore City Paper*, 80 percent of the clientele is African American, was never realized.[27] The principles listed by David Wallace, the planning director for the Charles Center complex, in a 1960 article about the project for *Traffic Quarterly*, include a focus on an "intensive mixture of uses"— but only retail and office space are mentioned to support the case that Charles Center accomplishes this aim.[28] According to Wallace, the assumptions of the project's economic and urban impact included the expectation of 20,000 new employees and 5,000 visitors per day to the shops and hotels, with special events drawing as many as 13,000 people downtown. There is entertainment, in the form of the theater and adjacent Civic Center area, and eventually in the extension to the Inner Harbor, but there was no housing onsite that would help generate something like a true twenty-four-hour use cycle.

Another principle in Wallace's article for *Traffic Quarterly* was that the plazas would operate as "pedestrian precincts, or islands, free from traffic, within which the pedestrians can move unhindered"; they would all be tied together by the skywalks, "an interconnecting walkway system."[29] In the extension of the Charles Center development model to the Inner Harbor, it became necessary to create more "islands" along the way. One of those islands, at the intersection of Pratt and Light Streets, would be the key to linking the Charles Center and Inner Harbor Projects, and the potential key to creating the kind of heterogeneous provisional street life envisioned by Jane Jacobs (see Figure 22).

Albert Copp was executive vice president at Charles Center-Inner Harbor Management, Inc., the nonprofit group set up to run Charles Center and bring about new development at the Inner Harbor from the 1960s onward. After the cancellation of the highways that would have formed the "ring road system" embraced by Jacobs, traffic engineers had to account for even more cars at ground level, and planners like Copp relied on the skywalks and "islands" to shelter pedestrians from them. At McKeldin Plaza, one of these islands was designed as the link connecting pedestrians to the waterfront. The plaza was built in 1982, but its origins are in a traffic study conducted in 1968. "We had to get people across [Light Street], so we ran a skywalk," Copp remembers, and at the plaza, "we needed a big mass to the south, something like a mountain,

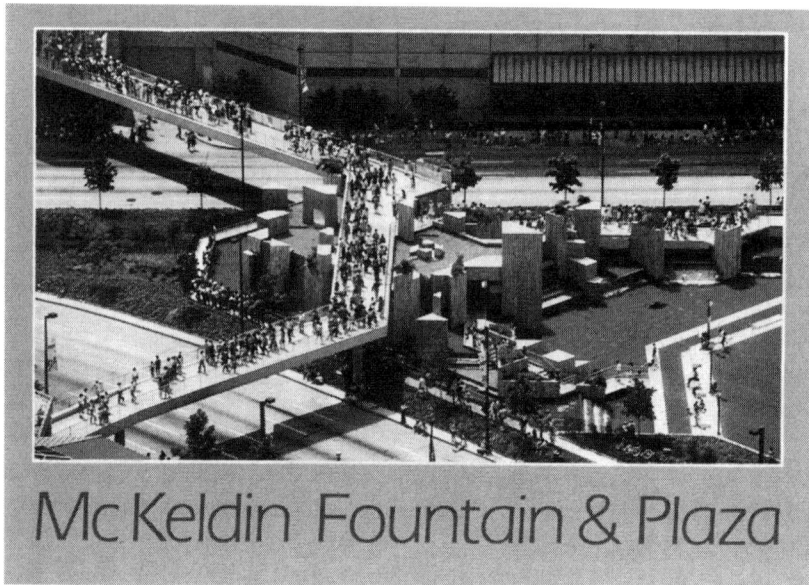

FIG. 22 McKeldin Fountain and Plaza, postcard, D. Traub & Son, Inc. Photo by Bob Willis, circa 1982.

to block the sound and exposure to traffic."[30] Someone had the idea to run water through it: the white noise would mask the sound and presence of car traffic, and the mountain at the island became a piece of public art. This concrete fountain—titled "The Waterfall" and designed by architect Thomas Todd, with skywalks, pools, and platforms at multiple levels—sheltered the plaza on two sides. Unlike the speculative skywalk system at Charles Center, the skywalks and traffic islands at the Inner Harbor were designed after some real-world testing. Copp and a traffic engineer watched the behavior of cars at rush hour when stoplight times were adjusted to lengths needed to allow the expected visitors to cross streets at grade. Their simulations showed that wait times were untenable and cars were in danger of backing up onto Interstate 95. Since the space had already been given over to the cars, there was less room left for people walking. The planners at the Inner Harbor realized they could put either the cars or the pedestrians on the ground plane, but they could not put both.[31]

At this plaza and at the Inner Harbor, over the next decades, many groups of heterogeneous users and visitors mixed. The original intended audience for the Inner Harbor project was city residents, according to contemporary accounts. Charles Center-Inner Harbor Management's chief executive Martin J. Millspaugh wrote that this space would be "a public playground for Baltimoreans along the shoreline."[32] To try out the use of the city as a playground, planners created an urban version of a traditional country fair. The "City Fair" attracted hundreds of thousands of people from the region to Charles Center and was eventually moved to the Inner Harbor. David Harvey points out that the language in the fair's publicity and reporting seemed built around the idea that Baltimore had to be "reborn" after the riots and unrest in 1968 following the assassination of Dr. Martin Luther King Jr. For Harvey, these spaces were created to make a new public life that was not based around politics or protest.[33]

Nevertheless, these same kinds of racial social tensions have haunted interactions in this public space in recent decades. In 2012, a General Assembly delegate in nearby Harford County accused Baltimore police of covering up a rash of "attacks" from "roving mobs of black youth" at the Inner Harbor. He said the area should be declared a "no travel zone" in an era when actual crime statistics showed violence was at record lows.[34] At the same time, many Baltimore youth reported stories of police harassment there. In 2010, a Baltimore city police officer was fired over a 2007 confrontation with skateboarding teenagers—in which he knocked one to the ground—that was later uploaded on video to YouTube.[35]

In response to the tone of confrontations like this, a youth-led initiative, the Inner Harbor Project, began programming and activism to promote better dialogue between police and young people in this area. A statement on its website reads in part: "The Inner Harbor Project focuses on public space because is the place where different social needs compete and where we can pioneer effective approaches to harmonious coexistence."[36] The project organizes events where youth themselves train police on ways to engage more respectfully. The group has raised funds to place a series of plaques with the "Code of Respect," a mutual agreement for behavior that applies to both kids and officers, beginning with "1. Your presence has an influence, choose positivity."[37] Despite the inclusion of stores in the Inner Harbor shopping pavilions that cater to young customers, a curfew enacted in 2014 criminalized the existence of teenagers (thirteen years and younger) in public space in Baltimore after 9 P.M. (this was later extended to 11 P.M. for kids ages fourteen to sixteen).

In 2014, a series of stories in the *Sun* revealed the millions of dollars that the city was spending to settle police harassment, brutality, and misconduct lawsuits.[38] The U.S. Department of Justice began a review of policing conduct in Baltimore that evolved to become a larger civil rights investigation after the unrest and uprising following the death of Freddie Gray while in police custody. The investigation uncovered years of systemic discriminatory policing practices in Baltimore that were illegal and unconstitutional. When Baltimoreans protested in the aftermath of the deaths of Trayvon Martin in Florida, Michael Brown in Ferguson, and Freddie Gray in Baltimore, the downtown area and the Inner Harbor were two of the places they came to march. The pedestrian traffic island at McKeldin Plaza is one of Baltimore's "Free Speech

Zones," areas where spontaneous group protest, leafleting, and other activity can take place without the need to obtain a permit in advance.[39] In at least one 2014 protest, police closed and blocked the stairs at the fountain and stationed themselves on the skywalks above the plaza, observing and filming the crowd below. For three months in 2011, Occupy Baltimore had camped out in the same fountain terraces and skywalks to protest income inequality and social injustice under capitalism. This all took place under the view of the bank headquarter buildings surrounding the plaza and harbor, whose existence and prominence were noted in David Harvey's 1991 essay for *The Baltimore Book*.

Those same institutions, Baltimore-based T. Rowe Price and PNC Bank, were among the first private donors to help fund the removal of the fountain and skywalks.[40] Earlier, as mentioned, the Downtown Partnership of Baltimore had removed skywalks in Hopkins Plaza at Charles Center, after supporting the removal of the Morris H. Mechanic Theatre. That concrete brutalist building had been a crucial supporting structure for stairs that allowed access to the skywalk system, so its removal facilitated the elimination of the other. At McKeldin Plaza, the same arrangement was in place, and the same strategy of removal applied. The skywalks there came down in July 2016, and the fountain was demolished beginning in October. Despite opposition from preservationists, architects, historians, and advocates for public space and public art, all of this was done without much solicited feedback from the people of Baltimore.

In the popular imagination, skywalks are places where the best and worst in urban public life become possible (see Figure 23). In science fiction and speculative design, they are signifiers of urban utopia and dystopia—*The Jetsons* or *Blade Runner*. Their origins are in the simple idea that creating separate levels, for people in cars and people on foot, would make the pedestrian experience safer and more pleasant. But in American cities split with divisions along racial and socioeconomic lines, there was always the concern that this class stratification would be reproduced in any multilevel urban spatial scenario. "The loss of the ground plane equals the loss of community," as architecture theorist and historian Thomas Schumacher used to tell his students.[41] Either the skywalks would become the exclusive domain of an elite tourist-business class, as Harvey's work suggests, or in more secular critique of skywalk urbanism, they would be "overrun" by drug users, the homeless, and criminals waiting to rob unsuspecting visitors, cut off from access to the stairs and the safety of the street below. Skywalks, even if they were successful, would, in the fears of many, pull activity away from the stores at grade. Renderings of the Baltimore skywalk system from the 1950s and 60s, in contradiction to the notion that the road below would be for service and delivery only, show people and storefronts at two levels. This was intended to be more like an outdoor mall with cars in the middle, than a desolate underground loading zone. In any case, skywalks are

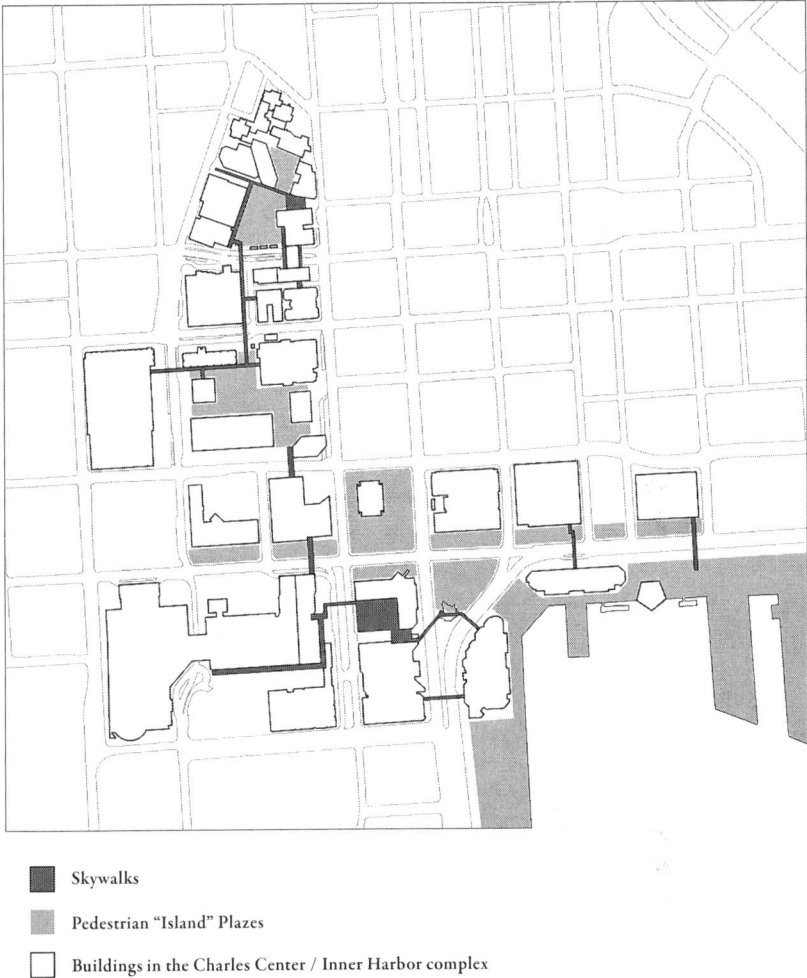

Skywalks

Pedestrian "Island" Plazes

Buildings in the Charles Center / Inner Harbor complex

FIG. 23 A map of Baltimore's downtown skywalks at Charles Center and the Inner Harbor, in dark grey, and the pedestrian "islands," in light grey, as they existed in the early 1990s at the network's height. Drawing by Fred Scharmen.

positioned in a double bind. They are either for the wealthy or for the poor, and they are either so active that they compete with the street or so vacant that they become unsafe. For many cities, it proved easier to take down the skywalk system than to disassemble the class divisions that made people fear this kind of public space in the first place.

In language around urban "revitalization," buildings become, at best, sources of property and income tax revenue or, at worst, vacant derelict eyesores. And people are depicted as either happy customers and office workers or dissatisfied potential rioters and criminals. In Baltimore, the answer to Harvey's implied question—Who is the public pedestrian space at Charles Center and the Inner Harbor for?—turned out to be very different from what he could have anticipated.

In August 2016, the Baltimore Bloc, a grassroots collective of activists, obstructed skywalk access to the Hyatt Regency hotel. Bloc members chained themselves to an escalator and unfurled a Black Lives Matter sign on the skywalk for traffic below to see as part of a protest against a Fraternal Order of Police convention downtown; this protest was seen by many on YouTube.[42] But skywalks are also the venues for parties. Every summer since 1999, the skywalks are overrun by fans of Japanese visual culture as part of the anime and science fiction convention Otakon, where most attendees dress as their favorite characters. At places like the architecture firm Gensler, with an office opening onto the skywalk system, staff organize office parties and happy hours to coincide with the spectacle. "Don't the homeless bathe there?" was an often-overheard comment about the fountain in McKeldin Plaza, before it was demolished.[43] In 2013, Otakon attendees emptied bottles of laundry soap into the fountain and jumped in for an impromptu swim party on a hot August evening.

There is also a ballet of sorts: the skywalks and fountain in McKeldin Plaza were popular recreation spots for practitioners of the urban free-running sport parkour, where people jumped from level to level and pushed themselves off the hard concrete surfaces. In 2007, Baltimore rap artist Rye Rye put dancers on the multiple levels of the skywalk and fountain, as part of the music video shoot for her song "Shake It to the Ground." The video also included shots of employees from Baltimore's Department of Public Works in hip waders, skimming the fountain's water clean. McKeldin Fountain, with its abstract geometry and multiple platforms was, like the skywalks, another of Susan Leigh Star's urban "boundary objects."[44]

"This was waiting to happen sadly," one Otakan attendee, Gaspar AKA Shiggitay, posted on an online message board, when news of the skywalk removal was announced, "I'm just as sad as the next person. . . . I guess we'll have the skywalk and the fountains in our memories. . . . >>."[45] Out of a system that once stretched over almost two miles downtown, only two or three skywalks remain, bridging Light Street, Pratt Street, and Hanover Street. Continuous travel from one to the other above the cars is no longer possible. While it existed, Baltimore's network of pedestrian "islands" linked by skywalks never quite succeeded in engendering anything like the sidewalk ballet described in Jacobs's book. But Jane Jacobs's Greenwich Village was not Sesame Street; her writing creates space for the homeless and the addicted alongside the kids on tricycles. The skywalks in downtown Baltimore created space for many different kinds of urban subjects, commerce-related and otherwise, but they never achieved the density and level of activity that are the prerequisites for becoming the "truly urban, concentrated, lively design" that Jacobs hoped they would be. Jacobs's sidewalk ballet, though, is less about the production of community than it is the production of an effect, the mutual visibility that is the result of the coexistence of difference in shared space: eyes on the street. The skywalks, as a platform for some kind of public life, did succeed in creating at least the potential for the partial visibility of some otherwise overlooked actualities in the contemporary city—like homelessness, police misconduct, public protest, income inequality, and simple urban play.

Notes

All URLs were accessed June 28–29, 2017.

1 Citizens' Committee for Charles Center and Civic Center Loans, *To Revitalize Downtown Baltimore*, 1958, accessed June 28, 2017.

2 Citizens' Committee, *To Revitalize Downtown Baltimore*.

3 Citizens' Committee, *To Revitalize Downtown Baltimore*.

4 Jane Jacobs, "Downtown Is for People," *Fortune*, April 1958, accessed June 28, 2017.

5 Kurt Andersen, "Fast Life along the Skywalks," *Time*, August 1, 1988, http://www.kurtandersen.com/journalism/time/fast-life-along-the-skywalks/.

6 Jacobs, "Downtown Is for People."

7 Jane Jacobs, "New Heart for Baltimore," *Architectural Forum*, June 1958, http://archives.ubalt.edu/gbc/pdf/12-11-26_Part1.pdf.

8 Jacobs, "New Heart for Baltimore."

9 David Alpert, "Skybridges Don't Make the Connection," *Greater Greater Washington*, February 28, 2008, https://ggwash.org/view/219/skybridges-dont-make-the-connection.

10 "This is still Palmer, though—he's applied for permission to connect the two parts of the BP with a pedestrian skybridge over Olympic Boulevard. Taking people off the street doesn't really jibe with the whole (largely very successful) project to revitalize Broadway, but considering the development falls in skybridge-enabler Jose Huizar's City Council district, don't be surprised if Palmer gets his bridge. The building is set to open in early 2017, assuming disgruntled Jane Jacobs acolytes don't burn this one down too." Ian Grant, "DTLA's Worst Developer Starts Work on Big Broadway Complex," *Curbed*, March 16, 2015, https://la.curbed.com/2015/3/16/9980318/broadway-palace-geoff-palmer.

11 Eileen Ambrose, "Downtown Baltimore Skywalk over Pratt Street to Come Down," *Baltimore Sun*, September 10, 2013, http://articles.baltimoresun.com/2013-09-10/business/bs-bz-skywalk-20130910_1_skywalk-downtown-baltimore-pratt-street.

12 Jane Jacobs, *The Death and Life of Great American Cities* (New York: Random House, 1961; New York: Modern Library, 1993), 66.

13 "But there is nothing simple about that order itself, or the bewildering number of components that go into it. Most of those components are specialized in one way or another. They unite in their joint effort upon the sidewalk, which is not specialized in the least. That is its strength." Jacobs, *The Death and Life*, 71.

14 Susan Leigh Star and James R. Griesemer, "Institutional Ecology, 'Transitions' and Boundary Objects: Amateurs and Professionals in Berkeley's Museum of Vertebrate Zoology, 1907–39," *Social Studies of Science* 19, no. 3 (August 1989): 387–420.

15 Archibald Coleman Rogers, "The Charles Center Project," *Journal of The American Institute of Architects*, March 1959.

16 Both of these schemes are published in English in Le Corbusier, *The City of To-morrow and its Planning* (New York: Dover Publications, 1987).

17 Le Corbusier, *The City of To-morrow*, 177.

18 Jacobs, *The Death and Life*, 484.

19 Anthony Flint, *Wrestling with Moses: How Jane Jacobs Took on New York's Master Builder and Transformed the American City* (New York: Random House, 2009), 125.

20 Barbara Mikulski, "Barbara Mikulski: The Senator as Community Activist," in *The Baltimore Book: New Views of Local History*, ed. Elizabeth Fee, Linda Shopes, and Linda Zeidman (Philadelphia: Temple University Press, 1991), 147–149.

21 Jacobs, "New Heart for Baltimore."

22 "Inventing Charles Center," in *The Architecture of Baltimore, an Illustrated History*, ed. Mary Ellen Hayward and Frank R. Shivers Jr. (Baltimore: Johns Hopkins University Press, 2004), 278–285.

23 Jacobs, "New Heart for Baltimore."

24 Olivia Klose, "Urban Renewal Renewed: A Makeover for Baltimore's Center Plaza," *Docomomo US National News*, Winter 2008.

25 Kevin Litten, "Downtown Partnership Wants a Hopkins Plaza Building Demolished to Make Way for Green Space," *Baltimore Business Journal*, March 11, 2014, http://www.bizjournals.com/baltimore/blog/real-estate/2014/03/downtown-partnership-wants-a-hopkins-plaza.html.

26 David Harvey, "A View from Federal Hill," in *The Baltimore Book*, 227–249.

27 "A majority of the customers have been coming to the market for more than 20 years. African-Americans make up a full 80 percent of the customers and a majority of those are middle-aged," Baynard Woods, "The Battles of Lexington," *Baltimore City Paper*, April 21, 2015, http://www.citypaper.com/news/features/bcpnews-the-battles-of-lexington-city-paper-goes-deep-inside-and-under-baltimores-oldest-market-20150421-story.html.

28 David Wallace, "Renaissance in Baltimore," *Traffic Quarterly*, January 1960, http://archives.ubalt.edu/gbc/pdf/12-11-26_Part1.pdf.

29 Wallace, "Renaissance in Baltimore."

30 Fred Scharmen, "Thinking of a Masterplan: A Look At How McKeldin Plaza Came to Be, and the Plans to Undo It All," *Baltimore City Paper*, August 31, 2016, http://www.citypaper.com/news/features/bcp-083116-feature-mckeldin-20160831-story.html.

31 Scharmen, "Thinking of a Masterplan."

32 Martin L. Millspaugh, "The Inner Harbor Story," *Urban Land Magazine*, April 2003, http://globalharbors.org/inner_harbor_story.html.

33 Harvey, "A View from Federal Hill."

34 "Maryland Delegate Refuses to Back down from Challenges to Mayor, Black Youth Mob Commentary," *Baltimore Afro-American*, June 6, 2012, http://afro.com/maryland-delegate-refuses-to-back-down-from-challenges-to-mayor-black-youth-mob-commentary/.

35 Peter Hermann, "Baltimore Cop Who Berated Skateboarder Fired," *Baltimore*

Sun, August 25, 2010, http://www.baltimoresun.com/bs-mtblog-2010-08
-baltimore_cop_who_berated_skat-story.html.

36 Inner Harbor Project, "Our Mission," http://www.theinnerharborproject.org
/mission/.

37 Inner Harbor Project, "Code of Respect," http://www.theinnerharborproject.org
/code-of-respect/.

38 Mark Puente, "Undue Force," *Baltimore Sun*, September 28, 2014, http://data
.baltimoresun.com/news/police-settlements/.

39 American Civil Liberties Union, "Free Speech Rights Significantly Expanded in
Baltimore's Inner Harbor," October 16, 2013, https://www.aclu.org/news/free
-speech-rights-significantly-expanded-baltimores-inner-harbor.

40 Fred Scharmen, "Brutal Reckoning," *Baltimore City Paper*, October 14, 2014,
http://www.citypaper.com/news/mobtownbeat/bcp-brutal-reckoning-20141014
-story.html.

41 Thomas Schumacher, in conversation with the author, 1999.

42 Brandon Soderberg, "#Stopfop Protest at the Hyatt Regency Further Illustrates
Police Misconduct and FOP Overreach," *Baltimore City Paper*, August 15, 2016,
http://www.citypaper.com/blogs/the-news-hole/bcpnews-stopfop-action-at-the
-hyatt-regency-further-illustrates-police-misconduct-and-fop-overreach-20160815
-story.html.

43 Fred Scharmen, "Thinking of a Masterplan."

44 Rye Rye, "Shake it to the Ground," https://www.youtube.com/watch?v
=fHAigWTZioI, accessed on June 29, 2017.

45 "Skywalk Bridge to Inner Harbor Being Demolished," *Otakon*, July 2016,
https://board.otakon.com/index.php?/topic/27727-skywalk-bridge-to-inner
-harbor-being-demolished/, accessed June 29, 2017.

23

Rethinking Gentrification in Baltimore, Sharp Leadenhall

•••••••••••••••••••••

MATTHEW DURINGTON
AND SAMUEL GERALD COLLINS

Much of the real applied work in community-based research is located in church basements during meetings and other events in which anthropologists work with our collaborators. That is where we found ourselves alongside student researchers in 2006 talking with community members from the community of Sharp Leadenhall in South Baltimore, one of the most historic African American communities in the city. As discussions ensued regarding the history of Sharp Leadenhall, urban renewal plans that had affected black communities in Baltimore, and current socioeconomic challenges facing individuals, the conversation shifted to all of the "newcomers" who were moving into the area who were literally and figuratively changing the complexion of Sharp Leadenhall. The neighborhood and other parts of South Baltimore had become "hot" in the real estate market as homes were being bought and rehabbed in the latest wave of gentrification in the city. This chapter discusses both the history of Sharp Leadenhall and contemporary issues concerning pressures that have emerged through processes of gentrification.

Gentrification is a tumultuous process whereby urban neighborhoods are restored and refurbished, usually in conjunction with an influx of new residents.

Much of this development centers on the acquisition, clearing, or rehabilitation of housing with the goal of increasing its market value. While often seen as a class-based phenomenon brought on by shifts in housing development, the process of gentrification often results in the racialized displacement of residents. This contemporary displacement because of higher home prices is historically preceded by discriminatory residential practices such as redlining, racial covenants, and blockbusting. Since the term "gentrification" was coined in 1964, the analytical concept has expanded in academia and common parlance. Gentrification was associated primarily with housing rehabilitation and residential areas until the mid-1980s, when its effects were analyzed in terms of broader societal restructuring and the changing nature of cities.[1] It can also involve large and small-scale business development by independent businesses or corporations.

Gentrification has also been analyzed in terms of its attachment to globalization and the effects of neoliberalism on urban and societal change. The concept has mutated as research expands to delve into its effects on rural environments, new building developments, and even the possibility of "super gentrification," which describes gentrification in its second-generation manifestation that affects the same locale.[2] A later stage of gentrification in the twenty-first century views it as inexorably tied to "intensified financialization of housing combined with the consolidation of pro-gentrification politics and polarized urban policies."[3] Gentrification researchers Mark Davidson and Loretta Lees claim that a holistic definition of the concept should include four elements: the reinvestment of capital, social upgrading of the locale by incoming high-income groups, landscape change, and the direct or indirect displacement of low-income groups.[4]

One of Sharp Leadenhall community activists' strategies to confront gentrification was to secure historical status for the neighborhood with Baltimore's Commission for Historic and Architectural Preservation (CHAP) in 2010. These efforts were successful, and the neighborhood now has signs adorning light poles on streets bordering the community that read "Historic Sharp Leadenhall." While this success was celebrated and discussed during the meeting described at the beginning of this chapter, folks were still worried about being able to stay in the community in the face of rising rent prices and other pressures brought on by gentrification. At one point a long-standing member of the community expressed her frustration by stating, "Well, you can't put history in if you're taking it out!" This sentiment embodies the tensions of gentrification in Baltimore. In essence, how can a historic black community in Baltimore exist if the actual members of that community can no longer afford to live there or feel unwelcome due to processes of gentrification that are highly racialized because the majority of new residents are white? Further complicating things, the different discourses on the city are not neatly divisible into "top-down" and "bottom-up": they overlap in significant ways, with different groups appropriating the language of other groups for their own purposes in a conflu-ence of perspectives brought on by the realities of political economy and gen-trification in the twenty-first century.

Alongside many other cities in the United States, Baltimore has suffered from post–World War II deindustrialization and the loss of a manufacturing economy while a huge segment of its urban population has migrated to the sub-urbs and beyond. Job opportunities have eroded over time, which undercut the tax base for the city and resulted in underfunded education and services. The steady demographic shift of "white flight" from Baltimore since World War II has also shaped a racialized perception of the city. As the formal economy has weakened, an informal economy has developed that fuels widespread neg-ative perceptions of the city as criminalized. The perception of Baltimore as racialized and criminalized further reinforces a stereotype of black men, result-ing in biased, problematic, and targeted law enforcement strategies and spiraling incarceration rates that concomitantly worsen unstable housing conditions. The dilapidation of the urban housing stock in Baltimore due to historic redlining and absentee ownership has become emblematic of these racial, economic, and population shifts. The oft-seen abandoned Baltimore row home with plywood boards on the windows has become a national symbol of urban blight. All of these material and symbolic conditions inform a view of the city as a dangerous space and become the fodder for a "representational burden" of Baltimore in popular culture as seen in shows such as *Homicide, The Corner,* and the land-mark series *The Wire.* Media footage from the Baltimore uprising of 2015 now compounds this representational burden—the slew of problematic media representations of the city and primarily of its black residents.

The process of gentrification parallels the social history of the city as wit-nessed in the historic African American community of Sharp Leadenhall. Since the neighborhood was first settled, the people and institutions of Sharp Lead-enhall have played a pivotal role in the history of African Americans in Balti-more. As many free blacks settled in the community it became a center for the antislavery movement; the Baltimore Abolitionist Society was founded there in 1789 by Elisha Tyson and others. That organization later became the Afri-can Academy of Baltimore, one of the first schools for free blacks in the United States. Despite this rich history and the recently acquired preservation desig-nation by the city of Baltimore, the last several decades have seen Sharp Lead-enhall under siege from socioeconomic and political forces that have shrunk the size of the community and population, most prominently because of vari-ous forms of gentrification.

The community has historically been subject to a number of urban renewal processes, including highway construction, urban homesteading, real estate expansion, and sport stadium construction, that have laid the groundwork for contemporary gentrification. The community of Sharp Leadenhall has a storied history of feminist activists that have taken on these challenges historically and contemporaneously as "centerwomen."[5] As Gregory describes this gendered construct developed from the work of Karen Sacks, a "centerwoman" embodies the "politicization of everyday life" in a community by strategically employing notions of family, kinship, and constructed women's roles as a tool in community activism with power brokers.[6] She may engage in such activities as hosting events within her home, where home cooking and local members may interface with politicians and stakeholders, or hosting cultural events in local churches or at block parties organized mostly by women in the community.

Mildred Rae Moon was the preeminent centerwoman in Sharp Leadenhall in the 1960s and 1970s. After much of the housing was razed in the 1960s for a proposed highway, she and other feminist activists were able to work with others, including Barbara Mikulski (later to become a U.S. senator), in the Movement against Destruction (MAD) organization, which succeeded in halting construction. The proposed highway spur from Interstate 95 in South Baltimore would have spanned Federal Hill and the Inner Harbor as part of the Robert Moses-designed federal highway system. Moon used her skill sets and tenacity in a constant battle with Mayor (and later governor) William Donald Schaefer, who would consistently tell her the highway was coming and could not be stopped. Moon and others persisted and eventually won, inadvertently helping create what would become a major tourist and economic engine for the city of Baltimore. Imagine if a highway span existed today across the Inner Harbor of Baltimore? One could only guess what the current socioeconomic climate would be if that were the case and Schaefer and others had succeeded in their plans. There would be no center for urban tourism in the city and the concomitant dollars that come with it. Ironically, while there is a statue of Schaefer in the Inner Harbor, which would not have existed if he had succeeded with his highway plans, a small bridge on Hanover Street named for Moon connects the Baltimore Ravens stadium—where destroyed houses once stood—to what still exists of the community in Sharp Leadenhall.

In the wake of the success of the Movement against Destruction, urban homesteading programs such as the "dollar houses" were offered in the neighborhood of Otterbein adjacent to Sharp Leadenhall. In this form of government-sponsored gentrification in the 1970s, middle-class people were encouraged to move back into the city by offering housing stock literally for one dollar, as long as individuals met the program criteria, agreed to reside there for eighteen months, and had a sufficient income to redevelop dilapidated properties.[7] While not perceived as racialized, the qualification requirements for this program excluded the majority of urban residents who already lived in these communities and ushered in another process of gentrification literally next door to Sharp Leadenhall. As it stands in the twenty-first century, the community of Sharp Leadenhall is hemmed in by development interests.

As in many other U.S. cities the hot housing market in Baltimore in the early twenty-first century was fueling redevelopment. Many Baltimore neighborhoods witnessed an influx of new residents and predatory lenders that swooped in with exotic financial instruments, claiming to make home ownership a viable opportunity for many. Sharp Leadenhall became a popular neighborhood on real estate speculation maps due to its proximity to nearby Federal Hill and local sports venues that were constructed on the former demolished homes of early residents of the community. The combination of loose lending practices from financial institutions and an overleveraged housing market all over the country led directly to the 2008 global economic crisis and recession. Baltimore suffered significantly in the financial aftermath of the housing-based recession in the United States, which forced another reckoning with the concept of gentrification. Ultimately, what type of neighborhoods will emerge from socioeconomic conditions in Baltimore in the twenty-first century? What will historic communities like Sharp Leadenhall become? The residents of Sharp Leadenhall are negotiating a cultural identity that relies on historic residency while confronting forces of displacement driven by both economic and symbolic forces.

The processes of gentrification have had a significant impact on the neighborhood of Sharp Leadenhall and many other neighborhoods throughout the city. As is the case with many other U.S. cities, Baltimore has systematically denied African American neighborhoods capital and removed much of the authority residents may have once had to define their own communities.[8] These results of gentrification are only exacerbated in the slow recovery from a global economic downturn. In response to these processes, grassroots community organizations and activists have worked to keep their communities intact, but face challenges as development persists.

Housing researcher Jason Hackworth asserts that the nature of gentrification has shifted as corporate developers are now more common than individual gentrifiers looking to buy homes, and the state is fueling this process directly. In addition, anti-gentrification social movements have become increasingly marginalized, while the land economics of urban investment have accelerated new types of neighborhood change.[9] Each of these processes can be witnessed in Sharp Leadenhall. Despite its current historical designation, much of Sharp Leadenhall was designated as light industrial zoning during the highway development schemes in the twentieth century. This enabled a major corporate development scheme of mixed-use development and high-rise condominiums supported by the city in the form of tax abatements. This development hit its stride in 2017 and continues as several construction projects unfold on former light industrial sites. While some community groups have partnered with developers in these efforts, others have not by choice or are excluded. Baltimore, along with many other urban locales, continues to rely on public–private partnerships for urban investment.

So, what happens to neighborhoods like Sharp Leadenhall that have gone through and continue to experience various waves of gentrification? Despite a growing awareness of this process by community groups, gentrification has not abated, but has merely changed in its complexion. Some developers now offer a small portion of new residences as "mixed-income"—usually less than 10 percent—but rarely follow through with these promises or only offer these as rental properties for current residents.[10] Mega-developments, such as the Port Covington project currently under development in South Baltimore, strike bargains with selective community leaders via questionable financial commitments that are often not sustainable to satiate critics. Unfortunately, certain community leaders fall in line with development agendas in exchange for deals ranging from the construction of cultural centers or support of other social programs.

Development is not done with the "right to the city" for all urban residents in mind, as discussed by David Harvey in a process where all voices are heard and respected in the remaking of cities.[11] The efforts of developers and city leaders still do not consider the input of local residents beyond the occasional and mandated community meeting to announce plans. In today's neoliberal era, housing more than ever reinforces the power of developers who possess the income to invest in cities when public budgets are depleted. In fact, these developments could be described as something much more nefarious than simple free-market practices. As Neil Smith details, processes of development can often be seen as "revanchist" processes that are racialized and discriminatory, if not by design or intent necessarily, but certainly in their respective outcomes.[12] In this sense, Smith shows how the process of gentrification feels more like "revenge" when it is highly racialized. Powerful stereotypes of the urban milieu are inscribed in popular culture and used to pathologize the poor: the city as dangerous, as sexualized, as nonwhite.

There are also discourses and representations that allow for expeditious capital expropriation: the city as the site of redevelopment, investment, and phantasmagorias of capital.[13] All of these "top-down" stereotypic representations have together wreaked havoc on the texture of neighborhoods in Baltimore over the last sixty years through the guise of urban renewal and other social engineering, transforming some working-class neighborhoods into pathologized ghettos and others into gentrified "rejuvenated" zones for capital investment premised on the absence of that neighborhood's previous residents.

But these are not the only representations being proffered by Baltimore residents. Baltimore residents variously seek to exert control over the way they are seen by the outside world, as well as by each other.[14] They may work to record their histories, to build solidarity with each other, to sponsor festivals and cultural events, to make their voices heard in City Council meetings, to challenge zoning, to demand more city services, to protest, or to form affinities with like-minded groups across the city, the nation, the world. Whatever the case, the stakes here are high. The very existence of neighborhoods, communities, and the city itself hinges on the ability of its inhabitants to demonstrate their worth to the world of power and capital outside them dominated by those with more financial capacity. These different interpretive frames bring together individual agency and institutions in powerful ways, denying some the ability to interpret their own lives, while others are able to author the city to their liking. As conceptual shifts in traditional gentrification continue to occur, the historically black communities in Baltimore continue to be under threat. If you find yourself at Solo Gibbs Park on a weekend in the spring or summer where kids play or witness the double- and triple-parking around historic black churches on a Sunday when former residents return for church services in Sharp Leadenhall, you can still see evidence of one of Baltimore's oldest black communities often hidden in between new development.

Notes

1 Loretta Lees, Tom Slater, and Erik Wyly, *Gentrification* (New York: Routledge, 2008); Loretta Lees, "Super-Gentrification: The Case of Brooklyn Heights, New York City," *Urban Studies* 40, no. 12 (2003): 2487–2509.

2 Lees et al., *Gentrification*; Lees, "Super-Gentrification."

3 David Harvey, "The Right to the City," *New Left Review* 53 (2008).

4 Mark Davidson and Loretta Lees, "New-Build Gentrification and London's Riverside Renaissance," *Environment and Planning* 37 (2005): 1165–1190.

5 Steven Gregory, *Black Corona* (Princeton, NJ: Princeton University Press, 1999).

6 Steven Gregory, "Race, Rubbish and Resistance: Empowering Difference in Community Politics," in *Race*, ed. Steven Gregory and Roger Sanjek (New Brunswick, NJ: Rutgers University Press, 1994), 383.

7 Michael Decourcy Hinds, "Baltimore's Story of City Homesteading," *New York Times* (1986 Archive).

8 Jeff Maskovsky, "Governing the 'New Hometowns': Race, Power, and Neighborhood Participation in the New Inner City," *Identities: Global Studies in Culture and Power* 13 (2006): 73–99.

9 Jason Hackworth, "Postrecession Gentrification in New York City," *Urban Affairs Review* 37, no. 6 (2002): 815–843.

10 See "Sharp Leadenhall: A Promise to Keep," Megaphone Project (2007), https://www.youtube.com/watch?v=OLFHq94GikE.

11 Harvey, "The Right to the City."

12 Neil Smith, *New Urban Frontier: Gentrification and the Revanchist City* (London: Routledge, 1996).

13 Saskia Sassen, "Whose City Is It? Globalization and the Formation of New Claims," *Public Culture* 8 (1996): 205–223; David Harvey, *Spaces of Capital: Towards a Critical Geography* (London: Routledge, 2001).

14 Matthew Durington, Shana Gass, Camee Maddox, Adrienne Ruhf, and Justin Schwermer, "Civic Engagement and Gentrification Issues in Metropolitan Baltimore," *Metropolitan Universities Journal* 1, no. 20 (2009): 101–114.

24

The Superblock

●●●●●●●●●●●●●●●●●●●●

A Downtown Development
Debacle, 2003–2015

P. NICOLE KING

From the Top Down

At fifteen stories, the Bromo Seltzer Tower was the tallest building in Baltimore when it was built in 1911. Captain Isaac Emerson, the inventor of the Bromo Seltzer headache remedy and hangover cure, modeled the grand tower after the Palazzo Vecchio in Florence, Italy.

Standing atop the iconic tower in 2017, I gazed down on the historic west side of downtown. I could easily see the buildings, but the people on the streets below were harder to make out. "The ordinary practitioners of the city live 'down below,' below the thresholds at which visibility begins," Michel de Certeau writes in *The Practice of Everyday Life*, "They walk—an elementary form of this experience of the city; they are walkers, *Wandersmänner*, whose bodies follow the thicks and thins of an urban 'text' they write without being able to read it."[1] To develop a city in just and equal ways, we must be able to see and critically read the "text" of those walking the city streets down below. This is the story of how politicians and developers, both inside and outside of the city, lacked the vision to read such a "text" in downtown Baltimore and to clearly see the people on the streets.

In this chapter I analyze the Superblock, a failed downtown development project proposed in 2003 and eventually canceled in 2015. In addition, I argue for a model of downtown development that is more connected to existing local communities by respecting the modest scale and historic fiber of independent business owners and the city they inhabit. The west side of downtown Baltimore is full of iconic historic buildings that are visibly in decline as new development projects such as Harbor Point and Port Covington, which are outside of the downtown footprint, boom with public and private investment and tax benefits. The west side's historic buildings include specimens from the colonial antebellum period, the factories of the industrial nineteenth century, and the theaters and the five-and-dimes of the twentieth century. Deindustrialization, suburbanization, disinvestment, and the unrest following more than a century of entrenched segregation and inequality throughout the city's neighborhoods have all scarred the commercial district of the west side of downtown Baltimore.

In the 1960s and 1970s, the city witnessed the rise of the Charles Center project in the city's central business district, and the 1980s saw Baltimore's working harbor refashioned as the Inner Harbor tourist destination of today. Yet the disinvestment in the city's neighborhoods and the decline of the west side of downtown clearly show that we need a new way—a more equitable and just way—to envision the redevelopment of our city centers and to rethink the true goals of downtown development in the twenty-first century if we are to avoid falling into the same pitfalls that devastated downtowns in the first place. It is what is going on in the streets, not the view from the top of the tower, that we must take seriously.

The Superblock Saga

In 1999, the Harry and Jeanette Weinberg Foundation, which is one of Baltimore's largest philanthropic funds, partnered with Grid Properties, a big New York developer, to debut a west side redevelopment plan called "Howard Street USA." The plan called for the demolition of 80 percent of the historic buildings in the west side of downtown. In 2000, local architecture critic Edward Gunts wrote an aptly titled story for the *Baltimore Sun*, "Keeping It Real: Does Baltimore Really Need to Demolish So Much of the West Side in Order to Revive It?" detailing the "$150 million, mixed-use development that would be the largest component of Baltimore's $350 million initiative to rejuvenate the west side of downtown."[2] City politicians and developers argued that the historic west side needed to be better integrated with the Inner Harbor and central business district redevelopments of recent decades while also connecting to the University of Maryland, Baltimore professional schools located in its footprint.

The project was inspired by Grid Property's Harlem USA—a development anchored by "big box" retailers on 125th Street in the historically African American neighborhood of Harlem in New York City—and by similar developments in San Francisco. New York and San Francisco are ground zero in the United States for hypergentrification, an extreme form of development that displaces longtime and often low-income residents of color from city neighborhoods.[3] The goal is to bring in residents and patrons who have more wealth than is possessed by the community's long-standing residents. In his article, Gunts pointed out potential problems of Howard Street USA: "In many ways, it comes across as an urban shopping center for people who don't like cities—flat, formulaic, hermetically sealed off from the street. It's the sort of prepackaged presence that poses a threat to urban culture: Death by Big Box."[4]

Local preservation nonprofits—such as Baltimore Heritage and Preservation Maryland—opposed the project as "urban removal," an outdated model of so-called slum clearance discredited by twenty-first-century urban planners and designers as racist and classist. The west side was mostly spared in the Great Fire of 1904, which destroyed much of the rest of downtown, and its built environment continued to hold a "richness and authenticity that help distinguish downtown Baltimore from the blandness of the suburbs," according to Gunts.[5]

The distinct aesthetic derived from the "richness and authenticity" of many layers of history accounted for the charm of the west side. The buildings are as diverse as the people. Howard Street USA would demolish much of this area's irreplaceable character and change its cultural landscape. A short video called "Baltimore's West Side Story," which focused both on the history of the area and the voices of local merchants, primarily Asian and African American small business owners, began to sway public opinion.[6] In January 2001, the city and the Maryland Historical Trust struck an agreement to preserve the area's host of historic buildings for the future. The Howard Street USA project returned to the drawing board as preservation efforts saved the west side, for the moment.

The pivotal events that led to the Superblock debacle started in 2003 with a Request for Proposal (RFP) put out by the Baltimore Development Corporation (BDC), a nonprofit private–public partnership formed by the merger of smaller development organizations in 1991 to focus on economic development in the city. The so-called Superblock development parcel included more than fifty properties (most of which were historic) across 3.6 acres of downtown, encompassing a five-block area bound by Clay and West Lexington Streets on the north, West Fayette Street on the south, Liberty Street on the east, and Howard Street on the west.[7] The BDC received four proposals for the entire parcel and nine proposals from current business or property owners in the Superblock footprint.[8] In 2004, the BDC recommended the winning proposal to Mayor Martin O'Malley; even though there was controversy that the proposed plan was both too big, but yet not strong enough to be feasible, and would tear down important historic buildings, the mayor approved the plan submitted by the Chera, Feil, and Goldman Group of New York, and this firm won the Superblock development rights. The Downtown Partnership, a nonprofit focused on revitalizing the city center, and WestSide Renaissance Inc., a group representing forty stakeholders in downtown real estate (including Peter Angelos, who owns the city's professional baseball team, the Orioles) were disappointed by the plan, but M. J. "Jay" Brodie, president of the BDC, was an unwavering supporter. Brodie told the *Sun*: "It's my strategy, and if it fails, you can blame it on me." Brodie also stated, "Chera made clear the families [the New York developers] would seek no public subsidies such as tax breaks," which is an important point to remember later.[9]

The Weinberg Foundation did not bid on the opportunity to develop the Superblock. The reason it later publicly gave for not responding to the RFP was that it and the city were then in negotiations over a "land swap" for properties on the north–south dividing line of Lexington Street: each party owned some land the other needed to do a large development. The plan for such a large project relied on having a single contiguous space to develop, which was a problem for the city, the billion-dollar foundation, and for small business owners who were kept in the dark about the "back door dealings" of developers and the city. Once the New York developers, reorganized as Lexington Square LLC, attained the exclusive negotiating privileges with the city for the Superblock property, the city planned to condemn and seize privately owned parcels within the Superblock footprint through eminent domain, a process in which private property can be taken by the government for public development projects. Small business owners had little to no say in these dealings. Young Ja Cho, co-owner of the Wig House Beauty Salon on the 100 block of W. Lexington Street, heard rumors for instance that the city would seize local properties by eminent domain, but she never received any official notice. "I'm just waiting and waiting and waiting," Cho said.[10]

A 2005 Supreme Court Case increased the legal reach of eminent domain for development projects.[11] The following year, Baltimore City made a bold move to begin the process of seizing the Weinberg properties using eminent domain when the negotiations for the land swap broke down. Taking property from small business or property owners has long been a regular practice of neoliberal city governments, of which Baltimore is a prime example. But in this case Baltimore City was departing from established practice by taking on a global, multibillion dollar foundation that had a long history of making investments in the city.[12]

John C. Murphy, a well-known Baltimore lawyer specializing in eminent domain/condemnation and historic preservation cases, filed suit on behalf of the nine businesses that had answered the original Superblock RFP and were now in danger of being condemned. The lawsuit claimed that the closed-door backroom dealings of the BDC were illegal and should be subject to Maryland's Open Meetings and Public Information Act. "It's always about the big guys pushing the small guys around," said Scott Mun, who co-owned Wig House on Lexington Street. "At the very least, they should consider the merchants and the people that are already here and not just push them aside."[13] One of the plaintiffs, Michael Epstein, co-owner of Shoe Fair in the 200 block of W. Fayette Street, had submitted a plan in response to BDC's RFP to turn the upper floors of his two buildings into apartments and to renovate their commercial ground floors. Like other small businesses owners he was upset that the BDC appeared not to have even considered his plan. The *Sun* reported, "Epstein says relocating is not an option he relishes because he grew up in the downtown shoe store that his father and grandfather once ran. 'We've been here for 35 to 40 years in the downtown area, and people are used to coming here,' said Epstein. 'We've got to fight for our right to exist.'"[14] In response to the lawsuit, the BDC described itself as a "separate nonprofit corporation" that is "not subject to the Maryland Public Information Act (MPIA)."[15]

The court sided with the downtown business owners' argument that the BDC was subject to MPIA laws, writing that the organization "receives as much as 87 percent of its budget from the city, meaning from taxpayers" and its members were appointed by the city's mayor. The ruling established that the BDC was a public entity and therefore must open its books and meetings to the public. If the Superblock debacle did nothing else, the ruling that the BDC must abide by the Maryland Public Information Act (MPIA) is a lasting legacy, even though activists, residents, journalists, lawyers, and small business owners continue to have to fight for transparency from the BDC.[16]

Race and racism are also determining factors in Baltimore's development policies. In a predominantly African American city, the developers making the decisions were mostly white, and few lived near the west side of downtown. In a 2004 opinion piece for the *Sun* titled "West-Side Renewal Doomed to Failure," architect Charles Belfoure points out a key difference between the west side development and other gentrified neighborhoods in Baltimore: "In the end—and no one wants to speak about it—race plays the real factor in the city's redevelopment. Research shows that the city's few successes such as Canton, Federal Hill, Fells Point, Brewers Hill, Locust Point, Hampden and Bolton Hill all retained majority white populations in their census tracts despite the white flight that began in the 1960s. The west side is perceived as black and dangerous, especially Lexington Market."[17] While I disagree that Lexington Market is dangerous, the west side of downtown remains a black social space, and Baltimore is a majority-black city. It would seem that white developers have been more committed to the equitable redevelopment of historically white communities, in contrast to their rather unequitable approach to redeveloping black neighborhoods and spaces. A city's downtown should primarily connect to, welcome, and serve its residents.

In 2006, the Superblock project and the contentious negotiations between the city and the Weinberg Foundation stalled. The local store owners were caught in limbo with the threat of condemnation looming and vacant spaces growing due to the standstill. Robert M. Reinhardt, general manager of New York Fashions on the 200 block of W. Lexington Street, described the slowdown of business: "There's been quite a bit of decrease in sales volume. If people walk up the street and see vacancies, the enthusiasm of going there to shop isn't there anymore. *It seems like it has taken so long to get nothing started* [emphasis mine]."[18] Samuel Klamner, the business co-owner whose father started Shoe Fair, a family-run men's footwear shop dating back to 1969, said his business earned annual sales of one million dollars despite the growing vacancy and inaction with the Superblock project. In 1999, "the city came to us and said to us, 'We have a plan and your days are numbered,'" Klamner told the *Sun*. In May 2006, Shoe Fair finally closed its doors for good. "We had gone as far as we could go," Klamner said. "It was a heartbreak for all of us."[19] Yun O. Park, who had owned Modern Mode at 105 W. Lexington Street since 1994, vowed in 2006 to stay in her store despite the Superblock slowdown. "I want to survive, that's what we want," Park told the *Sun*. "Most of the stores are gone. This area is getting harder and harder, but I'm still trying to survive. We're going to fight to the end."[20] The exclusive right to the Superblock development was to expire at the end of 2007, but the city granted the developers the first of many extensions. Some local store owners, like Klamner, could not keep their businesses open, while others, like Park, kept fighting for their rights as business owners and city dwellers.

The opposition to the Superblock was not limited to small businesses owners. In February 2007, Peter G. Angelos and WestSide Renaissance Inc. sued the city and the BDC. "This is a suit by people who are very concerned with the delayed and nonexistent development of the former heart of the Baltimore City business district," said M. Albert Figiniski, attorney for the plaintiffs. "This process began in 2003 and has netted, to date, no appropriate plan for redevelopment." Arnold Jolivet, president of the American Minority Contractors and Businesses Association and a founder of the Maryland Minority Contractors Association, also sued the city, alleging the process awarding Lexington Square the exclusive rights to develop the properties in the Superblock footprint "violated the city's competitive-bidding laws."[21] The Superblock plan seemed beyond salvation.

Then, ending their long-standing disagreement, the city and the Weinberg Foundation announced in 2007 that they had struck a land-swap deal giving the city the Superblock properties south of Lexington Street and Weinberg the properties north of Lexington.[22] Weinberg used the deal to rehab the historic

Stewart's department store and turn it into the Catholic Relief Services' world headquarters, which still occupies the building as of 2019. But, in contrast to retail stores, the Catholic Relief Services building does not inspire any street-level activity. While small business owners on the Superblock were left in limbo, the land swap and the booming real estate industry of the first years of the twenty-first century led to various deals and speculations on the west side. "I feel like someone is pulling me by the nose," Korean-American businessman and co-owner of New York Fashions Nam Koo stated. "I have to go this way, I have to go that way." Koo argued that the city had traded his land to the Weinberg Foundation because the city planned to either buy him out or condemn his property. "The person with development rights was supposed to be condemned along with us," Linn Koo says. "It's very upsetting. They should treat every business fairly and appropriately, and I don't think they've done either."[23]

As speculation grew on the west side in 2007, the *Sun* reported that Los Angeles billionaire David Murdock was selling One Market Center, the former Hutzler's Palace department store, and an adjacent seven-story office building. Murdock told the *Sun*, "There definitely is positive momentum in that part of town. And it's a good time to be a seller of commercial real estate in general."[24] The city felt so confident about this momentum that it put up a second Superblock property for sale.[25]

In 2007, three years after the development deal began, Lexington Square finally released its first written plan for the Superblock. The cookie-cutter development plan was a "$250 million mixed-use project with 400 one-and two-bedroom apartments, 900 parking spaces and 300,000 square feet of retail with small shops lining the street and destination retailers on two upper stories." The plan envisioned a major retailer such as "Circuit City or Best Buy, TJ Maxx, Marshalls, Victoria's Secret and H&M" anchoring the project. The BDC announced that it wanted both corporate retailers and local businesses—it also told Yon O. Park, owner of Modern Mode, that her shop could stay.[26] Today, Modern Mode is one of the only holdovers on the mostly vacant Lexington Street to survive the Superblock debacle, as big box retailers, like Best Buy, which never came to the Superblock, are closing stores nationwide due in part to the rise of online retailers.

To clear the final hurdles on the Superblock development, the city settled lawsuits and bought out small local business holdouts. The city bought out Carmel Realty, which owned the Valu Plus store on the 200 block of West Lexington Street, along with the rights to develop a property on North Howard Street, for $2.7 million. Nam S. Koo and Seon G. Good, co-owners of New York Fashions, sold their 12,000-square-foot flagship store and warehouse at the corner of Lexington and Park to the city for $3.75 million. "It's been a long struggle for the Koos, and I was glad to see some recognition was given to the fact that they had lost a great deal of money staying in that location," Murphy, their lawyer told the *Sun*. The Lexington Square developers also were allowed to deduct up to $10 million from the project's cost for environmental remediation and demolition associated with the Superblock.[27] This was in contrast to BDC president Brodie's 2004 statement that the New York developers needed "no public subsidies."

In 2008, the crash of subprime lending markets caused global markets to steeply decline, and the United States entered a Great Recession, the most devastating economic crisis since the Great Depression of the 1930s. In September of that year, despite assurances from the BDC that the Superblock project was moving ahead, Lexington Square revealed a "scaled down" version of the proposed development with "152,000 square feet of retail—half the original amount—360 apartments and a hotel." The developers said they would complete the project in 2011.[28] Many were doubtful. When the Great Recession still did not kill the Superblock development, preservationists revived their fight to save the west side's historic buildings and character.[29]

The preservation fight grew and intensified in 2010 after the city demolished the first buildings as part of the Superblock development and the state's high court dismissed the Angelos lawsuit.[30] At the end of 2010, the city's agreement with the Superblock developers was set to expire. Properties had been demolished, but no buildings had been constructed, and the project appeared to have stalled. Still, the city extended the development agreement again right before it was due to expire. In the beginning of 2011, the director of the Maryland Historical Trust approved the Superblock project while reserving for the trust the legal authority to block specific plans it did not see as complying with the agreement. The city extended the project completion date to 2014.[31]

The battle over preservation was far from over. Baltimore Heritage worked with local historians to conduct extensive research into the history of the Superblock area. Publicity about the sit-ins in which students from Morgan State College (now Morgan State University) fought to desegregate Read's Drugstore (at the corner of Lexington and Howard Streets) in 1955, one of the first civil rights sit-ins in the country, may have been the key historical impetus to preventing the demolition of the west side's historic buildings. The sit-ins at Read's were led by local university students and preceded by five years the more famous sit-ins at Woolworth's in Greensboro, North Carolina.[32] The sit-in movement "begins in Baltimore," stated Larry Gibson, University of Maryland Law professor and author of a book about Thurgood Marshall. "It begins with Morgan. It begins with Read's Drug Store. This is a national treasure."[33] While history can be exploited to serve gentrification, in the case of the Superblock recognition of the rich history of African American activism in Baltimore was essential to saving a part of downtown that still served the African American and immigrant communities of the city.

Ultimately, Read's Drugstore was added to the list of city historic landmarks.[34] In 2012, Mayor Stephanie Rawlings Blake asked the City Council to give the Superblock developers a "20-year, deep discount on property taxes," which represented yet another change from Brodie's assurances in 2004 that the developers "would seek no public subsidies such as tax breaks."[35] Brodie retired from the BDC in 2012.

The Lexington Square development group, which had spent millions of dollars on planning and other aspects of the Superblock development, remained committed to the project despite its many hurdles. But in 2013, the company sued the city after the mayor finally decided not to renew its exclusive right to develop the properties. In fall 2015, when the Maryland State Court of Appeals declined to hear Lexington Square's appeal, the Superblock debacle was finally officially dead. Within weeks, the city put out a new RFP for the spaces within the once super block. The RFP was open to single or group proposals. Kimberly Clark, vice president of the BDC told the *Sun*, "We want to get developers that [*sic*] are interested in moving forward, not sitting on properties."[36]

The Aftermath: Lessons Learned?

The city and BDC may have learned some lessons from the decade-long Superblock debacle. In 2010 before the deal was completely dead, the city funded a study by the Urban Land Institute Washington (ULI), which found that the west side's "wealth of historic buildings is its greatest asset" and that "redevelopment has suffered from a lack of vision and leadership." To address these issues, the authors of the study suggested a "building-by-building approach to revitalization." ULI panel member Betty Massey framed the recommended vision as a "thousand blooming flowers." This model opposes putting power into the hands of a few large-scale corporate developers and instead argues that the city "should award many parcels to different developers."[37] The recommended model would build the west side up from the streets through more grassroots and small-scale, more locally based, and historically relevant projects and business endeavors.

The Bromo Seltzer Tower, currently a city-owned art space with studios and a gallery, is the symbol of the Baltimore's newest arts district, the Bromo Arts and Entertainment District, which emerged in 2012. During the Superblock era, the historic Hippodrome Theater dating from 1914 was rehabbed and reopened as the France-Merrick Performing Arts Center in 2004, and the Everyman Theater moved from the Station North Arts and Entertainment district to the west side in 2013. There are currently several African American arts organizations in the district, including the following: the historic Arena Players theater group, which was established in 1953 and is one of the oldest continuously running African American theater groups in the country; the Eubie Blake Jazz Institute and Cultural Center, which dates to the 1980s; and the newer Downtown Cultural Arts Center, a nonprofit arts organization on Howard Street.[38] The 400 block of Howard Street may have finally begun to see the "thousand flowers blooming" model take off.

Another new arts organization is Le Mondo, "an artist-owned-and-driven project creating a multi-use community hub and experimental performance complex" located across the street from the Downtown Cultural Arts Center on the 400 block of Howard Street.[39] To create this space, local artists partnered with developer Ted Rouse, son of James Rouse, the famed developer who created the planned community of Columbia, Maryland, and Harborplace.[40] Current Space is another arts organization that is in a recently purchased building from the city located on the 400 block of Howard Street.

The opening of Le Mondo exemplifies the potential inherent in connections between these thousand flowers and the pre-existing culture and architecture of Baltimore's downtown. Outside another arts space on 219 Park Avenue (in the shadow of the failed Superblock development), Anthony Williams, a formerly homeless African American man who had lived among the abandoned buildings of Howard Street and then became a housing activist, had earlier approached Le Mondo's artistic codirector Evan Moritz. Williams told Moritz that he was writing a play about being homeless on Howard Street. His notebooks became the basis for Le Mondo's opening production, "The King of Howard Street," in May 2017.[41] The play was about a crew of Williams's friends who lived in a "bando," an abandoned building left vacant by ill-advised government policies and overly ambitious development schemes like the Superblock. And while the content of the play can serve as a warning about the human costs of these policies, its production serves as a symbol of the collaboration required for humane redevelopment.

Although later allegations of sexual misconduct against one of Le Mondo's artistic directors imperiled the project, the west side continues to flower with emerging projects because there is no one central organization controlling its development. One of those flourishing grassroots initiatives is the Charm City Night Market organized by the Chinatown Collective. On Saturday, September 22, 2018, the inaugural Charm City Night Market celebrated Baltimore's Asian American communities in a vacant lot at 200 Park Avenue and along Lexington Street right in the heart of the old Superblock redevelopment zone and near the city's historic Chinatown. More than ten thousand people flooded the area for live performances, art displays, and a plethora of food choices. People stood in lines for more than an hour at the numerous food booths, and the area was packed with people representing the future hopes of the city's west side.

Notes

1 Michel de Certeau, *The Practice of Everyday Life* (Berkeley: University of California Press, 1984, 1988), 93. For more on the politics of downtown development, see Stephen J. McGovern, *The Politics of Downtown Development: Dynamic Political Cultures in San Francisco and Washington, D.C.* (Lexington: University of Kentucky Press, 2015).

2 Edward Gunts, "Keeping It Real: Does Baltimore Really Need to Demolish So Much of the West Side in Order to Revive It?," *Baltimore Sun*, June 18, 2000; also see Edward Gunts, "Weinberg's Legacy: Howard Merchants; The Baltimore City Council has Recently Passed Legislation Allowing the City to Buy and Demolish 100 Buildings as Part of the Larger Redevelopment Plan," *Baltimore Sun*, November 5, 1990. Note: my research for this chapter primarily relies on the *Baltimore Sun*, the city's paper of record, and focuses on how the Superblock issue was reported to the public. Further research into the complex financial connections and nuances of this development project is ongoing. There is much more to this story that cannot be included in this brief chapter.

3 Grid Properties also developed DC USA. For more project see Grid Properties Inc.'s website, http://www.gridproperties.com/projects.html. Gina Bellafante defines hypergentrification as "the complicity between municipal government and big private money to reconfigure whole sections of a city, with dubious consequences, chief among them the ceding of space, goods and social currency from the ordinary classes to the ruling order" in her article, "Tracking the Hyper-Gentrification of New York, One Lost Knish Place at a Time," *New York Times*, September 27, 2017. The article reviews Jeremiah Moss's book, *Vanishing New York: How a Great City Lost Its Soul* (New York: Dey St./William Morrow, 2017). Also see Bethany Y. Li, "Now Is the Time! Challenging Resegregation and Displacement in the Age of Hypergentrification," *Fordham Law Review* 85, no. 3 (December 2016) 1189–1242; Rachel Brahinsky, "The Death of a City? Reports of San Francisco's Demise Have Been Greatly Exaggerated," *Boom: A Journal of California* 4, no. 2 (2014): 43–54.

4 Gunts, "Keeping It Real."

5 Gunts, "Keeping It Real."

6 Tom Pelton, "Mayor Spares Historic West Side," *Baltimore Sun*, January 9, 2001; Charles Belfour, "In Baltimore's West Side Preservation Story Unfold," *Baltimore Sun*, February 18, 2001; Baltimore Heritage and Preservation Maryland, "Baltimore's West Side Story," https://vimeo.com/9022133. The video also features Maryland comptroller and past mayor of Baltimore and governor of Maryland William Donald Schafer arguing for the historic buildings. In addition, Buzz Cusack, owner of the Senator Theater in Baltimore, played "Baltimore's West Side Story" before numerous movies to help spread the word and raise awareness of the issue.

7 Heather Harlan, "'Superblock' Spurs Interest," *Baltimore Business Journal*, November 10, 2003, https://www.bizjournals.com/baltimore/stories/2003/11/10/newscolumn1.html.

8 "Ideas Roll in for 'Superblock' Development," *Baltimore Business Journal*, March 2, 2004, https://www.bizjournals.com/baltimore/stories/2004/03/01/daily17.html.

9 Scott Calvert, "'Superblock' Team Plan Recommended to Mayor; Balto. Development Corp. Likes Four-Party Proposal," *Baltimore Sun*, November 25,

2004; Jill Rosen, "City Enhances West-Side Revival Plan," *Baltimore Sun*, February 2, 2005.

10 Eric Siegel, "Waiting and Waiting; West Side: Business Owners Who Have Yet to Learn Whether They'll Be Relocated by the Redevelopment Project Are Left with Plans on Hold," *Baltimore Sun*, May 25, 2002.

11 Linda Greenhouse, "Justices Uphold Taking Property for Development," *New York Times,* June 24, 2005.

12 It is difficult to determine in this specific case if the Weinberg Foundation was working for public good or profit. The "non-profit industrial complex" in Baltimore city has done damage to the residents it is supposed to serve. See Davon Love and Lawrence Grandpre, *The Black Book: Reflections from the Baltimore Grassroots* (self-published, Lulu.com, 2015); Patricia Fernandez-Kelley, *The Hero's Fight: African Americans in West Baltimore and the Shadow of the State* (Princeton, NJ: Princeton University Press, 2015).

13 John Fritze, "Open Books to Public, BDC Is Told; Development Agency Has to Disclose Details of Deals," *Baltimore Sun*, November 4, 2006.

14 Sumathi Reddy, "BDC Sued by Business Owners; 9 on Condemned Block on West Side Seek Data; Private Meetings Called Illegal; Plaintiffs Ask Court to Void Development Panel's Plan," *Baltimore Sun*, November 30, 2004.

15 Stephanie Desmon, "Shining Light on Private Use of City Power," *Baltimore Sun*, March 12, 2006.

16 Fritze, "Open Books to Public." The BDC was found in violation of the open meeting laws in 2016 during deliberations on the TIF for Kevin Plank's Sagamore Development Company plan in Port Covington. See Natalie Sherman, "BDC Violated Open Meeting Act," *Baltimore Sun*, May 23, 2016.

17 Charles Belfoure, "West-Side Renewal Doomed to Failure," *Baltimore Sun*, December 28, 2004.

18 Lorraine Mirabella, "Renewal Project Stalled in City; Baltimore Group Blames Weinberg Foundation for Superblock Standoff," *Baltimore Sun*, May 29, 2006.

19 Lorraine Mirabella, "Eminently Troubling; As City Officials Step up Their Use of Condemnation Powers, Some Property Owners Are Fighting Back," *Baltimore Sun*, July 9, 2006.

20 Lorraine Mirabella, "Concern Delays City OK on Sale; Comptroller Fears Cost of Superblock Land Deal May Be too Much," *Baltimore Sun*, December 21, 2006.

21 Erin Siegel and Jill Rosen, "Lawsuit Targets West-Side Project; Angelos, Developer Wants City to Scrap Superblock Deal," *Baltimore Sun*, February 28, 2007.

22 Lorraine Mirabella and Meredith Cohn, "West-Side Project Revived; Land Swap Will Restart Stalled 'Superblock' Effort," *Baltimore Sun*, March 28, 2007.

23 Jean Marbella, "Downtown Deal Leaves Business Owner Out," *Baltimore Sun*, April 6, 2007.

24 Lorraine Mirabella, "Howard St. Offices on Superblock up for Sale; Move Seen as Test of West Side's Appeal," *Baltimore Sun*, April 3, 2007.

25 Lorraine Mirabella, "Second Superblock Tract Offered; City Seeks Proposals for Land It Held back in 2003," *Baltimore Sun*, April 5, 2007.

26 Lorraine Mirabella, "Towering Vision for West Side; Plans Are Shown for Retail Shops, Apartment Towers," *Baltimore Sun*, April 12, 2007.

27 Lorraine Mirabella, "City Board Clears Superblock Deals: Board of Estimates Appears to Resolve Final Obstacles," *Baltimore Sun*, November 8, 2007.

28 Lorraine Mirabella, "Scaled-Back Plan for West Side Unveiled: Developer

Reduces Retail Space, Apartments, Adds Small Hotel to Proposal for 'Super-block,'" *Baltimore Sun*, September 26, 2008.

29   Lorraine Mirabella, "West-Side Project Meets Resistance: City Preservationists Say Old Retail District Should Be Saved," *Baltimore Sun*, December 12, 2008.

30   Lorraine Mirabella, "West-Side Project under Way: Vacant Buildings Razed as First Step in Renewal of Old Baltimore Shopping District," *Baltimore Sun*, January 15, 2010; Edward Gunts, "State's High Court Dismisses Challenge to 'Superblock': Ruling Clears the Way for Development to Resume on Downtown's West Side," *Baltimore Sun*, April 14, 2010.

31   Edward Gunts, "Superblock Developers Get 6 More Months," *Baltimore Sun* December 23, 2010; and "Superblock Developers Clear a Key Hurdle: State OKs Preservation Plan for Site on City's West Side," *Baltimore Sun*, January 5, 2011.

32   Edward Gunts, "Razing Historic Drugstore Decried: Civil Rights, Preservation Leaders Want Superblock Site of '55 Sit-In to Stand," *Baltimore Sun*, January 6, 2011.

33   Edward Gunts, "Read's Protest Blocks Plans for Superblock," *Baltimore Sun*, January 7, 2011.

34   Edward Gunts, "Drugstore Site Put on City's List of Landmarks: Preservation Ruling Stalls West-Side Development," *Baltimore Sun*, April 13, 2011.

35   Julie Scharper, "City Proposes Tax Subsidy for 'Superblock' Apartment Complex: Fayette Street Project Would Get 20-Year Tax Discount," *Baltimore Sun*, April 24, 2012.

36   Natalie Sherman, "Former 'Superblock' Parcels Re-Open for Redevelopment," *Baltimore Sun*, September 1, 2015.

37   Edward Gunts, "Urban Land Institute Offers Recommendations for City's West Side," *Baltimore Sun*, December 10, 2010; Urban Land Institute, *The West Side, Baltimore, Maryland*, 2010, http://uli.org/wp-content/uploads/ULI-Documents/BaltimoreReport.pdf, accessed July 23, 2017.

38   Arena Players website, http://arenaplayersinc.com/history/; Eubie Blake Jazz Institute and Cultural Center website, http://www.eubieblake.org/about.html; Downtown Cultural Arts Center, http://www.downtownculturalartcenter.org/, accessed July 23, 2017.

39   LeMondo website, http://www.lemondo.org/about/, accessed July 23, 2017.

40   I do not present Le Mondo or the arts as a panacea to solve Baltimore's problems, but rather as a small-scale development option that exemplifies the "thousand flowers" model. The art scene in our city is complicated and has been plagued by racial/gender disparities as well as issues of sexual assault. For more see Brittany Britto et al., "In the Age of #MeToo, Baltimore's Small Performing Arts Group Grapple with Sexual Misconduct Accusations," *Baltimore Sun*, July 18 2018; Maura Callahan and Rebekah Kirkman, "Abuse and Accountability in the Arts Scene: A Reckoning," *City Paper*, August 22, 2017; interview with Shelia Gaskins by Lauren Van Slyke, "Art-Part'heid: Bridging the Gap of Disparities in the Baltimore Arts Scene," *Bmore Art*, January 30, 2015.

41   Maura Callahan, "A Squatter's Story Becomes Theater in 'The King of Howard Street,'" *Baltimore City Paper*, May 23, 2017.

25

Under Armour's Global Headquarters and the Redevelopment of South Baltimore

• •

RICHARD E. OTTEN

Following the Baltimore uprising of 2015, Under Armour CEO Kevin Plank told shareholders that "the people of Baltimore are resilient, and we are going to be better because of it. This is not a rebuilding of our city. This is a continuation of building our city."[1] In this statement, Plank claimed for his corporation what urban social critics call "the right to the city," a term devised by sociologist Henri Lefebvre. However, Lefebvre was writing about average citizens'—not corporate billionaires'—right to the city. Plank's claim in the wake of the uprising is indicative of his view of his central role in the city's future.

Plank's biography presents him in the image of the "great man of history" fit for the new millennium. Having grown up in a prosperous suburb of Washington, D.C., Plank was a walk-on member of special teams for the University of Maryland football team where he got firsthand experience with sports apparel and its deficiencies. He built a sportswear company by experimenting with and developing textiles that would wick moisture more effectively than cotton. Now with a net worth of almost $2 billion, he seeks to cement his legacy as a hero of hardscrabble Baltimore, spearheaded by the redevelopment of Port Covington.[2]

Plank's Port Covington will be a "city within a city," a massive 260-acre planned redevelopment of a former railyard south of Baltimore's downtown: it will include Under Armour's corporate headquarters, high-rise apartments, retail, and a host of other amenities.[3] Plank's real estate subsidiary Sagamore Development Company planned and lobbied for the Port Covington development that will cost $5 billion, of which more than $500 million will be provided by public financing from the city. Ordinary citizens of Baltimore, such as those involved in Baltimoreans United in Leadership Development (BUILD), a self-described "broad-based, non-partisan, interfaith, multiracial community power organization rooted in Baltimore's neighborhoods and congregations," fought against the tax subsidies—building on their experience since 1977 fighting for social justice issues in the city.[4] BUILD saw Port Covington as a development driven more by Under Armour shareholders' concerns about profits and image than any interest in helping average Baltimoreans who are African American and working class. Port Covington's long-term benefits to the residents of Baltimore are unclear, and the use of public funds for a billionaire's development plan is controversial.

TIF Troubles

Tax-increment financing (TIF) is a powerful financing instrument by which private entities apply for and receive loans of public funds for infrastructure projects that are deemed necessary for a real estate development project to go forward. Proponents argue that cities and their residents should support TIFs because major capital projects such as sports stadiums and corporate headquarters like Under Armour provide benefits in the form of new jobs, tourist dollars, and new arrivals to cities. But critics of TIFs disagree, characterizing them as wasteful boondoggles that give away millions of citizens' dollars in exchange for economic gains for the elite few. These loans are supposed to be repaid over time with taxes paid by properties in the improved zone. As such, TIF is a typical neoliberal strategy through which the private sector aggressively seeks profits while transferring financial risks onto the public sector. Meanwhile, the municipality can claim that the TIF is neither an expenditure nor a "tax break," since it will be funded by a bond issue that should be repaid with tax revenue that would not exist without the TIF.

TIFs are not unique to Baltimore, and public officials' and corporations' enthusiasm for them is the object of critical scrutiny across the country. In their review of TIF case studies, public policy scholars Robert T. Greenbaum and Jim Landers find that, in terms of achieving the twin goals of boosting property values and stimulating economic activity, TIF-funded development schemes have "mixed" and "more mixed" track records, respectively. This is because property values tend to increase within urban zones that have been improved via TIFs, but not reliably, while broader economic benefits are less reliable and difficult to attribute to the TIF itself. Greenbaum and Landers conclude:

> The TIF financing mechanism is purposefully designed to help raise property values in order for it to be self-financing (and, a cynic might add, to help reward those land-owners pushing for the designation), so it may not be best-suited to accomplish other economic development goals, particularly if the increased property values represent a cost that is avoidable elsewhere.[5]

Theoretically, blighted neighborhoods in need of redevelopment are the necessary condition for TIF packages; practically, the necessary condition for a TIF package is an apex developer who stands to gain more from the redevelopment of a blighted neighborhood than does the municipality that grants the TIF and takes the associated risks.

A particular cost associated with TIFs is borne by public school districts.[6] In 2013, the Baltimore City Council controversially approved a TIF package worth more than $100 million to Beatty Development for Harbor Point, a remediated brownfield jutting into the east side of the Inner Harbor that now hosts the headquarters of the energy giant Exelon. The city funded infrastructural improvements to the area, including park space situated on the water side of Exelon's hulking headquarters that would be immediately accessible to workers at the adjacent Harbor Point's gleaming new offices, but farther away from residents of the neighboring low-income communities. The *Sun* revealed in 2015 that the property tax abatements and TIF funding for Harbor Point and smaller developments were negatively affecting the funding of Baltimore city schools, leading to $35 million in cuts from the state in 2016. The state funds local jurisdictions according to a formula tied to property values, at a time when the value of some real estate in Baltimore is skyrocketing because of these publicly subsidized development strategies. However, this formula is predicated on the assumption that rising property values will generate rising property tax revenues, enabling a jurisdiction to fund its public schools with less help from the state.[7] If landlords are excused from paying property taxes on a development, or if their tax revenues on that property are earmarked for decades for paying off the debt service, that development generates no new tax revenue to fund the schools. The Baltimore city school system would arguably be better off without the new TIF-supported developments. If such developments successfully draw new residents to the city, then the city cannot likely sustain its public school system without an adjustment to this formula, an adjustment that would have to be approved by legislators from around the state, which is unlikely.

If TIFs require the public to take risks to generate profits for corporate elites, then the TIF approval processes should be democratic. In 2010, voters in the state of California brought an end to three decades of aggressive deployment of this public financing method when they passed a referendum requiring that any further TIFs would need to be approved by voter referenda.[8] Unfortunately, Baltimore makes decisions on TIFs without voter referenda or any real community input.

Under Armour's Global Headquarters, Port Covington, and TIFs

In the spring of 2016, Plank's Sagamore Development Company submitted a request for a $535 million TIF, the third-largest TIF for a private entity in American history.[9] While community groups put up a valiant fight protesting the request, it was approved by both the public–private Baltimore Development Corporation; then by the Board of Finance, comprising the mayor, comptroller, and three appointees; and finally in September 2016, by the Baltimore City Council. This approval process is typical of downtown development projects in recent decades: it is the product of what Marc V. Levine, a professor of history and urban studies, characterizes as "a sort of Baltimore, Inc.: an urban redevelopment machine, fueled with public dollars, seeking to leverage private capital by offering numerous incentives and profit opportunities."[10] Public–private agencies arrange the terms of proposals that favor private ventures, and elected officials sell the Baltimore public on the notion that the expenditure is in their best interest.

In 2015, Plank felt that Under Armour was cramped at its Tide Point office park in Locust Point and pursued a site that would signify the company's aspirations. First, he attempted to take over the site of the Baltimore Museum of Industry (BMI), but after the museum's executive board refused to sell its prime waterfront parcel to him, the *Baltimore Sun* reported his frustrations with the BMI:

> "I'm sitting there and I'm thinking to myself this is awful. . . . They're stifling our growth," he said. "How could anyone not want us to grow?"
>
> The rejection came while he was in Dubai, a city that has experienced a massive building boom in the last decade.
>
> "I thought to myself, we could do something like that," he said. "Number one, I've got the engine in Under Armour. Number two . . . I can afford to make these decisions, so why am I waiting on the board of directors?"[11]

Plank's hubris is symptomatic of his sense of entitlement to the right to determine Baltimore's future. And if he "can afford to make these decisions," a $535 million TIF should not be necessary.

The massive and recently built urban environment that Plank encountered on his trip to Dubai conjured visions that Under Armour could make something similar happen in South Baltimore on the site of a former railyard, as if Under Armour's economic might were comparable to that of a petrostate. As the Maryland Historical Society describes it, "Port Covington long served South Baltimore as an industrial hub of the city. Sharing a peninsula with Locust Point and Fort McHenry, the port was for many years the Western Maryland Railway's 'junction with the world.'"[12] Large railyards in the Camden and Port Covington districts enabled South Baltimore to serve as one of the East Coast's major rail hubs, but the deindustrialization of Baltimore left both sites as decaying artifacts of a bygone era of capitalist accumulation.

Many of those who opposed the Port Covington TIF had earlier opposed the Harbor Point TIF, including BUILD, labor activists, and faith leaders: they questioned the wisdom of loaning vast sums of public capital and extending other financial sweeteners to fund private real estate development. The *Sun* quoted Councilman Carl Stokes's assessment of the City Council's decision to approve the Harbor Point TIF "as probably the worst piece of legislation I've ever seen. . . . We have polarized our city for no good reason."[13]

The approval of the Port Covington TIF coincided with the 2016 mayoral primary election. Candidates in the Democratic field that produced the city's new mayor expressed positions of varying degrees of skepticism. At a debate hosted by Morgan State University, Councilman Carl Stokes issued the strongest statement against the TIF, asserting that because it would support a brandnew development in a former railyard, not the rejuvenation of a neighborhood in decline, "the project meets none of the criteria [for the approval of TIF]. . . . If Sandtown, Penn North, Oliver and Broadway East get rebuilt first, then we'll consider it." Councilman Nick Mosby made a more specific demand that Under Armour establish a manufacturing plant in Baltimore in return for receiving such a generous loan. Eventual election winner Catherine Pugh joined other candidates in granting the TIF begrudging support, on the condition that it would provide jobs for local residents, especially those living across the Hanover Street Bridge in lower-income areas such as Cherry Hill. Former mayor and then-candidate Sheila Dixon said that the TIF should not be approved by the lame-duck administration of Mayor Stephanie Rawlings-Blake, who was not running for re-election.[14]

Even if Port Covington is successful on its own terms, the fear is that it will perpetuate Baltimore's history of segregation. Sagamore's proposed "affordable" housing was initially based on a median income far higher than Baltimore's average. After facing withering criticism at public hearings and negotiating with community activists, Sagamore agreed to make at least 10 percent of its housing affordable to residents earning less than $26,000 per year. Still, critics decry loopholes in the agreement, including a lack of a requirement that Sagamore construct this affordable housing at Port Covington itself, as opposed to other locations in the city.[15] Placing its affordable housing in East Baltimore, far from

Port Covington but near Sparrows Point, where Under Armour will soon build a distribution center, would only exacerbate existing racial and economic segregation.

Conclusion

Charly Carter, executive director of Maryland Working Families, an organization that opposed the TIF, accurately characterized Plank's broader agenda as an effort to appropriate Baltimore's scrappy working-class ethic and its gritty industrial decline aesthetic for the benefit of his Under Armour brand. Plank seeks to link his personal biography and his emerging brands to the history of labor and class in his adopted home city. Such a strategy would be fine, except that Plank predicates both the growth of his companies and the revival of Baltimore (on his own terms) on his receipt of the largest TIF in the city's history, approved shortly after an intense moment of urban unrest and cuts in funding to the city's struggling public schools.

Throughout the approval process for the TIF, Sagamore spokespeople insisted that they would be funding the construction of the new Under Armour headquarters themselves, and that they needed the TIF only to fund infrastructure such as streets and sewer and water lines, an elementary school, and world-class parks to attract partners who will build apartments, hotels, and office towers. And therein lies the saddest reality of this episode. As schools all over the city need remodeling, as water mains break and sinkholes devour downtown intersections and vacant houses adjacent to century-old city parks crumble, Port Covington is very unlikely to halt the decline of older and predominantly black neighborhoods in Baltimore.

Notes

1 Lorraine Mirabella, "Under Armour Remains Committed to Baltimore amid Unrest, Plank Says," *Baltimore Sun*, April 29, 2015.

2 "Kevin Plank: Chairman and CEO, Under Armour," *Forbes*, accessed May 14, 2018, https://www.forbes.com/profile/kevin-plank.

3 *Port Covington Master Plan Draft*, Baltimore City Department of Planning, June 16, 2016, https://planning.baltimorecity.gov/sites/default/files/PORT%20COVINGTON%20MASTER%20PLAN%20061616%20v11%206.22.16.pdf.

4 "About BUILD," Baltimoreans United in Leadership Development, accessed May 9, 2018, http://www.buildiaf.org/about/.

5 Robert T. Greenbaum and Jim Landers, "The Tiff over TIF: A Review of the Literature Examining the Effectiveness of the Tax Increment Financing," *National Tax Journal* 67, no. 3 (September 2014): 670.

6 Shari S. Lindsey, "Global-City Status at the Expense of Black and Latino Youth: How Chicago's TIF Districts Disparately Impact CPS Students," *DePaul Journal for Social Justice* 6, no. 1 (Fall 2012).

7   Luke Broadwater, "Baltimore's Quick Economic Growth Contributes to Loss in State Aid to Schools," *Baltimore Sun*, February 8, 2015.

8   George Lefcoe and Charles W. Swenson, "Redevelopment in California: The Demise of TIF-Funded Redevelopment in California and Its Aftermath," *National Tax Journal* 67, no. 3 (September 2014).

9   Sarah M. Cohen, "Under Armour's Slam-Dunk Deal: The Apparel Company's Owner Is Pursuing a Real Estate Deal That Will Expand Its Footprint and Help Transform Baltimore. Is He Asking too Much of the City to Do So?," *Slate*, June 20, 2016.

10 Mark V. Levine, "'A Third World City in the First World': Social Exclusion, Racial Inequality, and Sustainable Development in Baltimore," in *The Social Sustainability of Cities: Diversity and the Management of Change*, ed. Mario Polèse and Richard Stern (Toronto: University of Toronto Press, 2000), 129.

11 Natalie Sherman, "Port Covington Land Is Space for Under Armour to Grow," *Baltimore Sun*, March 2, 2015.

12 Maryland Historical Society Library Department, *Port Covington: Baltimore's Junction with the World* (Baltimore: Maryland Historical Society, June 30, 2016).

13 Luke Broadwater, "Council Gives Preliminary OK to Harbor Point Financing," *Baltimore Sun*, August 12, 2013.

14 Luke Broadwater, "Baltimore Mayoral Candidates Express Concern about $535M Public Financing Deal for Port Covington," *Baltimore Sun*, March 10, 2016.

15 Fern Shen, "Critics: Port Covington Deal Financially Risky, Worsens Segregation," *Baltimore Brew*, July 27, 2016; Luke Broadwater, "City Council Approves $660 Million Bond Deal for Port Covington Project," *Baltimore Sun*, September 19, 2016.

Part V

Democratizing
the Archives

• • • • • • • • • • • • • • • • • • • •

Baltimore Revisited concludes with a reflection on the raw materials of history, the primary sources that we collect and deposit into archives. Aiden Faust describes how the New Social History, a methodology that inspired *The Baltimore Book*, launched an "archival renaissance" in the 1970s by Baltimore's archivists who collected everyday primary sources from the city's working people and non-elites. Sadly, almost as soon as social history archivists could claim a few victories in Baltimore, conservative politicians cut much of the federal funding that provided the movement its lifeblood. Yet, as Faust points out, some of the city's social history archives still operate, highlighting the continued need for democratic and diverse archives of the everyday. To protect these resources, scholars and archivists have to collaborate, listen to one another, and move beyond turf battles over who takes credit. In short, we must work together to secure and protect the repositories that document our past and ongoing struggle for a collective right to the city.

As Denise Meringolo shows in the concluding chapter, sometimes we need to build archives in real time as history is happening. Her chapter describes a moment in her public history graduate course at UMBC from April 2015: "My students wanted to do something. They asked: What is the role of public history during times of unrest?" With the support of the Maryland Historical Society and an alliance of local scholars and public historians, Meringolo and her students built a digital public online archive to document the Baltimore uprising.

Meringolo's chapter—and the entire collection—cannot definitively answer this important question of what role history can or should play in times of struggle. But we hope to push readers to ask this question of themselves, to question the places they call home, and especially to question those in power as we build the cities and neighborhoods of the future.

26

Social History
in the Archives

• • • • • • • • • • • • • • • • • • • •

Baltimore's Enduring Legacy

AIDEN FAUST

> I have only two proposals for archivists:
> One, that they engage in a campaign to
> open all government documents to the
> public. . . . And two, that they take the
> trouble to compile a whole new world of
> documentary material, about the lives,
> desires, needs, of ordinary people.
> —Howard Zinn

When radical historian and activist Howard Zinn addressed the Society of American Archivists in 1970, he challenged them to take an active role in collecting records that reflected the experiences of everyday people, instead of simply perpetuating the histories of a powerful, moneyed elite.[1] Zinn's provocative message, which ran counter to archivists' traditional notions of objectivity and neutrality, advocated the intentional creation of new archives of social history. The democratic impulses within social history transformed not only the kinds of histories we write about ourselves but also the archival programs that support these histories.

This chapter considers how social history changed American archives in the second half of the twentieth century, using three archives in Baltimore between 1973 and 1984 as examples. All three of these archival programs are functional to date, despite modest staffing and resource challenges. As many of the country's social justice movements now celebrate significant anniversaries, the records collected and created by social historians in the 1970s and 1980s have begun to receive increased scholarly attention. It is the responsibility of a new generation of archivists to articulate the value of these records.

The mid-1970s witnessed a groundswell of public interest in archives that coincided with both the bicentennial anniversary of the United States and the popularity of Alex Haley's television series *Roots*.[2] Broadly speaking, popular attention turned to American history, both as a national story and in more personal, local terms. The mechanisms for government support of the cultural heritage sector had not yet been undermined, and federal funding flowed through the National Endowment for the Humanities (NEH) and the National Historical Publications and Records Commission (NHPRC) to libraries, archives, and museums at the exact point when scholars trained in social history were beginning their careers in archives. In the 1970s, American universities produced ten times the number of PhD historians as the job market could absorb, pushing many of these young new academics into applied fields, including archives and manuscripts.[3] With them, they brought fresh perspectives on the practice of doing history, including a school of thought known as the New Social History, which challenged notions of consensus history, emphasized the experiences of ordinary people, focused on previously marginalized groups, and took interdisciplinary approaches to analysis.[4]

The grassroots vision of documenting the histories of everyday people gave rise to a great enthusiasm within archival practice, including local archival practice. Baltimore experienced an "archival renaissance" that included the creation of the experimental Baltimore Region Institutional Studies Center (BRISC) by Theodore Dürr and a dynamic oral history program by Betty McKeever Key at the Maryland Historical Society (MDHS), as well as an overhaul of the Baltimore City Archives (BCA) by Richard Cox.[5] Popular interest in local history coincided with social history's impact on the archives. In Baltimore, experimental new archives and methods of historical documentation were implemented with bicentennial-era funding. In the decades since, Baltimore's social history archives—and the archivists who preserve them—have demonstrated a degree of resilience characteristic of the city itself.

Educated at Johns Hopkins University, William Theodore Dürr was an urban sociology professor at the University of Baltimore who opened BRISC there in 1973. By his own telling, the idea for BRISC originated in 1968, with his heroic salvage of the organizational records of Baltimore's Citizens Planning and Housing Association (CPHA) from the incinerator's flames.[6] In an interview Dürr recalled, "And then it hit me that probably many important records, especially [those] that deal with social history, were being lost and should be preserved."[7] This explicit reference to collecting and preserving documentary evidence related to social history clearly establishes Dürr's intentions.

When BRISC opened in 1973, University of Baltimore president H. Mebane Turner described it to local newspaper reporters as a research center for the "history and sociology of urban institutions."[8] Located on Baltimore's Antique Row at 847 North Howard Street, BRISC operated out of a 21,000-square foot building known as Howard Hall.[9] BRISC's collections focused on metropolitan records from organizations and related individuals, with emphases on urban planning, housing, social welfare, and city neighborhoods. While its focus on institutional records may appear to run counter to social history's concern with everyday people, Dürr and his staff took a keen interest in a broad spectrum of institutional structures. Citizen-led and grassroots groups were documented alongside nonprofits and religious organizations. Of particular interest were the records of quasi-governmental entities—boards, commissions, and other groups whose administrative histories spanned the public–private divide. BRISC's institutional focus on American liberalism also documented the neoliberal turn toward privatization and "shadow government."[10]

More than $130,000 in NHPRC funding was awarded to BRISC between 1977 and 1984 for archival collections that ranged from city planning records to metropolitan church records to local television news film.[11] From its inception, BRISC was a decidedly experimental archives and records management program. For one thing, many of its holdings included records less than twenty-five years old. By the standards of many archivists, these materials would have hardly been considered archival or eligible for permanent retention. Dürr, however, saw the future value of such records. BRISC took a very liberal approach to archival document selection, choosing to retain even the most trivial-seeming records: "We save it all—even laundry tickets we may find in a file once in awhile. But we save it all . . . you never know what future historians are going to be interested in."[12]

Another unorthodox aspect of the BRISC program was its approach to archival description. Making an intentional turn away from the historical manuscripts' tradition of cataloging documents at the item level, Dürr and his colleagues used early computer automation to tag files with words and phrases from an urban thesaurus they created.[13] This approach, which favored efficiency and aggregation of large datasets, was well suited to the extensive volume of modern records with which the program grappled. Dürr's ideas on subject-based access to archives and computer automation reached a national audience among archivists. He developed a software program called ARCHON, tested it against the profession's more widely adopted SPINDEX system for archival description and indexing, and discussed these results in the peer-reviewed publication, the *Society of American Archivists*, in 1984.[14] Social history's close alignment with the social sciences, including its inclination toward large datasets and qualitative analytical methods, demanded new approaches to archival search and retrieval. BRISC's early emphasis on automation signaled a shift in archival practice that would also align closely with information science and the movement of American archives toward American library practices.

During this period, BRISC was operating in a larger local context. Several local history groups and conferences also reflected the uptick in interest in Baltimore history in the 1970s. As archival historian Richard Cox notes,

> A renewed interest in Baltimore's history has surfaced in the 1970s. An outpouring of genealogical articles and books; a strong concern for historic preservation (led by the city's Commission for Historical and Architectural Preservation, created in 1954 and supported by the excellent homesteading program); conferences in 1975 and 1978 at the Maryland Historical Society devoted exclusively to the city's history; numerous dissertations on the subject; and the formation of such groups as the Baltimore History Research Group (1975) and the Baltimore Congress for Local Records and History (1976), all attest to this.[15]

In addition to the activity noted by Cox, another significant social history project that evolved out of BRISC with grant support was the Baltimore Neighborhood Heritage Project (BNHP), a community history program that documented predominantly working-class "ethnic" Baltimore neighborhoods in the late 1970s and early 1980s. The historians running BNHP wanted it to be more than an oral history project that sent interviewers into city neighborhoods to capture audio to later be preserved and transcribed in archives. Instead, the project's creators wanted to train long-standing members of those neighborhoods in the techniques of oral history to help the communities themselves articulate and maintain their histories. The project, which started in the Highlandtown neighborhood of Southeast Baltimore in 1977, expanded through CETA funds in 1979 to include twelve additional staff and five additional neighborhoods.[16]

Oral history as a method of archival documentation often seeks to collect narratives from underrepresented populations or fill gaps in existing historical records. BNHP demonstrated a clear social history approach by focusing on working-class urban neighborhoods undergoing demographic changes through deindustrialization and decades of white flight to the surrounding counties. Historian Linda Shopes, who helped create BNHP, subsequently critiqued the project thoroughly in the *Radical History Review* and other scholarly publications. Among her conclusions was the existence of a "tension between the kind of information historians think is important to recover about a community's history and what community residents themselves, however unconsciously, think is important to record about that history."[17]

After BNHP's interviews were complete, a theatrical production based on those interviews was developed and performed by actors from the Theatre Project in Baltimore. Known as the Baltimore Voices Company, this public history component of the project performed at almost three dozen local venues in 1980. After each performance, project participants would engage audience members in a discussion of what they had just seen. According to Shopes, whose work openly explored the radical potential of community histories for residents themselves, "Baltimore Voices was potentially the best tool for political consciousness-raising that our Project has yet produced."[18] In addition, copies of audiocassette tapes of several hundred BNHP interviews were placed with BRISC at the University of Baltimore, as well as the Maryland Historical Society, which was operating its own oral history program under the direction of Betty McKeever Key.

Betty Key began her career as an oral historian during the 1968 Eugene McCarthy presidential campaign. She recorded more than 750 hours of interviews with campaign workers for McCarthy—a project that was later deposited at Georgetown University. She then founded the oral history program at the Maryland Historical Society (MDHS) in 1971, "with restricted manpower and money."[19] By 1976, MDHS was awarded an $8,000 grant from the Maryland Committee on the Humanities and Public Policy to run an oral history project on civil rights in Maryland. The project focused on interviews about the former governor, Theodore R. McKeldin, and the former head of the Baltimore branch of the National Association for the Advancement of Colored People, Lillie Mae Carroll Jackson. Although both Jackson and McKeldin were deceased by that time, interviews were conducted with those who were close with both leaders.[20]

Key ran the Maryland Historical Society's oral history program from 1971–1983.[21] During that time, she published and presented practical guidelines for conducting oral history interviews, as well as processing and preserving these recordings in library settings.[22] Key's contributions as a mentor and educator are noted in the dedication to the 2006 book, *Preparing the Next Generation of Oral Historians*, edited by Barry Allen Lanman and Laura Marie Wendling.[23] The development of a major social history component to the archival program at the Maryland Historical Society was, in large part, due to the leadership of Key during these pivotal years of Baltimore's local archival renaissance. Known primarily as a repository for nineteenth-century history and a museum specializing in decorative arts, the history of MDHS is aligned with the American manuscripts' tradition of documenting elite, politically connected families. Yet, MDHS hosted local history conferences in 1975 and 1978. Writing optimistically about those programs, and the renaissance they signaled, was Richard J. Cox.[24]

Richard Cox, widely recognized as a contemporary archival leader and one of the profession's most prolific writers, began his archival career in Baltimore. Cox served as manuscripts curator at the Maryland Historical Society from 1973–1978 while working on his master's degree in history at the University of Maryland. He was subsequently appointed Baltimore City's archivist and records management officer, a position he maintained until leaving the state in 1983.[25] The period of time during which Cox was professionally active in Baltimore coincided with the city's archival renaissance: his contributions to the profession helped fuel those changes, and his prolific additions to the archival literature document this period.[26] Cox himself identified the role of BRISC and other local institutions in forming the Baltimore Congress for Local Records and History, a group that wrote a grant to help revitalize the city's municipal archives.[27]

The Baltimore's Bureau of Archives was formed in 1927, after which time it benefited from the efforts of the Works Progress Administration (WPA) and its Historic Records Survey. Under archivist Frank Sebald, six WPA workers surveyed, cataloged, and indexed records in the Bureau of Archives from 1935–1942. Their laudable efforts to organize and describe a vast sea of historical records, representing an archival backlog that reached back to the city's earliest years, were made possible by New Deal politics. This liberal vision of archives changed in the 1950s, when attention turned to records management and the space efficiencies afforded by the systematic destruction of nonpermanent records through records retention schedules. The Baltimore City Council created the Office of Records Management in 1954, and C. Frank Poole was hired as the city's first records manager the following year. Within his first twelve months on the job, Poole proudly reported to the local press that he had destroyed more than 8,000 feet of records. (The rule of thumb in records management is 90/10: 90 percent of records will be identified as ineligible for permanent retention and subsequently destroyed; only 10 percent will be deemed historically relevant and transferred to the archives.) Poole's work continued along these lines until his retirement in 1977.[28]

Poole's retirement, coupled with the growing public interest in local history, helped the Baltimore Congress for Local Records and History convince Mayor William Donald Schaefer to support a stronger archival program for municipal records. Richard Cox was hired in 1978 to lead the Baltimore City Archives (BCA). Over the next two years, with support from the local archival profession and several NHPRC grants, he hired William LeFurgy and Anne Turkos as assistant archivists, whose work focused on updating and expanding municipal records retention schedules. During this period, the revamping of the municipal archives included processing the records of the mayor and City

Council of Baltimore, the reorganization of records from the WPA's item-level cataloging system to a modern archival record group system, and the operation of an expanded records management program. *The Records of a City: A Guide to the Baltimore City Archives*, was published in 1984. This collection guide, more than 100 pages long, was the product of five years of work and two NHPRC grants.[29]

Despite the progress made during Baltimore's local history renaissance, national politics brought an abrupt halt to archival progress in Baltimore, just a decade after BRISC's creation. Federal funds for cultural heritage organizations were slashed by the Reagan administration, whose antipathy toward the national endowments was a well-publicized manifestation of the power struggle over the very terms of American democracy during the Conservative Ascendance. According to historian Cynthia Koch, "The NEH lost close to fourteen percent of its $151.3 million budget in 1982 and would not regain its 1981 level of funding until 1989. In an era of double-digit inflation this represented a real dollar cut of approximately fifty percent over the course of the 1980s."[30] The National Historical Publications and Records Commission, too, faced a funding crisis at the hands of Republicans. Although the NHPRC avoided political elimination in 1981, funding levels in 1982 were reduced almost 38 percent, from $4 million to $2.5 million, resulting in the loss of almost half of the commission's staff.[31] Locally, Betty Key's oral history program, Ted Dürr's BRISC experiment, and Richard Cox's municipal archives all depended on federal grants to hire staff and conduct the work needed to build their programs. In the absence of these funds, programmatic change came swiftly. In 1982, BRISC ceased operations at the University of Baltimore. The following year, Betty Key retired from the Maryland Historical Society, and Richard Cox resigned from his position at the Baltimore City Archives.

After the departure of Cox, the Baltimore City Archives witnessed a rapid succession of archivists—William LeFugy from 1983–1985 and Thomas Hollowak from 1986–1989, followed by two decades of near-defunct existence. In 2010, the Maryland State Archives received NHPRC funding to revitalize the City Archives, bringing descriptive information into the computer age by adding municipal collection guides to the state's online archival database.[32] The BCA is currently open for public research use, operating in North Baltimore under the auspices of the State Archives.

In the case of BRISC, the archival program was perceived as an unnecessary expense to the university, and its relevance to students was called into question. UB Law School dean Lawrence Katz summarized the situation after a November 1980 meeting held to discuss BRISC's future: "At present, BRISC's activities are directed largely to the outside world. It has not been integrated with the University programs, either at the faculty or the student level. . . . For the University to be willing to add financial support to BRISC, it (especially

President Turner) must be convinced of the value of BRISC to our faculty and students."[33] In its defense, Dürr claimed that more than a million dollars in local and federal funding had been obtained to support the center's activities at the university, including projects like the Baltimore Neighborhood Heritage Project and the Baltimore Voices Company. Despite his efforts to convince the campus administrators to continue operations, the Baltimore Region Institutional Studies Center was functionally closed in 1982, and approximately 1,500 linear feet of BRISC records were added to the Langsdale Library's Special Collections department.[34] In 1990, budget cuts again threatened the BRISC records, when library administrators attempted to close Special Collections—temporarily merging it with the library's reference department and transferring archival staff to other areas. Under new library leadership, the department was reconstituted and led by Thomas Hollowak, formerly of the City Archives, until his retirement in 2013. The department continues its operations out of Langsdale (now Robert L. Bogomolny) Library, where it is open to the public.[35]

In recent years, the Maryland Historical Society has also struggled financially, resulting in staff layoffs, museum closures, leadership turnover, and reduction in public access to its research collections. In 2003, seven employees were laid off. In 2006, a $1.2 million budget deficit led to the elimination of 20 percent of the staff, with the executive director resigning after just four months on the job. A year later, two satellite museums—the Maritime Museum and the Baltimore Civil War Museum—were closed to cut costs. In 2009, another round of layoffs prompted shorter operating hours and the departure of another director.[36] Despite these challenges, the MDHS Library and Special Collections remain open several days a week—free for those with paid memberships and open to the public with an admission fee.

Social historians' dream of building archives to document and preserve the experiences of ordinary people fell on hard financial times as the political pendulum in the country swung to the right in the 1980s. The local history renaissance of the mid-1970s, inspired by the democratic and radical impulses within social history, created an unfinished mandate for today's historians, archivists, librarians, and related cultural heritage workers. As keepers of Baltimore's social history, archivists at the Baltimore City Archives, Maryland Historical Society, and University of Baltimore must focus their attention on building sustainable archival programs.

In light of the very real challenges Baltimore's social history archives face, a new generation of archivists must address the urgent funding, staffing, and storage needs of their collections. While the first generation of social historians eagerly filled the archives, attention to acquisition often trumped organization and access to these records. Dürr's "we save it all" take on archival appraisal accurately captures the enthusiasm of social history archivists in the 1970s. And while it may be true that future research needs are impossible to predict, social history's vastly expanded universe of archival documentation demands rigorous archival management for it to be valuable to researchers. The work of organizing, describing, and providing access to these complex modern records goes on through the present day.

Baltimore's social history did not stop with federal funding cuts in 1982. The archival mandate to engage with communities and collect documentary material for future research continues. Where are the archives of Baltimore's crack epidemic? The AIDS crisis? The war on drugs? Who maintains the archives of mass incarceration? Who collects the primary sources that document the demolition of the city's high-rise public housing? What about the archives of predatory lending? Of eminent domain? Of gentrification? Social history archives must maintain relevance through social engagement and commitment to the historically underserved and underrepresented communities they document. Our archives should strive to be active spaces—not only for scholars but also for activists, artists, students, and residents—that build histories reflecting our communities and our lived realities.

How can a new generation of cultural heritage workers build on the foundation laid during Baltimore's archival renaissance of the 1970s? An ethos of cooperative collecting must guide our efforts on a metropolitan level. By defining clear collection development policies in our archives, we can collaborate across institutions to build complementary collections, rather than competitive ones. By working closely with our users, we can understand how research questions change as academic disciplines evolve. Our collections become recontextualized through use over time. We add materials to the archives to address gaps and silences in the historical record. We transfer out-of-scope materials to sister repositories with related collections. Through this process, archives become active sites of documentation and inquiry, rather than historical mirrors for wealthy and powerful elites. The ongoing project of articulating the social value of archives demonstrates commitment to the idea that history offers guidance for the future and for all members of our society.

Notes

1   Howard Zinn, "Secrecy, Archives, and the Public Interest," *Midwestern Archivist* 2, no. 2 (1977): 25, http://digital.library.wisc.edu/1793/44118. Zinn's 1970 speech was published in abridged version in 1971 by the *Boston University Journal*; a full version was published in 1977 in the *Midwestern Archivist*. The 1977 version is cited for its availability.

2   Alex Haley's popular 1976 novel reached even wider audiences through a 1977 television miniseries adaption. *Roots* was a story about an eighteenth-century slave named Kunta Kinte and seven generations of his descendants over the next two hundred years in the United States.

3   Robert B. Townsend, "History in Those Hard Times: Looking for Jobs in the 1970s," *Perspectives on History* 47, no. 6 (September 2009): 33.

4   Eric Foner, ed., *The New American History*, rev. and enlarged ed. (Philadelphia: Temple University Press, 1997), introduction to the first edition.

5   The term "archival renaissance" was applied to Baltimore by Richard J. Cox in "The Need for Comprehensive Records Programs in Local Government: Learning by Mistakes in Baltimore, 1947–1982," *Provenance* 1, no. 2 (Fall 1983): 14–34.

6   CPHA was organized in 1941 by citizens concerned about slum housing conditions in Baltimore. The history of the organization became the focus of Dürr's 1972 doctoral dissertation, and the salvaged organizational records later became the first archival collection of BRISC.

7   "Ted Dürr Interview," University of Baltimore Special Collections, https://soundcloud.com/ubarchives/ted-Dürr-interview, accessed June 25, 2016.

8   Mike Bowler, "UB Center Offers Mass of Civic Data," *Baltimore Sun*, April 11, 1973.

9   Howard Hall, at 847 North Howard Street, built in 1927, was originally the Baltimore College of Dentistry. Purchased by the University of Baltimore in 1929 to serve as its law school, Howard Hall was later sold to Maryland General Hospital. It currently serves at the home of the Eubie Blake National Jazz and Cultural Center. See Thomas L. Hollowak, *University of Baltimore* (Arcadia Publishing, 2000); Robert Hilson, "Blake Center Going to Howard Street as Anchor for the Avenue of the Arts," *Baltimore Sun*, December 21, 1994.

10 C. Fraser Smith and fellow journalists at the *Baltimore Sun* covered this topic extensively in the early 1980s.

11 "Maryland." National Archives and Records Administration, http://www.archives.gov/nhprc/projects/states-territories/md.html, accessed June 25, 2016.

12 "Ted Dürr Interview."

13 W. Theodore Dürr and Paul M. Rosenberg, *The Urban Information Thesaurus: A Vocabulary for Social Documentation* (Westport, CT: Greenwood Press, 1977).

14 Theodore W. Dürr, "Some Thoughts and Designs about Archives and Automation, 1984," *American Archivist* 47, no. 3 (July 1, 1984): 271–289, doi:10.17723/aarc.47.3.5v7421712822615q.

15 Richard Cox, "The Plight of American Municipal Archives: Baltimore, 1729–1979," *American Archivist* 42, no. 3 (July 1, 1979): 292, doi:10.17723/aarc.42.3.2512804653401xh3.

16 Linda Shopes, "The Baltimore Neighborhood Heritage Project: Oral History and Community Involvement," *Radical History Review* 25 (October 1981): 33–34.

17 Shopes, "Baltimore Neighborhood Heritage Project," 32.

18 Shopes, "Baltimore Neighborhood Heritage Project," 38, 40.

19 Earl Arnett, "Maryland Historical Society Wants to Begin Oral History Project," *Baltimore Sun*, January 12, 1976.

20 Arnett, "Maryland Historical Society."

21 The Director's Report of the Annual Report, 1982–1983, notes: "Three long-term staff members retired this year . . . and Betty Key, who brought to the Society statewide and national attention and respect through her accomplishments as Director of the Oral History Program." *Maryland Historical Society Magazine* 78, no. 4 (1983): 247.

22 See these publications by Betty McKeever Key: "Oral History in Maryland," *Maryland Historical Magazine* 70, no. 4 (Winter 1975): 379–384; *Oral History in*

Maryland: A Directory (Baltimore: Maryland Historical Society, 1981); "Oral History in the Library," *Catholic Library World* 49, no. 9 (1978): 380–384; "Practically Speaking: Alternatives to Transcribing Oral History Interviews," *History News* 35, no. 8 (1980): 40–41; and "Publishing Oral History: Observations and Objections," *Oral History Review* 10, no. 1 (January 1982): 145.

23 Lisa Krissoff Boehm et al., *Preparing the Next Generation of Oral Historians: An Anthology of Oral History Education*, ed. Barry A. Lanman and Laura M. Wendling (Lanham, MD: AltaMira Press, 2006).

24 Cox, "Plight of American Municipal Archives," 292.

25 "Curriculum Vitae." Faculty Website of Professor Richard J. Cox, September 22, 2010, http://www.pitt.edu/~rjcox/bio/index.html, accessed June 25, 2016.

26 See these publications by Richard J. Cox: "The Plight of American Municipal Archives"; "Need for Comprehensive Records Programs"; *Resources and Opportunities for Research at the Baltimore City Archives* (Baltimore, 1980); "American Archival History: Its Development, Needs, and Opportunities," *American Archivist* 46, no. 1 (January 1, 1983): 31–41, doi:10.17723/aarc.46.1.n43kl32721m250g1.

27 Cox, "Need for Comprehensive Records Programs," 24.

28 Aiden Faust, "'Archives Trouble': The Case of the Baltimore City Archives" (MLS thesis, University of Maryland, College of Information Studies, 2008).

29 Faust, "'Archives Trouble.'"

30 Cynthia Koch, "The Contest for American Culture: A Leadership Case Study on the NEA and NEH Funding Crisis," *Public Talk*, http://www.upenn.edu/pnc/ptkoch.html, accessed July 6, 2016.

31 *Documenting Democracy, 1964–2004* (Washington, DC: National Historical Publications and Records Commission, 2004), 34–36, //catalog.hathitrust.org/Record/004965854.

32 "Maryland." National Archives and Records Administration, http://www.archives.gov/nhprc/projects/states-territories/md.html, accessed June 25, 2016.

33 BRISC Correspondence, 1980–1985. University of Baltimore Langsdale Library Special Collections, University Archives, Office of the Provost Records (UR0006), Series 1, Catherine Russell Girra Subject Files.

34 BRISC Correspondence, 1980–1985.

35 Telephone interview with Thomas Hollowak, conducted June 29, 2016.

36 Mary Carole McCauley, "Historical Society Lays off 7 ; Plans Are to Refill Some Posts in Fall [Final Edition]," *Baltimore Sun*, June 13, 2003; Glenn McNatt, "Historical Society to Shut 2 City Museums; Civil War, Maritime Sites to Close Sept. 1 to Eliminate Deficit [Final Edition]," *Baltimore Sun*, July 3, 2007; Glenn McNatt, "Facing down a Financial Crisis ; Historical Society's New Chief Had to Make Difficult Decisions in a Hurry [Final Edition]," *Baltimore Sun*, August 2, 2006; Liz F. Kay, "Maryland Historical Society Cuts Staff and Public Hours," *Baltimore Sun*, December 3, 2009; Glenn McNatt, "Family Issues Led to Resignation; Maryland Historical Society Head Quits after Four Months [Final Edition]," *Baltimore Sun*, October 21, 2006.

27

Building a More Inclusive History of Baltimore

•••••••••••••••••••••

Preserving the Baltimore
Uprising

DENISE D. MERINGOLO

Black people, we are fully deserving of
the room and space to fully express our
humanity. This is what Black Lives
Matter is truly about. We support all of
our emotions, from our bliss to our anger
to our grief. All of it is welcome, as this is
what it means to be human, to love and
to lose those that we love so much. We
acknowledge that our uprisings are being
fueled by the love we have for ourselves
and for one another. A love that
challenges silence, repression and death.
—Opal Tometi, Patrisse Cullors, and
Alicia Garza, Formal Statement
Regarding Baltimore Protests

April, 2015: Graduate students in my Introduction to Public History course at the University of Maryland, Baltimore County (UMBC) were working on their final projects.[1] During a typical semester, I encourage students in this class to recognize public history as a profoundly collaborative practice. Through classroom readings and a semester-long project, they explore the complexities of practicing history with—not simply for—individuals and groups for whom an understanding of the past can have immediate, practical implications. I train them to think about public history as a dual effort to be responsible and responsive and to balance the standards of historical professionalism against the variability—and sometimes volatility—of community interests.[2] These lessons can seem abstract to students. But that spring was different. A local African American man named Freddie Gray died after rough handling by Baltimore Police Department (BPD) officers. Protests disrupted the city for two weeks. Baltimore news sources reliably reported on Freddie Gray's arrest, death, and the protests that followed. The *Baltimore Sun* established a timeline, and national news outlets used these stories as the foundation for additional reporting and analysis.[3]

On April 12, 2015, police officers saw Freddie Gray walking near the intersection of Pennsylvania and Mount Streets in West Baltimore and started chasing him. When they caught Gray, they arrested him for possession of a knife. It was not an easy arrest. Police twisted him as he screamed. Cell-phone video recorded by bystanders shows police dragging a handcuffed Gray to a transport vehicle.[4] They did not buckle him in, but stopped a block away to shackle his feet and load him back into the van on his stomach. Gray requested medical attention, but was ignored. The van made four additional stops. By the time it arrived at the police station, Gray had been in the back for thirty minutes. Gray was unresponsive, and police finally called for an ambulance.[5] He died a week later on April 19 from a severe spinal injury.

Peaceful protests began on Saturday, April 18. People assembled outside the Western District police station to demonstrate against Gray's rough treatment. Their efforts intensified after his death. Nonviolent marches and demonstrations continued. It is true that incidents of property damage and violence began to occur as well. An angry encounter took place outside an Orioles baseball game on April 25. Fans of the opposing team confronted protesters and hurled racial epithets at them. The atmosphere became increasingly tense. On Monday, April 27, the day of Freddie Gray's funeral, unsubstantiated rumors began spreading on Twitter that Baltimore school students were planning a lawless "purge."[6] By early afternoon, city officials abruptly shut down most of the city's public transit, leaving hundreds of students stranded in front of a wall of BPD officers. As frustration and confusion grew, violence and property damage increased as well. People lit fires, looted local businesses, and damaged vehicles.

The next day there was a clean-up of the affected area, and the marches and rallies continued.

While the events comprising the response to Freddie Gray's death were largely peaceful, some local politicians and national media reporters conflated the demonstrations with criminal activity and violence. Reporters and pundits repeatedly used the words "riot" and "rioters."[7] Governor Larry Hogan declared a state of emergency. Mayor Stephanie Rawlings-Blake issued a curfew, describing those engaged in civil disobedience as "thugs."[8] But photographs and videos seemed to show something else. Police wearing riot gear and members of the National Guard confronted peaceful marchers in T-shirts and tennis shoes. While some students threw water bottles and rocks at the police, protesters (including those associated with the Black Lives Matter movement), students, parents, and relatives of Freddie Gray objected to the broad mischaracterization of young black Baltimoreans as criminals.[9] This stereotype has underscored and justified police violence against African American men and women across the country for centuries.[10]

My students and I became increasingly concerned about the portrayal of local people and their role in the unrest. Many historians hesitate to write about current events.[11] It can be difficult to correctly identify their significance, particularly under volatile and unpredictable conditions. Similarly, archivists, museum curators, and others practitioners of public history can be slow to collect, preserve, and interpret current events, particularly when these events unfold in communities long overlooked by local cultural institutions.[12]

Understanding this fraught context, my students nonetheless asked, How might we offer a respectful, authentic, and professional response to the unrest of April 2015 and the problems of representation and interpretation it illuminated? We looked for models in public history practice. Most often, the history of unrest has been filtered through official records, emphasizing the perspectives of police officers, government leaders, and mainstream activists. These records, held in state and city archives or museums, tend to simplify and obscure the experiences of people directly affected by injustice and violence. The stature and legitimacy of the collecting institutions lend a sense of objectivity to records that are incomplete and, therefore, potentially misleading. Complicating this problem further, the majority of state and municipal collecting institutions have long neglected to collect history from poor and minority communities. Collections policies and collections committees have only reinforced this problem, rejecting the experiences of average people, activists, and others as insufficiently significant or representative to warrant inclusion in permanent collections. At the same time, there is a limited but significant history of radical, community-based collecting that has sought to challenge the status quo. Often tied to social justice movements and rooted in the practices of social history, projects like Out History and the Freedom Archives have sought to document the experiences of the marginalized and oppressed.[13] Over time, projects like these moved from the margins to the center of museums and archives and became increasingly relevant to the legitimacy and professionalization of their institutions. As a result, their preservation and interpretation are driven more often by experts than by those directly affected by poverty, inequality, and injustice.[14]

Since at least the turn of the twenty-first century, radical collecting practices have become more broadly collaborative. The expansion of digital public history practices has led to the adoption of "crowdsourcing" as a method for engaging people in the processes of collecting, allowing them to define the artifacts, documents, and images that best represent their lived experiences. While the term "crowdsourcing" originally described new forms of business practice enabled by the expansion of e-commerce, it quickly become valued as a method for documenting current events because it acknowledges people's inherent intellectual and interpretive authority to identify and define their own experiences.[15] By enabling individuals and community-based organizations to gather materials directly in digital collections, crowdsourcing holds promise for democratizing collections and, in turn, creating broader and more inclusive perspectives on the past. Early efforts—*The 9/11 Digital Archives* (2001) and the *Hurricane Digital Memory Bank* (2005) that documented the devastating effects of Hurricane Katrina in New Orleans—encouraged individuals to contribute audio, video, textual, and photographic representations of their memories and experiences to a digital repository.

The success of these projects inspired the 2008 development of Omeka by the Roy Rosenzweig Center for History and New Media at George Mason University.[16] Omeka is an open-source collections management system with a capacity for crowdsourcing. Since 2013, a variety of organizations and individuals have used Omeka to facilitate public collections efforts in response to traumatic events, including the Boston Marathon bombing and the death of Michael Brown at the hands of police in Ferguson, Missouri.[17] Inspired by these examples, we built an Omeka site, *Preserve the Baltimore Uprising,* as a digital space in which local people could preserve their own experiences and ideas about the death of Freddie Gray and the events that followed.[18] The site went live on May 1, 2015, twelve days after Gray's death while protests were still ongoing (see Figure 24).

Preserve the Baltimore Uprising began as a student-driven response to our fear that these local perspectives would be lost, flattened under the weight of words like "thug" and "riot." We reached out to members of the UMBC community, and the first contributors submitted images of students making protest signs and participating in demonstrations. Shortly after the site went live, Joe Tropea, digital projects manager with the Maryland Historical Society and a graduate of the UMBC public history program, approached me. The

FIG. 24 Baltimore uprising, 2015. Photo by J. M. Giordano.

Historical Society had put out a call for photographs, and local people had begun to send digital images and other material by email. We agreed to partner on the project, and together we publicized *Preserve the Baltimore Uprising* on social media, on local public radio, and through our home institutions.[19]

Through a collaboration of the Public History track of the UMBC Department of History and the Maryland Historical Society Archives, *Preserve the Baltimore Uprising* works to advance several overtly political goals. First, we focus our efforts on gathering digital materials that represent African American perspectives, emphasizing the experiences of protesters and activists, as well as, more broadly, the residents of the West Baltimore neighborhood where Freddie Gray lived and died. We see our collection as the foundation for a counternarrative that will challenge and complicate official interpretations of unrest by amplifying the too-often neglected perspectives and experiences of the people most directly affected both by the unrest of 2015 and by the history of segregation and injustice that preceded—and predicted—it.

Second, we see our project as part of an effort to challenge and transform the collections practices of the Maryland Historical Society. Collaboration with the society is crucial, because it ensures that the collection will be permanently protected and broadly accessible. However, throughout most of its 175-year history, the Maryland Historical Society has never fully represented Baltimore City history. Like many similar institutions across the country, its collections tend to represent white Marylanders and elite experiences and to emphasize official history. *Preserve the Baltimore Uprising* is a vehicle by which city residents can begin to influence and transform the institution, diversify its collections, and build a more inclusive understanding of city life over time.

Third, we also insist that *Preserve the Baltimore Uprising* serve as a mode of communication through which the Maryland Historical Society, UMBC, and other cultural and educational institutions can earn the trust of long-ignored and disrespected neighborhoods, organizations, and individuals by allowing contributors to submit materials to the collection with minimal intervention or mediation.

What is the role of public history during times of unrest? In the specific case of the 2015 Baltimore uprising, we sought to collect, protect, and amplify the experiences of local African American people in order to begin to create more inclusive cultural spaces and to influence the way the history of these events will be written.

Notes

Epigraph: Lily Workneh, "#BlackLivesMatter Co-Founders on Baltimore Uprisings: 'We Stand in Solidarity,'" *Huffington Post*, April 29, 2015; updated December 6, 2017, https://www.huffingtonpost.com/2015/04/29/black-lives-matter-baltimore_n_7170352.html.

1   "University of Maryland, Baltimore County," *Explore Baltimore Heritage*, https://explore.baltimoreheritage.org/tours/show/24#.WVaApoqQy8U; "UMBC Campus Stories on Explore Baltimore Heritage," *UMBC News*, June 8, 2016, http://50.umbc.edu/news/?id=60575.

2   While students in my class examine a variety of professional perspectives on public history, I tend to emphasize—in my teaching and in my own practice—what Cathy Stanton has described as progressive public history. Cathy Stanton *The Lowell Experiment: Public History in a Postindustrial City* (Amherst: University of Massachusetts Press, 2006).

3   "Timeline: Freddie Gray's Arrest, Death, and the Aftermath," *Baltimore Sun*, http://data.baltimoresun.com/news/freddie-gray/.

4   Eyder Peralta, "Timeline: What We Know about the Freddie Gray Arrest," *The Two Way: Breaking News from NPR*, National Public Radio, May 1, 2015, http://www.npr.org/sections/thetwo-way/2015/05/01/403629104/baltimore-protests-what-we-know-about-the-freddie-gray-arrest.

5   "Freddie Gray's Death in Police Custody—What We Know," *BBC News*, May 23, 2016, http://www.bbc.com/news/world-us-canada-32400497.

6   According to the rumors, students were calling for a so-called purge, a day of lawlessness inspired by a 2013 film of the same name depicting a totalitarian government that grants its citizens a twelve-hour period once a year in which they can break any laws they want.

7   The mayor attempted to explain her comments and eventually apologized. Marina Fang, "Baltimore Mayor Apologizes for Calling Protesters 'Thugs,'" *Huffington Post*, April 29, 2015, http://www.huffingtonpost.com/2015/04/29/baltimore-protesters-thugs_n_7172562.html.

8   Kevin Rector, Scott Dance, and Luke Broadwater, "Riots Erupt: Baltimore Descends into Chaos, Violence, Looting," *Baltimore Sun,* April 28, 2015.

9   Justin Fenton and Erica L. Green, "Baltimore Rioting Kicked off with Rumors of 'Purge,'" *Baltimore Sun,* April 27, 2015, http://www.baltimoresun.com/news /maryland/freddie-gray/bs-md-ci-freddie-gray-violence-chronology-20150427 -story.html; Jenna McLaughlin and Sam Brodey, "Eyewitnesses: The Baltimore Riots Did not Start the Way You Think," *Mother Jones,* April 28, 2015, http:// www.motherjones.com/politics/2015/04/how-baltimore-riots-began-mondawmin -purge/; P. Kenneth Burns, "Douglass Students Say They Got a Bad Rap," WYPR, April 30, 2015, http://news.wypr.org/post/douglass-students-say-they-got-bad -rap#stream/0.

10 While the arrest, and subsequent death, of Freddie Gray was an outcome of historical forces specific to Baltimore, it was also one in a number of similar incidents that had gained national attention in the early decades of the twenty-first century. These included the death of Eric Garner in New York City, on July 17, 2014, and Michael Brown in Ferguson, Missouri, on August 9, 2014. See Jeremy Hobson, *Here and Now,* National Public Radio/WBUR, Boston, July 11, 2016, http://www.wbur.org/hereandnow/2016/07/11/america-police-shooting -timeline.

11 Recently, there has been a noticeable increase in the number of historians willing to comment on and provide context for current events in newspaper columns like "Made by History" in the *Washington Post*, on public radio programs like "BackStory" on National Public Radio, as commentators on news talk shows, and on podcasts. It is also the case that this work can put historians at risk. Several have been accused of bias and unprofessionalism, and their home institutions have had to choose whether or not to defend their actions.

12 For example, Andrea Burns led a session at the 2018 Annual Meeting of the National Council on Public History, describing insufficient efforts by museums and archives to collect materials related to the Flint water crisis.

13 See, for example, https://freedomarchives.org/ and http://outhistory.org.

14 Andrea Burns, *From Storefront to Monument: Tracing the Public History of the Black Museums Movement* (Amherst: University of Massachusetts Press, 2013). Burns demonstrates that as black museums move from a grassroots to a professional focus, they tend to lose touch with the communities they serve. Her work suggests that a similar observable movement away from community-based and politically oriented collection in favor of disciplinary recognition and expertise has limited the potential of contemporary collecting to serve as a conduit and a site of dialogue between underserved communities and cultural institutions. Local people become objects of study, rather than equal partners in a historical process.

15 See "Crowdsourcing," Wikipedia, https://en.wikipedia.org/wiki/Crowdsourcing. Jeff Howe and Mark Robinson at *Wired* coined the term "crowdsourcing" to describe the ways in which internet-based businesses were outsourcing work to end users. Howe wrote, "Simply defined, crowdsourcing represents the act of a company or institution taking a function once performed by employees and outsourcing it to an undefined (and generally large) network of people in the form of an open call. This can take the form of peer-production (when the job is performed collaboratively), but is also often undertaken by sole individuals. The crucial prerequisite is the use of the open call format and the large network of

potential laborers." http://crowdsourcing.typepad.com/cs/2006/06 /crowdsourcing_a.html.

16 See http://911digitalarchive.org/; http://hurricanearchive.org; https://omeka.org; https://rrchnm.org.

17 See http://marathon.neu.edu/; http://digital.wustl.edu/ferguson; http://www .archivingpoliceviolence.org.

18 See http://baltimoreuprising2015.org.

19 See https://omeka.org/blog/2016/04/07/op-preserve-the-baltimore-uprising; Stephanie Shapiro, "Fix the City," *Urbanite*, November 2015, http://www .urbanitebaltimore.com/100/fix-the-city/#sthash.b4HyEppG.9OV7Dv5P.dpbs; Lekan Oguntoyinbo, "Baltimore Higher Ed Institutions Fight to Restore the City," *Diverse Magazine*, August 10, 2015, http://diverseeducation.com/article /77088; Mary Carole McCauley, "Witnesses to Freddie Gray Protest Submit Nearly 1,000 Items to Historical Society," *Baltimore Sun*, June 18, 2015, http:// www.baltimoresun.com/entertainment/arts/bs-ae-freddie-gray-photos-20150623 -story.html#page=1; Aaron Henkin and Andrea Appleton, "Crowdsourcing History," WYPR Midday, April 19, 2016, http://wypr.org/post/crowdsourcing -history.

Afterword

Weaving Knowledges

We are each contributors to this earthly narrative that we weave.
Connected, we move forward fighting for democracy.
Different gifts, loves, and passions working in the name of freedom and equity.
Collectively, listening and lifting up the journey of the "I" so that it can become
    "we"
Stories intersecting and intermingling, we examine all points of entry.
For, no one story is bigger than the whole; words beautifully chronicled in time
    and place.
Threaded and weaved, we make meaning in our being.
Awakening the inner ear and third eye for the most intimate seeing.
Enlightenment is not all joy, but a call and challenge to make real the ideal of full
    participation.
Now that you have been birthed again through the seeing of stories, fight for-
    ward towards justice.

—Shawntay Stocks

Acknowledgments

This book grew out of our shared and complicated love for the city of Baltimore, and it is to the city we give our first thanks.

We feel this is an important book because it crosses the boundaries of the bureaucracy to bring together people from local universities—University of Maryland, Baltimore County (UMBC), University of Baltimore, Morgan State University, Towson University, Maryland Institute College of Art, and Johns Hopkins University—and other city institutions, as well as scholars from across the United States. We are aware that *institutions cannot love you back*, but strongly feel that the humans who make up institutions can do more to work together to build better cities. Let us all seek models of real collaboration and fight to make our institutions more human and more equitable.

For Nicole and Kate, UMBC is their institutional home and where they met, taught together, and rode the campus shuttle to work. Many people at UMBC have been supportive of this project. The Dresher Center for the Humanities brought us together in a rare chance to co-teach a course for the humanities scholars program. Co-teaching helped us see a need to revisit Baltimore's stories, and it was out of this experience that this project was born. We thank the incoming humanities scholars of 2014 for inspiring this book. The Dresher Center for the Humanities also provided a summer faculty fellowship for Nicole that supported the completion of this book. We are fortunate to work with incredible colleagues across the university, especially in the College of Arts, Humanities, and Social Sciences. The Dean's Office provided research funds for Kate in support of the web-based components of this project. Our home departments of American Studies and Gender, Women's, + Sexuality Studies provided supportive intellectual spaces, and our colleagues and friends have supported our work on Baltimore.

We are all first and foremost teachers, and we are incredibly grateful for our students. They have gone along with us on our walking tours and museum visits, produced brilliant podcasts about the city, done original research about Baltimore, and engaged in service and activism in the city. We do what we do because of our students. Thank you for sharing your curiosity with us. Shawntay Stocks, Calvin Perry, and Andrew Holter offered their skills as researchers, editors, organizers, and writers in the early stages of this project, and we appreciate their work.

Rutgers University Press has been a welcome home, and we thank our initial editor Leslie Mitchner for believing in this project and Peter Mickulas and everyone at Rutgers University Press for shepherding it through the publication process. Thanks to Westchester Publishing Services and especially our fine copy editor Gail Naron Chalew for making this a better book. Rahne Alexander's editing and Jaimes Mayhew's map-making (see these maps at baltimorerevisited.org) greatly added to early versions of the book. We enjoyed working with these two talented Baltimore artists. UMBC's cartographer Joe School worked to develop the maps for the book, and we shared some great conversations about cities in the process.

Baltimore is a city of storytellers and historians. We thank Baltimore Heritage for its steady reminder that historical research really can save neighborhoods and neighbors. The Chesapeake American Studies Association (CHASA) meeting in 2014 and the Bmore Historic unconference in 2015 gave us occasions to think with scholars across the region about how—and why—to do this project. We thank the Baltimore City Historical Society for a space to tell these stories together as contributors in 2017. The vertical files at the Enoch Pratt Free Library have been a research home for us. We are grateful for the work that the Pratt does all over the city and for being a creative heart for it. We are all researchers, and they know it. That is why we will donate all royalties from this interdisciplinary project to the Enoch Pratt Free Library. Our public libraries and all those who work there make this a better city.

Finally and foremost, we would like to thank our contributors. Their research inspired this collection, and it is their work that inspires us to move forward. We read their chapters not just as histories but also as demands: to think harder, do better, and to never, ever leave history in the past.

We also have some individual thanks to share.

P. Nicole King: Baynard Woods is my most essential collaborator in many ways. He helps me navigate the world. In these troubled times, it is essential to have him on my team. I have a wonderful network of friends in Baltimore who are like family. Thanks to my friends and family, especially my mom Frances Earle King, for support and encouragement during the years I worked on this project.

Kate Drabinski: I was diagnosed with breast cancer just as this project was entering its most grueling phase of final revision. Terrible timing, as is any time one gets a diagnosis like this. So much gratitude for my coeditors: to Nicole for continuing her leadership of the project and to Joshua for stepping in to take the reins so I could focus on my health. Thank you to Carole McCann and Amy Bhatt for mentoring me through the hard process of recognizing my limits and letting myself be helped. Emily Drabinski has read and responded to everything I have written since I was old enough to write a single letter, and being her twin sister is my favorite thing. John Drabinski was a tormenting older brother, but he has since become a close friend and intellectual partner. Sarah Burgess has thought next to me for close to twenty years, and for that I am grateful. I am lucky to have a huge community of friends and supporters, but I wanted to thank these three for being my constant companions, making me laugh, and making me think better and harder for decades. And to Nicole Stanovsky, thank you for being my home.

Joshua Clark Davis: First and foremost, I want to thank Nicole and Kate for inviting me to join this project. I was surprised and honored when they asked me to be a coeditor for the book in December 2017, and I am grateful to have received the opportunity to help produce this work. I also want to thank Lou Galambos of Johns Hopkins University for inviting me to present my chapter for this book to the Institute for Applied Economics, Global Health, and the Study of Business Enterprise. Thanks to all of my colleagues at the University of Baltimore—especially my chair Betsy Nix—for their support as I unexpectedly assumed the duties of coeditor in spring 2018. Finally, thanks to both Andy Holter and Jessica Douglas for providing reassurances and expert counsel as I struggled to figure out how to be a good editor.

Notes on Contributors

LAWRENCE BROWN is an associate professor in the Morgan State University School of Community Health and Policy. His scholarly work focuses on the impact of historical trauma on community health and development. Brown received a BA in African American studies from Morehouse College in Atlanta, a master's of public administration from the University of Houston, and a PhD in health outcomes and policy research from the University of Tennessee Health Science Center. He is completing a book titled *The Black Butterfly: Why We Must Make Black Neighborhoods Matter* and is engaged with redlined Baltimore communities as an activist for equitable redevelopment.

DANIEL BUCCINO is a graduate of the Johns Hopkins University Humanities Center, an assistant professor in the Department of Psychiatry and Behavioral Sciences at the Johns Hopkins University School of Medicine, clinical manager at the Johns Hopkins Broadway Center for Addiction, and the director of the Johns Hopkins Civility Initiative.

MICHAEL CASIANO earned his PhD in American studies from the University of Maryland, College Park. His current book project is an interdisciplinary exploration of Baltimore that examines the ways that property rights and regulations were bound up in the criminalization of black life and culture during the first half of the twentieth century. He is a 2018–2019 postdoctoral fellow in Rutgers University's Center for Historical Analysis.

SAMUEL GERALD COLLINS is a cultural anthropologist interested in the information society and globalization, primarily in the United States and Korea. His MA and PhD are from American University in Washington, D.C. Before becoming a professor at Towson University, he taught at Dongseo University in Pusan, South Korea. He spent a Fulbright year from 2006–2007 at Kook-min University in Seoul.

SHANNON DARROW is a community development professional and independent scholar who lives and works in Baltimore. She studied American studies at the University of Maryland, College Park, and community studies and civic engage-ment at the University of Baltimore. Over the past ten years she has worked at the Association of Community Organizations for Reform Now (ACORN), Civic Works, and the Southeast CDC. She is currently the Maryland Project Coordinator at the National Fair Housing Alliance.

JOSHUA CLARK DAVIS is an assistant professor of history at the University of Bal-timore and the author of *From Head Shops to Whole Foods: The Rise and Fall of Activist Entrepreneurs*. Davis's writing has appeared in the *Atlantic*, the *Washington Post*, and *Jacobin*.

KATE DRABINSKI is a senior lecturer in Gender, Women's, + Sexuality Studies at UMBC, a member of the Baltimore Heritage LGBT History Committee, and a cofounder of the Baltimore Queerstories Collective; she also writes a regular blog about bicycling in the city. Her research interests include the histories of slavery, segregation, and sexuality and how those histories and our memories of them shape urban and rural environments. She earned her PhD in rhetoric with an emphasis in gender and sexuality from the University of California, Berkeley in 2006.

MATTHEW DURINGTON is a professor of anthropology at Towson University. He received his BA in the humanities, specializing in film, anthropology, sociology and African and African American studies at the University of Texas in 1994. He completed his MA in 1999 and his PhD in anthropology from Temple Uni-versity in 2003 specializing in urban and visual anthropology. He completed a postdoctorate at the University of KwaZulu-Natal in South Africa in 2004 and arrived at Towson University in the fall of that year. Durington is the director of the International Studies program in the College of Liberal Arts at Towson University and the coordinator for the anthropology concentration in the department. He has several research interests in the fields of urban, visual, and cultural anthropology.

NICOLE FABRICANT is an associate professor of anthropology at Towson Univer-sity. She received a BA from Mount Holyoke College in 1999 in urban anthro-pology and a PhD from Northwestern University in 2009. She completed a presidential postdoctorate at the University of South Florida in 2010 where she focused on the global water crisis and then joined Towson University in the fall of 2010. Fabricant's teaching interests include revolution in Latin America, life in the city, resource wars of the twenty-first century, environmental (in)justice, and gender and labor in Latin America. She has been working on a participatory action research project since 2016 with United Workers, Free Your Voice, and youth from Benjamin Franklin High School in Curtis Bay: its aim is to excavate the historic and contemporary layers of environmental toxicity in the region.

AIDEN FAUST is the head of Special Collections and Archives at the University of Baltimore. He received his MLS in archives and records management from the University of Maryland, College Park in 2008 and his MA in historical studies from the University of Maryland, Baltimore County in 2015. His work focuses on community histories and the sustainability of modern archival records programs.

JENNIFER A. FERRETTI is the digital initiatives librarian at the Maryland Institute College of Art. She is a first-generation American Latina whose librarianship is guided by critical perspectives and a disbelief of neutrality. Her work at MICA and beyond is focused on social justice and equitable access to information, as well as closing the knowledge gap between artist and archivist. Jennifer is a *Library Journal* 2018 Mover & Shaker.

LEIF FREDRICKSON received his PhD in history from the University of Virginia. He is working on a book on the history of lead poisoning in Baltimore and the nation based on his dissertation, *The Age of Lead: Metropolitan Change, Environmental Health, and Inner City Underdevelopment,* which won the Council of Graduate School's Distinguished Dissertation Award in the category of Humanities and Fine Arts.

ROBERT J. GAMBLE earned his PhD in history from Johns Hopkins University and currently teaches at the Park School of Baltimore. He is working on a book project, *American Bazaars: Urban Political Economy in the Early American Republic,* that explores the relationship between urban space, regulation, and capitalism in late eighteenth- and nineteenth-century Baltimore and Philadelphia. In addition to studying nineteenth-century public markets and food access, he has published on secondhand goods, street peddlers, and lotteries. He has been a research fellow at the McNeil Center for Early American Studies, Library Company of Philadelphia, and Maryland Historical Society and a faculty member at the University of Kansas, Maryland Institute College of Art, and St. Albans School in Washington, D.C.

MARISELA B. GOMEZ received a master's degree in public health in 2001, became a physician in 1999, and earned a PhD in immunopharmacology in 1995, all from Johns Hopkins University. Gomez's research and publications address the social factors of race, class, and community building and their impact on community health. She is the author of *Race, Class, Power and Organizing in East Baltimore: Rebuilding Abandoned Communities in America* (2012). In addition to her community-engaged action research and organizing, she has served as a consultant to community organizations and institutions in regard to racial equity, mindfulness and justice, organizational development, and strategic planning in Baltimore and beyond.

APRIL KALOGEROPOULOS HOUSEHOLDER is director of Undergraduate Research and Prestigious Scholarships at the University of Maryland, Baltimore County. Householder, a native of Baltimore, is an educator, filmmaker, and media scholar. She received her PhD in 2006 in comparative film studies from the University of Maryland, College Park. Her research interests include gender, race, sexuality, media, and feminism.

JODI KELBER-KAYE is the associate director of the Honors College at the University of Maryland, Baltimore County. She received both her PhD in comparative cultural and literary studies in 2003 and her MA in art history in 1994 from the University of Arizona. Her research and teaching focus on queer and feminist theories, critical race studies, and cultural studies. With coauthors Householder and Nix, she oversees the Baltimore Collectives and Communes Project, an oral history collection from people involved in radical movements in Baltimore in the 1970s.

LOUISE PARKER KELLEY is a writer and editor and has been a LGBT community organizer since 1975. She was a founder and editor of the *Baltimore Gay Paper* of GLCCB, wrote for *Women's Express*, and was a board member of the Chase Brexton clinic, coordinator for women's programming at GLCCB for more than ten years, Pride Festival Chair for two years, and an HIV educator for the state AIDS Administration and HERO. She served on Mayor Kurt Schmoke's Task Force for Gay and Lesbian Issues, was active in the Baltimore Justice Campaign, and contributed more than twenty panels to the NAMES Project. Her LGBT plays have been performed in Baltimore, Pittsburgh, Washington, D.C., Amsterdam, and London.

P. NICOLE KING is an associate professor and chair of the Department of American Studies at UMBC. She received her PhD in American studies from the University of Maryland, College Park in 2008. Her research and teaching interests focus on issues of place, power, and economic development. She is the author of *Sombreros and Motorcycles in a Newer South: The Politics of Aesthetics in South Carolina's Tourism Industry*, and her research on Baltimore has been published in the *Journal of Urban History* and the collection *Engaging Heritage: Engaging Communities.*

JACOB R. LEVIN, a teacher and lecturer, received his MA in historical studies from the University of Maryland, Baltimore County in 2011, and his BA in secondary education and social studies/history in 2006. He is currently pursuing his doctorate in history from American University. His research focuses on race, social justice, and religion, and his earlier publications have addressed the intersection of civil rights activism and sports.

EMILY LIEB received her PhD in history from Columbia University in 2010 and her BA in history from Brown University in 1999. She teaches history and urban studies at Seattle University. Her work focuses on the ways in which housing and school segregation have shaped (and continue to shape) American cities and neighborhoods. Her book manuscript, *"The City's Dying and They Don't Know Why,"* is a biography of West Baltimore's Rosemont neighborhood from the Progressive era through the 1970s, and her writing on Baltimore has appeared in *Politico* and *CityLab.*

TERESA MÉNDEZ graduated from Princeton University with a degree in cultural anthropology and received her MSW from the Smith College School for Social Work, where she is on the adjunct faculty. She has published and presented on the intersection of race, ethnicity, and culture; therapeutic impasse; and education. A former journalist, she currently maintains a private practice of psychotherapy in Baltimore.

DENISE D. MERINGOLO is an associate professor in the History Department at UMBC and the director of public history. She teaches courses in community-based public history practice, museums and material culture, and digital public history. Her book *Museums, Monuments, and National Parks: Toward a New Genealogy of Public History* won the 2013 National Council on Public History prize for the best book in the field. She is creator of *Preserve the Baltimore Uprising*, a digital collection project that allows individuals to gather and preserve images, videos, and stories about the protests that erupted after the death of Freddie Gray in police custody in April 2015. She received the prestigious Whiting Fellowship for 2018–2019 to activate the *Preserve the Baltimore Uprising* collection and promote community-based, collaborative historical reflection and interpretation.

ASHLEY MINNER is a community-based visual artist, folklorist, and storyteller from Baltimore, Maryland. She earned her MFA in community arts at the Maryland Institute College of Art in 2011. She is currently a PhD candidate in the Department of American Studies at the University of Maryland, College Park, where she is studying folklore, museum scholarship and material culture, and relationships between place and identity. An enrolled member of the Lumbee Tribe of North Carolina, she has been active in the Baltimore Lumbee community for many years and regularly visits communities throughout the U.S. South and Latin America. Ashley works as a folklorist for the Maryland Traditions Program of the Maryland State Arts Council and is a lecturer in the Department of American Studies at the University of Maryland, Baltimore County.

ELIZABETH MORROW NIX is an associate professor in the Division of Legal, Ethical and Historical Studies at the University of Baltimore. To commemorate the fortieth anniversary of the urban unrest that followed the assassination of the Rev. Dr. Martin Luther King Jr., Nix collaborated with colleagues, students, and community artists to create the *Baltimore '68* project. The steering committee held a community conference and published the anthology *Baltimore '68: Riots and Rebirth in an American City* in 2011. She is the coauthor of *Introduction to Public History: Interpreting the Past, Engaging Audiences*, published in 2017.

RICHARD E. OTTEN has a PhD in cultural studies from George Mason University. His dissertation offers a socio-semiotic analysis of Baltimore's decline. He received his MA from the University of Virginia, Charlottesville in English and American studies in 2001. He teaches American studies and gender & sexuality studies courses at Anne Arundel Community College and the University of Maryland, Baltimore County.

ELI POUSSON is the director of preservation and outreach at Baltimore Heritage, the city's nonprofit preservation advocacy organization. Before moving to Baltimore, Eli worked for the D.C. Office of Historic Preservation and completed graduate work in anthropology and historic preservation at the University of Maryland, College Park in 2009.

MARY RIZZO is an assistant professor of history and director of the Graduate Program in American Studies at Rutgers University-Newark. Through projects like the Telling Untold Histories Unconference, Queer Newark Oral History Project, and the Chicory digital archive of African American poetry, she has created inclusive public and digital history that centers stories that are often marginalized in traditional narratives. Her book *Class Acts: Young Men and the Rise of Lifestyle* was published in 2015. Her forthcoming book examines battles over cultural representations of Baltimore by writers, artists, and policy makers from 1953 to the early twenty-first century.

FRED SCHARMEN is an associate professor at Morgan State University's School of Architecture and Planning. His teaching, writing, and research focus on mining the speculative and utopian impulses of the recent past for ideas relevant to the contemporary built environment. His article "What is a Big Dumb Object?" was published in the *Journal of Architectural Education* in 2015, and his recent Baltimore *City Paper* feature, "Thinking of a Master Plan: A Look at How Mckeldin Plaza Came to Be, and the Plans to Undo It All" was given the President's Award for Architectural Journalism in 2016 by AIA Baltimore. Scharmen received a bachelor's degree in architecture from the University of Maryland, College Park and a master's degree in architecture from Yale University.

ALETHEIA HYUN-JIN SHIN received an MFA in community arts from the Maryland Institute College of Art in 2015 and explores the transnational, intercultural nature of the Korea Diaspora through her community-based art practice. Incorporating the methodology of community organizing and storytelling in her artistic praxis, she focuses on building local leadership through creative platforms that promote solidarity and community voices in Baltimore.

LINDA SHOPES is an editor, with Elizabeth Fee and Linda Zeidman, of *The Baltimore Book: New Views of Local History*, published in 1991. She currently works as a freelance editor and consultant in oral and public history. Shopes has written widely in in these fields; coedited, with Paula Hamilton, *Oral History and Public Memories* (2008); and served as coeditor of Palgrave Macmillan's Studies in Oral History series.

MICHELLE L. STEFANO is a folklife specialist (research and programs) at the American Folklife Center, Library of Congress (Washington, D.C.). She earned her BA in art history (Brown University, 2000), MA in international museum studies (Gothenburg University, Sweden, 2004) and PhD in 2010 from the International Centre for Cultural and Heritage Studies at Newcastle University (UK). From 2011–2016, Stefano worked for Maryland Traditions, the folklife program of Maryland, and led the partnership between Maryland Traditions and the University of Maryland, Baltimore County, where she was a visiting assistant professor in American studies. She coedited *The Routledge Companion to Intangible Cultural Heritage* (2016), *Engaging Heritage, Engaging Communities* (2016), and *Safeguarding Intangible Cultural Heritage* (2012).

JOE TROPEA is a public historian and documentary filmmaker. He received a MA in historical studies at the University of Maryland, Baltimore County and is currently the Maryland Historical Society's digital projects manager and curator of film and photographs. He is known for his feature documentaries

Hit and Stay: A History of Faith and Resistance (2013) and *Sickies Making Films* (2018).

AMY ZANONI is a PhD candidate in history at Rutgers University. She received an MA in historical studies from the University of Maryland, Baltimore County in 2013 and a BA in English and Latin American and Caribbean studies from McGill University in 2008. Zanoni's research examines the history of social movements, welfare and health care policy, and political economy in the postwar United States. She is currently working on her dissertation, which explores the welfare state's decline and those who fought against it in the late twentieth century through the microcosm of Chicago's only public hospital.

Index